Asia and the
International System

Edited by

WAYNE WILCOX

LEO E. ROSE

GAVIN BOYD

Winthrop Publishers, Inc.

Cambridge, Massachusetts

Cover by: Donya Melanson

Contents

iii

Introduction

This book seeks to portray the foreign policies of the Asian states, and the superpowers in Asia, in both their domestic and global contexts. The variety of governments in Asia makes this region fundamentally unlike any other "region" in international politics, and the security and developmental problems and opportunities of Asia are significantly different from those of any other area of the globe. Because of the importance of the Asian peoples to world history, and to the twentieth century's quest for peace and a greater equality of responsibility for world development, it seems appropriate to discuss Asia in the international system by emphasizing its foreign policies and politics.

The variety of Asian states necessitates a variety of authors, each a specialist on the countries or problems about which he has written. The editors have established general guidelines and boundaries, but they have responded to each author's estimate of the relative importance of the various factors identified as salient in Asia's world politics. Above all, the editors have not imposed a false unity upon a diverse world, nor have they insisted that Asia be treated as if it were not part of a global political system. Our concept is of a partially integrated world, its units hostage to one another in their insecurity, yet seeking autonomy in their cultural, economic and political values. The growing interdependence of human societies is accompanied by nationalism's injunction that would have each state follow its own "distant drummer."

In the absence of common interests, total isolation, or the general acceptance of the principle of "to each, his own," the relations between states are characterized by continuous bargaining. "Bargains" are sometimes the free product of mutually advantageous trades between governments maximizing their own values, but they are often the forced trades between the weak and the strong. The world of nation-states in Asia, as in Europe, is a very unequal world. Asymmetrical relationships of power, wealth and international status abound.

Since the beginning of the twentieth century, Asia has been at war. Coercive bargaining has pitted Japan, the Czarist and Soviet Russias, China and almost all of the smaller countries of the region against external powers and against each other. While Europe, Latin America and sub-Saharan Africa have been relatively peaceful since World War II, Asia has experienced a continuity of war, revolutionary violence and coercive bargaining.

Nationalism's "distant drummer" and the gross inequalities of inter-dependent and neighboring societies have left Asia with vast security problems and disputes, and have colored the foreign policy alternatives for most governments khaki. Post-colonial governments have to provide for development and defense outside imperial "protection," while providing increasing access to competitive world trade and technology. Their foreign policy choices have been filled with contradictory requirements and competitive demands.

Foreign policy is the arena in which these contradictory trends meet and must be resolved. Domestic goals must be reconciled with external imperatives; developmental funds must be measured against security expenditures and political values must be harmonized with the preferences of alliance partners. For these reasons, foreign policy almost always constitutes a burden for governments. Leaders must somehow convince their own citizens that compromises in autonomy, outlook and expenditures must be made to meet international challenges, opportunities or risks. And in the making of foreign policy, governments must deal with more uncertainty, less power and greater risks than in their domestic politics.

Each government in Asia lives in a "different" world; its perceptions of international politics are filtered through distinctive worldviews, and are measured against different experiences and assessed by unique criteria. Each set of leaders, even within the same national society, brings their own "mix" of domestic and foreign policy allocations; a regime change can be as fundamental to a nation's foreign policy as a major change in its resources.

Few governments can manage a vigorous foreign policy without wide support from other political "actors" in their domestic society. Whatever might be the theoretical possibilities available to a particular governing elite, the political possibilities are much more narrow. It is, therefore, necessary to study not only the "sitting government," but its allies and rivals who might constitute strengths or liabilities in the pursuit of a particular policy. This holds true as well for interest groups and segments of civil and military bureaucracies that dominate the foreign and security planning process.

No Asian state is capable of presenting an entirely coherent, factionless foreign policy decision-making process. The cold war has polarized Asians as it has Europeans, and contemporary techniques of covert action have led to governments becoming increasingly "penetrated" by the agents of other states. Quite frequently, penetration is by invitation, with a faction within the state inviting support from an external power in its quest for domestic success. Within the Communist states, the Sino-Soviet rivalry is the functional equivalent of the east-west rivalry in the rest of Asia.

In each author's analysis, specific attention is directed to the strategic setting in which the state, or group of states, conducts its foreign policy. The internal determinants of choice are then described, and the domestic political process by which they are made is portrayed. The policy process is not insulated from the past, or from its own natural history of obligations and responsibilities, however, and therefore it is necessary to portray trends and developments in foreign policy behavior. A final consideration, difficult to assess, is the relative success, failure and prospect for the country, or group of countries of functional problem management.

In order to provide a standard reference source on the quantitative measures of various state capacities, the data in Table One are useful. Such measures have an unfortunate quality of appearing more reliable and more directly translatable into "power" terms than is justified. The national accounts of all countries hide as much as they reveal, and no country in Asia is dependent solely upon its own resources in world politics. Alliances offer "multipliers," just as social disorder or governmental indecision constitutes "subtractors" from national capabilities. In any case, the question that precedes the arithmetic of power is "power to do what, when, where and to whom?"

The geography of conflict and cooperation is also important in organizing general notions of world politics in a given region. The many dimensions of political geography include much more than topographical and spatial factors. They also include the ethnic configuration of states and frontier areas, the movement of goods, services and

TABLE 1

Country	Area Sq. Miles	Population Thousand[2]	Population Per[1] Sq. Mile	Population %[2] Growth Rate	GNP U.S. $[2] Per Capita	GNP Average[2] Annual Growth (1961–67)	Budget Million[3] U.S. $	Defense Budget[4] Million U.S. $	Defense %[4] of G.N.P.	Defense Military[5] Manpower	Exports[6] Million U.S. $	Imports[6] Million U.S. $
Burma	261,970	25,811	100	2.1	70	0.6	309	$100,600,000	3.3	143,500	127	137
Cambodia	69,900	6,415	93	2.4	130	1.1		$336,000,000		179,000	83	96
Ceylon	25,232	11,701	488	2.4	160	1.3	443			6,000[b]		
China (mainland)	3,691,500	720,000[a]	198	1.5	90			$7.6 to $8.55 billion	9.5	2,880,000	2,100	1,900
China (Taiwan)	13,885	13,145	961	3.1	250	6.7	741	$601,250,000	8.8	540,000	665	716
India	1,226,600	511,125	422	2.5	90	0.9	6,329	$1,656 million	3.4	980,000	1,640	2,744
Indonesia	575,900	110,079	194	2.4	100	0.6	1,080	$272,000,000	2.3	319,000	771	806
Japan	142,770	99,918	704	1.0	1000	9.3	14,730	$1,864 million	0.8	259,000	10,228	9,070
South Korea	38,000	29,784	791	2.7	160	4.8	770	$411,000,000	4.0	634,250	335	909
North Korea	46,540	12,700	276	2.6	230	8.6[c]	2,182	$849,400,000		401,000	149	127
Laos	91,400	2,763	31	2.5	90	–0.1	68	$21,600,000		55,000	67	34
Malaysia	128,430	10,071	80	3.1	290	2.7	856	$186,000,000	4.6	50,000	1,202	1,029
Nepal	54,330	10,500	180	1.9	70	0.1	53			10,000[d]	70	90
Pakistan	400,500	120,042	273	2.6	90	2.9	1,704	$714,000,000	3.8	392,000	569	1,114
Philippines	115,800	34,656	307	3.4	180	0.8	646	$135,500,000	1.9	34,600	838	1,062
Singapore		1,956		2.6	600	2.9	245	$158,170,000	5.8	16,000	1,058	1,355
Thailand	198,500	32,680	167	3.1	130	3.9	812	$260,300,000	3.9	175,000	664	1,056
Vietnam (South)	66,000	16,973	261	2.7	120	1.8	808	$564,000,000	n.a.	500,000	38	750
Vietnam (North)	61,300	20,100	333	3.2	100			$584,000,000		492,000	62	140

Sources

1 *100 Edition Commercial Atlas and Marketing Guide* (New York: Rand McNally, 1969), pp. 568–571.

2 *World Bank Atlas 1969.*

3 Unless otherwise indicated, all data in this column are converted from local currency as given in *Statistical Yearbook 1969*, Twenty-first issue, Statistical Office of the United Nations, Department of Economic and Social Affairs, United Nations (New York, 1970).

4 *The Military Balance, 1971/72*, (London, Institute for Strategic Studies, 1971). The expression of defense expenditure(s) as a percentage of GNP has been calculated in terms of market prices, and the percentages may thus differ in some cases from those published by national governments and international organizations. Conversions from local currencies into US$ have usually been made at the current exchange rates as reported to the International Monetary Fund.

5 *Ibid., 1971/1972.*

6 Unless otherwise indicated, all data in this column are derived from International Monetary Fund, *Balance of Payments Yearbook*, Volume 21 (Washington, D.C., 1970), pp. 3, 10–12.

a The relevant data for some categories on Mainland China and North Vietnam are either unavailable or vary so greatly in different sources that they have not been included in the table. The relationship of the data for most of the other countries is only comparatively better, and different sets of figures can be found in alternate sources.

b The figure used in Ceylonese news reports during the "Che Guevara" uprising in 1971.

c Robert A. Scalapino and Chong-sik Lee, *Communism in Korea* (Berkeley: University of California Press, 1972). The authors warn, however, that the figure may be considerably too high because of the problem of calculating the inflation factor in Communist societies.

d The estimate given in various Nepali newspaper sources in the 1967–71 period.

peoples between political units, the cultural zones and linguistic channels that link as well as separate people, and the distances, modes and costs of movement from one area to another.

The following map attempts to portray topographical characteristics and relative distances. It also portrays the principal arenas of conflict that have involved the Asian peoples in war and violence since 1945. They cannot, unfortunately, show "eskimo maps;" that is, maps which show distances as a function of the time it takes to go between two points on the earth's surface. This factor, as the authors show, is of crucial importance in both continental and maritime Asia, and affects both security and development aspects of foreign policy.

If the authors and the book appear to be inconclusive, it is because the political process, both domestic and foreign, is without conclusion. It is a continuous requirement of governments to reconcile ever-changing domestic and foreign goals, just as it is a continuous requirement to adapt to the implications of technological and economic change in the world. The tasks of reconciliation and accommodation are especially severe in the absence of security, and for that reason Asian politics and foreign policies are unusually dynamic and fluid. Our view is that Asia is likely to continue to be highly turbulent, but that the sources of the factors making for such turbulence and their evolution can and should be understood, because they set the limits and the opportunities available for external powers, such as the United States, in their dealings with a large part of humanity.

PART ONE

The Foreign Policies of the Larger Asian States

China

GAVIN BOYD

In Asia's international politics, China plays the most prominent role. This vast and rapidly modernizing revolutionary state, with a population approaching 800 million, manifests a unique dynamism in its economic, political and military development. It gives vigorous encouragement to revolutionary movements that are striving to seize power in other countries, and especially in nearby states such as Burma, Thailand and India. Its armed strength, which is much greater than that of any of its neighbors, except the USSR, is felt throughout East and Southeast Asia. The foreign policy orientations of countries stretching from Pakistan to Japan are thus directly affected, and several manage their external relations mainly with a view to preserving their security in the face of Peking's challenges. The Chinese have had little meaningful interaction with most of those neighbors, however, since the start of the Great Proletarian Cultural Revolution in 1966, for the spirit of that extraordinary upheaval was expressed in foreign affairs by an almost exclusive concern with encouraging Communist insurgencies.

China's dynamic radicalism expresses total dedication to what may be called fundamental revolutionary values, as affirmed in the Thought of Mao Tse-tung, who has been the regime's supreme ideologue and charismatic leader. His doctrine, an application of Marxism-Leninism to problems encountered as his movement waged its peasant-based war to gain control of the nation from the Kuomintang government, gave great attention to building up revolutionary will power and fighting spirit within the Chinese Communist party on the basis of continual renewals of personal and group commitments to the ideals proclaimed by Marx and Lenin. The supreme end in view was the establishment of a "dictatorship of the working class" which would eliminate all forms of exploitation in China and transform her into a modern Socialist state that would no longer be vulnerable to attack by aggressive foreign powers. When Mao Tse-tung gained leadership of the Chinese Communist movement in 1935 Manchuria had been conquered by the militaristic regime in Japan, which was about to launch a full scale war against the rest of China. The distinctly Chinese version of Marxism-Leninism which Mao formulated in order to inspire his movement did not challenge Moscow's ideological leadership of International Communism, but since the development of bitter antagonisms between China and the USSR during the 1960's the Thought of Mao Tse-tung, as it is called, has been expounded in bitter opposition to the Soviet Union's "revisionism"—its alleged departures from Marxist-Leninist principles which have introduced "bourgeois" values into its social system. Such degeneration is claimed to have been prevented in China by the Cultural Revolution.

The prime international concern of the Chinese leaders is to communicate their radicalism, "the spiritual weapon of Mao Tse-tung's Thought" to foreign Communist movements, especially in Asia. With the Maoist ethos, those revolutionary organizations will develop tremendous capabilities for political violence and will triumph over all obstacles in their struggles for power. Western military intervention is to be discouraged by China's strong position in the continental strategic balance.

The policy of building up new forms of radical power that will displace non-Communist governments in other countries does not exclude temporary adjustments, compromises and co-operation with such administrations. The necessary flexibility is allowed by the ideology, and there is awareness that it can help prevent the formation of hostile alliances in Asia, assist the expansion of China's foreign trade, and open up opportunities to influence the political development of neighboring states. The compulsion to express solidarity with Marxist-Leninist movements that are struggling to gain control of other Asian countries, however, limits interest in official dealings with most of these states.

The Strategic Setting

The Chinese leaders see the rest of Asia primarily as the setting of the international revolutionary struggle which they are leading. They evidence sensitivity to the *strategic* realities in their part of the world, notably the presence of US armed forces in South Korea, Japan, the Philippines, Thailand, and South Vietnam, and the proximity of large Soviet military formations along the vast frontier stretching from near Vladivostok to the western end of Sinkiang. All that armed strength, however, is asserted to be of secondary importance. The future, it is claimed, will be shaped by the Maoist parties which are to replace by popular violence the "bourgeois" political structures in the rest of Asia and throughout the Third World. Each process of violent change is expected to re-enact the basic features of the long civil war which brought the Communist party to power in China during 1949, and is to contribute to the eventual establishment of a Peking-centered Communist world order. Overall progress towards that ideal is conceptualized as an increasingly effective exploitation, by China and the genuine Marxist-Leninist parties, of the basic contradictions which Peking sees in world politics, viz. those between the Socialist states and the "imperialist" nations; between the "imperialist" states themselves; between the peoples of the developing areas and their oppressors; and between the working classes and their rulers in the advanced capitalist countries.[1]

The Chinese regime's ideological perspective reflects the doctrinal evolution of its Communist movement. The concept of interconnected national and international revolutionary struggles derives from Marxism-Leninism, long established as the basic philosophy of the Chinese Communist party. The belief in Peking's entitlement to leadership of the global process of violent change has developed out of zealous opposition to perceived Soviet betrayals of the revolutionary cause through excessive interest in co-existence with the west; that, it is claimed, has meant holding back support for Communist insurgencies, especially the one in Vietnam. To meet the theoretical demands of the regime's new role, as the main center of inspiration for genuine Communist movements, Mao Tse-tung's strategy for revolutionary struggle has been given higher status than the Marxist-Leninist principles which it applied to conditions in China. At the same time, the national experience of violent change has been projected into Peking's understanding of the outside world. The relative simplicity of all this can be explained largely by the degree to which the Chinese system is closed to international influences. More awareness of external realities would no doubt have led to the formulation of a worldview that would be less China-centered and that would identify more with

[1] See "A Proposal Concerning the General Line of the International Communist Movement," Central Committee, Chinese Communist party (Peking: Foreign Languages Press, 1963) p. 6.

the outlooks of diverse revolutionary forces in the emerging nations. Memories of the distant and recent past influence the doctrinal perspective. The Chinese leaders, partly because of their isolation from the outside world, have a deep historical consciousness, and seem to view several adjacent areas primarily as parts of their former empire which were lost through European aggression. The humiliations imposed on the country by colonial powers, including Tsarist Russia, Britain and France, during the 19th century are recalled with much bitterness on the part of the Chinese. Government statements directed at the Soviet Union and India have expressed specific resentments at large Russian seizures of territory, most of which is now in the Soviet Far East, and at British encroachments on Himalayan border areas. There have been signs of ill feeling also regarding the English and French conquests which destroyed the tributary relationships of the mainland Southeast Asian states with imperial China. The political tradition of the old empire, which justified the forcible extension of sovereignty over neighboring peoples in order to give them the benefits of a superior civilization, probably survives to some extent, and may find expression in the assertion of China's revolutionary greatness and its obligation to lead all the Communist movements which have remained faithful to Marxism-Leninism.[2]

Because the Chinese leaders project their national experience into their world outlook with great faith, trusting in their capacity to transform the outside world by spreading their radicalism, they are evidently disinclined to investigate closely all the external factors that affect the prospects for their grand design. This no doubt partly explains why many of their pronouncements on international affairs are mainly polemical. The cultivation of faith in the ideology is accompanied by disdain for what might be called "professionalism" in the management of external relations. That, it is evidently feared, would mean less reliance on doctrine, and a lower capacity to communicate Maoist zeal to foreign Communist movements. External events, particularly the US's reduction of its involvement in East Asia, are apparently challenging the Peking leaders to develop a more realistic international outlook, but they clearly believe that their present world-

[2] See Marc Mancall, "The Persistence of Tradition in Chinese Foreign Policy", *The Annals of the American Academy of Political and Social Science*, Vol. 349, Sept. 1963, pp 14–26 and Benjamin I. Schwartz in John King Fairbank, ed., *The Chinese World Order*, Harvard UP, 1968, pp 276–288. See also Tang Tsou and Morton H. Halperin, "Mao Tse-tung's Revolutionary Strategy and Peking's International Behaviour", *The American Political Science Review*, LIX, 2, Mar. 1965, pp 80–99, and Robert Jay Lifton, *Revolutionary Immortality* (New York: Random House, 1968), pp 101–125.

view must be maintained if they are to work effectively for the advancement of the international revolution.

Because China's territory is so large, stretching from the Pacific to the Pamirs, and from the USSR to southern Asia, its environment is continental, not regional. China's neighbors include numerous states, of varying sizes, with differing social systems, levels of economic advancement, and military power. The most prominent are the three which China might consider inevitable rivals, i.e., the Soviet Union, and the two major democracies, Japan and India. The USSR is identified as a potent ideological enemy, and as a superior opponent militarily, whose influence contributed to the degeneration of numerous Chinese Communist party leaders into "capitalist roaders" before the Cultural Revolution. The chief victim of that upheaval, former Head of State Liu Shao-chi, is referred to contemptuously as "China's Khrushchev." Branded a "social-imperialist" power, the Soviet Union is accused of having global hegemonic ambitions which it is seeking to further through its influence on numerous revolutionary movements, and by collaborating with as well as opposing the US. Japan, the only advanced state in Asia economically and militarily, is viewed as a "reactionary" and "aggressive" capitalist power that is rearming and experiencing a revival of militarism, and is accused of following a neo-colonialist policy and taking over part of the US's imperialist role in Asia. Unlike the Soviet Union, however, Japan is also regarded as a valuable source of capital goods and materials necessary for China's industrialization; nearly 30 percent of Peking's imports came from this country in 1970. India, the largest adjacent non-Communist state, is viewed as a threat to China's Himalayan border areas, but not apprehensively, because New Delhi is evidently not considered to be pursuing a broadly expansionist policy, and its military development is supported by a relatively small industrial base. There are indications of anxiety, however, about the Congress government's ties with the Soviet Union, and especially about the flow of Soviet military equipment, including ships and aircraft, to India's armed forces, which had become quite substantial before the 1965 Indo-Pakistani war and which continued afterwards despite the mediatory role which the USSR assumed in relation to that conflict.

China's other neighbors in southern Asia are mostly regarded as essentially hostile states which are ripe for Communist violence. The major exceptions are North Vietnam, a friendly Socialist regime, and Pakistan, a state whose left wing administration, backed by its army, is viewed with approval because of its willingness to accept Chinese political support against India. For strategic and historical reasons, Chinese attention seems to focus on the Southeast Asian countries, whose national Communist movements, excluding those in Indochina, have aligned with Peking.

The United States, the most advanced capitalist nation, is seen as an outside power which has penetrated the environment, economically, politically, and militarily, with the support of "reactionary" Asian governments, and which is seeking to dominate the globe through aggression, intervention, subversion, and sabotage, especially in Asia, Africa and Latin America. The US's military presence in East Asia is regarded as threatening evidence of its animosity; China's security is felt to require the withdrawal of US forces from South Korea, Japan, Taiwan, Indochina, Thailand and the Philippines as well as South Vietnam. The US's military protection of the Kuomintang government on Taiwan is especially resented as a form of interference in China's *internal* affairs. The drastic modifications of the US's former non-recognition and embargo policies by the Nixon administration are attributed by the Chinese to international pressures rather than to a change of basic attitudes. It is not specifically acknowledged that the United States is endeavoring to *reduce* its military involvement in Southeast Asia, but this trend is given oblique recognition and is in effect explained by references to Washington's failures in Vietnam and to popular demands within the US for disengagement from Indochina.

China sees itself confronting the major antagonistic states in the environment and the US military presence without any substantial outside support but with the solidarity of affinitive Communist movements in neighboring countries which are gaining strength as popular hostility to the US and the local "reactionary" governments becomes stronger. The Chinese evidently expect the Maoist parties in Southeast Asia to wage more and more effective struggles which will force total American disengagement from the area, while reducing and eventually removing Soviet and Japanese influence. For the present, however, no progress seems to be anticipated in China's struggles against the USSR and Japan, and the close relationship between Moscow and New Delhi is probably expected to become a more serious danger. On the whole, therefore, the state of the outside world appears to be viewed as a challenge to build up China's own resources for defense, and for the activation of violent change throughout the underdeveloped Asian countries.[3]

[3] See outlook reflected in *Renmin Ribao, Hongi,* and *Jiefangjun Bao* editorials, *Peking Review,* 19, May 7, 1971, pp 10–12, and 21, May 21, 1971, pp 4–5.

Internal Determinants of China's Foreign Policy

Ideology and nationalism are the main determinants of Chinese foreign policy. The first is the most prominent, and the main principles of the regime's statecraft are formulated in terms of its concepts. The second, a strong emotional force with a basis in traditional Chinese culture, finds expression in the ideology and in the international projection of Mao Tse-tung's role as a charismatic leader. The manifestations of nationalism in doctrine and policy reflect the closed character of the system, and tend to limit the possibilities for rapport with Communist movements in other countries, but evidently help to generate support for the regime within China.

Peking's external policy is authoritatively stated to be based on Marxism-Leninism, creatively developed and brought to a high stage in the Thought of Mao Tse-tung. China's philosophy has been so designated since the early stages of the Cultural Revolution. Before that upheaval, the official doctrine was Marxism-Leninism *and* the Thought of Mao Tse-tung, and was understood to include a major text by Liu Shao-chi, the now purged Head of State. In upholding and extolling Mao Tse-tung's thinking, the regime asserts the fundamental revolutionary values which he has articulated and in particular affirms the importance of *revolutionary will power*, which he sees as the decisive factor in state building, modernization, social development and external relations. In the regime's foreign policy, as in its domestic affairs, the ideals proclaimed by Mao Tse-tung are to be given full expression, and especially are to be communicated to the Marxist-Leninist movements of the developing areas, whose struggles are to receive full support.

Chinese communications at three levels articulate the commitment to generate revolutionary power within "bourgeois" states and thus change their social systems by internal violence. *Ideological* pronouncements, which relate Maoism to external situations in order to set policy guidelines, are the most informative. Peking directs them at foreign Communists and well-indoctrinated sections of the domestic audience. Thus far, the most significant document in this category is one issued by the Central Committee of the Chinese Communist party in 1963; it stresses each Socialist state's obligation to support Marxist-Leninist parties that are struggling for power in other countries.[4] *Government* statements on external affairs are mostly couched in terms of the ideology, but do not elaborate its imperatives; as exercises in diplomacy, they express constructive international inten-

[4] "A Proposal Concerning the General Line of the International Communist Movement", *op. cit.*

tions, an altruistic concern for "oppressed" peoples, and a defensive attitude towards the danger of western and especially US "aggression." Finally, the routine output of the Chinese media blends the substance of communications at the first two levels for the benefit of mass audiences, and provides much enthusiastic coverage of Communist insurgencies in Asia and other developing areas.

As expressed in the different levels of communication, especially the first, the imperative to spread Maoist radicalism through the non-Communist countries has three aspects: it necessitates opposition to the west, especially the US, and the USSR, and it requires co-existence with numerous middle-powers on a basis of expediency. Activities under each heading are to help the promotion of violent change in Asia, Africa and Latin America, which is thought of as *the support of peoples who are waging armed struggles for liberation from oppressive governments*. Chinese aid is given principally to Peking-oriented parties which are leading such insurgencies, but these organizations are expected to rely mainly on their own resources, which they will be able to utilize with decisive results if they remain faithful to Maoist principles of strategy and accept Peking's guidance.[5] Communist parties which still co-operate with the USSR are not to be helped—most of them, indeed, are treated as enemies. The major exception in Asia is the Vietnamese Dang Lao Dong, whose struggle against the Saigon administration is aided militarily, and politically.

Hostility to "imperialism" complements the endeavor to spread revolution, for the advanced capitalist states, especially the US, are alleged to express their class character by pursuing aggressive policies against China and the Asian Communist movements. Peking is obliged to counter US and other interventionist activities, as well as the direct American military threat to its own regime. This is done by building up broad international opposition to Washington's activities in Asia and other developing areas, and by increasing China's own armed strength to make it a more significant deterrent. Meanwhile, Communist violence throughout the under-developed countries inflicts defeats on the "imperialists," thus increasingly discrediting and restricting their international roles. Any western military intervention to help suppress a revolutionary uprising, it is claimed, with special reference to Vietnam, will have important negative advantages, in that it will dramatize the unpatriotic and reactionary character of the assisted government, to the advantage of the insurgents.[6]

Opposition to "revisionism" is an obligation that concerns the future

5 See Lin Piao, *Long Live the Victory of Peoples' War* (Peking: Foreign Languages Press, 1967), pp 37–58.

6 *Ibid.*, pp 54–58.

vigor and development of all the genuine Marxist-Leninist parties. The Soviet Union's dilution of the ideology is considered such a grave and fundamental danger that there can be no question of partial co-operation with Moscow. *Total* hostility toward the USSR is viewed by the Chinese as the only correct response. Peking considers it must also work as effectively as possible against Soviet diplomacy in the developing areas, which allegedly seeks to advance Moscow's great power aims at the expense of the national Communist movements, in some cases with their unwitting co-operation. Any strengthening of the Soviet Union's influence in emerging nations such as India and the radical Arab states is clearly expected to make its ideological deviation a more serious danger for the world revolution. The Chinese associate the struggle against "revisionism" with a duty to build up friendship and co-operation with other Socialist states on a basis of *proletarian internationalism.* This term, long used by the Soviet Union to justify its hegemony in international Communism, is understood with reference to *China's* claimed role as the center of the world revolution. The main practical concern, however, is to encourage anti-Soviet attitudes in the east European states, including those which are quite "revisionist," such as Yugoslavia. This evidences the intensity of Chinese hostility towards the USSR, but needs not indicate any lack of conviction behind Peking's opposition to "revisionism."[7]

Peaceful co-existence, according to Chinese ideological pronouncements, is a line of diplomacy that facilitates expedient compromises and settlements with the "imperialists" and their allies, while safeguarding the basic interests of foreign revolutionary movements. The diplomacy itself expresses formal commitment to certain *principles* of co-existence, for example, respect for the territorial integrity and sovereignty of other states, non-interference in their internal affairs, non-aggression, and the management of relations with them on a basis of equality and mutual benefit. These norms, it is made clear, concern the *regime's* dealings with other *governments* and do not impose any limits on the support which the Chinese *people* give to the awakened masses in other countries who are waging revolutionary wars. The expansion of the global Communist struggle is indeed to bring about another kind of co-existence: it will gradually *force* the "imperialists" to desist from their "aggressive" activities. This, in the Chinese view, could not be achieved by the "one-sided" Soviet policy of co-existence, which is basically a form of collusion with Washington. For the present, however, peaceful co-existence as an element

[7] See, for example, denunciations of Soviet revisionism in "Long Live the Victory of the Dictatorship of the Proletariat," *Peking Review,* 12, Mar. 19, 1971, pp 9–11.

of Chinese policy involves tacit restraint on expressions of the regime's hostility towards the US, and in that respect makes it all the more urgent for China to build up great militancy in the affinitive Asian Communist movements.[8]

While co-existing with certain middle and small powers and working to change their social systems China seeks to exploit the antagonisms between Washington and Moscow. This is implied in Peking's doctrinal statements on foreign affairs, which evidence a belief that the "contradiction" between the superpowers is the dominant conflict in the present international situation, and which indicate that all potential allies must be recruited for struggle against the *main enemy* of the moment. The USSR is not specifically identified as playing that role, but meaningful interaction with Moscow is clearly not intended; dealings with the US, however, have probably been envisaged since the mid 1971 decision to welcome a visit by President Nixon. Through dialogue with Washington the Chinese regime can expect to strengthen its position in relation to Moscow, and yet may be able to prevent any losses of morale in the Asian Maoist parties by credibly representing that the US is being dealt with from a position of strength, and that Washington is seeking to withdraw from a totally unsuccessful involvement in Indochina. These points have been emphasized in commentaries by sympathetic external sources, such as the North Korean press, which have been carried by Chinese domestic media.[9]

NATIONALISM

While the most meaningful and authoritative formulations of Peking's foreign policy have an international quality which helps them to identify with revolutionary movements across the world, their significance for the regime's leaders is determined primarily with reference to the Chinese mandate to lead all the genuine foreign Communist movements. This expectation seems to be understandable in the atmosphere of the Chinese system, which is one of exultation at its revolutionary greatness, its attainment of a level of Socialist advancement far higher than that of any other Communist state, due to the leadership and wisdom of Mao Tse-tung.

[8] For the Chinese view on co-existence, see "A Proposal Concerning the General Line of the International Communist Movement," *op. cit.*, pp 12–36.

[9] Peking Radio's domestic service August 10, 1971, carried the full text of an article in the North Korean Nodong Sinmun which claimed that the US President was visiting China because his policy in Asia had failed.

Nationalism, a strong force long-present in the Chinese Communist movement, gives impetus to the elite's striving for economic and military development, and is both anti-American and anti-Soviet. The strongest appeal of Marxism-Leninism within and outside the party in China has always been its promise of transforming the country into a powerful modern state and thus overcoming the backwardness and weakness which necessitated the acceptance of humiliating defeats by European colonial powers and Japan during the past two hundred years. Since the Chinese civil war, patriotic desires to modernize on a Socialist basis have been linked with animosity towards the US. Deep hostility towards the USSR, however, has also been present since the late 1950's. This ill-feeling has been caused by the Soviet Union's perceived malice, especially as expressed in the termination of its large economic aid program in China during 1960, and has also developed out of the regime's strong ideological objections to Moscow's revisionism. Because of the intensity of the Chinese bitterness towards the Soviet Union, there is probably less rational calculation in this area of policy than in any other, and this no doubt helps to explain Peking's willingness to accept the economic and military costs of relying on its own resources rather than working towards a resumption of co-operation with Moscow.[10]

Peking's nationalism makes it also actively concerned with problems of external security. Despite the nation's under-development, defense spending, it is estimated, is about 9½% of the Gross National Product. Military expenditures are believed to have approximated $8000 million in 1970. The armed services, including ground forces numbering 2.5 million men, backed by a modest stock of nuclear weapons, are much larger than those of India and Japan. China's advances in weapons technology, however, may not be rapid enough to warrant hopes of eventually catching up with the Soviet Union or the US. For this reason Peking may wish to participate in arms control talks with the superpowers at some future date, and could see some advantage in removing obstacles to strategic arms limitation agreements between Moscow and Washington.

For the present, the Chinese ideology sustains hopes for increasing security as revolutionary wars remove the US presence from Asia. If these expectations are disappointed, however, frustrations within the leadership may produce a crisis of faith, especially as the narrow perspective of the ideology has allowed little scope for gains through

---

[10] The influence of nationalism on Chinese policy is discussed by Ishwer C. Ojha in, *Chinese Foreign Policy in an Age of Transition* (Boston: Beacon Press, 1969), especially chapter 2, and by Marc Mancall, *op. cit.*

diplomacy. Drastic modification of the ideology on the basis of strong nationalist reactions to external problems and opportunities may well occur after Mao Tse-tung's leadership has weakened, especially if the atmosphere of ideological consensus which the regime is striving to create is disrupted by a struggle for succession.

CAPABILITIES

While shaped primarily by ideological compulsions and nationalist impulses, China's foreign policy is influenced by understandings and expectations about its capabilities. The ruling elite appears to have tremendous confidence in the regime's capacity to inspire other Asian Communist movements, but only modest faith in its resources for economic and cultural diplomacy. There seems to be prudent understanding of the nation's strategic inferiority in relation to the superpowers, but this is to a large extent concealed by triumphal pronouncements about the spread of revolutionary wars.

During the half decade before the Cultural Revolution, China demonstrated a capacity to inspire what might be called *internationalist* anti-Soviet militancy in Third World Communist movements. Important allies were won over among the Asian Marxist-Leninist parties, such as the ruling Vietnamese Dang Lao Dong, the Communist party of India (Marxist), the Japanese Communist party, and the Indonesian Communist party. Each of these endorsed Peking's denunciations of the USSR, but in relatively independent ways, and without accepting China as the new center of the international Communist movement. Subsequently the Indonesian party was suppressed, and none of the others accepted Maoism as expounded by Peking after the start of the Cultural Revolution. The Indian and Japanese parties were alienated by Chinese attempts to guide their policies, and the Hanoi leaders, obliged to accept heavy military dependence on the USSR, switched to a neutral position vis-à-vis Moscow and Peking. When the Cultural Revolution ended, China was left with the allegiance of the small national Communist parties in Burma, Thailand, Malaysia and the Philippines. As underground organizations with no prospects of switching to legal political methods, they had evidently been quite receptive to Maoist logic and promises of support. Most of the leaders of Pakistan's extreme leftist National Awami party had also been won over, but partly because of enthusiasm for China as an ally against India, and not merely on the basis of agreement with the Maoist philosophy. For the present, the Chinese doctrine does not seem to be inspiring great dynamism in the Asian Marxist-Leninist parties which have remained loyal to Peking, but some of them may be able to attract wider followings if further Communist military gains are made in Indochina and if the US continues to reduce its involvement in the region.[11]

China's resources for meaningful interaction with non-Communist states, which could assume more importance if the southern Asian Maoist parties fail to develop effective campaigns of political violence, are less substantial than they were before the Cultural Revolution. The militant spirit of the new order is suspicious of expertise in the foreign affairs ministry, and diplomats who survived the purge are under pressure to display Maoist zeal rather than an interest in constructive relations with non-Communist governments. Formerly, when the regime was developing friendly relations with neutral Asian states such as India and Burma on a basis of peaceful co-existence, the staffs of its embassies and consulates included personnel who were capable of building up understandings with politicians in those countries by identifying with their values and policies, while at the same time conveying favorable impressions of the Chinese system. Such officials could emerge again, if Peking shifts to a new statecraft of goodwill towards non-Communist Asian governments. As has been stressed, however, the single-minded concern with spreading revolution which has dominated the regime's policy since the Cultural Revolution suggests that such a change would be difficult, as it would mean readjusting strong ideological beliefs and risking some penetration of "bourgeois" culture into the Chinese system.[12]

The regime's capacity to project a persuasive nation-building appeal through *cultural* and *popular* diplomacy is affected by the general orientation of its policy. Major opportunities for publicizing Chinese achievements in non-aligned Asian countries that were utilized during the 1950's no longer exist. As Peking is openly hostile to India, Indonesia and Burma, audiences in those states can be reached only through radio broadcasts and underground or semi-

[11] See studies of southern Asian Communist movements in Robert A. Scalapino, ed., *The Communist Revolution in Asia*, 2nd ed. (Englewood Cliffs, N.J.: Prentice-Hall, 1969). See also Sheldon W. Simon, "Maoism and Inter-Party Relations: Peking's Alienation of the Japan Communist Party," *The China Quarterly*, 35, July–Sept. 1968, pp 40–57, and *Current Scene*, VIII, 6, Mar. 15, 1970.

[12] Peking's former co-existence statecraft is discussed by Herbert Passin in "China's Cultural Diplomacy," *The China Quarterly Press*, 1962. The regime's diplomatic resources are examined by Kenneth Young in *Negotiating with the Chinese Communists: The United States Experience, 1953–1967* (New York: McGraw-Hill, 1968), pp 338–370. The effects of the Cultural Revolution on the foreign affairs establishment are studied by Melvin Gurtov in "The Foreign Ministry and Foreign Affairs during the Cultural Revolution," *The China Quarterly*, Oct.–Dec. 1969, pp 65–102.

clandestine publications, which must compete against larger flows of information about China from critical non-Communist sources. The economic assistance programs which helped Chinese publicity work in Indonesia and Burma are no longer operating, and there are no substantial Chinese aid programs elsewhere in Southeast Asia which could attract wide attention. Peking, however, does have access to mass audiences in West Pakistan, where it is providing considerable capital and technical aid, and where its cultural and information activities are in effect supplemented by local media that manifest much enthusiasm for its social and economic achievements.

If friendly relations were built up again with neighbors such as India and Indonesia, there would be new opportunities to make their populations aware of China's advances. However, in many southern and East Asian countries, living conditions have improved during the past decade and a half. Japan's tremendous economic progress has become widely-known, and Soviet information activities have persistently discredited the Chinese regime. Economic progress in China itself, moreover, has been slow during the past decade and a half because of the severe effects of the Cultural Revolution.[13]

Peking's *military strength* is a major element in its international role, and is evidently being felt more by neighboring countries as the US's involvement in East Asia diminishes. Rapid advances in nuclear arms programs dating from the 1950's have made possible the production of a modest stock of hydrogen weapons and possibly one hundred 20KT atomic bombs. Short, middle range and intercontinental missile delivery systems are being developed. The ground forces, comprising principally 115 line divisions and 20 artillery divisions, are adequately supplied with light and medium weapons, but lack heavy equipment and transport. The navy is very small, but the air force has some 2,500 combat planes, and although many are of Korean war vintage there is a growing number of locally made MIG-21's, and—since 1971 —TU16 bombers.[14]

With defense allocations which are more than double the combined Indian and Japanese totals (see chart page viii) the Chinese leaders are striving to build up their regime's nuclear capability and strengthen its large conventional forces. This military power is already sufficient to inhibit most of the non-Communist Asian states from

[13] See Alexander Eckstein, *Communist China's Economic Growth and Foreign Trade* (New York: McGraw-Hill, 1966), pp 41–86, and *Current Scene,* VIII, 11, June 1, 1970, and IX, 1, Jan. 7, 1971.

[14] See *The Military Balance, 1971–1972* (London: The Institute for Strategic Studies), pp 41–42.

attempting to develop an alliance system for their own protection. With the US's partial disengagement, moreover, China's position in the strategic balance is tending to become stronger, thus causing small Southeast Asian states such as Thailand and Burma to explore the possibilities of accommodation with Peking. In this new situation, sensitivities to China's armed strength can be increased in its environment by displays of hostility towards outside powers such as the US and the USSR, or towards large neighbors such as India and Japan. By precipitating a crisis in the Taiwan Strait, for example, or on the Himalayan border, Peking could expect to make several Southeast Asian governments quite anxious to develop mutual understandings, and perhaps more disposed to allow China some influence in their policy-making. Peking, however, evidently would not wish to display its power in ways that would provoke the US to *extend* its modified Asian security role, or that would lead to military build-ups in India and Japan, assisted respectively by the Soviet Union and the US.

China's capabilities for the advancement of its external aims are substantial, but are affected by significant limitations. Its capacity to generate revolutionary power in foreign states is considerable; it can do much to mold the psychology of other Asian Communist movements, but it is less capable of identifying with them than it was previously because of its intensified nationalism, and is unwilling to see them develop their own styles and policies. Resources for diplomacy towards non-Communist states are lacking, and evidently will not be developed unless the present Maoist approach to foreign policy undergoes a major change. The regime's military power, however, makes its presence felt throughout southern Asia, and awareness of that can probably be increased without serious risks by limited displays of force, and possibly also by working towards a resolution of the Indochina conflict with the US, using a combination of pressures and conciliation in order to demonstrate that the settlement is being largely imposed by China. For the present, however, Peking cannot openly use its armed forces to assist revolutionary movements in nearby countries; that would meet broad international disapproval, alienate potential supporters of Maoist movements elsewhere in Asia, and risk some form of retaliation by the US.

DECISION-MAKING

China's new militancy and fundamentalism appear to have simplified the making of foreign policy. The range of options available to the decision-makers has been reduced by the concentration on spreading revolution, and inclinations to experiment within the restricted framework of current doctrinal guidelines are evidently being held in check by the simplistic and extremist Maoist approach. The relative isolation of the decision-makers and their staffs from social and political realities in other Asian countries tends to protect their ideological premise from challenge, and must also limit critical evaluation of the methods chosen to further the regime's external aims. Upward communication to the high decision-makers from the working levels, moreover, is undoubtedly quite restricted, because the new pressures for ideological conformity must inhibit the expression of critical views and proposals for innovation. Insecurity, due to the unsettled atmosphere, probably causes many officials to adhere strictly to instructions and observe carefully the Maoist rituals.

The *institutions* through which foreign policy is made were severely affected by the Cultural Revolution, which was aimed especially against officials who were considered to be more interested in diplomacy than in the spread of violent change through the developing areas, and who were suspected of favoring a resumption of co-operation with the USSR. Foreign Minister Chen Yi was denounced and subjected to much humiliation during 1968. Four of his ten Vice-Ministers were reportedly suspended, and several senior officials in the regional departments of the Ministry and in related party departments are believed to have been replaced.[15] Chi Peng-fei, a Vice Minister of Foreign Affairs, formerly Ambassador to East Germany, who had apparently escaped censure during the purge, was appointed Acting Minister of Foreign Affairs on April 1, 1971. There has been considerable reorganization within the Ministry since 1966 but Asian Affairs are believed to be still the responsibility of Vice-Minister Han Nien-lung, a former Ambassador to Sweden, who received his present rank in 1964, and who was not personally affected by the Cultural Revolution.

The main lines of foreign policy are evidently decided by 74 year old Chou En-lai, the highest ranking leader after Mao Tse-tung. As Prime Minister since 1949, Chou has had extensive experience in managing both peaceful and hostile forms of Chinese diplomacy. The now very powerful military establishment, for reasons which will be indicated next, probably has a strong influence on Chou's decision-making, through the General Political Department under the General Staff of the People's Liberation Army and the Foreign Affairs Bureau within the Defense Ministry. The party apparatus, over which military leaders appear to have much control, is involved in external affairs

---

[15] See Melvin Gurtov, *op. cit.*, and Donald W. Klein, "The Ninth Central Committee," *The China Quarterly*, 45, Jan.–Mar. 1971, pp 37–56.

through its Central Committee's Foreign Relations Department, headed by Keng Piao, who became a member of the Central Committee in 1969.

Domestic Politics and Foreign Policy

As the imperatives which shape China's external policy derive mainly from the ethos of the new order, there are significant interconnections between the management of its foreign relations and its internal political processes. The projection of the regime's dynamism into the outside world is clearly felt to be necessary for its own vitality and stability; total commitment to Maoist values must be expressed—externally as well as domestically. The advances made by Marxist-Leninist movements in other countries, moreover, are expected to help sustain popular enthusiasm within China. All the zeal roused among the Chinese population on behalf of the affinitive Communist parties, meanwhile, is to protect the revolutionary culture against contamination by the "bourgeois" ideologies of the emerging nations and the west.

The Chinese regime's foreign policy is influenced by the complex effects of its evolution into an intensely radical Socialist state. This transformation has occurred through a process of internal struggle over issues concerning the generation and application of political power within the country and abroad. Under Mao Tse-tung's leadership, and in opposition to Liu Shao-chi and other "capitalist" minded figures, there has been a striving to assert the supremacy of the kind of power which the Communist party has exercised as a movement, by molding and activating individuals through manipulation of their psychology, using indoctrination and group dynamics. *Institutionalized* power has been viewed with suspicion; it has been felt that those possessing it tend to develop "bourgeois" outlooks while enjoying its rewards and developing their own expertise, and are inclined to alienate the masses by bureaucratic behavior. Yet the new order's capacity to develop the forms of direct and intimate social control preferred by the Maoists seems to have been reduced by structural and functional changes during the Cultural Revolution that have weakened the role of the Communist party.

When the Chinese Communist leaders began to build up a Socialist system during the early 1950's they were evidently agreed that the Soviet Union should be accepted as a model. They had long respected Moscow's primacy in international Communism, and apparently saw a need for a close economic and military partnership with the USSR. Its party and government hierarchies were virtually duplicated, China's industrialization followed its pattern, and there was close co-operation with its external policies. After the death of Stalin, however, the Chinese leaders were evidently unwilling to recognize that Stalin's ideological authority had passed to the USSR's unstable "collective leadership," and in 1956 their doctrinal convictions and their increasingly independent views on international Communist strategy caused them to disapprove of Khrushchev's liberalization in the USSR, and his new foreign policy, which stressed co-existence with the west and the promotion of Communism in the Third World by "peaceful" methods. Public respect for Moscow's leadership continued, but an extraordinary new program of accelerated Socialist economic development was launched in China, apparently in the hope of demonstrating that the regime had a superior dynamism which had been restricted by imitation of the Soviet system, and that it would now give great inspiration to Communist movements in Asia, Africa, and Latin America. Because the new drive placed great emphasis on activating the workers and peasants through intensified indoctrination, and ignored technological and administrative factors, however, the economy was severely disrupted, and the experiment terminated early in 1960. A long period of recovery then began, but by this time a split had developed in the higher levels of the party. A group headed by its Chairman, Mao Tse-tung, whose personal prestige had been committed to the discredited policy, remained convinced that the development of intense revolutionary dedication at all levels was the main requisite for economic growth, and that institutional controls should allow much freedom for workers and peasants to express their creativity under party direction. Other leaders of the party were in opposition, including Liu Shao-chi, Mao Tse-tung's successor as Head of State in 1959, who favored somewhat pragmatic economic policies, like those which had previously been in effect, and which had been responsible for impressive development on a planned basis between 1953 and 1958. This section of the ruling elite also apparently wished to continue in a modified form the established partnership with the Soviet Union, but by 1960 this was being dangerously strained by public Chinese criticisms of Moscow's policy that were evidently inspired by Mao Tse-tung's group.[16]

The Great Proletarian Cultural Revolution launched by Mao Tse-

[16] See Herbert Dinerstein in Steven L. Speigel and Kenneth N. Waltz, eds., *Conflict in World Politics* (Cambridge, Mass., Winthrop, 1971), pp 78–95; R. G. Boyd, "Revolutionary Nation-Building: The Chinese Model," *International Journal*, XXV, 1, Winter 1969–70, pp 69–93; and Philip Bridgham, "Mao's Cultural Revolution: The Struggle to Consolidate Power," *The China Quarterly*, 41, Jan.–Mar. 1970, pp 1–25.

tung in 1966, with the support of the military establishment headed by Lin Piao, was a large-scale campaign in which Liu Shao-chi and many of his alleged supporters were publicly discredited and removed from their posts. Approximately half of the party's Central Committee members were dismissed, together with most of the officials on its governing committees at the provincial level and below. The monopoly of power which had been exercised by the party was then assumed by the military establishment, whose representatives dominated new temporary organs known as *Revolutionary Committees.* As the party was slowly rebuilt, beginning in 1969, strong army influence was evident at its higher levels, and there were indications that it was intended to become virtually a political extension of the military establishment. Theoretical justification for this was provided by statements in the official press to the effect that the highest standards of revolutionary dedication were attained in the People's Liberation Army, because of its discipline, austerity, and exacting demands.[17] The media, which operate under strong military influence, exalt the Army's role as a powerful arm of the "dictatorship of the proletariat" which is protecting the regime against internal as well as external dangers. In 1971 the 44th anniversary of the Army (August 1) was given much more publicity than the 50th anniversary of the party (July 1), and the great qualities of the military forces were praised, but the party was warned that its members at all levels had to strive for greater dedication to the ideology.

The emerging system has assumed its fundamentalist character because the Maoist ruling elite, having conducted the severe purge in the name of basic Marxist-Leninist values, is seeking to construct a new order which would realize those ideals and overcome any tendencies towards "bourgeois" degeneration. This is being attempted by a process of "continuing revolution," i.e., ceaseless promotion of class struggles throughout the society to raise levels of revolutionary dedication and encourage complete renunciations of non-proletarian attitudes and beliefs. Through this social engineering, the new polity is to generate, in a purer and more effective manner, the kind of political power which the Communist movement had previously striven to develop. The nation is thus to reach higher and higher levels of Socialist advancement, and become even more dynamic; its external activities to spread revolution will thus become more effective.

The internal process of political development through social struggle is reflected in the distinctive foreign policy orientation which has been described in the previous section. The ideals which are being

[17] See Editorial, *Peking Review,* 31, Aug. 2, 1968, pp 5–8.

realized in China are to be promoted in the outside world, without compromises like those which caused Soviet policy to become "revisionist," and the achievements of the regime's statecraft are to assist its internal consolidation and growth. The intended linkages between domestic and external activity, however, are affected by problems which the ruling elite faces in its efforts to generate popular support and maintain its authority.

The compulsion to express Marxist-Leninist fundamentalism externally as well as internally, at the likely cost of neglecting national interests which could be advanced through diplomacy, appears to be based on profound convictions that, at all levels, beliefs in the regime's basic revolutionary ideals will weaken if they are not constantly given full expression, and that the radical power which is to transform foreign "bourgeois" states will not be generated within those societies unless China continues to build up her own system and communicates revolutionary zeal to Communist movements in the outside world. Hence there can be no question of restraint on the public expression of Chinese solidarity with Marxist-Leninist forces that are waging *peoples' wars.*

The development of the new order is assisted by giving the population experiences of vicarious involvement in successful struggles for power by foreign Communist movements, together with intense awareness of the nation's role as the center of inspiration for those revolutionary organizations. A policy that allowed much scope for peaceful co-existence with other states, it is clearly felt, would not be compatible with the continuing internal revolution, for that must be hostile to external as well as domestic manifestations of "bourgeois" ideology, and its objectives would be defeated if the Chinese population were given any basis for viewing non-Communist regimes in favorable light.

The ruling elite seems confident that support within its own power structure as well as among the bulk of the population will be increased by external revolutionary triumphs. Unless there are impressive achievements by affinitive Communist parties, however, especially in Asia, anxiety about the loyalties of persons in the higher levels of the regime may cause the new leaders to increase tensions in the confrontations with hostile states, especially the USSR, in order to elicit stronger expressions of solidarity from senior Chinese military, party, and administrative officials. Failures by Maoist parties in the environment will no doubt make the ruling elite quite apprehensive about the attitudes of its subordinates, and therefore probably more inclined to adopt tension-producing measures externally, so as to stir up more patriotic fervor within the system. Dissent in the higher and middle levels, even if major revolutionary gains were being achieved in nearby areas, would almost certainly be countered by a similar strategy, in the expectation that a new unity would be forged on the basis of intensified nationalist sentiments directed against outside threats. When the new order was being set up, during the final stages of the Cultural Revolution, intensive efforts were made to dramatize the country's external dangers, especially those presented by the Soviet Union after clashes on the Issuri and Amur rivers and the Sinkiang boundary. Border talks with the USSR began in late 1969, but Peking's domestic media continued to depict the Soviet Union as a hostile state.[18]

There is also a danger of instability in the Chinese polity because it has assumed some of the characteristics of a radical praetorian system. With the heavy concentration of authority in the military establishment, army leaders are evidently tending to divide into competing loyalty groups. The Chinese Communist party, being rebuilt as an extension of the military establishment, does not have a corporate life of its own, and evidently can do little to restrain and resolve army rivalries. At the same time, military domination is evidently having an adverse effect on the party's capacity to indoctrinate and mobilize the population, and yet problems of social control may well be increasing. The new order, by comparison with the pre-Cultural Revolution regime, lacks institutions for political participation, especially as the former mass organizations have not been revived, yet its demands for ideological conformity are stricter, and the restructured party is oriented more towards dominating rather than identifying with the masses. Finally, Mao Tse-tung's role as a charismatic leader is weakening, as age and ill health prevent him from further developing his philosophy and political style; Prime Minister Chou En-lai, the next most prominent figure, has the image of a relatively flexible administrator and politician, not that of a forceful or inspiring personality.[19] He appears to have become responsible for the overall direction of the regime's affairs since the disappearance in late 1971 of Defense Minister Lin Piao, who was to have succeeded Mao Tse-tung. The military leaders evidently feel obliged to rely on Chou's expertise and utilize his international status, but his position may not be strong enough to challenge their wishes on any important issue or to moderate their rivalries. High level conflicts involving very senior army personnel are believed to

[18] See Chinese Foreign Ministry document, *Peking Review*, 41, Oct. 10, 1969, pp 8–15, and article, "Leninism or Social Imperialism," *Peking Review*, 17, April 24, 1970, pp 5–15.

[19] See Thomas W. Robinson, "Chou En-lai's Political Style: Comparisons with Mao Tse-tung and Lin Piao," *Asian Survey*, X, 12, Dec. 1970, pp 1101–1116.

have been responsible for the unprecedented cancellation of the national day celebrations on October 1, 1971.

China and the World Community

To the outside world China presents the image of a highly unified radical system with an immense potential for revolutionary modernization. Its statecraft is portrayed as the expression of a supreme historical mission, to be proclaimed rather than defended against "revisionist" and "bourgeois" critics, and yet well understood by and intimately linked with the aspirations of "oppressed" peoples throughout the world, who respond enthusiastically to its inspiring appeals. While representing that it is operating from a position of strength in the contemporary international system, however, it endeavors to develop an effective combination of what its theorists call "alliance and struggle methods" in its foreign relations, to overcome tacitly recognized weaknesses in its role and gain ascendancy over the west, the Soviet Union, and the "reactionary" governments in the developing areas. The global revolutionary struggle, conceived as an integrated process under China's leadership, is to draw support from all the political forces in the outside world that can be won over as allies, and is to be directed principally against the "main enemy." This is an extension of a basic principle of the *people's war* doctrine, i.e., that of recruiting potential supporters among the "middle of the road" elements, in order to build up the "progressive" forces and to isolate and strike against the main opponents.[20]

The expedient duality in China's statecraft has another dimension because of the foreign policy requirements of the country's modernization. These receive oblique but significant recognition in ideological pronouncements, which indicate that the regime needs international conditions which will be favorable for "Socialist construction." The nation's economic development requires large imports of capital goods, iron and steel, chemicals, raw materials, and fuels. Because of the Chinese aversion for the USSR, most of these items have to be obtained from the middle powers in the capitalist world. Such purchases are given little publicity by Peking's media, but diplomacy towards those states seeks to exploit the opportunities for this commerce, and to increase the exports by which it is largely financed. Revolutionary aims, meanwhile, are served by encouraging anti-US attitudes in these major trading partners.

[20] See Tang Tsou and Morton H. Halperin, *op. cit.*, and "Long Live the Victory of People's War."

While in effect drawing on the resources of the advanced private enterprise states in the "intermediate zone" between the superpowers, the Chinese regime gives most of its attention to promoting revolutionary violence and cultivating potential allies in the rest of that vast sector of the international system. Ongoing and incipient peoples' wars in India and several other neighboring states are publicly encouraged, while distant new states are mostly shown goodwill and are urged to support China's opposition to "imperialism" and especially to the US. In general, the developing countries which are closer appear to be considered by the Chinese to be better-prepared for, or more vulnerable to, revolutionary violence, and only a few are objects of Peking's "alliance" diplomacy.

THE MIDDLE POWERS

With the more advanced West European countries, which comprise the main group of middle powers, relatively cordial relations are maintained, facilitating substantial imports of plant, machinery, construction materials, instruments, and other items vital for industrialization. Purchases from West Germany, Britain, France, Italy, the Netherlands, Sweden, Switzerland, Belgium, Finland, Norway, Austria, and Denmark in 1970 totalled $535.5 million—about one third of China's total imports from the non-Communist world.[21] Commerce with these states is not affected by the encouragement of peoples' wars in southern Asia, as the European trading partners have only secondary interests in that region, and seek to expand their business with Peking; indeed they compete against each other, especially by extending or underwriting credits that assist Chinese purchases. Their enthusiasm, moreover, is politically advantageous, for most of them respect the People's Republic's international interests. Only France, however, has given significant support to Peking's anti-US policies and this has been done principally in relation to the Indochina war, but as a manifestation of Gaullist nationalism, rather than an expression of rapport with China. The Maoist regime, as has been stressed, lacks resources for meaningful interaction with administrations in advanced open societies, and its hostility to "imperialism" has little in common with the moderate anti-American economic nationalism of the major West European states.[22]

Japan is accorded separate treatment, as a major capital exporter and as a neighboring middle power aligned with the US. Industrial imports

[21] *Current Scene*, IX, 8, August 7, 1971.

[22] See Arthur Lall's comments on Chinese diplomacy in *How Communist China Negotiates* (New York: Columbia University Press, 1968), pp 3–8.

from Japan are very large, and indeed exceed those from all the West European states. Much is done by Tokyo to expand these sales, which totalled $568.9 million in 1970,[23] yet Peking, while showing a clear preference for Japan over the other advanced trading partners, displays extreme hostility to its Liberal-Democratic government, accusing that administration of having "imperialistic" designs and collaborating with the US's "aggressive" policies. This animosity is clearly intended to discourage Japan from assuming a more active political role in South and East Asia, especially in line with Washington's hopes for co-operation in security matters between Peking's non-Communist neighbors. Tokyo is pressured by Chinese threats to end the trade, which represents a major element in its foreign commerce. A further Chinese objective is to help the extreme left Japanese Socialist party attract more popular support. This organization, a leading opposition force in the Diet, is somewhat receptive to Maoism; Peking has been developing contacts with it for more than a decade, and especially since 1966, when the Chinese denounced the Japanese Communist party for advocating a new Sino-Soviet alliance to assist North Vietnam.[24]

THIRD WORLD NEIGHBORS

While the Chinese regime endeavors to prevent the development of what must realistically be called the constructive Japanese role in its environment, which has developed mainly through economic assistance programs, its revolutionary statecraft is directed principally at southern Asia. Strong encouragement is given to Maoist parties which are claimed to be waging vigorous armed struggles in Burma, Thailand, Malaysia, Indonesia, the Philippines and India. Peking's attitudes towards most of these states are hostile, and, on behalf of the Communist insurgents in the first three, clandestine radio stations in South China broadcast appeals for support among their populations and direct propaganda against their governments. For strategic reasons, the developing peoples' wars in these mainland Southeast Asian countries are probably considered to be highly important. Although they are being waged by small guerrilla forces estimated to number between 500 and 2,000 men, they can be given military assistance from China and North Vietnam, and it will evidently be feasible to expand this aid if further Communist gains are made in Laos and Cambodia, where the US is

---

[23] *Current Scene,* IX, 8, August 7, 1971.

[24] Peking's relations with the Japanese Socialist party are discussed by Chae-Jin Lee in "Factional Politics in the Japanese Socialist Party: The Chinese Cultural Revolution Case," *Asian Survey,* X, 3, Mar. 1970, pp. 230–243.

unwilling to intervene. In Peking's view, the insurgency in Burma is presumably the most significant, as this is an adjacent country under an oppressive military dictatorship which faces acute internal security problems, including serious disaffection among the relatively large minorities along the Yunnan border. The struggle in Thailand probably ranks next in importance because of this state's proximity to Indochina, and its significance as the nearest active ally of the US.

For the present, however, because the Maoist parties in continental Southeast Asia are small, China's designs for the spread of violent change depend very much on co-operation with the independently minded Communist leaders of North Vietnam, as armed forces under their direction or inspiration which control large areas of South Vietnam, eastern Cambodia, and the eastern half of Laos, may well be able to extend their authority over the whole of Indochina as the US reduces its active military support of the Saigon government. Such a victory would have a major impact on the politics of the region, and would no doubt greatly encourage the Peking-oriented Communist movements in Thailand, Burma and Malaysia. China, accordingly, is endeavoring to develop closer bonds with Hanoi, but understanding is hindered by Peking's insistence on the supremacy of Maoism and North Vietnam's evident desire to maintain friendly relations with the Soviet Union, its main source of military aid and, more importantly, of support against possible Chinese pressures.[25]

In South Asia, Soviet competition is a much more serious problem and is partly responsible for a major exercise in alliance diplomacy. "Struggle" methods are used in relation to India, to defeat Moscow's aims and effect violent change, but Pakistan is treated as a potential ally. The two lines of strategy are evidently intended to be complementary, but the second appears to work against some of the first's objectives, yet produces more significant results. The contrast reflects highly effective identification with anti-Indian Islamic nationalism in West Pakistan, and exclusive involvement with a small narrowly based Maoist movement in India.

Peking is openly hostile to Indira Gandhi's Congress administration in New Delhi, and denounces it as a "reactionary" government which serves the interests of India's exploiting classes and collaborates with the superpowers against China, striving especially to hold territory seized from the old Empire by the British. Chinese broadcasts and publications directed at India keep alive memories of the 1962 Hima-

[25] See Donald S. Zagoria, *Vietnam Triangle* (New York: Pegasus, 1967), and Robert A. Rupen and Robert Farrell, eds., *Vietnam and the Sino-Soviet Dispute* (New York: Praeger, 1967).

layan border war, in which New Delhi's forces were rapidly overcome by Chinese thrusts into the Northeast Frontier Agency and the Ladakh area of Kashmir. While expressing determination to maintain control over all frontier territories that have historically belonged to China, Peking adds another threatening dimension to its stance by affirming solidarity with the army-backed regime in West Pakistan and endorsing its claims that India is endangering its security while supporting the independent Bengali government. During the 1965 Indo-Pakistani war China threatened military action against New Delhi's forces at a point on the border with the Indian protectorate of Sikkim, demanding the removal of Indian fortifications allegedly set up on the Chinese side of the boundary, and this earned much gratitude in Islamabad.

To push forward the revolution in India encouragement is given to the Communist party of India (Marxist-Leninist), which is engaging in terrorism and small-scale guerrilla warfare, mainly in West Bengal. This pro-Peking organization was established by extreme militants whom the Chinese encouraged to split off from the Communist party of India (Marxist) after it had refused to endorse a resort to violence in the countryside by its extreme left wing during 1967. The Communist party of India (Marxist) representing mainly the left wing of the country's original Marxist-Leninist party, however, has remained the strongest radical force in the country, and its parent organization, the Communist party of India, towards which it is bitterly hostile, is the only other important social protest movement. The Maoist body, handicapped by its identification with China, has not spread far out of West Bengal, and for the present does not seem capable of developing into a national organization. Peking's incitement of the Maoists suggests excessive optimism regarding their capabilities and the prospects for revolution in India. The long-term intention is probably to bring about the establishment of an affinitive regime, thereby thwarting Soviet policies in the region. The expressions of Chinese hostility, however, tend to strengthen ties between New Delhi and Moscow. The ruling Congress party looks to the Soviet Union for military and political support, especially under the terms of the 1971 Indo-Soviet Friendship Treaty, and the USSR seeks to strengthen the relationship in view of India's need for security against China, and of the extensive opportunities which New Delhi's friendship allows for Soviet information and cultural activities directed at the Indian public.[26]

China's links with Pakistan are directed against India and, obliquely, against the US and the USSR. The association with Islamabad became

[26] See Chester Bowles, "America and Russia in India," *Foreign Affairs*, 49, 4, July 1971, pp 636–651. See also *Current Scene*, VIII, 6, Mar. 15, 1970.

very active and very close after China's defeat of India in the Himalayan war of 1962. The Chinese, avoiding reference to their revolutionary aims, began a diplomacy based on common hostility to India, and in 1964 expressed solidarity with Pakistan's long-standing demand that the Kashmir dispute should be settled by self-determination. This evoked much gratitude, and very favorable publicity was given to China by Pakistani media, especially during and after the 1965 war with India. Popular admiration and enthusiasm for China contributed to the emergence of the leftist People's party as the leading political organization in the West Wing at the 1970 elections. The upheaval in East Pakistan during 1971, however, presented the Chinese with a difficult problem. There were opportunities for Maoist elements to gain leadership of the Bengali freedom struggle but the way was open to strengthen ties with the Yahya Khan government by supporting its extremely repressive policy in the East Wing, and this course was taken. The friendship with Pakistan had helped the development of strong pro-Chinese leadership in the extreme leftist National Awami party in the East Wing, however, and members of this organization were reportedly active in the Bengali resistance movement.[27]

Of India's small neighbors, Nepal is of some significance to Peking, because of its monarch's desire for external support to counter military and economic pressures from New Delhi that threaten its independence. Chinese diplomacy exploits this need with some success, and there are incidental benefits for a small local Maoist party which operates with some caution in view of Peking's interest in Nepalese goodwill. A friendly relationship with Ceylon's Socialist administration, which had developed partly because of commercial links that helped the island expand its rubber sales, has been strained since mid 1971 when the Bandaranaike government was threatened by a leftist insurgency that drew some inspiration from China.

OTHER NEW STATES

Revolutionary objectives are to a certain extent concealed in Chinese diplomacy towards numerous states in southwest Asia and Africa. Many of these are "progressive" in varying degrees, most are receptive to Soviet economic assistance and cultural exchange, and also to western aid, and there are few significant local Maoist organizations which can be encouraged. Friendships with these states are developed by pro-

[27] The positions of the People's party and the National Awami party before the upheaval in East Pakistan are reviewed by Craig Baxter in "Pakistan Votes," *Asian Survey*, XI, 3, Mar. 1971, pp 197–218.

viding modest economic assistance and identifying with their antipathies towards the west. Those benefiting from Peking's foreign aid programs include Tanzania, Zambia, Somalia, Southern Yemen, the Yemen Arab Republic, and Afghanistan. The radical Arab states, especially the United Arab Republic, Algeria and Syria, have been receiving special attention, but Peking is unable to compete against the large-scale economic and military assistance which they obtain from the Soviet Union.[28]

Achievements, Failures and Prospects

China's statecraft has achieved significant results in Asia, but thus far mostly *not* through inspiring and building up Maoist parties. As these advances have been made outside the main line of revolutionary statecraft, it is unclear how Peking evaluates their significance. They would seem to indicate a need for flexible methods that would facilitate identification with a wide range of "progressive" forces in neighboring states, and that would be aimed at the development of only partially affinitive forms of revolutionary power within other social systems.

The gains which must be quite apparent in the Maoist perspective relate mainly to Southeast Asia. Peking has won over and retained the loyalties of the national Marxist-Leninist parties in this area, with the exception of the Vietnamese Dang Lao Dong, and its affiliates in Cambodia and Laos. Support for Hanoi, notwithstanding its co-operation with Moscow, has contributed to the potentially decisive achievement of forcing the US to reduce its engagement, thereby lowering the credibility of its containment strategy, and giving encouragement to revolutionary movements in nearby countries. The shift in US policy may be opening the way for direct confrontations between the Chinese regime and the forces of nationalism in its area, but thus far it has been prompting small Southeast Asian states to seek understandings with Peking.

China evidently considers that the struggle to build up Maoist influence within the Vietnamese Communist movement must go forward, and that the achievements of the "liberation wars" in South Vietnam, Cambodia and Laos have been possible *despite*, rather than *because* of the Dang Lao Dong's strength as a nationalist and ideologically independent organization. To the extent that this attitude remains

[28] See Joseph E. Khalili, "Sino-Arab Relations," *Asian Survey*, VIII, 8, Aug. 1968, pp 678–690; *Current Scene* V, 15, Sept. 15, 1967; and G. T. Yu, "China in Africa," *Yearbook of World Affairs* (London: The London Institute of World Affairs, 1970), pp 125–137.

evident, however, it will no doubt continue to prevent understanding with Hanoi, and, therefore, effective exploitation of the opportunities for further revolutionary gains after the anticipated extension of Communist control over the whole of Indochina.

Because of their stress on the universal validity of Maoism, the Peking leaders are disinclined to recognize that other Asian Communist movements, like their own, must develop effective nationalist appeals in order to build up their capabilities for revolutionary action. The Maoist perspective, however, is being challenged not only by the Dang Lao Dong's achievements but also by Peking's successes in contributing to the growth of the leftist People's party in Pakistan. The emergence of the new leading political organization in West Pakistan, a loosely structured body which is largely a projection of Bhutto's personality, suggests that the Chinese regime, by identifying with major forces of nationalism in a friendly country, can stimulate the growth of strong, relatively affinitive movements, thereby generating more usable political power than could be developed through mere extensions of its own system like the Maoist parties in southern Asia. Other conclusions at variance with the Maoist outlook are suggested by Peking's achievement in developing understanding and co-operation with the Japanese Socialist party. The rapport with this organization appears to be based mainly on shared internationalist militancy, and it is evidently not being strained by demands for acceptance of the Chinese leader's doctrine. The organization would clearly lose some of its distinctive appeal and be less creative in developing its role if it were to become totally identified with the Maoist regime. If it can be persuaded to continue responding to the Marxist-Leninist internationalism that is still present in the Chinese ideology, this party may well become a very useful ally.

Relatively affinitive leftist parties like those in Japan and West Pakistan are not being encouraged to develop in other Asian countries; that, for the present, does not seem to be a major Chinese objective. Yet while Peking's policy remains oriented towards molding the psychology of foreign Communist movements and guiding their activities its results will probably continue to be limited by the restrictions which Maoism tends to impose on their growth because of its distinctively nationalist character and its extremism. Hence the Chinese-inspired Marxist-Leninist parties of continental Southeast Asia, although encouraged and aided by the reduction of the US's involvement in Indochina, may not be able to develop significant capabilities for political violence. China's efforts to transform these parties and those of South Asia into strong revolutionary organizations moreover may be affected by domestic problems. Mao Tse-tung's charismatic role is ending and is not likely to be effectively assumed by his successor; some of the praetorian features of the new order on balance seem to hinder rather than assist the development of public support; and there is a danger of serious conflict within the military elite. The Asian Maoist parties will no doubt experience losses of confidence and direction if there is grave disunity in China, and they may react unfavorably if Peking, because of anxieties about their attitudes, urges them to show more and more loyalty to its leadership.

For ideological reasons, China's policy is oriented away from potentially useful interaction with major non-Communist political forces in most of the area. Yet on account of internal tensions, and in response to opportunities and problems in Asia, Peking's external policy may have begun to move into a transitional stage. Within the ruling elite there may be groups which believe that, to strengthen morale and loyalties at all levels of the system, substantial increases in the regime's international status and influence are needed, and that there must be sufficient ideological flexibility to secure these by the most expedient means. A readiness to introduce new lines of diplomacy may be encouraged by the attempts of small Southeast Asian states to reach understandings with China regarding their futures as the US's presence in their area decreases. More importantly, opportunities to profit from Washington's new quest for meaningful dialogue may well have a powerful effect, because of the importance of the potential gains. What has been the dominant concern with showing total hostility to the imperialist enemy may be modified to attain recognition as the leading continental power which can settle the affairs of Asia in virtual collaboration with as well as struggle against the US. At the same time, there may be an increasing disposition to manage the relationship with Washington in ways that will prevent more active Soviet involvement in China's part of the world. Such purposes might be obscured by reiterations of loyalty to Maoist principles, and by phases of indecision and experimentation, but could lead to significant "revisionist" changes in Peking's foreign relations.

Japan

HANS H. BAERWALD

The Strategic Setting

Japan's foreign policy in the post-World War II era
can be viewed from a variety of perspectives. Officially,
Japan has been guided principally by its relationship
with the United States, as exemplified in the Treaty
of Mutual Cooperation and Security, 1960 (and its
earlier version, 1951). Economically, the requirements
of an ever-expanding economy and the concomitant
necessity for trade have helped to shape the broad
outlines of Japanese foreign policy. Politically, the
chasm that has separated the worldview of the governing
Liberal-Democratic party from that of its major
opposition, the Socialist party, has contributed
substantially to the constraints imposed on the
formulators of Japanese foreign policy.

Geographical factors have also influenced to varying
degrees the course of Japanese foreign policy. As an
island country, Japan has natural boundaries that have
allowed it periodically (as in the Tokugawa era,
1603–1867) to isolate itself from the rest of the world.
These have also provided it with several alternative
paths for foreign expansion in the past century. The
ocean has been important for fishing, and the
requirements of Japan's expanding foreign trade have
made the Japanese extremely sensitive to the maintenance
of open sea lanes.

Korea, across the Tsushima straits, is Japan's closest
neighbor, although this proximity has not provided a
solid basis for friendship. Rather, it has produced

a compound mixture of concern, desire to control[1] (culminating in Korea's annexation as a colony of Japan between 1910 and 1945), and, more recently, Japan's reluctant recognition that the Korean peninsula is "the dagger that points at the heart of Japan."

Historically and culturally, China has provided the major external influence on Japan. Traditionally, the Japanese considered themselves the moon to China's sun, but with the decline in Chinese power in the late 19th century and the concomitant rise in Japanese power, the Japanese attitude changed to one in which the Japanese thought of themselves more as the *sensei* (teacher) and the Chinese as the *deshi* (student). The post-World War II Japanese attitude toward China has been a curious combination of a feeling of guilt about the innumerable atrocities committed during Japan's aggression against China (1936-45) and, in the past decade, a strong sense of self-confidence in any comparison with China—cultural, political or economic. China's bifurcation since 1949 into the People's Republic and the Nationalist Government on Taiwan has added a further dimension to the complexity of this attitude.

Russia, although a neighbor, is more of an historical rival than a friend. Competition for control of Northeast Asia has bred more fear and suspicion than amity in this relationship. Retention by the Soviet Union of former Japanese territory—the Kurile Islands (to the northeast of Hokkaido) and the southern portion of Sakhalin (Karafuto to the Japanese)—after World War II remains a factor impeding the reversal of these attitudes.

Increasingly the Japanese have been looking southward to Southeast Asia and to Australia both for access to raw materials and for a market. Historically, this is a relatively recent area of concern, as most of that area was under the control of western imperialist powers prior to the 1950's. Indeed, one impetus for Japanese expansionism in the 1930's and early 1940's, was to counteract this control, as reflected in "The Greater East Asian Co-Prosperity Sphere" slogan.

While Japan is located off the coast of Asia, for the greater part of the post-World War II era Japanese official policy has been directed more toward the United States and thence to Europe than toward Asia. Indeed, the Japanese have had to face a paradox: they are an Asian people, but as a highly-industrialized society they are also part of the "developed" world—the developed "north" in contrast to the

---

[1] Japan's first attempt to bring Korea within its sphere of influence came in the early 17th century, coinciding with—but counteracting—the expansion of the Ch'ing (MANCHU) dynasty into the area. Competition over Korea on the part of Japan, China and Russia has a long, historical background.

less developed "south" in economic terms—as are North America and Europe. Notwithstanding its geographic location, Japan is a member of the Organization for Economic and Cooperative Development (OECD), which is. centered around the Atlantic. This paradox has reflected the uncertainty on the part of the Japanese concerning where their national interests lie and what their real national identity is in the world political context.

Internal Determinants of Japanese Foreign Policy

SOCIETY AND ECONOMY

Japan is a geopolitical anomaly; it consists of an island chain in the northwestern Pacific with a population of about one hundred and three million people who are spread unevenly over an area approximating the state of Montana (two-thirds of them live in the major industrial-commercial zone extending from Tokyo in the northeast to Kyushu in the southwest). Japan has an extraordinarily narrow base of the raw materials that are generally believed to be an absolute prerequisite for industrialization. Despite Japan's scarcity of natural resources and its relatively late (by contrast to western nations) modernization, it became, in the latter half of the 1960's, the third largest nation-state, as measured in terms of gross national product (GNP). The fact that this feat was accomplished not only in the face of a paucity of nature's bounty, but also in spite of Japan's defeat in war, is generally attributed to the Japanese people, who by their plain hard work provide their nation's single most substantial asset.

Several possibilities emerge from a consideration of the economic miracle that the Japanese have wrought. First, it is clear that their economy has expanded at a prodigious rate—well in excess of ten percent annually during the 1960's. Second, it is likely that their pattern of expansion will continue. Third, it is also likely that the rate of growth of their economy may decline as popular concerns with environmental pollution begin to impinge on governmental and industrial decision-makers. As a consequence of these divergent pulls, projections of the absolute size of the Japanese economy do vary.

What is obvious, however, is that Japan is well on the way to becoming an economic giant—certainly in Asia, and to a somewhat lesser degree on a global scale. What used to be said about the relationship between the United States and Japan—that when the American economy has a cold, Japan's has pneumonia—can already be said with considerable justification about Japan's role vis-à-vis South Korea, Taiwan, and most of the countries of Southeast Asia. Furthermore, the relationship between the Japanese and American economies itself is in the process of a shifting and not entirely amicable adjustment, as was clearly evident in the events surrounding the floating of both the dollar and the yen in 1971.

Hence, Asians and Europeans—as well as Americans—will probably have to become used to coming to terms with Japan as a significant factor in their economies. It is an open question, however, whether the Japanese will want to play a diplomatic and political role commensurate with their economic power.

CAPABILITIES AND EXTERNAL RESTRAINTS ON FOREIGN POLICY

Certain broad patterns of Japan's foreign policy problems emerge and divide by era. During its occupation after World War II, Japan did not really have a foreign policy. Instead, the government had to deal with the foreigners—mainly American—who were trying to govern their country. The period of occupation can be divided into two nearly equal parts. In the first, government efforts sought to protect the traditional polity (especially the bureaucracy's authority) to every possible extent. For instance, diplomats who spoke English and who could communicate directly with the occupiers were in a fortunate position and were extremely useful to the government, although it meant in effect that the Foreign Ministry had to become the Central Liaison Office through which most of the day-to-day contact between Occupation Headquarters and the Japanese Government was channeled. In this context it is not surprising that three of the occupation-era prime ministers (Shidehara Kijuro, Yoshida Shigeru and Ashida Hitoshi) had had lengthy careers in their country's diplomatic service. In the second part of this era, government attention was spent—at least in part—on an effort to blunt the effects of the "reverse course" in American occupation policy (from "reform" to "rehabilitation"). The most notable instance of this effort was Premier Yoshida's temporizing on the question of Japan's rearming precipitously and on a large scale, as was called for by Special Envoy John Foster Dulles during negotiations on the 1951 Peace Treaty with Japan that formally ended World War II.

On neither occasion did the Japanese public fully endorse its officialdom. During the occupation's "reformist" era (1945–48), the "traditionalists" believed their government had not done its utmost to protect the traditional polity (the definition of which verges inevitably on the mystical), whereas the "modernizers" believed too little support had been given to the wholesale restructuring of their society. During the rebuilding "rehabilitation" era (1948–51) the principal source of dissent came from Japanese progressives, for whom abiding by the strictest interpretation of the new "Peace Constitution" had become an article of fundamental faith.

Similar divisions and concerns surrounded the peace settlement. Even the dissenters were pleased that a peace treaty had been negotiated, signed and ratified by 1952. That was not the problem. Questions were raised, however, regarding the exclusion of China, the Soviet Union, Czechoslovakia, India and Burma from the signatories. China's non-inclusion was, in a sense, a victory for the Japanese negotiators in that it permitted them to participate in the final choice regarding which China, Nationalist or Communist, was to be recognized as the inheritor of the government against which they had waged war for over a decade. They speedily decided on the Nationalist Government in Taiwan. Neither India nor Burma presented a major issue, except regarding reparations. What did create concern—and has continued to do so—was the Russian absence. (It must be recalled that the negotiations, principally by and with the United States, transpired during the height of the Korean war.) The Russians and Japanese have still not negotiated a formal peace treaty with each other, though formal diplomatic relations were re-established in 1956.[2] This move enabled Japan to overcome Soviet vetoes in the United Nations, which had blocked Japan's applications for membership but had not resolved disputed issues such as the status of the "northern islands," which remains in abeyance to this day.

Because it was difficult for the dissenters not to agree that a peace treaty, incomplete though it might be, was more desirable than an occupation of possibly indefinite duration, their criticism went beyond the document itself and focused on the 1951 bilateral Security Pact with the United States. From their point of view the pact's inclusion in the peace settlement in effect forced Japan to take sides in the then highly-inflamed "cold war," and they argued that the new alliance merely replaced one form of Japanese subservience to the United States (the principal agent of the occupation) for another. For them it seemed an insubstantial substitute.

[2] For a full discussion, please see Donald C. Hellmann, *Japanese Domestic Politics and Foreign Policy, The Peace Agreement with the Soviet Union* (Berkeley and Los Angeles: University of California Press, 1969).

As Japanese dissatisfaction with the alliance became more general, two issues became the focus and symbol of that feeling: the continued presence of American military bases on Japanese soil; and American control over Okinawa. Both issues are now (twenty years after the peace settlement) well on their way to being satisfactorily resolved, at least from Japan's perspective. Since these two issues have been very significant for the Japanese a brief elaboration of the substantive issues involved seems necessary.

As late as 1968 the United States still retained close to one hundred and fifty military installations throughout Japan's home islands. They ranged in size from such major complexes as the naval base at Yokosuka, south of Yokohama, and the Tachikawa air base on the western outskirts of Tokyo, to minor complexes (as far as displacement of land is concerned) like radar or other communication sites. Few Japanese, outside of official circles in Japan's foreign and defense communities, continued to view these installations favorably.

Various factors influenced the Japanese: in the 1950's the continued presence of the bases was viewed as either the price Japan had to pay for the Peace Treaty or as the perpetuation of the occupation, or both. American pronouncements to the effect that the bases provided Japan with defensive capabilities which would otherwise not be available were all too readily dismissed on the basis that until the latter half of the 1960's no external threats were perceived or that the bases increased their country's vulnerability by being possible targets of attack.

Many Japanese supported a policy of nonalignment and friendship. And, although America itself might have benign intentions vis-à-vis Japan, it had enemies. Why should Japan open itself to the possibility of becoming involved in hostilities that might be a consequence of American foreign policy? Such a situation might be acceptable only if there was a substantial congruence of interests between the two countries.

The existence of a fundamental affinity of interests was subject to increasingly serious doubts in the 1960's in the aftermath of the new pact's acceptance at the beginning of that decade. As Japan's GNP continued its spectacular upward climb, so did the nationalist aspirations of many Japanese for greater autonomy. Furthermore, America's seemingly ever-deepening involvement in Indochina in the latter half of the decade spread doubts in some quarters about the senior partner's wisdom and its ability to cope with Asian problems.

Okinawa, the largest of the Ryukyu Islands, acquired a status similar to the base issue, that is, as a symbol of the strains and stresses in the alliance. In 1945, near the close of the war in the Pacific, American forces had taken Okinawa from the Japanese in the bloodiest encounter of that conflict. It became an area of direct military government, unlike Japan's home islands, where the occupation exercised control through the existing government. In the peace settlement the United States recognized Japan's "residual sovereignty" over the Ryukyus, but no terminal date was set for the possible reversion of Okinawa to Japan (or alternative dispensations).

"Keystone of the Pacific" became the sobriquet bestowed on Okinawa by the US military. The Pentagon poured billions of dollars into the installations located through the chain of islands, but especially on Okinawa itself. With the enlargement of the conflict in Indochina, especially after the commencement of the B-52 raids on North Vietnam (many of which originated from Okinawa), these islands became increasingly important supply, staging and training areas for the US military.

It was not only their strategic location and their day-to-day utility (for another possible war in Korea as well as Indochina) that made the Ryukyuan bases valuable to the US. Of equal importance was the capability to use them without restrictions ("free use") so long as they remained under American administrative control. This is to say, the American authorities were not hampered by the requirement for "prior consultation" with the Japanese government in the event of a major change in the disposition of US military forces. Presumably the latter restriction referred expressly to movement of nuclear weapons into or out of the area, although this was never entirely understood by everyone.

Japanese enthusiasm on the Ryukyu Islands reversion question remained lukewarm until the latter half of the 1960's—even if Okinawan inclinations were being forcefully expressed considerably earlier—for essentially the following reasons. First, the Japanese government did not wish to antagonize its senior partner. Second, the Japanese home-islanders retained some element of prejudice vis-à-vis their Okinawan brethren. Third, so long as the Americans found it useful to have nuclear weapons in the area, it was just barely possible that the Ryukyus would be the major target of attack rather than the home islands themselves.

Thus the Japanese acquiesced with the arrangement, but with increasing reluctance after the enlargement of the Indochinese conflict; and the role that Okinawa played in it had become the object of public concern in Japan. Pressure on behalf of administrative reversion to Japan mounted steadily; so much so that fears were expressed concerning the future of the alliance if the issues were not resolved in a manner satisfactory to Japanese nationalist aspirations.

President Nixon and Prime Minister Sato, at their meeting in November 1969, agreed in principle to the proposition that the Ryukyus would revert to Japan by 1972 and that any American bases on the islands would come under the Security Pact's "prior consultation" clause governing the use of bases in Japan. This agreement defused the issue and averted, for the time being, an end to the alliance, although there was some grumbling in Japan because their government had apparently formally recognized South Korea's and Taiwan's importance to Japanese security.

Both of these issues seem to be well on the road to resolution. Some American military bases still remain in Japan, but their number is constantly being reduced. It can also be anticipated that the endless details of Okinawan reversion to Japan will have been worked out by 1972 (barring unexpected dramatic new developments in East Asia), and that the two governments will adhere to the timetable established in the 1969 Nixon-Sato communiqué. Friction will be an inevitable by-product of the alliance, but it may take strikingly different forms in the 1970's in view of the Nixon Doctrine and Japan's own more assertive foreign policy.

Domestic Politics and Foreign Policy

World War II resulted in the destruction of Japan's major industrial cities, including the awesome fire-bomb raids on Tokyo and the dropping of the atomic bombs on Hiroshima and Nagasaki, the psychological trauma of defeat, profound for a people to whom the concept and historical memory of defeat was alien, and the shock of finding their country occupied by foreign military forces.

Participation in a devastating—almost suicidal—war, and the resultant defeat and occupation of the Japanese home islands, not to mention the loss of empire (Taiwan, Korea, Manchuria, Karafuto and the Kurile Islands, and even, until recently, territory considered part of Japan such as the Ryukyu and Bonin Islands) has set the parameters for the direction of Japanese foreign policy over the last twenty-five years. Indeed, as determinants of the broad outlines of foreign policy the factors associated with the road to and from the Pacific war have been of equal importance to the requirements of economic survival and growth defined in geopolitical terms, such as the location of Japan, its insular character, and the ratio of population to available land and resources.

The Japanese people, including their policy-makers, have asked themselves why their pre-1945 foreign policy failed. Their answers have been varied. Some (and possibly their number is increasing) would maintain that the policies of the western powers—particularly the United States—frustrated the grand design of The Greater East Asia Co-Prosperity Sphere by means of which Japan was to have gained hegemony over Asia and, presumably—with her German and Italian partners—the world. Most, however, believe that the fault lay with the adventurism of their own military—aided and abetted by segments of the business community, the expansionist ideology of ultranationalist ideologues, and the weakness of opposition to the "military-industrial-intellectual complex" of the 1930's. Undoubtedly the presumed penchant for pacifism together with a "nuclear allergy," both of which have been important in the post-war era as baggage carried by the Japanese, owe more to defeat and occupation than to geopolitical imperatives. Faint whisperings of bygone aspirations are beginning to be heard, as dramatized in 1970 by the dramatic ritual suicide of the erratically brilliant novelist-essayist-playwright-actor Mishima Yukio, who seems to have manifested most of the contradictory longings of the Japanese soul. For the present, Japanese foreign policy remains weighted down by the baggage of defeat and occupation, which is made feasible in security terms by the American nuclear umbrella. It is to these inputs that attention must be given at the outset.

DEFEAT AND OCCUPATION

Japan's dream of empire—one of the dominant themes in its modern history—can be traced back at least as far as the Sino-Japanese war of 1894–95 in which its control over Taiwan was recognized by the Chinese. Korea had been another objective from the period of the Meiji Restoration (1867–68), but the tri-cornered competition among Japan, China and Russia for a dominant influence in this area of Northeast Asia prevented the absorption of Korea into the Japanese Empire until 1910, after Russia's defeat in the Russo-Japanese war of 1904–5. Japan also acquired Karafuto (the southern half of Sakhalin Island) in the peace treaty that ended that war.

An attempt to seize the Shantung peninsula from China during the first World War was frustrated at the Versailles Peace Conference, largely due to American opposition. This rankled the Japanese deeply and contributed to their seizure of Manchuria in 1931 and to the outbreak of full-scale (if undeclared) war between China and Japan in 1936. Japan's foreign policy in the pre-World War II period was dominated by an expansionist-minded military clique which brought the country into a major confrontation with the United States leading to the surprise attack on Pearl Harbor on December 7, 1941 and to Japan's eventual total and disastrous defeat.

Given this background, it is no wonder that Japan's World War II antagonists laid down certain terms of surrender in the Potsdam Declaration of July 26, 1945 which have left a deep imprint:

There must be eliminated for all time the authority and influence of those who have deceived and misled the people of Japan into embarking on world conquest, for we insist that a new order of peace, security and justice will be impossible until irresponsible militarism is driven from the world.

Defeat not only ended the imperial dream. It also brought in its wake, at least initially, an occupation the policies of which were designed to carry out the Potsdam Declaration: Japan was to be rendered impotent, both militarily and, to a considerable extent, economically. It was completely demilitarized; all armed forces were abolished, and most of the leadership, tainted with war guilt, was either tried as war criminals or removed and barred from positions of public responsibility.

Nothing less than the wholesale restructuring of the Japanese polity was contemplated by the victors. It was presumed that the end result of occupation reforms would be a democratic and peaceful Japan. Official policies guiding these efforts frequently linked these goals. Thus, any potential revival of militarism was viewed not only as a problem in itself but also as inimical to the germinating of democratic tendencies. Article IX of the 1947 Constitution provides the quintessential expression of this policy:

Aspiring sincerely to an international peace based on justice and order, the Japanese people renounce war as a sovereign right of the nation and the threat or use of force as means of settling international disputes.

In order to accomplish the aim of the preceding paragraph, land, sea and air forces, as well as other war potential, will never be maintained. The right of belligerency of the state will not be recognized.[3]

---

[3] The Constitution of Japan (1947) is available in numerous sources. See, for instance, Theodore McNelly, *Contemporary Government of Japan* (Boston: Houghton Mifflin Company, 1963), pp. 211–220.

In retrospect, the Japanese people have been truer to this mandate in their attitudes than those (principally American) tutors who insisted that the clause be incorporated into that document which provides the foundation for Japan's contemporary political system. It can be—and, of course, has been—argued that Article IX is dead. Japan does maintain ground, sea and air "Self Defense Forces" (SDF). Their development has progressed so far in recent years, in fact, that whether or not Japan will go nuclear is a lively topic of debate in certain restricted circles. However, although legal legerdemain has permitted the establishment of the SDF, and thereby vitiated the purposes of this constitutional provision, the provision still retains high potency in the realm of politics.

A two-thirds majority of both Houses of the Diet (Parliament) is required to initiate amendments to the Constitution. One segment— probably as yet a minority, but attitudes are shifting—of the governing Liberal-Democratic party (LDP) has been advocating constitutional revision for some years. A leading figure in this movement is former Prime Minister Kishi. All of the opposition (Japan Socialist, Democratic-Socialist, Komeito, and Communist) is, however, firmly opposed to constitutional changes, not so much because they believe the document to be perfect, but rather because of the importance that they attach to the retention of Article IX. Their stance, and that of the LDP moderates who fear that constitutional revision is not worth the political upheaval which they—probably realistically—consider a likely consequence were it to be attempted, have thus far been sufficient to deter any serious move to amend the Constitution.

If one set of major determinants of Japanese foreign policy is provided by defeat in a major war, demilitarization and Article IX of the Constitution, a second—if countervailing—set of determinants has flowed from Japan's relationship with the United States. Epitomizing the latter are the 1951 and 1960 Treaties of Mutual Cooperation and Security between the two countries.

Originally, this pact came into being in conjunction with the conclusion of the Peace Treaty between Japan and her former belligerents (except for the Soviet Union and the People's Republic of China). A commonly-held belief in Japan is that the Security Pact was the price that the Japanese Government had to pay for the Peace Treaty. More recent evidence, however, indicates that some Japanese policymakers had their own reasons for supporting the pact—principally that it could provide for American help in countering domestic subversion, especially though not exclusively that of the Communists,[4]

[4] Martin E. Weinstein, *Japan's Postwar Defense Policy, 1947–68* (New York and London: Columbia University Press, 1971).

and because of apprehensions concerning Communist (and particularly Soviet) objectives in launching the attack on South Korea in June 1950.

Officially, as stated in the preamble of the 1951 treaty, the following circumstances made the pact a necessity. First, Japan was reentering the world of international relations after having been disarmed. Second, Japan would be endangered in so doing because "irresponsible militarism has not yet been driven from the world." Third, Japan as a sovereign nation has the right to enter into collective security arrangements, a right recognized in the UN Charter. Fourth, that Japan desires the protection provided by the stationing of American armed forces in Japan so as to deter aggression against itself.

It is interesting to note that some of the wording in this preamble— e.g., the reference to "irresponsible militarism"—does, in fact, parallel the wording of the Potsdam Declaration—thus buttressing the belief that if the latter was what Japan had had to accept in surrendering, the former was the price to be paid for the Peace Treaty. In the intervening six years, however, it was no longer Japanese militarism that was found to be "irresponsible," but rather that of North Korea and its allies, the Soviet Union and the People's Republic of China.

Furthermore, in recognizing Japan's inherent right to enter into collective security arrangements, and presumably its right to self-defense, the pact provides a counterpoint to the motif of Article IX of the Constitution. It is small wonder that the interweaving of these themes has created more dissonance than harmony. From a practical standpoint, it is the Security Treaty, as amended in 1960, which has prevailed as far as the development of Japan's foreign policy is concerned. Without the treaty, Japan would probably not have had the presumed protection of America's nuclear umbrella, nor is it likely that the Japanese Self-Defense Forces would have developed in the way that they have.

By the same token, from a Japanese perspective, the Security Pact has locked Japan into bilateral and multilateral military security arrangements authored by the United States over the last twenty years. It is this circumstance which brought about the imbroglio surrounding the ratification of the revised Security Treaty by the Diet in the spring of 1960, as well as the anguish occasioned by the negotiations over Okinawan reversion to Japanese jurisdiction and the formula of "automatic extension" (on a year-to-year basis) of the treaty's life in the autumn of 1969 and spring of 1970. For, even if one were to accept the need for some form of military power as a necessary condition for the inherent right to self-defense, problems do remain if that right is to be exercised and at the same time circumscribed by Japan's status as a junior partner of the United States.

Not all Japanese believe that this politico-military alignment is either necessary or desirable. Some prefer the pristine purity of Article IX. Others see in the pact a limitation upon Japan, keeping her subservient to foreign (i.e., American) interests and hampering her capacity to act independently, especially in developing closer ties with China and the Soviet Union. It is within these confines and those provided by Japan's absolute need to trade (for access to raw materials as well as for markets) that much of the debate over Japanese foreign policy has taken place.

POLITICS AND FOREIGN POLICY-MAKING

On the surface Japanese politics give the appearance of being the very model of stability. Both chambers of the Diet and its executive, the Cabinet, have been controlled by the Liberal-Democratic party (LDP) since that party was formed in the autumn of 1955. Indeed, the LDP has a nearly two-thirds majority of seats. Not only that, but throughout the post-war period, conservatives in the LDP or its antecedents have dominated the government with the exception of a relatively brief inter-regnum in 1947–48 when two coalition cabinets in which the Socialists participated held the reins of government.

For all practical purposes, then, it has been the conservative LDP, articulating and responding principally to the interests of the business and farming communities and supported (some would maintain, dominated) by the bureaucracy, which has controlled Japanese politics since World War II. It is a formidable and neatly inter-locking coalition. Many LDP'ers began their careers as bureaucrats in various key ministries (especially Finance). Campaign funds flow from the business community and, thanks to an apportionment of Diet seats which penalizes residents of the large metropolitan centers such as Tokyo, Osaka, Kyoto and Kobe, rural-based support for the party provides it with a stable group of voters who enjoy a disproportionate share of representation.

Several destabilizing factors lurk beneath this seeming sea of tranquillity. First, the LDP is not monolithic. It is a federation of contending factions which, while they vote together in the Diet, are constantly maneuvering for position. In so doing they manage to complicate the policy-making process within the party by limiting the ability of the LDP's leadership to move freely. Prime Minister Kishi, for example, lost his position as chief executive after overseeing the ratification of the revised American-Japanese Security Pact in the summer of 1960 chiefly because dissident factions within the party could play upon dissatisfaction with his leadership in that situation.

Second, the bureaucracy—though it may be among the world's best educated and highly-trained, dedicated (albeit occasionally overbearing) and honest—is also not monolithic. In matters affecting foreign policy, disputes between the Foreign Ministry, on the one hand, and the Ministry of International Trade and Industry (MITI) are not uncommon. In the negotiations over textiles with the United States, for example, the Foreign Ministry was considerably more anxious to accede to American requests for voluntary restrictions on Japanese imports to the United States than was MITI, which, in turn, was more responsive to the views of the Japanese textile manufacturers. Inevitably, the issue became entangled in LDP factional politics, adding its quotient to the set of constraints affecting the formulation of public policy.

Third, the business community may be united in its financial support of the LDP, but this does not mean that it is united on substantive aspects of policy. What is best for those corporations which trade heavily with the United States may not be advantageous to those interested in expanding trade with the People's Republic of China—to mention only one area of controversy. Furthermore, this lack of unity within one of the principal support pillars of the LDP also feeds factionalism within the party since certain business interests have closer ties with one or another faction or set of factions, thus adding to the latter's autonomy.

Fourth, though the LDP has been constant, broadly speaking, in its support for the alliance with the United States, and has thereby provided a stable base for Japanese foreign policy, none of the opposition parties lends its full approval to this basic posture of recent Japanese foreign policy. Their criticism ranges from relatively moderate to radical with the Democratic Socialists at the former, the Komeito (literally, "Clean Government party,"—the political arm of the Nichiren Buddhist Soka Gakkai) toward the middle, and the left-wing of the Japan Socialist as well as the Communist parties at the other end of the spectrum.

Disarray within and among these opposition forces seriously affects their ability to provide the public with a coherent alternative foreign policy. The Japanese Socialist party (JSP), which has been the largest "renovationist" element, is possibly even more seriously wracked by internal factional strife than the LDP, because the JSP's disputes are ideological as well as personal. At one pole are the near-Maoists under the leadership of former chairman Sasaki Kozo, who espouse policies that have been far friendlier to Peking than those of the Japanese Communists in the post-1965 period. At the other pole are those led by former Secretary-General Eda Saburo, whose views are closer to the moderate Democratic-Socialists, who were one faction inside the JSP before its split at the beginning of the 1960's. Indeed, so serious is the current controversy within the JSP, that it may well have split once again by the time these lines appear in print.

As an alternative, voices are again being heard advocating the formation of a new party consisting of the moderates within the JSP, the Democratic-Socialists and the Komeito, and possibly including dissidents within the LDP. For a variety of reasons[5] a party combining these elements, while conceivable, is considered unlikely. It is worth mentioning only as an indication of the extent to which there is a feeling of dissatisfaction with the current situation.

Each of the major and minor parties faces, to varying degrees, a period of disequilibrium at the beginning of the 1970's. The LDP has managed to do extremely well in the last two general elections. Nonetheless, its popular vote, and, more importantly, its percentage of the popular vote, has continued a steady but unspectacular decline. Moreover, it is anticipated that Prime Minister Sato's tenure will come to an end with his current (fourth) term as LDP President, i.e., some time prior to November 1972. Problems attendant to the selection of his successor could and probably will create uncertainty. It is entirely possible that foreign policy issues will become embroiled in the resultant jockeying for power.

The JSP faces even more serious difficulties. Its drastic decline in the general election of 1969 has exacerbated its fratricidal proclivities. A further reduction in its strength is considered likely, thereby diminishing the party's capacity to bring into established channels that disaffected portion of the public which is oriented to direct action. That this is no idle speculation, was demonstrated by the activities of the Hansen Seinen Iinkai (Anti-War Youth Committee). Its adherents attempted to barricade the building in which the JSP was scheduled to hold its convention in the spring of 1970, and were only dispersed after the riot police were called, a recourse to which the JSP's leadership resorted with considerable embarrassment.

The JSP's moderate Democratic-Socialist (DSP) offshoot, while maintaining itself, is relatively stagnant. Its founder Nishio Suehiro's tight control over the DSP, which lasted for nearly ten years, has ended; and the succession went smoothly. Nonetheless, the degree to which its leadership is in the vanguard of those advocating a new mod-

---

[5] To explain them fully would require a separate essay. One factor that presents a formidable obstacle, however, is Japan's multi-member electoral district system which forces ideological comrades-in-arms to run against each other instead of against their presumed ideological enemies. For further details please see my "Ittō Nanaraku: The 1969 General Election in Japan," *Asian Survey*, March 1970, pp 179–194.

erate coalition grouping is seen as reflecting some pessimism about their party's future as an independent entity. Should their party not grow the question would have to be raised as to where the moderate intellectuals and unionists will go.

The Komeito, Soka Gakkai-nurtured, ambiguous in its ideology, increasingly moderating its former militancy, may be approaching a growth plateau. Its parent body is no longer certain that active involvement in politics is successful in gaining converts to Nichiren Shoshu, the neo-Buddhist doctrine of Soka Gakkai. Nonetheless, the Komeito's existence as a political party having a group of religious believers as its principal support is, at least partially, reflective of disorientation in one segment of the Japanese voting public. Whether the Komeito can continue to capitalize on the hardships experienced by recent immigrants into the large metropolitan regions and/or can find new sources of support in the semi-rural countryside remains to be seen.

Miyamoto Kenji's *Jishu-Dokuritsu Rosen* (Autonomously-Independent Line), initially propounded in the mid-1960's, has brought renewed prestige, purpose and respectability to the Japanese Communist party (JCP). For the time being, the JCP is playing a cool game vis-à-vis both Peking and Moscow. It is again committed to electoral politics. Observers are not agreed on the meaning of these developments for the 1970's. Some argue that the JCP's current posture buttresses overall political stability, as measured for regularized political processes. Others see danger signs in the party's substantial growth, because it would result in the increasing injection of alien doctrine into the mainstream of Japanese politics.

At the outset of the 1970's it could be said that Japanese domestic politics are becoming increasingly unstable, but it must also be recognized that Japanese politics are unpredictable. For example, during the troubles in the spring of 1960 over the Security Pact, which appeared to be a training period for a violent upheaval in the years ahead, it would have been extremely difficult to foresee the relative tranquillity of the political scene during the decade as a whole.

Ratification of the revised US/Japan Security Treaty was one of the focal points of the serious disturbances which rocked Japanese politics at that bitter time. Since an issue in the realm of foreign policy was involved, a brief recapitulation may provide greater meaning to the relationship between domestic political trends and the basic thrust of Japanese foreign policy. Events surrounding the 1960 treaty's approval remain controversial.[6] Prime Minister Kishi and his mainstream coali-

[6] For a comprehensive analysis please see George R. Packard III, *Protest in Tokyo: The Security Treaty Crisis of 1960* (Princeton: Princeton University Press, 1966).

tion of LDP factions were clearly opting for treaty approval at almost any cost. Equally clearly, the JSP—supported and abetted by Sohyo (the major trade union federation) Zengakuren (the national student association), and varied groups of intellectuals—and the JCP were committed to disapproval, also at almost any cost. In the resultant collision, considerable damage was done to parliamentary procedure, and societal strands were severely strained.

Prime Minister Kishi's interest in approval was readily understandable. He had staked his political future on achieving treaty revision and had managed to eliminate provisions in the 1951 pact which had been an affront to Japan's autonomy—such as the clause which permitted American armed forces to be used in controlling domestic turmoil in Japan. From his perspective, the new treaty placed Japan on a more equal footing with the United States.

His opponents objected to the treaty itself because they considered it a tool to remilitarize their country and thereby undermine the continued stability of parliamentary democracy—which some opposition activists seemed equally ready to sacrifice in the struggle. Furthermore, Kishi's prior career as a Cabinet Minister in the wartime Tojo Cabinet confirmed their fears: how could their nation remain true to its Peace Constitution, which epitomized their conception of democracy, under leadership compromised by war guilt?

In the end, the new treaty was ratified, but with each passing year of the 1960's, it became increasingly apparent that roughly half of the public voted for candidates that ran on party platforms which at a minimum were opposed to the indefinite duration of the treaty (DSP and Komeito) or, at a maximum, advocated its abolition (JSP and JCP).

This critical divergence on the single most important aspect of Japanese foreign policy has been partially obscured by the vagaries of the political process which enabled the LDP to win over sixty percent of the seats in the House of Representatives with less than fifty percent of the popular vote. Nonetheless, as any recent public opinion poll on Japanese foreign policy reiterates, the chasm that divides the Japanese public into two relatively equal camps whose foreign policy goals differ sharply is a harsh reality for her foreign policy-makers. As a leading LDPer and potential Prime Minister, Ōhira Masayoshi, has succinctly stated, "Our first task is to create consensus at home."[7]

[7] Interview, September 6, 1968. At the time, Mr. Ōhira was chairman of the LDP's Policy Council.

An aura of mystery tends to surround the actual process of decision-making in the Japanese political system. The formalistic approach is the simplest one, and will be dealt with first. In constitutional terms, it is the Diet (Parliament) which is the "highest organ of state power;"[8] of the two chambers, the House of Representatives (491 members, elected from 124 districts) is far more powerful than the House of Councilors (252 members, 150 of whom are elected nationally with the others chosen from prefecture-wide constituencies). The House of Representatives officially elects the Prime Minister—although here formalism already breaks down, because since 1955 the LDP convention has in effect been making that decision when it selects the party president, due to its preponderant majority of Diet seats. Ratification of international treaties—constituting the most formal expression of foreign policy entered into by Japan—is basically the responsibility of the Representatives; their approval of a treaty is final, regardless of contrary action by the House of Councilors, if at least thirty days of a Diet session remain.[9] Further, with only one exception (Fujiyama Aiichirō was a private citizen at the time of his initial appointment but subsequently became a Member of the House of Representatives) all recent Foreign Ministers have been members of this chamber. It is, of course, the Foreign Minister who—in his executive capacity—presides over the *Gaimushō* (Foreign Ministry), which is the presumed official formulator and executor of foreign policy.

All of the foregoing is true insofar as constitutional and formal procedures are concerned, but the synthesizing of foreign policy involves a far broader and more complex pattern of persons and institutions. So convoluted does it all become if attempts are made to analyze specific cases of decision-making in detail, that one has to accept the disheartening conclusion that our understanding—as well as that of the Japanese—is at best incomplete, at worst misleading and a game of blind man's buff.

One alternative to the formalistic approach (which all agree is incomplete), is to perceive Japanese politics as a series of concentric circles, with the public at the broad outer rim. Within the central core—where presumably real decision-making power rests—would be found representatives of three groups; the senior bureaucrats, the leadership of the LDP (so long as it continues to govern), and the industrial-business community. None of these elements speaks with one

---

[8] The Constitution of Japan (1947), Chapter IV, Article 41.

[9] *Ibid.*, Articles 60 and 61.

voice to each other or the public (to the extent that the latter is consulted), but little can be achieved without a reasonable degree of consensus among them. If Japan does have an "establishment," or at any rate a congerie of individuals who are more influential than the well-washed masses, this triad might well be it.

A generally noted tendency among Japanese is to seek the broadest possible area of consensus; conversely, an effort is made to avoid decisions should a consensus be lacking. It is also true, however, that when a sufficiently large segment of the "establishment" considers the adoption of a policy or a treaty to be vital, it has been willing (for some players the appropriate verb would be "eager") to grapple with the opposition with every element of power at its disposal. Such was the case in the approval of the revised Security Pact with the United States in 1960 as well as the 1965 treaty re-establishing diplomatic relations with South Korea.[10]

As has been suggested, avoidance of decision-making is frequently considered less painful for the Japanese. For example, prior to 1970, some leaders of the LDP had given serious consideration to having the Security Pact with the United States extended for a specific time period, five or ten years. But this would have required action by the Diet. With the anguish of the spring of 1960 still a vivid memory, it was considered advisable to extend the pact on a year-to-year basis, already provided for in the original treaty and thus not requiring Diet action. For entirely different reasons, there has been only the slowest perceptible change in Japan's approach to the establishment of diplomatic relations with the People's Republic of China. In this instance a policy goal that is desired by many elements both inside and outside the establishment thus far has been blocked by dominant elements in the latter group. That the 1970's are likely to witness at least a limited rapprochement between Washington and Peking, however, is bound to have a profound impact on Tokyo's "China policy" as well.

It is worth noting that the exact mix of key actors depends, at least in part, on the specific issue at hand. On matters related to the reduction of agricultural, e.g., grapefruit, tariffs as part of overall trade liberalization, for example, the voices of the Ministry of Agriculture and Forestry and the various farm lobbies will be augmented by that of the *natsumikan* (the closest Japanese counterpart to grapefruit) growers who are heard loudly and clearly through the channels of the LDP. (As Premier Sato's electoral district, Yamaguchi's second, is one of the major producers of this bitter, oversized mandarin orange, the *natsumikan*

---

[10] For the latter, please see my "Nikkan Kokkai: The Japan-Korea Treaty Diet" in Lucian W. Pye, ed., *Cases in Comparative Politics: Asia* (Boston: Little, Brown, 1970), pp. 19–57.

growers have a substantial advantage in that body.) Obviously this combination of interested forces is aided by the continuing importance that the LDP attaches to the support of rural voters.

In contrast, the capacity of industrial workers to exert veto power is considerably less. For example, substantial segments of the trade union movement opposed the normalization of relations between Japan and the Republic of Korea, partly because of the fear that this move would result in Japan's being flooded with low-priced products made with cheap Korean labor. Neither their efforts, nor those of the JSP—their parliamentary representatives—were sufficient to block the re-estab- lishment of diplomatic ties between the two countries.[11] This failure is due, in large part, to the fact that the trade union movement is almost totally interlocked with opposition parties and thus has no effective channels of communication and influence within the ruling party.

In this age of instant transmission of sight and sound, one additional factor—the media of communication—requires consideration. The Japanese people, with their penchant for technology, must be among the most communications-oriented people in the world. They have three major national newspapers (the *Asahi, Mainichi,* and *Yomiuri*), virtually countless weekly and monthly magazines (ranging from the serious to the obscene), and possibly more important—one of the most sophisticated television and radio networks in the world.

One of the endlessly debated topics relating to the formulation of public policy is whether the final arbiters are the government, and/or the "establishment," and/or the media. Probably a fair answer would be a combination of all three. In any case, public opinion—unless so stringently defined as to make the term meaningless—is more the victim than the influencer of public policy.[12]

In summary, decision-making in Japan is not sufficiently understood, unless one's vision is restricted to the formal institutions of government. A critical role in determining the "national interest" on a particular issue of foreign policy can be played by a group of *natsumikan* growers as much as by the Prime Minister or senior Foreign Ministry official. It depends on specific circumstances which particular constellation of forces and interests have a major say in the final decision-making process.

[11] *Ibid.*

[12] During the course of several visits and periods of residence in Japan (1945–49, 1954–55, 1963, 1964, 1965–67, 1969–70), I had numerous occasions to discuss the material for this section with Japanese parliamentarians, journalists (especially those assigned to the Prime Minister's Office and the Foreign Ministry), academic colleagues, businessmen, and trade union officials. It is impossible to list them all but I want to express my profound appreciation for their willingness to assist me in seeing their country, and its place in the world, from a variety of perspectives.

Such a system may be confusing to the Japanese and even more confusing to foreign students of Japanese politics. Nonetheless, the system would appear to have worked far better than the system which existed in Japan in the pre-war era. The latter was simpler and more readily comprehensible because the military—in the field of foreign affairs—had a preponderant share of power. It performed so well that it came perilously close to destroying the society it was intended to serve.

Japan and the World Community

TRADE AND FOREIGN POLICY

As we have noted, the paucity of Japan's raw material resources is the single most important motivation for an ever-expanding foreign trade. Concurrently, the need for hard currencies with which to purchase iron, oil, coal, copper, zinc, and lumber has driven Japanese businessmen all over the world in a frantic search for markets to which its products, such as ships, radios, television sets, computers, cars and motorcycles can be exported.

Japan has pursued a two-pronged policy in the search for markets and foreign exchange. First to make certain that its relations with the industrialized nations, mostly in North America and Europe, enable it to have ready access to these markets. In effect, this meant that Japan sought (successfully by the 1960's) to become a partner—even if a lesser one, measured in per capita income terms—in the world's "rich men's club." Roughly half of Japan's exports has gone to countries in these two geographic regions. Prime Minister Yoshida (especially during the latter years—1949–54—of his tenure) devoted himself assiduously to the view that people who enjoyed a relatively high standard of living would have more money to spend on Japanese-made products than those who were living in economies which were in the throes of development.[13]

This aspect of foreign trade policy has paid handsome dividends. Europeans and North Americans have become accustomed to purchasing a seemingly ever-increasing number and range of Japanese products which are usually somewhat less expensive but as well, or better, made than local manufactures. Sales resistance is making itself felt, however. Natural and synthetic textiles have become a cause célèbre in Japanese-American trade, and symbolize an aspect of prob-

[13] For a challengingly optimistic assessment, please see Herman Kahn, *The Emerging Japanese Superstate* (Englewood Cliffs, New Jersey: Prentice-Hall, Inc., 1970).

lems that lie ahead. Negotiations over this issue have been excruciatingly complicated, possibly unnecessarily so. But it is probable that economic relations between the two states will replace the alliance system as the principal cause of friction between the two states in the 1970's, and possibly with both sides taking increasingly "national interest" positions on the issues involved.

American official policy on Japanese textiles has been designed to make the Japanese understand that if they themselves do not impose a voluntary quota on their exports to the United States, they will face US congressional legislation which would be far more stringent. Japanese official policy sees either alternative as a negation of America's fundamental commitment to free trade. Furthermore, they are all too ready to believe that textiles became entangled in the settlement regarding Okinawa. Put crassly, there is a widespread and probably mistaken belief that textile quotas are a necessary quid pro quo for Ryukyuan reversion. (There has apparently been some mendacity by both partners on this last point.)

Americans have countered with assertions that the Japanese should be the last to accuse others of a lack of commitment to free trade, given the snail-like pace of Japan's response to requests that it liberalize its regulations concerning the importation of foreign goods and capital. The Japanese in turn have replied that, while their economy, as measured in GNP, might be the third largest in the world their standard of living was still far behind that enjoyed by Europeans and Americans, as measured in per capita income, on which scale their country was still fifteenth or sixteenth.

Furthermore, if the United States originally attempted to justify its trade policy on the basis of domestic political and economic requirements, that game could also be played by the Japanese, with some differences. First, the Japanese have consistently tried—at least officially —to separate "political" and "economic" questions (presumably the latter should be resolved on the basis of, for example, the "real damage" suffered by the American textile industry from the importation of Japanese goods). Secondly, the Japanese Government—specifically Prime Minister Sato and Japan's Embassy in Washington—had only belatedly discovered the political muscle of their own textile manufacturers and their representatives, who were politically closer to elements in the LDP anti-mainstream than to Sato's own mainstream coalition.

The influence of domestic opposition became clearly evident in the breakdown in negotiations in the late 1960's over the imposition of a "voluntary quota" formula under which limits would be set upon the scale of Japan's textile exports to the United States. The Japanese press in this instance extolled the government's refusal to make this concession, interpreting it as an indication that Japan was no longer prepared to accept a "junior partner" role in economic relations with America.[14] While Tokyo eventually had to agree to the "voluntary quota" formula on a temporary basis, an end to this and similar economic crises is not in sight.

Many Japanese, including in their ranks people who have been intimately involved in their country's post-war trade with and security orientation towards the US and (to a lesser degree) Europe, have never forgotten that they do live in Asia. To be sure, money could be made in the west, but the money-makers were an Oriental people who had deep cultural bonds with other Asians. They had fought a war for the sake of establishing an East Asia Co-Prosperity Sphere with the slogan "Asia for the Asians."

That, of course, was part of the problem and one that remained a reality in various Asian states. Some (not all) Indonesians, Filipinos, Koreans, Chinese were not prepared to forget—in the first post-war decade—the havoc that Japan's military masters had wrought. With the notable exceptions of the Chinese Nationalist Government on Taiwan and of India, reparation became the first item of business. Negotiations led to settlements with all involved except the government of the People's Republic of China (PRC), which insisted that reparations should remain as an agenda item for future disposition.[15]

Another element of the problem was the bifurcation of Asian states. Korea became and has remained divided into South and North Korea (Kankoku and Chosen, respectively, for the Japanese); China consists of Taiwan and the PRC, and no one is yet certain of Indochina's future contours. In each instance, the Japanese have attempted to pursue a dual policy consisting of formal diplomatic ties and trade with the non-Communist countries (Nationalist China, South Korea and South Vietnam), and business dealings—to the extent possible—with the Communist states.

Trade and other relations with the PRC and Taiwan have tested Japanese ingenuity to the utmost. It was with the Nationalist Government of China that the Peace Treaty was signed. It was the Nationalists who absolved Japan from paying any reparations. It is with the Nationalists that the Japanese have formal diplomatic ties and government-approved business relations. None of these conditions pertain to Japan's relations

[14] Gerald L. Curtis, "The Textile Negotiations: A Failure to Communicate," *Columbia Journal of World Business*, Vol. VI, No. 1, pp. 72, 75–78.

[15] For a full discussion, please see Lawrence Olson, *Japan in Post-War Asia* (New York: Praeger, 1970).

with the PRC. Nonetheless there has been a substantial and increasing level of trade with the mainland along two channels.

One of these channels is the "Memorandum Trade" negotiated, on the Japanese side, by semi-official groups. Fujiyama Aiichiro, who had been Kishi's Foreign Minister, led the 1971 delegation. A joint communiqué with the Chinese—who extract a quota of political agreements from the Japanese in Peking, which are then denied or explained away by the government spokesmen in Tokyo—has become the contractual basis for a given year's memorandum trade.

Business conducted by "friendly firms" (as defined by the Chinese) provides the second channel. Presumably, it is not sponsored—even semi-officially—by the Japanese government. It is alleged that a percentage of the profits from this trade went into the coffers of the Japanese Communist party (JCP) during the first half of the 1960's when amity prevailed between the JCP and Peking, and after 1967 when JCP-Peking relations became frosty, into the Maoist-oriented wing of the JCP. In its way, this multifaceted approach to "China," whether Nationalist, Communist, or both, is an index of Japanese capabilities to respond pragmatically and flexibly to a problem that some others find virtually insoluble.

Japan's flexible approach will be tested substantially in the years ahead should both China and Taiwan continue giving priority to political, as opposed to "purely economic" considerations. Trade with both has reached a level of near parity, $950 million with Taiwan as opposed to $825 million with China in 1970. Insofar as possible, the Japanese would also prefer to cope with any Chinese threat—diplomatically, militarily, or economically—through negotiation rather than confrontation. This preference might of course become less plausible should China's hostility go beyond the level of rhetoric and adversely affect Japan's access to Southeast Asia. Nonetheless, an avoidance of confrontation with China or Taiwan remains as a strongly-felt wish of the Japanese.

Japanese efforts to expand their business opportunities have provided the impetus to probe into areas in which they had little or no pre-war experience. Joint development efforts with the Soviet Union to exploit Siberian natural resources (especially natural gas and oil) have thus far foundered on the shoals of the "Northern Islands" issues,[16] and the terms and extent of Japanese capital and management investment in Siberian development. It is an option that the Japanese wish to keep

[16] David I. Hitchcock, Jr., "Joint Development of Siberia: Decision-Making in Japanese-Soviet Relations," *Asian Survey*, XI:3 (March, 1971), pp. 279–300.

open for the day when alternative sources may become closed or present providers become insufficient.

In their relations with the Soviet Union, the Japanese have encountered a variation of the non-separability problem of politics and economics that has plagued their relation with the PRC. They have been reluctant to give any impression of joining a Russian-sponsored coalition directed against China. Even if the Kremlin might wish to give primacy to such considerations, the Japanese search for trading partners—admittedly an almost overwhelming desire—has not succumbed to that particular siren-song.

Australia, and, to a lesser degree, New Zealand are two other countries with which strenuous efforts to expand trade have been made. Similar exertions are being conducted in Latin America and Africa. In the latter continent a flourishing trade with white South Africa has partially blocked opportunities in Black Africa.[17] In Africa the temptation to deal with a rich country has superseded any presumed interest in assisting developing countries or notions of Afro-Asian solidarity which are occasionally enunciated.

Somewhat platitudinous pronouncements periodically emanate from official circles regarding Japanese foreign aid efforts. There is an acute awareness of what is sometimes called the "North-South problem." Broadly speaking, this refers to the growing gap between the developed "northern" and developing "southern" half of the world. Pledges have been made that Japan will contribute one percent of her GNP to foreign aid programs by 1975—it is about half that in 1971—but doubts persist that this goal can be achieved. Domestic pressures toward larger budgetary allocation on behalf of public housing, education, welfare services and transportation, or a larger share for the military (about eight percent or .8 of 1% of GNP at present), or both may preclude the fulfillment of pietistic promises of aid.

Southeast Asia looms especially large in the Japanese approach to the "North-South problem." The countries in this area have been the primary recipients of Japanese economic and technical assistance programs. Simultaneously, Japanese private entrepreneurs have been extremely active, especially in Thailand, Indonesia and—to a somewhat lesser extent—the Philippines, particularly with respect to the development of off-shore oil resources in Southeast Asia. Japan could, and probably will, play an increasingly important role in this area, but to do so the spectre of an economic version of "The Greater East Asia Co-Prosperity Sphere" will have to be laid to rest and the behavior of

---

[17] Based on private information provided by an American businessman active in Japanese-African trade.

Japanese businessmen will have to become more sensitive to local feelings. There is a growing consciousness of these desiderata, but it has proved difficult to combine them with aggressive business practices. They face a problem that is by no means unique.

There is little doubt, however, that the Japanese industrial and commercial entrepreneurs are being extraordinarily active in their search for new sources of raw materials, particularly natural gas, petroleum and coal. A substantial segment of these efforts is privately conducted. The interlocking interests of the *zaikai* (financial and business community), the Ministry of International Trade and Industry, and the leadership of the LDP are believed sufficient to support the conclusion that they are an integral part of Japanese foreign policy.

Achievements, Failures and Prospects

Over a quarter-century has elapsed since Japan's earlier exertions to become one of the world's major powers ended in the rubble of her industrialized urban areas and the lethal ashes of Hiroshima and Nagasaki. The memories of that catastrophe still cast a long shadow and have made Japanese post-war foreign policy-makers extremely cautious and prudent. This attitude may be ending. It is not just that a new generation is coming to the fore, although this factor cannot be dismissed even in a society in which seniority—or, at least the need to wait for one's turn—still provides a powerful constraint. It is also that the Japanese have begun to reassess their international status subsequent to their becoming one of the world's major economic powers.

Japan's relationship with the United States, both for purposes of military defense (the Security Pact) and trade, still remains the single most important ingredient in its foreign policy. Whether the pact's continued existence after June 1970 under the automatic extension formula is to be viewed as an achievement or failure is dependent largely on which segment of Japanese political opinion is consulted. To Prime Minister Sato and his allies in the LDP, the relative tranquillity surrounding the pact's survival was a striking success. To the varied forces of the opposition, especially the left-wing of the JSP and the anti-JCP but nonetheless radical student militants, its continuation as the fulcrum of their country's foreign relations was a resounding failure.

This division within Japan's body politic cannot be overemphasized, for it too has contributed its consequential share to the circumspection with which Japan's foreign policy-makers have acted. In a very real sense, the pact's survival came to be tied to the reversion of Okinawa and the other Ryukyu Islands to Japan's administrative jurisdiction.

American acceptance in principle of the Japanese resolution to this dispute (which had come close to tearing the alliance as well as Japanese domestic politics into tatters) can be viewed as a victory for Japan.

Anti-establishment dissenters greatly influenced the negotiations on whether or not Okinawa would again become an integral part of Japan in 1972. Initially, Prime Minister Sato's exploration of this issue had been delicate. He strengthened his resolve only after ascertaining that his domestic situation required it. Other elements in the establishment assisted his position by utilizing the media to create a broadening consensus. He also temporized until he was reasonably certain that the US would not be fundamentally affronted.

From another perspective, the anticipated settlement of the Okinawan issue signalled the end of Japan's quarter-century of subservience to the US. To be sure, some of this subservience was less real than imagined, or could be used as a convenient excuse not to embark on new foreign policy ventures—for example, establishing relations with Peking—which the Prime Minister or Foreign Ministry believed to be premature.

Japanese formal acceptance of South Korea's and Taiwan's security as important to its own (officially acknowledged for the first time in the 1969 Sato-Nixon communiqué) poses a counterpoint to the theme that reversion of Okinawa serves as a coda ending the post-World War II era. Japanese policy-makers supposedly calculated that the acceptance—in principle—of these security commitments was a necessary price that had to be paid. Dissenters argued that the cost was too high. This aspect of the debate will undoubtedly grow in intensity when and if American military entanglements in Asia loosen.

In non-official American commentaries this supposition is frequently linked to the proposition that Japan would somehow shoulder the responsibilities from which the United States is presumed to be in the process of withdrawing. American official policy-makers apparently remain divided on the question of whether a fully rearmed—including nuclear weapons—Japan is desirable. To be sure, the possible consequences of a potential power vacuum are lengthily debated in Japan. Their discussion by no means indicates that a new consensus has been achieved; to assume so would be misleading as well as a misreading of Japanese foreign policy trends.

Article IX of Japan's present Constitution (prohibiting the use of military force in the settlement of international disputes) remains a real restraint. It does so despite the fact that its intent was twisted to make legal allowances for the creation of the Self-Defense Forces which have become an establishment of considerable potency. The existence of such forces—and their use in cases of domestic turmoil—is one thing; their possible use outside Japanese borders is quite another. Considerable changes would have to take place in the perceptions of Japanese policy-makers, regarding the domestic political environment and the limitations that it imposes, before Japanese military action abroad can even begin to be contemplated.

For the vast majority of Japanese, this set of Constitutional (buttressed by political) restraints has been a blessing. Japan's policy-makers have responded accordingly, and have been adept at avoiding—so far, successfully—any centrifugal pulls into the military conflicts that have scarred the face of Asia in the last twenty years.

Instead, they have concentrated on rebuilding their economy, with astonishing success. This great economic achievement is beginning to have repercussions on Japan's foreign policy. They have discovered that being the third largest national producer of goods and services has not brought a commensurate degree of respect among the world's powers. This imbalance rankles, for the Japanese are a proud—and increasingly nationalistic—people. Nonetheless, they have not yet arrived at anything even approaching a consensus—within as well as without the establishment—on how this disequilibrium between being an economic giant and a diplomatic dwarf is to be rectified. Furthermore, their "transistor-salesmen" or "economic animal" reputation abroad has not satisfied their self-image or aspirations.

Japan's two principal foreign policy guidelines, that is, the alliance with the US and "business first" are no longer meeting the needs of the Japanese people. No one is certain what is to replace them. One option is for Japan to develop an independent nuclear capability, and certainly this is possible from a technical and probably even a financial standpoint. Undoubtedly, the domestic political fallout would be extremely grim, conceivably sundering the current experiment with parliamentary democracy. Some Japanese decision-makers might be willing to pay this price if they were convinced that a nuclear capacity would guarantee big-power status. Few are convinced of the validity of this equation, however, citing other nuclear powers—China, England and France—none of which have attained superpower status. Furthermore, especially by comparison to China, the Soviet Union or the United States, Japan is far more vulnerable to nuclear attack, they assert. Hence, why court risks that would be costly and of questionable utility?

Another alternative would be to emphasize a strict posture of neutrality. For some proponents this would include the abolition of all Japanese military forces. For others it would mean retaining at least the present level of military capabilities. Frequently, this neutrality option is coupled with a renunciation of the US/Japan Security Pact which would then be replaced by a series of non-aggression pacts with all countries, particularly the Soviet Union and the People's Republic of China. No permutation of this combination of options as yet appears preferable to an expanding trade anchored to the alliance with the United States.

Japan's achievements in rehabilitating itself at home and, to varying degrees, in reestablishing significant trading relations with other nations are important ingredients in judging its success in international relations. The Japanese people nonetheless feel a sense of malaise, partially because of their presumed excessive dependence on the United States, partially because of their perceived imbalance between economic power and diplomatic influence. Neither can probably be cured without a broader base of agreement among themselves of what constitutes their nation's interests. They hope and need to achieve at least a working consensus on these questions in the 1970's if Japan is to assume the role in Asian and global politics that its economic strength could and should lead them to expect.

India

LEO E. ROSE

Modern India constitutes the heartland of the South
Asian sub-continent, the massive "peninsular" area to the
south of the great Himalayan range. Situated between an
Islamic cultural area to the west and a Buddhist cultural
area to the east, India is *Aryavarta*—the homeland of
the Indoaryan people and their highly-structured,
complex social and religious system, Hinduism, and its
various offshoots such as Jainism, Sikhism and Buddhism.

For much of the past millenium, however, the
sub-continent has been ruled by foreigners—first Muslim
dynasties which invaded India from the northwest and
then later the British who came by sea. It was only in
1947 that an independent Indian state, assertively secular
in constitutional theory but overwhelmingly Hindu in
composition, was established. The world's second largest
polity (and largest democratic political system), with an
estimated 550 million people in 1970, India's population
also includes several large minority communities of
various types—fifty million Muslims, eight million Sikhs,
forty million "tribals," and perhaps another sixty
million Hindus of Dravidian (non-Indoaryan) origin
concentrated in the southern section of the country.
Variety, thus, is not only the spice of life in India; it is a
basic social and political factor of vital importance to
the state's rulers in both foreign and domestic policy
decision-making.

The Strategic Setting

The worldview of a society with as diverse a cultural,
ethnic and political background as India's is certain to
reflect this pluralist framework. The complexity of India's

national self-image is further reinforced by the fact that the sub-continent was never a unified political entity prior to 1947 *except* under alien rulers with a worldview distinct in many respects from that of Hindu India. In this regard, India contrasts sharply with China, Japan and several Southeast Asian states that have long histories as centralized polities with common political traditions.

India's rich historical experiences, however, do provide a traditional perspective on the world that has had a significant impact upon the country's contemporary definition of its international position and its foreign policy goals and principles. These have been largely shaped by salient geopolitical factors that were as important to India 2300 years ago, at the time of the abortive Alexandrian invasion of South Asia, as they are today.

One of the most critical facts of political geography is that then, as now, South Asia is a peripheral area to the vast Euro-Asian continent. India was never an integral part of the well-developed land communication system from the Mediterranean area, through Central Asia to East Asia. Indeed, while Indian cultural and intellectual influences (primarily Buddhism) had a considerable impact on China, Japan and Southeast Asia, these were not transmitted directly from India but only indirectly after first gaining currency in Central Asia via Kashmir and Afghanistan.

There were limited commercial and other relations between South and West Asia by land routes (such as the famous Khyber Pass), but these were always of minor significance in economic terms to both areas. Far more crucial was South Asia's role in the sea routes between the Mediterranean area and Southeast Asia. It was India's status as the principal entrepôt in this complicated trade structure that made the western coastal areas of the sub-continent so vital to a succession of maritime empires, from the West Asian Muslim commercial communities in the 12th–14th centuries to the Portuguese, Dutch, French, and British. India became the "jewel" of the vast British Empire not only because of its wealth but even more important because it was the fulcrum upon which the entire British imperial and trade system in the Asian area was balanced.

Given the importance of South Asia's sea communications and its vulnerability to seaward assault, it is surprising that none of the littoral Indian states ever emerged for more than brief periods as naval powers. Indian commercial communities played a major role in the trade with both Southeast and West Asia, but South Asia, surrounded on three sides by water, has never developed a strong sea-going tradition. The extensive Indian influence in Southeast Asia prior to the western colonial period was not due to military or naval power but rather to the intellectual force of Indian Buddhism and Brahmanic Hinduism (even Islam entered Southeast Asia after being "Indianized" in some respects), and to the entrepreneurial activities of migrant Indian merchant communities.

The failure to capitalize on the possibilities of the sea is still evident in contemporary India, which tends to view the ocean's distances as a barrier to communications rather than as a linkage system of vital importance to India's own security and economic interests. This is even more striking since South Asia's land communications are vastly more difficult, passing through some of the world's most inhospitable terrain. And yet, for good historical and strategic reasons it is these land frontiers that have largely dominated the perspective of India's rulers for hundreds of years, down to and including the present generation of political leaders.[1]

South Asia's only viable land communications with the external world lie through the northwest to Central and West Asia; these routes have played a vital role in Indian history, for they were followed by the various invading armies that conquered South Asia from at least the era of the Indoaryans more than 3000 years ago up to—but not including—the British in the 17th and 18th centuries. The significance of this land communication system was thus largely political and strategic in character. It is not unreasonable, therefore, that contemporary India is deeply concerned with the fact that these traditional invasion channels are in the hands of a neighboring power—Pakistan. While India conceives of no immediate threat to its existence from areas *beyond* Pakistan, it cannot help but be dissatisfied with a situation in which one of the principal physical barriers to South Asia is controlled by an unfriendly power that has demonstrated a readiness to cooperate with India's enemies, at least on a limited basis, in the recent past. New Delhi's "intransigence" on the Kashmir question, for instance, should be partly perceived in geopolitical terms, as the loss of Kashmir would expose India strategically to an even greater extent than at present.

To both the north and northeast, there are massive physical barriers that have long deterred substantial and continuous contact with East and Southeast Asia. The Himalayas and the Assam/Burma ranges

[1] There would appear to be a significant difference in the southern and northern Indian perspectives in this respect. In the north, the focus is almost exclusively on India's land frontiers, particularly to the northwest, while in the south there is much greater awareness of Southeast Asia and India's sea communications with the outside world. The north has predominated, however, both politically and in the definition of the Indian worldview in the development of a common Indian national identity in the 19th and 20th centuries.

are exceedingly rugged, constituting a major deterrent to communications.[2] Moreover, much of the border area is inhabited by tribal communities which, in the northeastern section at least, are unassimilated into any of the surrounding major cultures—Indian, Tibetan, Burmese or Chinese—thus further deterring the use of the few routes that traverse the imposing terrain. This has been an important factor in the boundary disputes that have arisen between India, China and Burma in recent decades, for the task of defining political borders in this area was taken up only late in the British period of rule in India and Burma and was never completed to the satisfaction of all the powers concerned, nor could it become ethnographically "logical" given the social complexity of the mountain peoples.

India's geopolitical situation in this northern border area was undermined to some extent by two factors in the immediate post-independence period. The first of these was the partition of Bengal and the merger of the Muslim-majority area of East Bengal into Pakistan. This virtually isolated India from Assam and the eastern and northeastern borders with Burma and China (i.e., Tibet) except for a narrow corridor between East Bengal and the sub-Himalayan hill area, with disastrous consequences in the brief 1962 border war on the northeastern border with China. The second was the decision by New Delhi to allow the Himalayan border states of Nepal, Sikkim and Bhutan to maintain a separate political identity rather than to insist upon their accession into the newly-formed Indian Union. While India has continued to exert a dominant influence in the border states, its position has been seriously weakened by the presence of China across the Himalayan border in Tibet. Chinese determination to wield at least a minimal influence in this "buffer" area has led to a limited confrontation that has had an adverse effect upon Indian interests in the border states.

The government of India's attention in geopolitical and strategic terms in most of the period since 1947 has been focused on its western boundary with Pakistan and the northern border with Chinese-controlled Tibet. Two limited wars with Pakistan over Kashmir (1948 and 1965) and one with China (1962) have reinforced this tendency, as the disputes with both these powers on the boundary question are still unresolved. But while the issues have been kept alive, a de facto settlement has been achieved which, while not publicly recognized by any of the participants, is accepted in fact by all three.

---

[2] That most of the Indians in Southeast Asia, including Burma, are of South Indian origin demonstrates the greater importance of India's sea communications with this area.

Verbal disputations are certain to continue, but any major conflict over these frontiers would now appear to be unlikely except in the context of such fundamental political developments as political chaos or disintegration in India or Pakistan, or a major internal challenge to Chinese control of Tibet and Sinkiang.

Prior to 1971, East Bengal (East Pakistan) posed a much less serious problem for New Delhi, at least in security terms, as there was never any question of India's capacity to occupy that area if the need should arise. Indeed, in some respects, East Bengal served as a hostage, limiting the alternatives available to the Pakistan government in its dispute with India over Kashmir. However, the series of events in East Bengal in March/April 1971 that led the Pakistan government to attempt the suppression of what it denounced as a "separatist" movement and, as a consequence, the declaration of the independence of "Bangla Desh" by the dominant political party in the area, has added a new area of instability and danger on India's borders. The course of events in late 1971 that led to the third Indo-Pakistani war secured the independence of Bangla Desh but did not guarantee political stability in this region. The problems raised for India both internally (i.e., Bengali nationalism within India that may be attracted by the establishment of an independent "Bengali nation") and externally (i.e., competition with China and other major powers for influence in the new state) are incalculable. In any case, it is probable that there will be a switch in India's strategic priorities from the northwest and north to the northeast, and the political implications of this within India are far greater than were the more clear-cut disputes with Pakistan over Kashmir or with China over Ladakh.

Moreover, this tension is occurring simultaneously with the prospect—if not likelihood—of "big power" competition for influence and control in the area of the Indian Ocean which would raise another serious geopolitical and security problem for New Delhi. India virtually ignored the Indian Ocean as an area of concern until about 1964, when a limited but effective alliance between China, Indonesia and Pakistan with distinctly antiIndian overtones finally alerted New Delhi to its strategic interests in this area. The overthrow of the Sukarno regime in Indonesia in 1965/66 ended that particular threatening situation, but India has continued to place considerable emphasis upon the development of a navy with a limited but not insignificant capability. With the Soviet Union demonstrating some interest—if as yet little capacity—in becoming an Indian Ocean naval power, and with the United States, Britain, and Australia preparing countermeasures, India does not want to be caught in a position in which it could exert little influence over the course of events in this area except through admonitions and complaints to the various great powers involved.

Thus, the outside world continues to impinge upon India in spite of the latter's obvious preference (since at least 1962) for minimizing its direct involvement in international affairs, even in Asia. New Delhi's intense preoccupation with defense and security problems is likely to continue in the years ahead, even if peace returns to Southeast Asia and there is a gradual diminution of Chinese hostility in the post-Maoist period—neither of which is a certainty by any means. Nevertheless, India faces the future with a greater degree of confidence than has been evident at any time since the breakdown of relations with China around 1959–1960. This is due in part to substantial improvements in its own military capability and to the remarkable recuperative powers demonstrated by its democratic political system, but also to a greater understanding of strategic realities as they affect the sub-continent.

Historically, South Asia has been relatively isolated from the rest of Asia, and Indians still are not particularly inclined to link their fate with that of other Asians. Prior to 1947, for instance, South Asia had only very limited contacts with China, and was never part of a Sino-centered cultural region as were Japan, Korea, and much of Southeast Asia. India, thus, views its Communist neighbor to the north with an inherent sense of equality and difference, that is not always as evident in the elites of these other areas which still tend to think of China as the "middle kingdom." Nor is India a part of the Islamic cultural area of West Asia even though it had Muslim rulers for several centuries and has two Muslim-majority states as neighbors within the sub-continent itself.

Pan-Asian sentiment, while frequently expressed in contemporary India, would seem to have little real substance in the historic tradition or contemporary worldview of the Indian people. It is rather a consequence of the 20th century reaction to Western colonialism in its political, economic and cultural forms. The propensity to lump all of Asia (or the "Third World") into one cultural category ignores the basic distinctiveness of these regions and their widely differing responses to external intrusions, both past and present. This is evident, for instance, in the Indian reaction to the intrusion of massive western influences in the 18th to 20th centuries, which contrasts sharply with that of China or Japan. India's intellectual elite proved to be more accommodative and receptive, not only for pragmatic political and economic reasons but also because of the greater eclectic qualities of the Hindu culture and its frequently demonstrated capacity to absorb the novel while retaining intact its basic character.

South Asia has been to a great extent a civilization unto itself in which changes and innovations have taken place at a comparatively moderate pace even during periods of maximum external intrusion, and then often on the initiative of the Indians themselves.

Internal Determinants of India's Foreign Policy

India became independent from Britain in 1947 administratively ill-prepared to function effectively in international relations. Under British rule, South Asia's foreign relations had been handled almost exclusively by London rather than by New Delhi.[3] Even the Political Department of the government of India, which handled relations with Nepal, Tibet, Afghanistan and the Indian princely states, was a virtual preserve of British members of the Indian Civil Service. There was, thus, no core of Indian administrators with experience in the foreign policy field as there was within the internal administration.

The foreign service structure, incorporated in the Ministry of External Affairs (MEA), had to be developed and expanded from the bottom to the top commencing in 1947 and this took several years to accomplish. In the interim, procedures and instruments of supervision and control over the nation's foreign diplomatic service functioned haphazardly, allowing a number of ambassadors—such as K. M. Panikkar in China and V. K. Krishna Menon in London—to operate as virtually autonomous agents responsible only in a personal capacity to Prime Minister Nehru. Some of these ambassadors played an important role in the evolution of India's diplomatic relations in a vital period, and occasionally in ways that did not strictly conform to the nominal foreign policy objectives of the government they ostensibly represented.

Such "free wheeling" operations at the ambassadorial level were largely eliminated once the MEA had defined rules of procedure more precisely and had formalized its administrative structure. Nevertheless, the foreign service still retains a special status in comparison to the Indian Administrative Service which assures it greater autonomy in the selection of personnel and in internal administration than is allowed the other departments of government.

[3] The British Government of India did appoint an Indian, S. C. Bajpai, to a post in Washington during World War II, but his responsibilities were largely restricted to non-political matters. Nevertheless, Bajpai's experience was so unique among Indian officials that he was entrusted with the task of organizing the foreign service after independence.

The Ministry's role in the formulation and implementation of foreign policy is restricted in several important respects. In the first place, all major foreign policy decisions require the approval of the cabinet, and the MEA's prerogatives can be effectively challenged at this level. This was not too important during the long period when Nehru served as both Prime Minister and as Foreign Minister, as his policy decisions, made in consultation with the MEA staff, were usually accepted without serious controversy within the cabinet. Since his death in 1964, however, the two ministries have not been held jointly, and the influence of the MEA has consequently declined. Decision-making in foreign policy now is largely the responsibility of the prime minister and several cabinet colleagues, usually including the ministers for External Affairs, Defence, Finance and Home, and the secretaries of their respective departments. On some of the most vital questions concerning foreign aid and trade, departments other than MEA may wield a more decisive influence.[4]

The definition of the fundamental principles of India's foreign policy was largely a post-independence exercise. The Congress party, which had led the struggle for freedom, had rarely lifted its attention above the internal political level to considerations of foreign policy issues prior to 1947. Nor was there any deeply-ingrained historical perspective on relations with other states, even India's neighbors, to set the framework within which foreign policy could be formulated, as this had been the responsibility of the British for the previous two centuries. Of all the Congress party leaders, only Jawaharlal Nehru had devoted much attention to international politics in the pre-independence period. His views were a curious and somewhat contradictory blend of Fabian Socialist theories and an aristocratic British view of the world (from whence in part his low esteem of the United States derived), combined with strong anticolonial and anticapitalist sentiments. Fortunately for India, his proclivity for abstruse generalization on broader policy questions was usually moderated by a strong pragmatic sense in those situations in which his own country's vital interests were concerned.

The task of defining the broader principles of Indian foreign policy was eagerly taken up by Nehru. There were, of course, important external constraints upon the alternatives available to him, for India was hampered from the beginning by a series of dependency rela-

[4] Ashok Kapoor's fascinating analysis of the negotiations between the Indian and US governments and a private American-led consortium on the construction of fertilizer plants in India illustrates the relatively minor role played by the MEA in India's external economic relations. See Ashok Kapoor, *International Business Negotiations* (New York: New York University Press, 1970).

tionships that could not be ignored. Internal constraints upon the prime minister were relatively insignificant, however, except on certain questions concerning relations with immediate neighbors in which several other Congress party leaders held views on India's basic interests that varied from those expounded by Nehru. Occasionally, these other leaders voiced dissident opinions within the cabinet and the party, but usually only with limited success.

The opposition parties, whether of the right or left, were no better prepared than the Congress party to offer a real alternative to Nehru's foreign policy, nor were they even able to use foreign policy issues effectively in domestic politics. Until Stalin's death in 1953, the Communist party (CPI) faithfully reiterated the criticisms of the Nehru government and its foreign policy emanating from the Soviet Union. The virtually total turnabout in Moscow's attitude on this subject in the 1954–56 period, however, was accepted (with considerable reluctance) by the CPI which thereafter limited its attacks on the Nehru regime to specific domestic questions and generally supported the government on foreign policy.

The right-wing, Hindu-oriented Jana Sangh party has consistently and vehemently criticized the Indian government's "soft" policy toward Pakistan, while several leaders of the moderate Indian Socialist party expressed distress over Nehru's acceptance of China's conquest of Tibet in 1951. But neither party was able to engender sufficient public response on these issues to pressure Nehru into a reconsideration of policy. The fact was that it was only Nehru, supported by a small coterie of advisors both within and outside the MEA, that had a sophisticated foreign policy. Few Indians could challenge the prime minister's foreign policy expertise.

India is a democratic polity with institutions modelled closely after the British parliamentary system, with certain American institutional appendages such as federalism and the principle of judicial review. In formal constitutional terms, therefore, the prime minister, cabinet and various departments of government are ultimately responsible to the popularly-elected parliament on foreign policy issues. But for the first decade after independence, parliament used its power only very sparingly, seldom serving even as an effective debating society on foreign policy issues. On the few occasions that attempts were made in this direction, the Congress party used its huge majority to stifle the criticisms emanating from opposition (or dissident Congress) party sources. Thus, the fundamental principles of Indian foreign policy, such as non-alignment, peaceful coexistence, and the insulation of Asia from the East-West "cold war," were all accepted by Parliament in the 1947–54 period virtually without debate. Even some issues vital to

India's own immediate interests, such as Nehru's 1949 pledge to hold a plebiscite in Kashmir or the Chinese conquest of Tibet in 1950–51, were not the subject of extended discussion in either House of Parliament although a few lonely voices were raised on such occasions warning of the possibly dire consequences for India. For his part, Nehru usually demonstrated great respect for Parliament as an institution, but was not always prepared to take its members into his confidence, as we know from his failure to keep the House informed on the border dispute with China in the 1954–59 period.

The Indian press and public, operating in a democratic political system and invariably very outspoken on local issues, was no less reticent to express its views on foreign policy. The general tendency, with the exception of a few individual journalists, was to accept the government's policy on these matters without serious inquiry. There was, moreover, a broad consensus within the politically articulate public on foreign policy issues, indicative more of its comparative disinterest in the subject than of serious reflection. Even in the academic community, there appeared to be little independent thinking on external issues until the late 1950's when a number of institutions were established to conduct research on international relations and specific foreign countries. Until that time, India was almost totally dependent upon western source materials on international relations, whose biases in their lines of analysis were, to be sure, often reinterpreted to accord with Indian views.

This is not to say that the Indian government could blithely ignore parliamentary, press or public opinion in formulating foreign policy, for on matters of direct concern to India, some internal constraints did apply. Nehru's attempt to "liberalize" his policy on the Kashmir question in 1951, for instance, was seriously inhibited by the strongly antiPakistani attitude of broad sections of the Indian public, particularly in the north where a large number of refugees from Pakistan had settled. The continued existence of a large Muslim minority (approximately 50 million) that usually voted overwhelmingly for the "secular" Congress party also had an indirect but important influence on the evolution of Nehru's Middle East policy. But these were the exceptions, and even they could have been circumvented if other factors had not been generally supportive of the policy line taken on these two issues.

But if the first post-independence decade was one of comparative freedom for Nehru on foreign affairs, the course of events in the second decade posed greater problems for the government in this respect. The issues in dispute became increasingly complex and immediately important to India, and the automatic support of the Congress party, parliament, press and public was no longer assured. This first became evident in the parliamentary debate on Russian intervention in Hungary in 1956 during which Nehru was finally obliged to take a position more critical of the Soviet Union than he had originally intended.

Far more serious, however, was the deterioration in relations with China over several border disputes, which were first made public by Nehru only in 1959 although they had been "active" since at least 1954. The dispute eventually led to a short border war in 1962 in which India suffered a humiliating defeat that deeply embittered the Indian public and seriously undermined its confidence in the Nehru government's foreign policy. In the 1959–62 period, severe criticisms of both the principles and implementation of Indian foreign policy were voiced in Parliament, which was particularly incensed over Nehru's efforts to settle the dispute without even the formality of consulting the legislative body. It is probable, indeed, that this parliamentary and press criticism, and the opposition of the Home Minister in the cabinet, were decisive factors in Nehru's rejection of a Chinese offer of settlement in 1961 that would have made the Chinese aggression in 1962 unnecessary.[5] After the defeat in the war, the uproar in Parliament and a threatened revolt in the Congress party forced Nehru to dismiss his unpopular Defence Minister, V. K. Krishna Menon, essentially as a scapegoat for the defects in the prime minister's own handling of the situation.

By the time of Nehru's death in 1964, his foreign policy was in tatters, and was under increasing attack from all sides. This was directed both at its basic principles, and particularly the nonalignment policy which was held to have failed India at its hour of need, and at the manner of implementation. His successors, Lal Bahadur Shastri (1964–66) and Mrs. Indira Gandhi (1966–present) have had to reconstruct and reorient the policy line and regain the confidence of the public. This has been accomplished to a considerable extent, although not so much through a change in principles or goals as through expanding their definition and exercising greater flexibility in their implementation.

Decision-making on foreign policy now involves a much more complex network of interests than in the 1950's, both because the external environment is much more diversified and internal constraints

---

[5] If China had made the same offer in 1956 or even 1959, there is little doubt that Nehru could have accepted it without arousing a serious public outcry in India. It was, therefore, Peking's failure to understand the dynamics of a democratic political system, and the limitations this imposed on Nehru's freedom of action, that was partly responsible for the failure of the 1961 negotiations.

can no longer be as easily ignored. This latter factor was particularly crucial during the 1969–71 period, following the split in the Congress party, after which Mrs. Gandhi's party held only a plurality in the lower House of Parliament. This gave some of the opposition parties an unprecedented influence in decision-making as the government depended for its survival upon the tacit support of the pro-Soviet CPI, the dominant State party in Tamil Nadu (the DMK), and even the Socialist parties on occasion. The situation led to a virtual moratorium on decision-making in the foreign policy field for the government desperately sought to evade all issues that required new initiatives but brought it limited political rewards in terms of increased support from the Indian public.

The slogan of "self-reliance" in foreign policy and defense has a strong appeal to Indians and overt signs of dependency on any foreign power is bound to elicit a barrage of criticism of the government. But India is not yet capable of total self-reliance in these fields without sacrificing essential economic and military development goals. The government, thus, on several occasions has dramatized some minor event that presumably demonstrated its independence from external constraints or its impartiality in dealing with all foreign powers. Or, conversely, when New Delhi had to introduce some unpopular domestic economic measure, such as devaluation of the rupee in 1966, by implication the blame was placed upon what was depicted as irresistible foreign influence (the World Bank and the United States in this instance) which the government had sought to resist but to which it had finally to submit. Thus, in a variety of ways, internal political factors played a major role in several post-1962 Indian government decisions on foreign policy, and New Delhi was increasingly sensitive to the trend of opinion in the country on such questions.

Mrs. Gandhi's overwhelming victory in the March 1971 general elections, however, has provided her with greater flexibility in foreign affairs. Dependence upon Communist support, at least at the Center,[6] was no longer crucial, and the severe electoral setbacks to the right wing parties raised doubts about the political efficacy of the broadsides they had been directing at the government on foreign policy issues. While foreign policy played only a minor role in the election cam-

[6] It should be noted, however, that the Congress party is in a de facto alliance with the CPI in Kerala and West Bengal because of the strong challenge posed in both states by the more extremist wing of the Communist movement, the CPM. These alliances are probably more important to the CPI than the Congress, and it is unlikely that the former party could use these arrangements effectively as leverages on foreign policy issues in its dialogue with the Central Government.

paign, Mrs. Gandhi and the Congress party interpreted the results as a broad mandate on both foreign and domestic policy. This raised the possibility of new initiatives by the government of India in its foreign relations, particularly with reference to Pakistan and China. The Indo-Pakistani war in late 1971 resulted in worsened relations, with both of these countries, however, and made any overtures in their direction both inappropriate and inexpedient for the time being.

If Mrs. Gandhi's scope for maneuverability has substantially improved since the elections, the internal constraints she must contend with are still formidable. The public debate on foreign policy (e.g., nuclear weapons, relations with China and Pakistan) is more intensive than ever before, serviced in part by the growing number of non-official specialists on international relations and defense in both the universities and the press. Their criticism of the government policy is now more often to the point, based upon substantive research and study, and thus deserving of government consideration.

Parliament, on the other hand, while more vocal than in the past on foreign policy issues, is no more capable either structurally or psychologically to play a significant role in the decision-making process, except in a negative sense—as a body whose views have to be placated on occasion. There is, for instance, no real equivalent of the US Senate or House committees on foreign relations constantly submitting the executive's policy and actions to intensive public scrutiny. Even the Parliament's powers over the budget are comparatively nominal, as party discipline assures passage once the ruling party has extended its approval. Furthermore, India's straitened domestic economy and the grandiose if ambiguous promises to "wipe out poverty" made by Mrs. Gandhi in the 1971 election campaign would have given primacy to internal problems and only secondary priority to foreign policy issues under most sets of circumstances. Unfortunately for Mrs. Gandhi, the East Bengal crisis and the flow of nearly ten million refugees into India forced her government to divert both energy and resources away from India's social and economic development to relief programs and an expanded military budget, at least temporarily.

India and the World Community

Like the other states in southern Asia, most of India's foreign policy decisions, and many internal policy decisions as well, are strongly conditioned by an external environment over which New Delhi has only a limited influence, much less control. This status is a result of complex economic and political factors that are so intricately intertwined as to defy disentangling.

India has a vast economy (GNP approximately $50 billion per annum, or about that of France) and one that can, on the basis of human and material resources and market factors, at least aspire to a high degree of "self-sufficiency" and "self-reliance." But this is only a potential, for in fact the Indian economy is heavily dependent in many crucial respects on externally-derived inputs of various kinds for its expansion and prosperity. Moreover, the Indian population, over 550 million and growing at the rate of more than 12 million per year, places a heavy strain upon existing resources, particularly in rural areas where cultivable land is at a premium. It is only through a rapid and substantial expansion of manufacturing and service industries that the country's increasingly critical unemployment problem can be kept within reasonable bounds.

With a huge domestic market that is capable of absorbing virtually everything that the Indian economy can produce, the tendency has been for a relatively low priority to be placed upon exports. But much of Indian industry and agriculture is still heavily dependent upon foreign imports of machinery, equipment and some raw materials, with the result that the country has a persistently unfavorable balance of trade and foreign exchange deficit. Foreign aid from a wide variety of sources, while only a small proportion of India's annual GNP or even capital investment, is nevertheless of great importance in minimizing the adverse effects of the trade imbalance, and indeed is critical to growth in vital areas of the economy, whether it is machinery for industrial expansion or fertilizer for the "green revolution."

Foreign aid, which has averaged around $1 billion per annum since 1958, entails a wide range of economic commitments as well as parameters upon the range of options open to India politically. The aid has imposed upon the economy enormous repayment costs that are now reaching such proportions that they offset a substantial percentage of all new assistance. There is also the problem of the vast US holdings (on paper) of Indian currency, the so-called P.L. 480 rupees that accrue to the US government's account in India as payment for imported American food grains. In theory, although probably not in practice, the US could use these holdings to undermine the Indian currency and release strongly inflationary pressures within the economy.

The general situation has led a number of India's reputable economists to propose a moratorium on further foreign aid, or at least the restriction of aid to those purposes that will have an immediate economic payoff or earn foreign exchange. But this could have unacceptable social and political consequences, and would further reduce India's already low rate of economic growth. The government, thus, has opted for a different approach under which it seeks to increase the quantity of foreign aid, improve the terms upon which aid is obtained, and divert as much of the aid as possible to import substitution that will lessen dependence upon external sources either by producing commodities for export or those that are now being imported.[7] It has also sought to diversify the sources of foreign economic aid to the greatest extent possible in order to minimize the political and economic effects of the aid programs. India has achieved some success in this endeavor, primarily through expanded economic relations with the Soviet Union and Eastern Europe. Yet, aid from the United States and from sources that essentially take their lead from Washington—such as the World Bank, International Monetary Fund, a "consortium" of western European countries, and even the Asian Development Bank—still provides approximately 75–80 percent of economic aid offered to India and nearly 85 percent of the aid actually utilized.[8]

The suspicion that both the United States and the Soviet Union use their foreign aid programs to influence India's foreign policy has long agitated important elements of the Indian public. The evidence advanced in support of these allegations has been inconclusive, while India's determination and ability to resist superpower pressure has generally been underestimated. New Delhi's refusal to submit to Soviet and US pressure on the Nuclear Non-Proliferation Treaty, and to the suspension of a portion of the US aid program when the Indian government refused to accept a UN-imposed ceasefire and withdrawal resolution during the 1971 war with Pakistan, was a clear indication of the limitations on superpower capabilities. In defining its policy toward the Asian region, India obviously cannot ignore the USSR and US, but it is a serious misreading of the situation to assume that New Delhi *must* accept advice and guidance from either source.

[7] This policy has led to the introduction of strict regulations on imports, what Indians call "permit raj" (rule by permits), because virtually everything an industrialist must import from abroad requires a government license. The potential for wholesale administrative corruption and inefficiency in the operation of this system is, of course, obvious to everyone involved.

[8] These estimates are based on figures for the period up to March 1970, but the breakdown by source would not vary significantly for the period thereafter. By country or institution, the figures were: U.S., 50.9 percent; World Bank and I.D.A., 12.6 percent; USSR, 8 percent; West Germany, 7 percent; U.K., 6.8 percent; Japan, 2.8 percent; and others, 11.9 percent. *Records and Statistics* (New Delhi), 22:1, November 1970, p. 48.

The situation is further complicated by the Indian government's own uncertainty over the role it should and can play within Asia in furthering its foreign policy objectives, which in any case have often not been defined in sufficiently concrete terms to constitute a guide to action. The extent to which India should become involved in regional cooperation movements on both the economic and political level, for instance, has engendered a continuing debate within government circles for several years. Even more sensitive is the question of involvement, directly or indirectly, in security arrangements implicitly directed at China, whatever their source of inspiration. India has maintained its long-term opposition to any form of military alliance involving western states, and New Delhi's response to a Soviet proposal in 1969 for an "Asian mutual security system" was equally negative. New Delhi even refused to attend the Djakarta conference of May 1970, at which a number of Asian powers discussed the crisis caused by the massive foreign intervention in Cambodia, ostensibly on the grounds that India's nonalignment policy might be compromised in the process. New Delhi's predilection is for noninvolvement to the greatest extent possible in all difficult international disputes, but it also recognizes that India's strategic situation in southern Asia, great size, potential power, and its own national interests make isolation impossible. The question, then, is when and on what terms India should become involved.

INDIA AND NEIGHBORING STATES

India's international relations in the Asian area can be divided into two distinct categories in decision-making terms: those that are local to South Asia—i.e., relations with Pakistan, Bangla Desh, the Himalayan border states, Ceylon, as well as with China and Burma on frontier delimitation questions—and those that are broader in scope, involving relations with China, Southeast Asia, Japan, West Asia and the superpowers. In a broader strategic sense, the latter set of problems will probably prove to be more crucial, but it is also the arena in which India has only limited capability or influence. The really serious questions, thus, are more local in character. The decision in April 1971 to support the Ceylon government against what was defined as an extremist leftist insurrection, for instance, was indicative of New Delhi's determination to discourage challenges and threats both from within the area and outside to India's hegemony in South Asia.

Pakistan and Bangla Desh: Since independence in 1947, Pakistan has usually absorbed an inordinate amount of attention from Indian decision-makers. The nature of this problem has changed over the past two decades, but the basically divergent worldviews of the political elites of the two states and, perhaps even more important, their widely different interpretations of the criteria that underlay partition, have served to maintain their mutual relations at a constant level of restrained hostility with occasional outbursts of open conflict. To the Pakistanis—or at least the West Pakistanis—religious community formed the basis for partition, and thus any area of the sub-continent (such as Kashmir) and East Bengal in which the Muslims form a majority by rights should be part of the Muslim state of Pakistan. For India, the division was territorial rather than communal, and Pakistan's continued insistence upon the application of the "two nation" theory is unacceptable. To admit the legitimacy of Pakistan's position in the Kashmir dispute, the Indians argue, would undermine the secular state concept, one of the fundamental principles upon which the Indian political and legal system is based.

In addition to the dispute over Kashmir, which has led to armed hostilities on two occasions, there are numerous other conflicts of interest between the two countries that frequently heighten tensions. The partition of the sub-continent was carried out on territorial principles that ignored certain practical considerations. For instance, disputes over control of water resources, essential to agricultural development in both states, have been chronic, first in the west, where a division of water supply under the Indus River Project was made possible only through the massive input of foreign aid for this specific purpose, and more recently between East Bengal and India.

The differing political perspectives of the two governments have had a significant impact on their economic policy as well. British India, if underdeveloped, at least had a continental economy that was not constrained by internal boundaries. But the economies of the two successor states since partition have grown increasingly competitive rather than complementary, and indeed, for long periods there have been virtually no economic relations between them. This economic autarky has been an irritant to India in some areas adjacent to Pakistan but, in broader developmental terms, has been of minor significance. For West Pakistan, the break in economic ties with India, after some initial difficulties, has been the catalyst for a substantial industrialization program; for East Pakistan, however, it had been an economic disaster. The inability of the two countries to collaborate even on some mutually beneficial economic programs is indicative of the depth of distrust and incompatibility that still marks their relationship.

In foreign policy, the biggest problem for New Delhi (other than the endless debates over Kashmir in the United Nations) that Pakistan poses is the latter's persistent efforts to attain parity in military power with India—through the military alliance with the United States prior to 1962 and through support from a variety of sources thereafter. This was not acceptable to India even before the 1962 border war with China, and much less so once military cooperation between China and Pakistan against India became a possibility, no matter how remote. Pakistan's policy in this respect was counterproductive in the long term, because of the substantial modernization and expansion of the Indian army, and a steady widening of the gap in military power between the two states, particularly after their costly wars in 1965 and 1971. Even the addition of China's limited military capacity in Tibet would no longer tilt the balance in Pakistan's favor, at least in terms of conventional weaponry.[9]

There is, thus, no real possibility of Pakistan gaining its objectives by military means barring wholesale political chaos or disintegration in India. India's hegemony, however, has not contributed to progress toward a settlement, and indeed may have hardened lines in both countries. Moreover, the issues in dispute are central to their domestic politics, and there has been no occasion since 1951 in which both the Pakistan and Indian governments felt strong enough internally to risk the potentially dangerous political fallout from a compromise settlement. Nor has the external environment made a positive contribution. Both China and the Soviet Union have played with considerable skill upon the differences between the two powers to their own advantage. The United States has usually favored an overall settlement, but has lacked—or has been reluctant to use—the capacity to induce a basic resolution of the issues in dispute.

The upheaval in East Bengal in 1971, which promises to add another irreconcilable dispute to Indo-Pakistani relations for years to come, has dimmed what little hope there may have been for an improvement in their relationship. The pressure on New Delhi to intervene in support of the Bengali separatist movement became increasingly difficult to resist, both because of the tremendous economic

---

[9] There are serious climatic and topographic obstacles to military collusion between Pakistan and China, even assuming the two governments were prepared to act jointly. During the winter months (December–March), for instance, most of the Himalayan border passes are snowbound, and China would face immense logistic problems in supporting a major military campaign across the Himalayas at that time of year. This is the dry season on the Gangetic plain, however, and Pakistan would have to contend with the full weight of Indian military power for approximately four months on its own.

burden imposed by the flight of millions of East Bengali refugees to India and the strategic political and military factors involved.

Of course India welcomed any development that weakened the viability of the Pakistani government and, particularly, the Pakistani army, but New Delhi's initial response to the situation in East Bengal was marked by considerable restraint. The East Bengali demand for more regional autonomy *within* Pakistan was warmly endorsed by the Indian authorities, but New Delhi was more ambivalent on the independence question. The operating principle may be summarized as: "autonomy for East Bengal—yes; independence—preferably not."

Why this reaction? The most important factor was that an independent Bangla Desh raised a new complex of difficult problems for New Delhi without significantly improving India's position vis-à-vis its principal regional rivals—West Pakistan and China. Moreover, the Indian political elite, like their counterparts elsewhere in Asia and Africa, are profoundly disturbed by national disintegration and "Balkanization" anywhere in the area, for these set a precedent for divisive forces within their own societies. New Delhi was particularly sensitive when the area involved was adjacent to northeastern India, where political dissidence has long flourished and where there is considerable scope for Chinese assistance to subversive activities.

Moreover, an independent Bangla Desh, with a population of 75 million, would inevitably serve as a rallying point for Bangla "nationalist" sentiment among the 35 million Bengalis in India. In particular, it would be likely to further encourage the extremist, pro-Maoist forces in West Bengal, which already have rather tenuous ties with both the Chinese and similar groups in East Bengal. The elimination of much of the moderate leadership in East Bengal by the Pakistan government's campaign against the "separatist" movement has provided the extremist forces with an unprecedented opportunity to seize the leadership of the political movements in both areas of Bengal. It is not an entirely implausible scenario that the Indian government might eventually find itself intervening, either directly or indirectly, in Bangla Desh to prevent the establishment of a pro-Chinese regime at the eastern end of the Gangetic plain.

Whatever its preferences may have been on the subject, New Delhi will now have to accommodate itself to an independent Bangla Desh. What will be India's policy in this new situation. Primary emphasis, it seems reasonable to presume, will be placed upon developing intimate economic ties with the new state which in many respects would be advantageous to both. The political repercussions, however, may prove serious, for the East Bengalis would soon shift their complaints about West Pakistani economic exploitation to India. The Chinese might then be provided with the opportunity to serve as a counterweight, and in a context far more threatening to India than that posed by the existing Sino-Pakistani "alliance." For New Delhi, therefore, the developments in East Bengal opened few channels for the advancement of long-term Indian interests, created many new problems in its relations with all neighboring states, and further complicated its own serious domestic political problems in eastern India.[10] The prolongation of the civil war in East Bengal led to a continued influx of refugees into India as well as the progressive radicalization of the Bengali resistance movement. Once the Pakistani Army had demonstrated its inability to bring the situation under control and the major powers had failed in their efforts to arrange a political settlement, New Delhi decided that direct intervention in support of the Bangla Desh forces was unavoidable. This led to full-scale war with Pakistan in December 1971 and the establishment of an independent nation, Bangla Desh. The repercussions on Indo-Pakistani relations in the short-run were disastrous, but it is possible that these events may contribute eventually to a political settlement throughout South Asia.

China: Asia's largest state, which shares a 1500 mile border with India and the Himalayan border states, has been a constant puzzle to the Indians, who have never satisfactorily defined the terms of their relationship with the People's Republic of China. Nehru made a concerted effort for over more than three decades to "understand" the Chinese, but with only limited success. Indeed, the humiliations of 1962 were to some extent the consequence of his misperception of Chinese interests and behavior.

The Indian response to the People's Republic of China has fluctuated widely, depending upon the status of their relationship at a particular moment. More recently, a better balanced appraisal has been reached, but there is still considerable uncertainty in New Delhi (as in other capitals) over China's own perception of its proper place in Asia and how this conforms to or conflicts with those of India. China has been the primary focus of India's Asia policy since 1949, and it remains the single most important, if imponderable long-term factor in New Delhi's calculations.

The history of the relationship between these two powers since

[10] The course of developments in the Naga, Mizo and other tribal areas in eastern India that have long been in a virtual state of rebellion is sure to be strongly influenced by events in East Bengal. See Gordon P. Means, "Cease-fire Politics in Nagaland," *Asian Survey*, XI:10 (October, 1971).

the victory of the Communist regime in China presents a cyclical pattern. In the 1949–52 period, India's friendly overtures to Communist China were treated with considerable suspicion by Peking, and New Delhi's bona fides as a nonaligned power were questioned. From 1953–58, Chinese policy toward India shifted drastically, and Nehru played a leading role in Peking's efforts to establish relations with the Afro-Asian world on the basis of the principles of "peaceful coexistence." There was in this period what virtually amounted to a de facto coalition between the two states on some world and Asian problems, and the working relationship between them was closer than any that Peking has had either before or since with a non-Communist power.

The boundary dispute on the Sino-Indian Himalayan frontier, which first arose in 1954, assumed increasingly serious proportions in the context of the 1959 revolt in Tibet against Chinese rule. Relations deteriorated rapidly thereafter, culminating in a brief border war in 1962. The border disagreements, although conducive to rampant emotionalism on both sides, were comparatively minor and probably could have been settled peacefully if they had not coincided with (a) the Sino-Soviet split, and (b) a divergence between the Chinese and Indian views on the role of the Afro-Asian states in an increasingly multipolar international political system.

By the late 1960's, New Delhi had largely surmounted the traumatic effects of its defeat in the 1962 border war, and had a more realistic appraisal of the limitations imposed on Communist China's war-making capacity in South Asia by logistic, climatic and topographical factors, as well as by Peking's continued disputes with both superpowers. Even the potential application of Chinese "nuclear blackmail" is not taken too seriously as long as broader strategic factors in Asia do not change substantially. For India, it is Communist China's potential as a support base for internal subversion in South Asia that causes greater concern, particularly in the context of recent developments in East Bengal.

Despite the background of animosity surrounding Sino-Indian relations in the 1960's, New Delhi assumes that a new approach to Peking will probably become necessary in the next decade. During its period of comparative weakness in the border area itself, India borrowed an old Chinese tactic—that is, avoiding a settlement until a better balance has been achieved and the adversary appears to be in a more reasonable frame of mind. New Delhi realizes that the territory lost to Communist China in 1962 is not likely to be regained under existing conditions, and would now seem to be prepared to consider a compromise settlement, perhaps along the lines offered by Chou En-lai in 1961. Mrs. Gandhi's overwhelming victory in the 1971 elections made this a more distinct possibility if Chinese support for Pakistan in the conflict over East Bengal had not intruded. In any case, it would appear that Communist China is not interested in a settlement that leaves India entangled in what Peking perceives as New Delhi's subordinate role in the Soviet Union's "containment" policy, as exemplified by the 1971 Indo-Soviet Friendship Pact.

Some Indian circles not particularly friendly to Communist China also feel that a lack of flexibility in New Delhi's China policy is due to an excessive dependence upon the Soviet Union, and argue that this has been disadvantageous to India in certain respects. The success with which Pakistan has used Communist China as a counter to India and as a bargaining factor in relations with both the United States and the Soviet Union has been cited as a useful example for New Delhi. There is also some apprehension that either or both superpowers may eventually reach an accommodation with Peking that would force a complete revision of India's strategic and political calculations. New Delhi considers it essential to move in conjunction with the major powers in any overall political settlement in Asia, which explains the great concern with which India reacted to Nixon's announcement of his intention to visit Peking in 1972.

While China is a major factor in all of India's decision-making on foreign policy, there is as yet sufficient room for maneuver to provide New Delhi with a variety of alternatives. Communist China is of minor significance to India in economic terms, and the political and strategic challenges it presents can be met as long as the power balance in Asia does not shift too far in Peking's direction. Furthermore, there are no significant domestic political forces pressuring the government on this issue, and it is the external environment that will largely shape India's China policy in the next decade. New Delhi would welcome a settlement with Peking that eased the drain on resources caused by India's military build-up and that undermined the China-Pakistan axis, but not on any terms and certainly not a manner which might endanger its more important relations with the United States and the Soviet Union.

Southeast Asia and Japan: In the early 1950's, Nehru set the transformation of Southeast Asia into a "zone of peace"—in which western influence and the "cold war" would be excluded—as a primary goal of Indian foreign policy. This was to be accomplished through cooperation between India and Communist China. Peking's acceptance of the principles of "peaceful coexistence" with the new states of Southeast Asia would, Nehru argued, induce the latter to adopt a nonaligned policy modeled after New Delhi's. This decade was, then, a period of intensive activity for India in Southeast Asia; it strongly supported Indonesia's struggle for independence, played a crucial intermediary role in international conferences on the area, and served as the chairman of the Internation Truce Commissions set up for Vietnam, Laos and Cambodia by the 1954 Geneva agreement.

A number of factors intruded to frustrate Indian policy in the area. Several of the Southeast Asian states did not accept Nehru's reassurances about Communist China's peaceful intentions, and preferred to stake their existence upon more tangible sources of support through military and/or political alliances with the western powers led by the United States. Rather than a "zone of peace" Southeast Asia became a scene of wars and disputes, most of them internally based but fed by the rivalries of the major powers. India's own involvement declined substantially after the 1962 war with Communist China, due in part to indecision in New Delhi over what became a primary objective thereafter—forestalling the establishment of a Chinese sphere of influence throughout Southeast Asia.

Uncertainty about India's role also was reflected in the cautious position taken on the Vietnam war. New Delhi's immediate response to American involvement was mildly critical of certain tactics, such as the bombing of the north, but was implicitly supportive of the effort to maintain a non-Communist regime in the south. By mid-1967, however, India's appraisal of the situation seems to have changed substantially, as it then concluded that a unified Indochina, even under Communist control, would be better able to withstand Chinese pressure. More recently, New Delhi's position has shifted again to some extent, as it is now assumed that the US military will be out of Vietnam but that the Communists lack the strength to establish an effective control over Indochina. It is expected that hostilities will continue on at least a low scale for some years to come, but in a context of limited superpower involvement.

The "neutralization" of Southeast Asia, guaranteed by all the great powers involved, is still the ultimate objective of India, but New Delhi perceives no very positive role for itself in the attainment of this goal. India recognizes that it has a vital stake in the region, both politically and economically, but it has demonstrated a basic reluctance to contribute—even to the most limited possible extent—to the process of stabilization. Not only are all forms of political involvement eschewed, but India has usually even refrained from participation in multinational efforts to establish an institutional superstructure for regional economic cooperation. As a result, Indian influence and prestige in Southeast Asia is at a nadir. The largest state in southern Asia, with a powerful military and naval force, has been deprived—or deprived itself—of any significant role in the area.

Indecisiveness in India's Asian policy is also apparent in its relations with Japan, although in this instance Indian caution is matched by that of Japan. These two Asian powers, which have many obvious interests in common, have never marched in step in policy terms. In the 1950's, India's nonalignment policy and advocacy of the Peking regime was not viewed with enthusiasm by Tokyo, while in the 1960's it was India's concern with potential Chinese expansionism that disturbed the Japanese government which was then making its own overtures to Peking. India's evaluation of Japanese foreign policy has been no less negative. The alliance with the United States has been decried on the same basis as other western-Asian military pact, and Japan is also considered to be excessively opportunistic in its China policy and overassertive, economically, in Southeast Asia to India's disadvantage. Only very recently have the two governments begun to perceive a broader community of interests and a need to work together on at least limited goals.

It is probable that this cooperative spirit will become stronger in the 1970's. India considers Japan an attractive alternative source of foreign aid, but has been deterred previously by the comparatively unfavorable terms Japan extracts for its assistance. For its part, Tokyo has been apprehensive about any major economic commitment to a society as vast and omnivorous as India, but both political and economic considerations are likely to push Japan toward greater involvement in South Asia, including India. Japan, the only really "great power" in Asia at this time both economically, and politically, is sure to play an increasingly important role in all aspects of Indian policy in Asia.

The superpowers: The United States and the Soviet Union have been the pillars of India's foreign policy since at least the mid-1950's, and New Delhi's flexibility in dealing with troublesome neighbors has been to a considerable extent determined by the state of its relationship with the superpowers at any given moment. Their aid programs, economic and military, are a constant factor in Indian decision-making, both in the positive sense of aid received and in the negative sense of aid withheld from its principal rivals—i.e., Pakistan and Communist China.

The history of India's relations with the United States and the Soviet Union has been marked by varying degrees of intimacy. New Delhi's basic objective has usually been to maintain a position approximately equidistant between the superpowers, but this has not always been possible, usually for reasons the Indian authorities could not control. In the 1947–53 period, the balance tipped heavily in the direction of the western powers as the Soviet Union's attitude during all but the last few months of the Stalin era was distinctly unfriendly to the Nehru government. With Stalin's death in 1953, however, a basic change occurred in the Soviet's position on India, dramatized by the successful B & K (Bulganin and Khrushchev) campaign tour of India in 1955. Subsequently, India has constituted the key to Soviet policy in southern Asia. Economic assistance was inaugurated at this time, and B & K explicitly supported India in its dispute with Pakistan over Kashmir.

These enthusiastic endorsements from the Soviet Union coincided with, and indeed were partly inspired by, a serious deterioration in US-Indian relations. In 1954, Washington had brought Pakistan into two of its anti-Communist military alliances—the Southeast Asia Treaty Organization (SEATO) and the Central Treaty Organization (CENTO). Under these agreements, the United States supplied Pakistan with massive military aid during the next decade—in theory for use against Communist aggressors but with no adequate safeguards to prevent their use against India, as they were in 1965 and 1971.[11] This threatened India's highly-valued dominant power status in South Asia, and compelled India to divert resources to the expansion of the Indian army to match the Pakistani military build-up. Moreover, India interpreted the alliance as having been inspired by a pro-Pakistani bias which was also evident in American and British support in the United Nations for a plebiscite in Kashmir. Nehru also apprehended that his nonalignment policy, the only hope for peace in Asia in his view, had suffered a setback by the association of a South Asian state in a western-dominated military alliance system. He was, furthermore, very skeptical of the efficacy of a "containment" policy in the Asian setting, and doubted Pakistan's bona fides in opting for inclusion.

A more acceptable balance in South Asia was established by the Kennedy administration in the early 1960's under which India advanced several steps on the scale of US values. During the Sino-Indian war in 1962, Washington was strongly supportive of India despite the strain this placed on US-Pakistan relations. American guarantees of air support against Chinese air attacks on Indian cities was sought and received by New Delhi, and an extensive US military aid program designed to assist in the strengthening of India's mountain warfare capability (i.e., against China rather than Pakistan) was inaugurated.

---

[11] Some Indian commentators have been prone to infer an antiIndian motivation to US policy in South Asia, alleging that Pakistan was brought into the anti-Communist alliance system in 1954 primarily because of Washington's displeasure with Nehru's nonalignment policy. There is little substance to this, for American policy on this question was conditioned by a completely different set of perceptions in Washington than that suggested. The fact was that India played a relatively minor role in American, Asian and world policy at that time, and could be and was virtually ignored.

The Soviet Union was considerably slower in clarifying its position on the 1962 war, as it was still attempting to disguise the severity of its own dispute with Peking. Finally, however, Moscow did criticize the Chinese (although rather obliquely) and, more important to New Delhi, agreed to extend military aid (including a jet aircraft factory) to India. Suddenly, India found itself the recipient of substantial military assistance from both the superpowers, and for the same reason —to build up the strength of the Indian army deployed on the northern border with China.

The operating principles of Indian foreign policy could not escape unscathed in this drastic change of circumstance. Given the diverse sources of support, and the motivations thereof, the nonalignment policy required reinterpretation. It was retained with respect to India's relations with the United States and the Soviet Union, but New Delhi accepted a de facto bi-alignment with both of the superpowers in their separate but supportive "China containment" policies. The relationship was not formalized, of course, but there was a broad degree of cooperation and consultation at the official level, and on a well-balanced basis to India's considerable satisfaction.

The 1965 Indo-Pakistani war upset this balance to some extent as it substantially reduced US support, thereby expanding the relative importance of Soviet influence in South Asia. It was Moscow rather than Washington or London that intervened successfully, organizing the Tashkent conference between the belligerents and serving as a "nonpartisan" but assertive mediator in the negotiations. While the United States had played a constructive role in the UN-sponsored ceasefire that brought the fighting to a halt, Washington adopted a hands-off but supportive position on the settlement process itself.

During the conflict, the United States suspended all military assistance to both India and Pakistan, and has retained the ban—with certain minor exceptions—subsequently. New Delhi understood that this was more to Pakistan's disadvantage than to its own and did not raise strong objections. But the Indian government was disturbed because the US ban made India increasingly dependent upon the Soviet Union as a source of military assistance and reduced to that extent India's flexibility in both defense and foreign policy. This even had an impact on domestic politics, as the CPI gained greater leverage with Mrs. Gandhi's government because of the intermediary role it occasionally plays in relations between India and the Soviet Union.

By 1971, India's military expansion program had virtually reached its planned expansion goal and had achieved greater self-sufficiency in military production, reducing, to some extent, the degree of dependence upon Soviet sources. Nevertheless, most of the more sophisticated weaponry still has to be obtained from abroad, and the Soviet Union continues to be the main source of supply. Thus, given the vital importance India places upon improving its defense posture in the southern Asian region, the policy that sought to avoid exclusive dependence on either superpower in any aid category had to be modified.

Of more long-range significance, perhaps, is the Indian perception of the relative depth of the American and Soviet commitment in Central and South Asia. The credibility of the US involvement had been questioned by Indian officials long before the Nixon Doctrine raised the issue in more critical form. Washington's concern with this region is presumed to be primarily reactive in character, rather than based upon vital national interests. The Soviet Union, in contrast, has a territorial imperative that makes withdrawal from the region inconceivable.

A series of events in 1971, including developments in East Bengal, small-scale US arms aid to Pakistan, and what appeared to New Delhi to be the opening stage of a rapprochement between Washington and Peking, convinced both India and the Soviet Union of the need to place their relationship on a more formal basis. A 20-year treaty of "peace and friendship" was signed between the two powers in August 1971. The most important clauses in the agreement were those providing for "mutual consultations" in the event of an emergency in either country's relations with third powers and obligating both states to refrain from supporting "any third party that engages in armed conflict with the other party."[12] While the Indian authorities strongly (and correctly) denied that the treaty constituted a military alliance with the Soviet Union or even an abandonment of nonalignment, it certainly placed Indo-Soviet relations on an unprecedented basis of intimacy, in the process providing New Delhi with greater freedom of maneuver in its relations with Pakistan and China. It also marked the recognition of a broadly-based community of interests between India and the Soviet Union in the southern Asian region.

This does not mean, of course, that India is assured of Soviet support in any particular crisis situation or on a permanent basis. Indeed, New Delhi must operate on the assumption that Moscow may at some point find it expedient to reactivate the alliance with China or mollify Pakistan at India's expense. It continues to be vital to India, therefore, to encourage at least a minimal American presence in South Asia if New Delhi's principle of countervailing forces is to be effective. The treaty with the Soviet Union has modified but not eliminated this basic Indian

---

[12] *The Statesman Weekly* (Calcutta), August 14, 1971, p. 6.

perception of their self-interest and it continues to be essential to the success of New Delhi's foreign policy to avoid a total commitment to any of the contending blocs in the arena of word politics.

Achievements, Failures and Prospects

The success or failure of the broader objectives of Indian foreign policy have been mixed. In the immediate post-independence period, Prime Minister Nehru set a series of ambitious goals for his country that were intended to contribute to the cause of world peace and the amelioration of tensions in the international community. This reflected his strong sense of responsibility, as well as his feeling that India was peculiarly qualified to serve as a buffer between antagonists and as a middleman in the settlement of international disputes. That there was some substance to Nehru's role-perception was indicated by India's contributions to the Korean war cease-fire (1953), the Geneva agreement on Indochina (1954), and the Middle East crisis (1956).

Nevertheless, in the long run, Nehru's efforts to transform Asia into a "zone of peace" were a failure—in part because of some serious misperceptions of his own. Under his definition, the zone of peace concept required the virtual exclusion of the western powers and the Soviet Union from any significant political role in the area. This ignored the fact that both the United States and the Soviet Union are Pacific as well as global powers with direct political and economic interests in the region that neither are prepared to surrender.

India's Asian policy also depended heavily upon Chinese cooperation in minimizing the influence of non-Asian states, including the Soviet Union. Nehru's denunciations of military alliances were usually directed at those initiated by the western powers but the Sino-Soviet alliance was equally obstructive to the broader goals of his policy. Underlying his approach to China in the early 1950's was the hope that Peking could somehow extract itself from a dependent status upon Moscow and become instead a status quo power in Asia. Ironically, the first objective was achieved at New Delhi's expense, as by 1962 Peking was sufficiently independent from Russian influence to ignore the latter's warning against hostilities with India over a minor border dispute. China has also accepted the principle of "peaceful coexistence" with several Asian states, which in essence is supportive of the status quo, but there is some skepticism that this can easily be combined with its *verbal* support of wars of "National Liberation." India still hopes that Asia can become a zone of peace, but now this is to be accomplished through the time-honored "balance of power" principle rather than by a unified response from the Asian states to external intrusions.

A corollary to the zone of peace strategy was Nehru's plan to maintain Asia as a "nuclear free" area in which all countries renounced the acquisition or use of nuclear weapons. China's decision to "go nuclear," therefore, has forced India into some hard decisions of its own on this question. India is well-advanced in the technology of the peaceful use of atomic energy and could, in a short time, develop a nuclear weapons program as well. Moreover, there is substantial public support for this in India, particularly among intellectuals and politicians.

The arguments in support of a nuclear weapons program usually focus around three main points. First, with China having the bomb and using nuclear diplomacy, at least implicitly, all of India's previous calculations, based upon the presumption of a "balance of terror" between the superpowers that neutralized their capacity to use the bomb, must be reexamined. India, it is argued, cannot safely renounce nuclear weapons in a multinuclear world in Asia without seriously jeopardizing its security. Second, the credibility of the tacit US and Soviet guarantees to India with respect to Chinese nuclear weapons is questioned. Would the superpowers really intervene to prevent the use of "nuclear blackmail" by Peking in another confrontation with India? Third, there is strong support for India asserting a more prominent role in Asia and this would be possible, it is contended, only if India goes nuclear. The benefits the Chinese have derived in world prestige through its nuclear program is cited in this regard.

There is an equally strong group within the vocal Indian public that opposes any nuclear weapons program, and a variety of arguments are advanced in support of this position. The relatively small number of intellectuals who still adhere to Nehru's and Gandhi's approach to international relations point out that a nuclear program would be totally inconsistent with all the moral principles that India has expounded since independence. Some of the more pragmatic opponents use two practical arguments. First, that China's possession of the bomb has not in fact significantly altered the power balance in Asia since Peking cannot even threaten to use the few bombs it possesses against Asian countries without weakening its defenses against the superpowers or inviting massive retaliation, by either or both the US and the USSR. China's cautious avoidance of any kind of physical confrontation with the United States in the Vietnam war even after its acquisition of the bomb is used as supportive evidence. The second argument stresses the cost factor, and maintains that while India might be able to afford a few bombs it cannot afford the delivery system required to make them operable. The estimates on costs have varied widely, but it is agreed that a medium-range delivery system would be a serious drain on India's resources. The supporters of the program, however, argue that India does not need an elaborate delivery system but merely a bomber force capable of destroying China's vulnerable supply lines to Tibet and perhaps to threaten southwest China.

The government's policy on this issue has been characterized by deliberate temporizing and vacillation, intended to delay the need to make a decision. Its public position is that India will not make the bomb at this time but reserves the right to do so later if this is considered necessary. New Delhi has refused to sign the Nuclear Non-Proliferation Treaty, despite considerable pressure from both the United States and the Soviet Union, on the grounds that the treaty does not offer sufficient safeguards to nonnuclear powers, or limit the capacity of the existing nuclear powers. Despite the ambiguous language used, it would appear that New Delhi has made a tentative decision to go nuclear by the end of the 1970's if the external security environment does not improve substantially. This is indicated in the huge allocation of resources, both human and material, to develop the scientific and technological facilities that will enable it to produce both the bomb and a delivery system if the need arises.

Nehru's nonalignment policy has also been the recipient of widespread criticism in the past decade. Nonalignment had been conceived as the policy best suited to advance the cause of world peace by removing an ever larger number of states from direct participation in the cold war. The great diversity of views and interests within the Afro-Asian area, however, has raised doubts about the validity of this approach. The most serious disputes, it is pointed out, are intraregional. The ludicrous events surrounding subsequent efforts to organize Afro-Asian conferences since Bandung (1955) and the meaningless slogans emanating from these quarters are indicative of the problems faced in reconciling differences *within* the region, and nonalignment is irrelevant to this situation by and large.

Even India, which first formulated the principle of nonalignment in conceptual and tactical terms, has had to modify its policy substantially. From Nehru's early advocacy of keeping contacts with the western powers and the Soviet Union to the unavoidable minimum, New Delhi now seeks to maximize them to the greatest extent possible. The shift in India's position on Soviet participation in Afro-Asian conferences between 1955 and 1967 is one symptom of this change in attitude. As a working principle, nonalignment has been considerably reduced in scope to mean nonalignment between the United States and the Soviet Union, but alignment with either or both of these powers on a series of specific issues. The rhetoric remains the same, and the government still insists that India is nonaligned. But this almost amounts to the pious mouthing of an ineffective but ritualistic *mantra* (magic formula) as it is quite evident that New Delhi has no hesitation to abandon this principle when India's interests are at stake, such as the 1971 treaty with the Soviet Union.

The third major facet of Nehru's foreign policy was his belief that India could serve as an effective ideological bridge between the contending powers in the cold war. This never occurred in the sense in which Nehru used the phrase. India was a useful instrumentality in certain crisis situations, but all of Nehru's admonitions and advice did not serve to achieve a meeting of the minds between the cold war blocs. But in another sense, India did contribute to the US-Soviet détente, for it was in South Asia that the China policies of the two superpowers converged in the 1961–71 decade, making tacit cooperation between them possible in selected sets of circumstances in this area.

If India has not had too much success in the broader aspects of its foreign policy it has much better reason to be satisfied with its regional policy. India's dominant power status in South Asia has been preserved against a variety of challenges, if at a high price. The real gap in military strength and capacity (including productive capacity and the ability to sustain conflict) between India and Pakistan, for instance, is probably greater today than a decade ago. The substantial Chinese military presence in Tibet has been largely neutralized, at least in terms of major operations south of the Himalayan crest. Because of this, India's preeminent influence in the Himalayan border states has been enhanced. Even India's relations with the various major powers provides some cause for satisfaction, for all of these must now define their role in South Asia on the assumption of India's dominant power status in this region. New Delhi still has many grounds for complaint, particularly with respect to US and Chinese support of Pakistan, but there is increasing realization in India that this is more of symbolic significance than a serious threat to the existing power balance in South Asia.

In the view of the Indian authorities, the greatest security problem India faces today is no longer overt military aggression but external support for internal political dissidence. The viability of its foreign policy is not at stake here, but rather that of the political system itself. The effective utilization of diplomatic channels, however, can be of assistance by reducing both the quantity and the accessibility of foreign support of revolutionary elements. This could best be achieved through a settlement with Communist China that neutralized that source of external assistance. Peking may be responsive to an overture on this subject, as it has paid a high price (in continued tension with India) for the support it has given to various Indian rebel groups (Nagas, Mizos, Naxalites, etc.), and for very meager returns.

India's foreign policy problems remain very complex and threatening both on the local (South Asian) and international level, but a cautious optimism does not seem unwarranted. Southeast Asia seems destined for years of conflict, but it now is possible that this will remain localized with no contender emerging as the dominant power. This is the best of a bad situation as far as New Delhi is concerned, for it would not endanger India's vital lines of communication through Southeast Asian waters or pose a serious political challenge to the Indian political system. The importance of India to the superpowers has, if anything, increased since the 1971 Indo-Pakistani war. Relations with Washington deteriorated seriously during this conflict, but should improve after an extended period of recuperation. There is even some ground for optimism with regard to relations with Communist China, particularly if Peking should decide to encourage New Delhi to modify its present pro-Soviet policy by reducing tensions between the two countries. The only seemingly unresolvable conflict is that with Pakistan, as the harmful effects of the partition of the sub-continent continue to disrupt the whole of South Asia, making intraregional cooperation—vital to both economic development and political stability—unlikely, for many years to come.

Pakistan

WAYNE WILCOX

Pakistan was created in 1947 as a result of the partition
of the British Indian Empire at the time of the
withdrawal of the British from South Asia. The new
state was the product of a successful "foreign policy"
pursued in the pre-independence period by the
leadership of the Muslim League, which argued that
the Indian Muslims were a "separate nation" of one
hundred million people, divided from the Indian
Hindus by culture, history and values. The "diplomacy"
of separatism pitted the Pakistani movement against
both the British and the Indian National Congress,
and in a series of conferences and campaigns, it
was successful.

Few states have been created with as many endemic
problems as Pakistan. The communal violence that
accompanied partition led to a massive slaughter of
Muslims and Hindus and millions of refugees—
flowing in both directions. Over forty million Muslims
remained in India, where they constitute a significant
minority and a continuous source of controversy
between the two states. Moreover, Pakistan was divided
into two regions, one in the northwest and the other
in the northeast areas of South Asia, separated by a
thousand miles of Indian territory. Pakistan began its
existence as a divided, incomplete and partial homeland
for the Muslims. Periodic wars, border strife and rivalry
with India have weakened Pakistan's domestic security
and economic viability. The transformation of an
autonomy movement into a separatist movement in
East Pakistan (Bangla Desh) in 1971, and the strong

suppressive measures taken by the Pakistani government, destroyed the very national existence of the Pakistani state and led to its division into two national entities.

Until these events in 1971, one of the more positive aspects of Pakistan's existence had been the comparative success of its foreign policy. Its security, its voice in the world and its economic development had all profited handsomely from foreign policy ingenuity. It is the only major state in the world that has received significant amounts of military and economic assistance from the United States, the Soviet Union and the People's Republic of China. Deprived of such assistance, Pakistan would be without influence even in its region, and its woefully underdeveloped economy would be stagnant. It would lack the means to defend itself or perhaps even to keep domestic order. Foreign policy, therefore, is more than a burden to Pakistan; it is a major pillar of public policy and national life.

The Strategic Setting

The most distinctive and troublesome aspect of Pakistan's creation was its division into two "wings." This curious geography was the product of the religious basis of the partition of British India, since the areas in which the Muslims were a majority were in the Indus valley of western India, and in the lower Gangetic valley of eastern India. Pakistan was at its creation a country of two parts related to one another *only* by a common faith.

East Pakistan, which constituted about 55 percent of the population of the state, is part of Bengal. Before Pakistan's creation, it was the rural hinterland of Calcutta's mills and factories and the principal source for jute production. Less than 5 percent of the East Bengal population lived in cities, and the cruel nature of the river delta topography subjected most of the provincial population to alternating floods and cyclones. Yet some of the districts of East Bengal had the highest population densities per acre of cultivated land in the world as well as some of the lowest per capita income and nutritional levels in the human family.

Culturally, East Bengal shares the pride of Calcutta in the glorious Bengali prose and poetry and in Bengal's image as the intellectual center of the Indian experience. From the early twentieth century, Bengali-Muslim families educated their children in Calcutta and took an active role in provincial political affairs. Since the Muslims were a majority in the province, the coming of political representation gave them an avenue to assert their power against the cultural and economic superiority of the Hindu community.

When in 1940 the Muslim League called for the creation of a Muslim state in the Indian sub-continent, the Bengali Muslims gave their support. The demand had the quality of a communal "trade union" demand, an outrageous first bid made so that it could be bargained away for more modest benefits. Moreover, it appeared to allow for an independent Bengal as well as a consolidated Muslim state in western India. Since the leadership of the Bengali Muslims generally spoke Urdu and English as well as Bengali, and since they shared common interests with other Muslim provincial leaders in pressuring both the British and the Hindus, the distinctive provincial qualities of East Bengal were not asserted during the Pakistan movement.

What became West Pakistan—part of the province of Punjab, the North-West Frontier Province, Sind, Baluchistan and ten small princely states—was in fact the Indus valley. This part of the Indian sub-continent is extremely arid, and would be desert but for the fact that it is the largest irrigated plain in the world. While Pakistan inherited the fields and lower river irrigation facilities, the headwaters of the Indus system fell to India. The 45 percent of Pakistan's population that lived in the west wing therefore were hostage to continued water supply from rivers that rise in the western Himalayas and flow through India before flooding into the rivers of the Punjab that meet to become the mighty Indus flowing into the Arabian sea.

Like East Pakistan, the western wing was almost entirely agricultural. Only Lahore, an agricultural marketing town, and Karachi, a small port very much in Bombay's shadow, qualified as more than district towns. But unlike East Pakistan, the people of the Indus valley spoke many languages and dialects. The tribal people inhabiting the gateway of India—the Khyber Pass—speak Pushtu as do their brothers in eastern Afghanistan. In the plains of the Punjab, the language is Punjabi and farther south along the lower Indus, the language is Sindhi. The high desert areas of Baluchistan find tribal peoples speaking Pushtu, Baluchi and Brahui. Many of the educated townspeople of the region can speak and read Urdu, the language of the North Indian Muslim community that stretched from Lahore and New Delhi to Patna in Bihar. After the great 5–6 million refugee influx at the time of independence, more Urdu speakers found themselves in the west wing, and Karachi gained a significant number of Gujarati-speaking Muslim refugees and immigrants.

Social and political change came to the Muslims of the Indus valley somewhat slower than to their brethren in the Gangetic delta, in part because Calcutta's vitality was unmatched by the regional towns of the west and because ethno-linguistic boundaries within the west kept unified politics and cultural currents from sweeping from area to area. In the Punjab, Muslim landlords combined with their Hindu and Sikh equals to organize a nonreligious, economically conservative Unionist party. In the northwest Frontier Province the Pathan peoples, over 90 percent Muslim, followed a self-styled "Frontier Gandhi" aligned with the Indian National Congress. In Sind, Muslim factions were so bitterly divided that Hindu politicians played important coalition roles, and in Baluchistan social conditions did not permit normal political participation.

When the Muslim League called for the creation of Pakistan in 1940 in Lahore, Muslim politicians in the western region were divided in their attitudes but for many of the same reasons as their Bengali colleagues, indicated support for it. The Muslim League leadership did not come from either Bengal or the Indus valley; it was drawn heavily from Muslim-minority provinces in India. Mohammad Ali Jinnah, the great leader, was from Bombay and Liaquat Ali Khan, the first prime minister, was from New Delhi and represented North Indian Muslims.

The paradox of the Pakistani movement is that its demand was asserted by leaders from outside the territories that it would in 1947 include. The difficulty was that the provincial Muslim leaders of Bengal and the Indus valley were reluctant partners in the creation of a state in which they would forfeit power to "immigrant" *national* leaders, and would do so in the name of Islam rather than their provincial constituents. Moreover, since Pakistani "nationalism" had to organize such disparate and divided groups, it had to use extremely general symbols and appeals, among them religion.

The Pakistani movement succeeded because Hindu-Muslim tension and conflict had become so widespread and threatening in the period after 1937. The dislocations of the depression and the inflation and social disorder of World War II further created conditions of distrust between the two large communities. In 1947, religious identity was socially more important than provincial origin or economic class because of communal violence and political uncertainty. There was, therefore, a considerable antiHindu element in the Pakistani movement, and it translated directly into an antiIndia element in the foreign policy of Pakistan after its creation. While the domestic diversity of Pakistan's many peoples would set the stage of domestic political turbulence and instability, the origins of the separatist movement would nourish the antiIndian element in a consistent foreign policy.

Few states have ever been created with as many problems and as few capacities as Pakistan. The holocaust of mass communal violence at the time of partition led to perhaps a million dead and ten million refugees. Despite the scale of population movements, millions of Muslims remained in India, and millions of Hindus remained in Pakistan. About 11 percent of the population of both states was comprised of religious minorities sharing the faith of "majorities" across the partition line. Because the population movements left large communities of the faithful in the "other's" state, the communal agony of riots, tension and charges of "second class" citizenship remained. Moreover, they were exaggerated by the behavior of the "neighboring" state.

Another major problem of the partition of British India concerned the princely state of Jammu and Kashmir whose Hindu ruler attempted to avoid integration with either India or Pakistan. In a series of actions, some polite, some politic and some conspiratorial, the new governments of India and Pakistan and the rival factions of Kashmiri politicians became entangled in conflicts which led to war—from which came Indian military victory and Pakistani frustration. Since the ruler of the state was Hindu and the majority of his subjects Muslim, Pakistan's leaders have charged that Kashmir was being held in bondage by the Indian police and army and that the state's accession to India was the product of conspiracy. India has charged that Pakistan was behind the invasion of the state by Pathan tribesmen in 1947–48, and that its claim to the state is both legal and the product of the choice of the Kashmiris. The leaders of various Kashmiri factions claim different things, but almost all champion more autonomy than either India or Pakistan would allow.

Pakistan thus began its existence as a divided, incomplete and partial homeland for the Indian Muslims. Its foreign policy stems directly from this strategic setting, and from the goals of a partially frustrated nationalist movement.

Internal Determinants of Pakistan's Foreign Policy

Pakistan was born, in the words of its first leader, as a "moth-eaten, truncated" version of the original design of the state. It contained 86 million people, with almost no industrial base from which to begin national economic growth or on which to build a defense capacity. The total electrical generating capacity of the country in 1947 was only

75,000 Kwh (kilowatts), and banking was so completely in the hands of the British and the Hindus that of the 487 offices that existed in Pakistan's territory before independence, only 69 remained thereafter. Although East Pakistan's fields produced 75 percent of the jute of British India, there was not one jute textile mill in the entire area that fell to Pakistan. Of the 395 cotton textile mills in British India, Pakistan inherited only 14. The country had no coal, iron ore, oil, natural gas or nonferrous metals, and had no defense industry. Just as the agriculture of the Indus valley depended wholly upon water from India, the industry and services of all of Pakistan required access to Indian fuel, raw materials, factories and markets. And after the communal riots and the Kashmir war, India was the enemy.

There was no Pakistan government three months before the state was created, and the British partition plan allowed 72 days in which the accumulated resources and institutions of 150 years of rule were to be divided. The Pakistan foreign service, civil service and army had to be created in slightly more than two months, with all government officials having the option as to which government they chose to serve. Only 82 members of the elite Indian Civil Service opted for Pakistan, and since the Indian foreign service was extremely small, the numbers of Muslim officers available to Pakistan was even smaller. Muslims were much better represented in the armed forces, having provided about 40 percent of the troop strength of the British Indian army in World War II, but these were heavy in infantry rather than in the technical specialties.

The political leadership of the state was also tiny. The Muslim League leaders were more experienced in agitation than in governance, and they were divided by provincial origin as well as by political competition. Since the Pakistani movement had succeeded at the expense of provincial governments as well as at the expense of Indian unity, the national government found itself almost immediately under siege from its provincial rivals in its new state. This would have been a great challenge under any circumstances, but was overwhelming for a group of men who "took power" without any of the authority of an established state. As the first prime minister said, when he arrived in Karachi he found no files, notes, office directories or even pens and paper. Indian currency had to be used for a year.

That Pakistan survived at all is a high tribute to a small number of politicians and civil and military officers, and is testament to the desperate efforts of the refugees, the populations of the provinces of the new states, and to the many British who stayed on to help the struggling new state. Although Pakistan was created as a homeland in which the Indian Muslims might more fully express their religious faith, it was so tenuous a creation that security considerations outweighed Islamic ideals. The first priority of Pakistan has been "state-building," the forced-draft construction of a national administration, military forces, a viable and independent economy and a foreign policy that supports Pakistan's existence. The operational motto of Pakistan has been "First, the garrison; then, the Muslim ideal."

The garrison has been necessary to hold together the scattered provinces and diverse peoples of Pakistan, and it has been necessary to protect the state from Indian power. For more than twenty-five years, Pakistan's governments have defined India as the principal security threat. Immediately after independence, the horrors of partition violence, the Kashmir war and Indian *machtpolitik* in Junagadh, Hyderabad and the Indus waters disputes[1] convinced Pakistan's leaders that India would exploit its power at Pakistan's expense. Since India is four times Pakistan's size in population, and considerably more than four times its size in industrial and military potential, the Pakistani garrison is viable only if supported by Pakistan's allies.

Almost all of the diplomatic initiatives of Pakistan since 1947 have been directed toward finding allies against India, and in building the garrison. Between 1947 and 1953, Pakistan hoped to find allies among the Muslim states of the Middle East. Because of the religious tone of Pakistan's nationalism, its leaders imagined that other Muslim states newly free of western domination would share an interest in a Pan-Islamic bloc. This unwarranted assumption caused Pakistan some grief in both Turkey and Egypt where governments were attempting to pursue secularism. A very successful Indian diplomacy to offset Pakistan's proto-alliance in the Muslim world found the Nasser-Nehru-Tito axis much more successful than Pakistan's clumsy cultural bid.

Indeed, India's vigorous international diplomacy offset Pakistan's efforts to win support in the Commonwealth, the United Nations and the Muslim world. During the same period, India was consolidating its new political order and "winning" in each territorial and economic dispute with Pakistan. Six years after partition, Pakistan had managed to survive, somewhat chaotically, but its position within the sub-continent and in the world was one of complete inferiority and vulnerability to India.

The determinants of Pakistan's foreign policies since 1947 have been in large part the consequence of its strategic setting, its domestic diversity and its enmity with India. If there is a shared worldview

---

[1] These disputes are traced in great detail from the Pakistan point of view in G. W. Choudhury, *Pakistan's Relations with India, 1947–1966* (New York: Praeger, 1968).

among the elites who manage foreign and security policy, it seems to be "through the garrison state glass, darkly" with India looming large, implacably hostile and increasingly dangerous and powerful.

While security considerations have been paramount in determining foreign policy choices, economic development goals have also been important. In the period immediately following its independence, Pakistan's foreign policy had to accommodate the need for some economic interchange between India and Pakistan, although this soon fell victim to economic nationalism on the part of Pakistan. By adopting a laissez-faire private enterprise economy, the governors of Pakistan hoped to attract Indian Muslim businessmen who otherwise might invest in India. The Korean war raw materials price boom made Pakistan's exports a mainstay of the new government, and when the war was over, Pakistan was on the eve of concluding an agreement with the United States that would lead to large-scale economic assistance. Where questions of trade and economic cooperation with India are concerned, Pakistan has continuously said "better poor and independent," but when opportunities for growth and integration outside South Asia have arisen, Pakistan has made the most of them.

Domestic Politics and Foreign Policy

While Pakistan's strategic setting and internal conditions and goals set the general terms of its foreign policy choices, the policy-making process is dominated by a particular regime and different regimes have different preferences within general limits. The distinctive "mix" between internal and external factors in foreign policy is specific to each regime and period, and much of Pakistan's foreign policy can only be understood by reference to domestic politics.

The domestic politics of a religious, separatist nationalism that led to Pakistan's creation also led its new leaders to an ultranationalist foreign policy. The nationalist symbols that were potent within the country were those which led Pakistan to seek friends in the Muslim world. But the necessities of survival and the building of a state forced the government to pursue a policy of subordinate cooperation with India until such time as great power alternatives became available to support an independent posture. The tasks of reconciling a Muslim political identity with building a strong state once led H. S. Suhrawardy, prime minister in 1956, to justify an alliance with the United States rather than with the Middle Eastern states on the grounds that sentiment aside, "zero plus zero equals zero." The Muslim states could not, even if they chose, offset Indian power vis-à-vis Pakistan.

The foreign policy managers of Pakistan were drawn heavily from the civil and military services which were themselves highly westernized. These men were pragmatic, searching for resources by which to consolidate the state, maintain its independence and sustain its economy. At the top levels of government, British officers on loan to the new state also exercised considerable influence. Since the politicians were extraordinarily burdened with establishing a new government, writing a constitution and managing domestic political competition and conflict, they delegated considerable authority to the technocrats of the ministries of foreign affairs and defense.

Public opinion was not an important factor in foreign policy. The literacy percentage was well less than 15 percent, and the English-speaking elite that dominated the national press, the universities, the government and the political life was less than one half of one percent of the population. This small English-speaking elite had been schooled in Britain or in the British tradition, and was predisposed to cooperation with the west. The religious leadership of the country could make its views felt in the foreign policy field only in blocking actions, charging the government with antiMuslim behavior; it could not mobilize the strength to force a foreign policy of panIslamism. And the proSoviet faction, a small segment of the secular, westernized, English-literate elite, was too small and isolated to produce more than criticism of the government's policy.

ProMuslim, prowestern and proSoviet foreign policies could not be simultaneously reconciled, especially in the 1950's when the cold war invaded Pakistan's domestic decision-making considerations and when the Arab states began their antiwestern, proSoviet foreign policies. Any foreign policy orientation, therefore, had a domestic cost. Of the available opportunities, the only orientation that had considerable *benefits* was cooperation with the west. Pakistan's diplomacy, therefore, became prowestern, with as little antiSoviet content and as much proMuslim content as possible. This maximized the chances of benefit, and the costs of orientation were minimized; it also accorded with the preferences of the westernized elite directing the state.

Mohammad Ali Jinnah, the founder of the state, died within 15 months of its creation, and Liaquat Ali Khan, the first prime minister, was assassinated in 1951. The regional politicians laid siege to the "national" seats of power in Karachi, and the diversity and divisions within the state became increasingly important. In the rapidly changing government, the civil service and the army came to play a greater role. They had been the beneficiaries of heavy investments in the "garrison," and they were much better organized and better led than the politicians. Moreover, they shared a common language and a national commitment, whereas most politicians were becoming more attentive to parochial constituencies. By about 1953, politics had become provincialized, and the national government had been captured by the technocrats.

At precisely this time, the United States was expanding its strategic posture along the frontiers of the Soviet Union and China as part of a global containment policy managed by Secretary of State John Foster Dulles. As the Americans looked for cold war allies, the Pakistan armed services were looking for military resources. The quite different needs of the two countries coincided, and in 1954 the United States and Pakistan became allied powers.

The sequence by which Pakistan became a member of the cold war alliances is important to remember. It started with General Mohammad Ayub Khan's self-directed mission in search of arms to Washington, and was legitimized within Pakistan as a Turko-Pakistan agreement before becoming a US-Pakistan relationship. By 1956, Pakistan was the most aligned country in Asia, belonging to the Baghdad Pact, the Southeast Asian Treaty Organization and having bilateral treaty relationships with the United States. The domestic cost of this foreign policy was minimized because Pakistan was allied with Turkey, Iran, Iraq and Britain as well as with the United States. Muslim opinion was mollified by notions of a Muslim alliance with some "stiffening." Pro-Communist opinion had been muffled since the Communist party of Pakistan had been banned for its alleged participation in an abortive coup d'état in 1951.

To a great degree, the alliance foreign policy was an army foreign policy vigorously pursued by its Commander-in-Chief, General Mohammad Ayub Khan. Within the Pakistani government, there was some disagreement about its prudence, especially since the Mohammad Ali Bogra-Jawaharlal Nehru talks in 1953 had begun to promise some political détente and movement toward the settlement of the Kashmir problem. Nehru's quid pro quo was that Pakistan not align itself with Washington, thereby "bringing the cold war" into South Asia, and militarizing the "political" disputes between the two countries.

On the other hand, Prime Minister Nehru was vague about the nature of the Kashmir settlement and Pakistan army leadership could point to the costs of continued military vulnerability even if some Kashmir settlement, from weakness, could be negotiated.

There was another reason why the military leadership wanted US arms, if need be at the expense of a negotiated settlement of Kashmir. In General Ayub Khan's words,[2]

The political turmoil which appeared in the wake of the Prime Minister's [Liaquat Ali Khan] death convinced me that we must not lose any time in building up the army which alone could hold the country together and defend it against possible attack.

A strong army was therefore a domestic as well as an external calculation in the mind of the commander-in-chief.

Another factor making the military alliance attractive was Ayub Khan's own role as the principal spokesman in the government for the army's claim on desperately short resources. If he was to convince his brother officers that he could "deliver the goods," he could strengthen his own leadership of the military forces.

In conditions of very considerable political instability and change, Pakistan did conclude an alliance with the United States that would lead, in the next decade, to a flow of military equipment worth $700 million and in the next sixteen years to economic grants and loans of almost $4 billion. By the stroke of a pen, Pakistan found itself aligned with the most powerful nation in the world. Its security assured, its leaders then began pushing for a settlement of the Kashmir dispute from their new-found position of strength.

India responded to the US-Pakistan alliance by announcing that Pakistan's actions had changed the whole environment of the Kashmir dispute and that previous Indian offers to conduct a plebiscite were no longer "necessary." The government of India violently condemned the United States for its involvement in South Asian regional quarrels, and began the courtship of the Soviet Union to offset Pakistan's patron. Kashmir became part of the agenda of the cold war as well as Indo-Pakistani relations.

Pakistan's politicians, having emphasized state-building priorities, soon found that the servants of the state—the civil service and the army—had become its masters. The army, by doubling its fire-power and by building strength from external resources, strengthened its independent position within the political system. The civil service, controlling the allocation of economic assistance as well as tax revenue, strengthened its power at the center of the decision-making process. Politicians, reluctant to authorize elections which might mean their

---

[2] Mohammad Ayub Khan, *Friends Not Masters* (New York: Oxford University Press, 1967), p. 42. My emphasis.

defeat, stalled in the writing of a constitution and in the building of popular support through parties and elections. As provincial tensions increased and economic change produced social instability, cabinets fell victim to factional struggles and the manipulation of the civil and military service leaders. In October, 1958, the army seized power and proclaimed its dominant position in the decision-making process.

Since 1958, Pakistan's foreign and security policy have been managed by civil and military officers, relatively independent of partisan criticism and with considerable freedom from the constraints of domestic public opinion. Changes in Pakistan's posture since that time show how pragmatic the roots of policy have been, and how little based on deep preferences for the west, or against the Communist states. Pakistan's leaders, within the broad limits of their goals, have attempted to build strength, increasingly by diplomatic arrangements, facilitate economic development, and maintain an autonomy of action which allows a measure of opportunism and the possibility of minimizing domestic criticism. It has been an attentive foreign policy, but not a responsible one; the government has attempted to meet public concern but it has not elicited support.

Pakistan and the World Community

Pakistan was one of the "new states" of 1947, while India fell heir to the status of British India in the world community. It therefore had to petition for admission to the United Nations and most of the functional international agencies, and to establish itself as a responsible member of international society. This was an especially urgent need for Pakistan because of its curious territorial division, because many observers of South Asia believed that Pakistan would soon re-merge with India and because Indian diplomacy seemed committed, especially after the Kashmir war, to deny Pakistan international recognition and influence. Since 1947, Pakistan's foreign policy has been heavily involved with three major countries; India, the United States and the People's Republic of China; its foreign economic policy has been intimately associated with the British Commonwealth and especially Great Britain and its principal areas of concern outside these powers has been with its neighbors to the west—Afghanistan, Iran and Turkey, Saudi Arabia and Jordan.

India: While Pakistan has considered India the adversary par excellence, and has fought three wars (1948, 1965, 1971) and a series of border clashes with India since 1947, there has been cooperation as well as conflict. The countries share not only frontiers and issues of separation, but a common past, similar cultural preferences and common languages. The fate of the nations of the sub-continent is in some measure intertwined. Jute and tea prices affect both economies, and both governments fear a major presence of a great power in the region. They share interests in water control, whether in the Indus or the Ganges, and they have been able to agree on many measures of pest control and public health. Ideas from one country flow into the neighboring one without suffering from translation, just as troubles in one country's border districts spill over into the other's, regardless of the foreign policy intentions of governments.

The period between 1947 and 1951 was marked by overt warfare and bitter relations. The streets of New Delhi and Lahore were full of people who had been dispossessed and who had lost relatives as well as land; their mood was murderous. From 1951 to 1954, some progress was made in cooling passions, asserting government control, settling refugees and searching for ways to establish contact without making Pakistan into an Indian satellite. Pakistan's economy was increasingly independent of India's, and the disputes of the period were more economic than "high politics." On the eve of the US-Pakistani arms agreement, India was reaching out for a settlement with Pakistan.

Despite bitter denunciations by New Delhi, the arms agreements helped to stabilize Pakistan's defense budget and to reassure its government about its survival prospects. The passions of partition continued to recede. Ayub Khan's coup d'état in 1958, while not publicly welcomed in India, was not cause for a round of Indian challenges, and after the 1959 Tibet revolt the government of Pakistan offered to discuss joint defense of the sub-continent with India, subject, of course, to a resolution of outstanding disputes. While Nehru rebuffed Pakistan's attempt to capitalize on India's problems with China, the offer was not merely an attempt to embarrass New Delhi.

In 1960, the governments signed the Indus Rivers agreement[3] and Ayub Khan and Nehru managed to have cordial discussions at the Commonwealth Prime Minister's meetings in London the next year. When 1962 brought a major Sino-Indian war, Pakistan did not attack the weakened Indian government even though it did pressure the United States and Great Britain to arm India only if it settled its quarrels with Pakistan.

The joint defense offer, forebearance at the time of the Sino-Indian

---

[3] The classic study of this dispute and the way in which it was solved is Aloys Michel, *The Indus Rivers* (New Haven: Yale University Press, 1967).

war and the Harriman-Sandys mission to lead Nehru and Ayub Khan into discussions on resolving the Kashmir conflict all came to naught. India did not have to accommodate Pakistan's interest and the great powers were ready to aid India against China regardless of its posture against Pakistan. This was especially true of the Soviet Union after the Sino-Soviet split widened into a chasm.

Pakistan had pinned its hopes on the United States, India's primary supplier of economic assistance, pushing the Nehru government into an accommodation with the Islamic Republic. The Sino-Indian war, instead of increasing American pressure on India for a détente with Pakistan, led instead to increased military and economic assistance from the west. The shock of the war quickened Indian nationalism while weakening the ability of the Indian government to publicly deal with either Pakistan or China. No democratically elected government of India could have negotiated away territory or status in the aftermath of the humiliation administered by China, and hope to survive.

The government of Pakistan, however, witnessing what it called the "desertion" of the United States as its ally, and the rearming of a nationalist India with weapons more potent against Pakistan than China, turned toward cordial relations with Peking. After the fact, this was labelled "Sino-Pakistan collusion" to destroy India, but as late as 1961 Ayub Khan was on record as offering India the prospect of sub-continental defense if sub-continental disputes could be ameliorated. Just as Pakistan was turning to China, it was also normalizing its relationships with the Soviet Union as if to proclaim to the world the end of its alignment with the United States.

In his memoirs, Ayub Khan calls this diplomacy one of "walking a triangular tightrope." Since no great power was wholly reliable and since each great power could be useful to Pakistan, it was necessary to cultivate good relations with all. The United States was necessary for continued economic and military assistance; China was useful as a source of strategic support that had the function of deterring the Indians from major military action toward Pakistan; and the Soviet Union could possibly be useful if Pakistan could normalize relations and exert some influence on Moscow to reduce its level of support for India, or, conversely, increase support for Pakistan. But the diplomacy was directed toward India rather than toward the bilateral relationships with the great powers, all of which Pakistan basically feared.

In March, 1963, Pakistan and China signed a border agreement and within a year Chou En-lai announced support for national self-determination in Kashmir. Factional politics in Kashmir boiled up in the winter of 1963/64 and a much weakened Nehru government, its leader rapidly failing, reacted by releasing Sheikh Abdullah. The Sheikh, called the "Lion of Kashmir," was perhaps the most powerful of nationalist-oriented Kashmiri politicians, and had been imprisoned (without trial) for eleven years previous. Upon his release, he asked permission to go to Pakistan to discuss the settlement of the dispute; on March 24th, he arrived to a hero's welcome in Rawalpindi. Two days later, he announced a June meeting at which Ayub Khan and Nehru would discuss the issue. While Sheikh Abdullah was in Pakistan, however, Nehru died. Despite efforts to arrange a similar meeting between Lal Bahadur Shastri and Ayub Khan, the Kashmir problem remained deadlocked and in May, 1965, Sheikh Abdullah was arrested once again, by the Indians.

In April 1965 fighting broke out between Indian and Pakistani forces in the Rann of Kutch, a salt marsh area on the Sind-Gujarat frontier. The hostilities occurred barely a month after Ayub Khan had returned from an extended visit to China, and the Indians believed that the fighting was part of Sino-Pakistan "collusion." While the Rann of Kutch fighting was ended and international arbitration accepted in settling the border dispute, tension between the two countries remained high. In June, border clashes took place in Kashmir, and in August and September a major war took place between India and Pakistan, first in Kashmir, and then throughout the West Pakistan-India border.

One expert has argued that[4]

By January 1965 it is reasonable to assume that President Ayub Khan of Pakistan had despaired of a negotiated settlement of the Kashmir problem.

It appears reasonably certain that the government of Pakistan planned and organized these efforts at coercive diplomacy to re-open the Kashmir question which the Indians, simultaneously, were attempting to close by extending certain provisions of the Indian Constitution to include Kashmir.

The Pakistan plan, to be successful, had to appear to be highly localized and as part of a domestic Kashmiri insurrection. The actual military phase had to be short, both because of its cost and the preponderance of Indian military power. The hope of the plan was that a weak Shastri regime would be forced to release Sheikh Abdullah or to directly negotiate with Ayub Khan.

None of these assumptions or hopes materialized. The war escalated

---

[4] Alastair Lamb, *The Kashmir Problem 1947–1966* (New York: Praeger, 1966), p. 112.

both in its scale and the areas which it engulfed, and on September 6 Indian forces launched attacks directed against Lahore. On September 22, a ceasefire came into force and troops from both countries were withdrawn to their positions before the fighting. The Soviet Union offered its good offices at Tashkent to conclude a peace agreement, but it was bitter for Pakistan to accept. India's strength was demonstrated and Pakistan was forced to almost double an already heavy defense budget—from $272.2 million to $542.0 million. Its material losses and battlefield casualties were matched by the political costs to the Ayub regime. Within three years the regime was tottering and within four years it was toppled.

The successor regime, led by General A. M. Yayha Khan, Commander-in-Chief of the Pakistan army, established martial law but called for nationwide elections which were held in the winter of 1970/71. The results testified to the great degree of political alienation of East Pakistan, where the Awami League party won 80 percent of the vote and 167 of 169 seats for parliament. Its platform was "the Six Points" all of which related to provincial autonomy. The West Pakistan vote was scattered among many parties, the largest of which was the People's party of Pakistan led by Z. A. Bhutto. Its platform was nationalistic, Socialistic and antiIndian.

The election outcomes left the army in a quandary. To accept a degree of provincial autonomy that left the defense and foreign affairs budget at the mercy of provincial legislatures was anathema. On the other hand, the grievances of East Pakistan were genuine and had been accepted; it had received much less than its due in the allocation of development resources, foreign exchange earnings and political power in the Ayub Khan decade. President Yayha Khan attempted, in the late spring, to arrange a constitutional settlement that would maintain a high level of support for the "national" activities of Pakistan—development planning and finance, defense and foreign affairs—while decentralizing allocation of budgets, management of programs and direction of public policy.

Sheikh Mujibur Rahman, leader of the Awami League, attempted to forestall the demands for secession which many of his militant followers championed, while at the same time pushing to the maximum his demand for the "Six Point" povincial autonomy plan. In March 1971, it appeared that a settlement was nearly reached, but in a series of tragic events, the negotiations broke down and widespread violence followed. The East Pakistan Rifles and East Pakistan Police provided recruits for a Bengali separatist army, while the units of the West Pakistan army in the province were reinforced and sent into action against centers of Awami League strength such as the university of Dacca and the Bengali press.

The Awami League was outlawed, Sheikh Mujibur Rahman was arrested and widespread fighting increased, especially in the districts bordering India. The government of Pakistan charged India with providing sanctuary for the "miscreants" and arming them for guerrilla war, while the government of India indicated moral support for the aspirations of the leaders of a free East Pakistan, "Bangla Desh." The civil war in East Bengal led to the outbreak of full-scale hostilities between India and Pakistan in December 1971, the defeat and surrender of the Pakistani military forces, and the establishment of a de facto independent Bangla Desh government.

Like the 1965 war, which almost destroyed the Pakistan economy and severely compromised its government, the Bangla Desh civil war and India's critical role in it has brought Pakistan once more to the point of total economic exhaustion. Development, for all practical purposes, stopped, and an immense international effort was needed to prevent famine and economic depression. The importance of foreign policy, and especially of relations with India, has been brought home with a vengeance.

The United States: The American relationship with Pakistan stemmed from the cold war alliance diplomacy being pursued by Washington during the first Eisenhower administration. At its origins, the military assistance agreement was more political than strategic; the United States wanted political friends in the Third World to offset the Soviet "national liberation" plan. Military aid as such was less important than the security "guarantee" that the US relationship implied, and was also less important than the large amounts of grants and loan economic assistance that flowed to America's "ally."

Pakistan continued to follow its own policies toward India and its immediate neighbors, and welcomed the Middle Eastern dimension of its alliance memberships. The change "bought" by the United States was "declaratory anti-Communism," and facilities for the Americans useful in their global posture against the Soviet Union. Since the Communist party of Pakistan was banned well before the alliance was signed and was extremely small in any case, this change in policy was not politically difficult.

In the first period of the alliance, 1954–1959, the emphasis was on developing working relationships and winning agreement on force levels, type of equipment, type of American facilities and political postures. The actual delivery of American military equipment was slow and the amounts were somewhat less than the Pakistanis had hoped. There was much more American political and diplomatic activity than military activity. Indeed, in the year before the 1958 coup d'état, an American, Charles Burton Marshall, was "Political Advisor" to the government of Pakistan. Immediately after the military coup, Mr. Marshall was returned to Washington, and General Ayub Khan moved to minimize American political influence in the country.

From 1959 to 1965, the alliance was turbulent and troubled. The original purposes of the alliance, cold war diplomatic maneuvering, had become less important to the United States in the era of the "Spirit of Camp David." In the next year, President John F. Kennedy would bury the rhetoric of the anti-Communist crusade of the 1950's. The electronic intelligence facilities necessary to monitor Soviet and Chinese nuclear and rocket tests were important, however, and Pakistan's economy was also a high priority to the US aid mission.

In 1960, a U-2 high altitude reconnaissance plane that took off from the US base in Peshawar, Pakistan, was shot down over Sverdlovsk in the Soviet Union. Premier Khrushchev threatened to destroy the bases from which it operated, and public opinion in Pakistan was forced to consider the "price" it paid for collaboration with the United States. President Ayub Khan was looking for ways to reduce tension with the Communist states, and after the U-2 affair, moved rapidly to seek some economic agreement with the Soviet Union. The year before, Pakistan had changed its vote on the admission of Communist China to the United Nations to accord with its own preferences and interests, not those of its American ally.

While normalizing relations with Moscow and Peking, President Ayub Khan was also courting the Kennedy administration. His emphasis was on economic development and political friendship, not military assistance and strategic alliances. This accorded with the priorities of the new administration in Washington, and Ayub Khan's personal diplomacy with the president and his wife was effective. This trend within the relationship was abruptly shaken at the time of the Sino-Indian border war in 1962.

The United States had come to India's aid and had cautioned Pakistan, its ally, not to interfere at the time of India's troubles. President Ayub Khan did not seek to pressure India as much as the United States, which he hoped would use its new-found influence in India to arrange a settlement on Kashmir. While the Harriman-Sandys Mission attempted that, unsuccessfully, it was clear that the United States was not going to withhold assistance to India if it did not settle with Pakistan. Moreover, the Indian military buildup was not accompanied by the redeployment of Indian forces on the Pakistani frontier, and Ayub Khan bitterly complained that its American friend was arming its colossal enemy in such a way as to completely compromise the 1:3 troop ratio that was Pakistan's defense posture. The Kennedy administration saw China as the threat to be met, and down-played the problems of Indo-Pakistani relations.

The government of Pakistan reacted violently to this set of American policies, and greatly increased their outreach to China and the Soviet Union. The standard Soviet history of Pakistan-Soviet relations notes that 1963 was a "breakthrough year" in good relations.[5] The Sino-Pakistan frontier dispute was ended by treaty in the same year, and cultural, diplomatic and military missions were exchanged. After President Kennedy's assassination and the escalation of American commitments in Vietnam, the United States attempted to discourage close Sino-Pakistani relations with the result that political disputes between Washington and Rawalpindi deepened. On the eve of the Indo-Pakistan war of 1965, the United States had "postponed" the meetings of the Aid Pakistan consortium as the two countries discussed issues of mutual "interest," such as Pakistan's deepening friendship with Peking.

The Indo-Pakistani war led to a complete embargo on economic and military assistance to both countries, and Pakistan charged that America's ally was treated with the same sanctions as neutralist India; India, meanwhile, charged that Washington accorded the victim (India) and the aggressor the same treatment. The embargo meant that Pakistan's wholly American-equipped armed forces had no replacements and no spare parts and ammunition. They could not fight on beyond the stockpiles of supplies in the country. Ayub Khan asked Washington to mediate the dispute; he was referred to the United Nations and, ultimately, to Moscow. The alliance was over, even though the documents remained.

Over the course of the year after the Tashkent agreement was signed, the United States eased its embargo of arms to Pakistan. Non-lethal spare parts were made available for sale in modest quantity, and then spare parts for lethal equipment, again on a restricted quantity and "cash and carry" basis. In 1968/69, Pakistan indicated that the lease on American facilities in the country would not be renewed, and that the US airbase facility at Peshawar would have to be closed in 1970.

In the meantime, both Communist China and Indonesia had provided some arms for Pakistan—China sending MIG-19 aircraft and T-55 medium tanks in a quantity that surprised western observers, since it was the first case of Chinese military assistance to a non-Communist country. After the Tashkent accord, the Soviet Union also indi-

---

[5] I. M. Kompantsev, *Pakistan i Sovetskii Souiz* (Moscow: Nauka, 1970).

cated a willingness to sell some arms to Pakistan but only after the US bases in the country were closed.

Since 1965 and the end of the military phase of the US-Pakistani relationship, economic assistance has been the principal activity bringing the governments together. Pakistan's economic performance in the 1960's was excellent, and it came to be known, perhaps too fulsomely, as a "development miracle." The $4 billion in grants and loans had led to high growth rates, but the distribution of their benefit within the country and the heavy defense expenditures after 1965 weakened the social benefits of growth. The Ayub Khan government became less popular because of unequal growth than it might have, had the economic performance been less impressive.

After the second coup d'état of General A. M. Yayha Khan, the International Bank of Reconstruction and Development (World Bank) and the United States found themselves redefining their economic strategy toward Pakistan. More equality of advantage within Pakistan was called for, and a special East Pakistan high priority set of projects was adopted in the summer of 1970. The onset of civil war in the spring of 1971, however, led to a suspension of economic and military sales assistance. In the aftermath of the destruction of that war the prime need is for relief and rehabilitation expenditures. The growth of Pakistan in 1971/72 will almost surely be negative, and its entire future is clouded.

As with India, Pakistan's governments have rediscovered the central importance of foreign policy in the disintegration of the American alliance and its associated military and economic assistance resources.

The People's Republic of China: Pakistan has cultivated the best relations with the People's Republic of China of any non-Communist state, and has done so despite its own basic fears of Chinese power and Chinese-sponsored internal insurrection. As early as the Bandung Conference in 1955, the government of Pakistan representatives assured Chou En-lai that the alliance with the United States was not directed at China, and that Pakistan hoped for good relations with its large neighbor. The Chinese reciprocated the view, and while basically ignoring Pakistan, did not charge it with anti-Chinese behavior.

As Pakistan began its search for other than US support, China responded with cautious acceptance of Pakistan's motives. Ayub Khan's offer to India of a "joint defense of the sub-continent" plan was obviously directed against China, but after it was twice spurned by New Delhi, the Pakistanis moved to accept friendship with China. After the Sino-Indian war of 1962, the Chinese interest in intimate relations with Pakistan was heightened, and Peking's support for Pakistan on the Kashmir issue won it many friends. Once the border agreement of 1963 was negotiated, new initiatives found Pakistan International Airlines "winning" route rights into Shanghai and Canton (at the expense of British Overseas Airways Corporation and others), cultural missions being exchanged and some Chinese economic assistance agreements being discussed.

After the Indo-Pakistani conflict developed in 1965, China made available aircraft and tanks, and in the latter stages of the September war made threatening moves on the Sikkim border. Indonesian naval units were also sent into Indo-Pakistan coastal waters as part of the Rawalpindi-Peking-Jakarta diplomatic coalition. This support had a greater psychological impact than a military effect, and Pakistan's public opinion veered toward the view that Chinese support was the primary defense against a full-scale Indian invasion in 1965.

When the Ayub Khan government was under siege from its domestic foes in 1968, Peking was prompt and full in its support of Rawalpindi. When the government was toppled, China accorded full support to its successor military regime. In the spring of 1971, shortly after the outbreak of civil war in East Bengal, Peking not only endorsed the "national" government's position against the secessionists, but made available a $20 million credit to ease Pakistan's economic crisis. Like the military support in the 1965 war, this was more psychological support than economic assistance, but it was relatively important to the regime in power.

Relations with China, which have gone consistently well since about 1960, have reinforced for Pakistan the importance of its foreign policy. Chinese support in actual terms has been small, but salient. Moreover, China has done more for Pakistan than almost any observer thought likely before the action, and China's image as a growing power in Asia allows even small *present* activities to be magnified in the light of *future* possibilities. Pakistan governments are therefore likely to continue to highly value relations with Peking.

Achievements, Failures and Prospects

Judged against any reasonable criteria, Pakistan's foreign policy for the first twenty-five years of its independence has been creative and successful. Its governments have consistently mobilized external support for domestically defined goals. This does not, of course, mean that Pakistan has attained all of its objectives. The achievement of gaining control of Kashmir and establishing strategic parity at the expense of India, four times the size and power of Pakistan, was an extraordinarily ambitious goal. The success of the foreign policy lies in the fact that it brought to Pakistan more economic and military support than Pakistan's resources, power and importance in the world would appear to justify, and it did so while allowing the consistent pursuit of Pakistan's interests vis-à-vis India.

Without any domestic defense industry in 1947, Pakistan has managed to field an army of a third of a million men, equipped with American and Chinese tanks. Its ordnance factories, one in each wing, were built by the British and the Chinese. The Pakistani air force flies American, Chinese and French aircraft, and American and Russian helicopters. The Pakistani navy has American, French and Italian equipment. Most of this military equipment came to Pakistan on concessional terms; much of it by grant, and most of the rest of it on easy credit and good prices.

With very little economic potential, Pakistan's economy grew during the 1960's at rates as high as 6 percent a year, in large part because Pakistan's domestic investments were being matched by external assistance. About half of the funds devoted to investment came from foreign aid, and it came from a dozen countries, including the major western industrial states and the Soviet Union and China. Pakistan is the only major country in the world that has managed to diversify its economic assistance support across both the cold war and the Sino-Soviet splits.

Pakistan has been able to consistently pursue its interests with India, and it has also been able to maintain good relations with Iran and Turkey, its cultural cousins in the Middle East. It has also been able to frustrate Afghanistan's on-again, off-again support for a Pakhtunistan (Pathan) state that would unite the Pathan tribes into one state.

All of the problems with which Pakistan was created continue to exist, and its major foreign policy goals have not yet been gained. The spatial and ethno-linguistic differences within Pakistan remain, and the civil war of 1971, which found the Indian government blocking access between the two wings, shows how important they were. Kashmir remains in Indian hands, and military efforts to wring it from them have proven almost disastrous to Pakistan. The great goals elude Pakistan's leaders, just as the great power of India remains and grows greater. Viewed in terms of its goals and challenges, Pakistan's successful foreign policy has been necessary to "keep up," without basically making major forward progress and by 1971, Pakistan appears to have dramatically lost ground.

The long-term realization of Pakistan's South Asian goals would require a fundamental change in India's political structure. Were India to divide into four or five states, Pakistan might be able to attain a parity on the issues of most interest to it. Since this is not in prospect, Pakistan's national unity is much more in doubt in the decade 1970–

1980. It is conceivable that a major Indian defeat in battle would allow Pakistan some opportunity for another Kashmir initiative, but India could only be defeated by a great power and Pakistan would have to make its peace with that country before it could assert its weak, secondary claim.

Pakistan's division into two states presents wholly new foreign policy problems for India and the great powers. Whether India's role as a "welcome midwife" can be transformed into that of a respected "mother" is doubtful. Bangla Desh will be even more weak than was Pakistan at its birth. Weakness in the world demands an active foreign policy, and Bangla Desh's internal problems will make its domestic politics turbulent as well.

While the prospects of Pakistan's foreign policy appear to be bleak, both because of domestic problems and insufficient resources, this prospect is not new. Since its creation, the state has operated under very great constraints and has been able to produce quite remarkable gains. Whether this will be possible in the future awaits tomorrow's opportunities. What is clear, however, is that Pakistan will continue to prove to be a dynamic state in world politics. Its setting, structure, domestic politics, and need for external resources are too great for it to become "isolationist." And the spilled blood of the communal riots, wars and clashes between India and West Pakistan do not appear to make a foreign policy of "subordinate reconciliation" possible. Neither peace nor war, but cold war will most probably continue to divide the two great countries of South Asia in the next decade.

Indonesia

FRANKLIN B. WEINSTEIN

Since the proclamation of independence in 1945, Indonesia's foreign policy has, in one degree or another, served three principal uses: defense of the nation's independence against perceived threats; mobilization of the resources of the outside world for the country's economic development; and the achievement of a variety of purposes related to domestic political competition.[1] While the degree to which each of the three uses has found expression in policy has varied from one period to the next, no Indonesian government has been able to sustain for long a foreign policy which does not give at least some consideration to all three.

Independence and development as uses of foreign policy express deeply-held attitudes on the part of the foreign-policy elite. Although there are complementary elements between independence and development, there is also fundamental conflict. Those who feel it necessary to use foreign policy to defend the nation's independence assume an essentially hostile world in which even "friends" pose a threat to the nation's capacity to set its own course; this view suggests that only by self-reliance can the nation's problems be solved without sacrificing its independence. A foreign policy of development assumes that cooperation with foreign friends is possible and that a reasonable amount of dependence on them can be accepted without jeopardizing the country's freedom. Independence and development reflect, in the first instance, the policymaking

[1] For an elaboration of this framework see Franklin B. Weinstein, "The Uses of Foreign Policy in Indonesia: An Approach to the Analysis of Foreign Policy in the Less Developed Countries," *World Politics*, XXIV, No. 3 (April, 1972).

elite's perception of a set of basic internal and external environmental givens, such as geography and natural resources, culture and history, economic and military capabilities, and the nature of the international system.

The Strategic Setting

Indonesia's geography and natural resources, in the view of the nation's leaders,[2] provide some justification for a foreign policy of development but suggest even more strongly the need for a foreign policy of independence. Indonesia's size, extending over 3000 miles from the tip of Sumatra to West Irian; its militarily and politically strategic location astride key trade routes at the crossroads of Southeast Asia; its population of more than 125 million, by far the largest in Southeast Asia; and its abundance of oil, rubber, tin and other natural resources are generally viewed as long-run assets, which will eventually help to assure Djakarta of an important role in international relations, besides bringing prosperity to the land. Indonesia's separation from the Asian mainland is now widely felt to guarantee a substantial degree of physical security. The country's strategic importance and material advantages facilitate a foreign policy of development by attracting the interest of outside powers; if no one were interested in aiding or investing in Indonesia, a development foreign policy would not be a possibility. Moreover, Indonesia's possession of natural resources which it has only a very limited capacity to exploit without assistance argues strongly for a foreign policy that will encourage outsiders to help the Indonesians draw benefit from their natural endowment.

But so long as Indonesia remains in a weak and economically underdeveloped condition, many leaders feel, its strategic location and natural resources will continue to be more a liability than a source of strength. Those "assets" place the country in an unusual state of jeopardy because they constitute incentives for larger powers to seek to dominate Indonesia. "Our wealth makes us vulnerable," Indonesian leaders frequently assert. Indonesia, in their view, is like a pretty young girl who is constantly being approached by men who want to take advantage of her. This sense of vulnerability is heightened by the fact that Indonesia is a chain of islands. With their popu-

---

[2] This characterization of the views of Indonesia's leaders, like other such judgments throughout this essay, is based on in depth interviews with the Indonesian "foreign policy elite" carried out by the author in Djakarta between 1968 and 1970.

lation and resources distributed unevenly among the islands, Indonesia's leaders have never been entirely free of the fear that outside forces may exploit this potential source of disunity to divide and to dominate Indonesia.

History and culture give rise to similar xenophobic pressures. Nationalist historical writings have made the Indonesian elite generally aware that the influence of what is now Indonesia has at times extended abroad. In particular, the Sumatran-based empire of Srivijaya, which reached its height in the ninth century, and the fourteenth-century Javanese kingdom of Modjopohit are extolled as reminders of Indonesia's past glory. A highly-developed literary and artistic tradition has reinforced this feeling of national self-confidence. This suggests an internal strength that would reduce the Indonesians' fear of domination as a result of foreign economic relations, but at the same time it makes an acceptance of dependence on outsiders especially humiliating.

Indonesia's history is read as overflowing with warnings of the dangers to the nation's independence. If the experience of 350 years of Dutch colonial rule has been interpreted as evidence that Indonesia's physical resources are an inducement to others to seek domination of their country, Indonesian leaders see the harsh Japanese occupation during World War II and pressures on Indonesia from both sides during the cold war years as proof that the danger of domination by outside powers did not disappear with the passing of Dutch colonialism.

Concern about dependence on the outside world has cultural roots as well. The historical experience of the Javanese has left them with a cultural legacy that contains a good measure of anti-foreignism, a theme which is kept alive in the popular puppet theater. Indonesia's ethnic diversity, like its geography, raises fears of disunity that might lead to a loss of independence. The presence of an economically influential Chinese minority also stimulates concern about Indonesia's vulnerability to threats from within. The Indonesians also fear that a cultural invasion that will destroy Indonesia's national identity would be the result of a foreign policy of development with its concomitant foreign economic relationships.

Economic and military capabilities have also suggested a need for both the independence and development uses of foreign policy. Indonesia's economy has experienced extraordinary difficulties, owing to a number of fundamental problems including: overpopulation and underemployment on Java; ubiquitous corruption; a dependence on world market prices for the several key export commodities; an almost total lack of industrial capacity; a lack of technical expertise; a sorely inadequate economic infrastructure; and, until the last several years, chronic runaway inflation.[3] There is a consensus among Indonesia's present leaders that their economic problems can be solved only with foreign aid and investment. Yet, the very condition of economic underdevelopment that makes cooperation with the outside world seem indispensable makes it dangerous. It is the weakness of Indonesia's economic institutions that lends substance to the fear that any economic relationship with outside powers will leave Indonesians subservient to foreigners. As for military capabilities, Indonesia has a sizeable army (more than 400,000) while its navy and air force have acquired some sophisticated equipment—from the Soviet Union, in particular, although much of it has already fallen into disrepair because of the absence of spare parts. The possession of a modern military establishment has given the Indonesians a flexibility in pursuing a foreign policy of independence which they would not otherwise have enjoyed. But at the same time, the acquisition and maintenance of its military force inevitably involves a continuing dependence on outside sources of equipment and training, to some extent it draws resources away from development.

The international system, in the eyes of most Indonesian leaders, is essentially an exploitative order, in which the more powerful nations seek to dominate the weak—the Communist powers through the installation of Communist regimes; the western powers through economic domination. The system is one in which the rich nations, whether Communist or capitalist, share important common interests which conflict with those of the poor nations, who are constantly subject to political and economic pressures from the rich and powerful. The implication, of course, is that a foreign policy of independence is essential. But the international system is also seen as marked by a measure of conflict among the big powers. To the extent that Indonesia can play upon those conflicts and balance the powers against one another, the international system is seen as providing a way out of the basic independence-development dilemma: by getting roughly comparable aid from two sides that cannot cooperate with each other to exploit Indonesia, Djakarta can avoid the kind of dependence it fears. But the possibility of following this course requires that the great powers continue to find their differences irreconcilable and that they display a roughly equal interest in cooperating with

---

[3] In 1966, the annual inflation rate reached a peak of approximately 650 percent. For the best discussion of the inflation problem, see J. A. C. Mackie, *Problems of the Indonesian Inflation* (Ithaca: Cornell Modern Indonesia Project, 1967).

Indonesia. The Indonesian leaders, however, see both a diminution in cold war conflict and a decline in the eagerness of the powers to extend aid, so they are not optimistic about the possibility of resolving their dilemma in such a manner.

The Indonesian foreign-policy elite, then, sees their environment as necessitating a foreign policy that will serve both independence and development, but the predominant view of the world is that it is basically hostile and cooperation with the great powers is very risky. Though some cling to the hope that a developmental foreign policy can be followed without sacrificing independence, few really believe so. There is, however, a good deal of ambivalence in the way the Indonesian policy-making elite views the world, with the competing impulses for independence and development coexisting in the minds of most Indonesian leaders.

Determinants of Indonesia's Foreign Policy

Indonesian foreign policy in the 1960's displayed two sharply contrasting faces. Under Sukarno's leadership in the first half of the decade, Indonesia aspired to leadership in an "anti-imperialist" international front. Sukarno condemned the prevailing international system as an exploitative order in which the old established forces (oldefos) of the world sought through economic, political, and military means to keep the new emerging forces (nefos) in subjugation. Nefos like Indonesia had to fight to preserve and perfect their independence. Sukarno led Indonesia into a foreign policy of confrontation against imperial powers, first against the Dutch in West Irian (New Guinea) and then against the British in Malaysia. Convinced that foreign aid was not intended to help Indonesia develop economically but rather was a means of gaining domination over his country, Sukarno exalted self-reliance and told the United States to "go to hell with your aid."

Since 1966 under Suharto, Indonesia has become something of a model of the new state that eschews controversy and orients its foreign policy to the needs of economic development. Western and Japanese economic aid and capital investment have been eagerly solicited, the anti-imperialist crusade has been virtually abandoned, and confrontation has been replaced by passivity and talk of regional cooperation. Where Djakarta newspapers had once carried headlines proclaiming Indonesia's determination to fight to the death against the oldefos, now they told of favorable International Monetary Fund (IMF) evaluations of Indonesia's economic performance, efforts to win larger aid commitments, and cooperation with the former oldefos. No longer was foreign policy described as a struggle to preserve Indonesia's independence and overcome the forces of exploitation. Indonesia entered the 1970's firmly embarked on a foreign policy of development.

This striking transformation of Indonesian foreign policy should not, however, be permitted to obscure important continuities that have marked the process of foreign policy-making in Indonesia since the proclamation of the Republic on 17 August 1945. For the whole of the Republic of Indonesia's national existence, foreign policy has been the product of a continuing interplay among independence, development, and political competition. A crucial role in determining the mixture of independence and development that will actually find expression in foreign policy is played by the competition for domestic political power.

Political competition energizes Indonesian foreign policy, reshaping independence and development to fit the needs of each political actor and giving expression to limitations imposed by the nature of the Indonesian political system. If weakness underlies both independence and development as uses of foreign policy, it is also a key fact of Indonesia's political life. Indonesia's political, military, and socioreligious groupings have been so beset by conflict with one another and by internal disunity that none has been able to generate the power to deal effectively with Indonesia's most pressing problems without outside help. Self-reliance as an approach to economic development has never really been an alternative for the Indonesians because no political group, with the possible exception of the Communists, has had the capacity to mobilize domestic resources. Moreover, for those who have succeeded in Indonesia's elitist political game, a developmental strategy which involves the mobilization of a whole society would carry inestimable political risks, for it could not fail to be profoundly destabilizing. There has thus been a great temptation for any incumbent group, confronted with the need to legitimize and sustain its governing position by dealing with Indonesia's economic and political problems, to seek outside aid. Incumbency also means control over the distribution of resources acquired from abroad, which can constitute an important political asset. As we shall see, practically every incumbent regime has solicited such aid.

But if the Indonesian political system has provided a strong incentive for incumbents to initiate a foreign policy of development, relying heavily on cooperation with the outside world, it has burdened such a policy with almost insurmountable political risks. The Indonesians' profound fear that reliance on foreign aid will compromise their independence has encouraged those out of power to use that popular sentiment to embarrass the leadership. The syndrome runs as follows: the greater the degree of competition in the

Indonesian political system and the more precarious the position of the incumbents, the more vulnerable they have been to this allegation, and consequently the less likely they have been to carry out a foreign policy of development.

Political competition occurs at three general levels of intensity: bureaucratic competition, a struggle for personal or factional advantage which is always present but does not by itself impose great limitations on the latitude of the incumbent regime is the least intense. In parliamentary competition stakes are moderate and some risks are acceptable. However, the most intense competition is death-struggle competition between forces committed to each other's destruction. As we look now at the internal determinants of Indonesian foreign policy over the last quarter century, we can see clearly how the level of political competition helps to determine whether Djakarta's foreign policy will be one which emphasizes independence or one which stresses development.

Domestic Politics and Foreign Policy

THE REVOLUTION (1945–1949)—AN EMBRYONIC FOREIGN POLICY OF DEVELOPMENT

Indonesian foreign policy during the fight for independence from the Dutch (1945–49) was, in effect, an embryonic foreign policy of development. At a time when the overriding goal of Indonesian politics was the achievement of unchallenged independence from the Dutch, Indonesia's foreign policy pursued a course that left the new republic's fate heavily dependent on outsiders. Despite repeated disappointments at the outside world's failure to help, the Indonesian government persisted in a foreign policy based on the hope that international pressures would force the Dutch to recognize Indonesia's independence. To facilitate the acquisition of that outside support, domestic programs were kept "moderate" and certain foreigners were permitted to intrude substantially into Indonesia's policy-making process. Though only minimal consideration was given to economic development, owing to the state of war and uncertainty, the assumptions and techniques of Indonesian foreign policy during the revolution were those of the foreign policy of development, and the hope of future economic aid was an important factor.

The revolutionary period illustrates well the basic dynamics of Indonesia's foreign policy-making process; for the fundamental conflict between self-reliance and dependence on others was evident from the revolution's first year.[4] The proclamation of independence had been issued by Sukarno on August 17, 1945, after a group of militant young leaders had kidnapped him and convinced him of the necessity to take such action immediately. These militants, the vanguard of the revolution, were particularly attracted to Tan Malaka, an older leader who had been a Communist in the 1920's and 1930's but had since severed his ties with Moscow. After it became clear that the Dutch would seek to reimpose their authority, Tan Malaka called for an all-out armed struggle to win "100% independence." He demanded the confiscation of all foreign factories and agricultural estates in order to inspire the masses to "fight as lions."[5] The Dutch would not leave until forced to do so, and those who believed that foreign powers would pressure the Dutch into giving up Indonesia were deluding themselves, he warned. Tan Malaka exhorted his countrymen to rely on their own efforts and to reject negotiations as long as Dutch troops remained on Indonesian soil. He urged, in essence, a foreign policy of independence.

Tan Malaka's view attracted wide support from political and military leaders.[6] But the government of Socialist Prime Minister Soetan Sjahrir had already opted, with the important backing of President Sukarno and Vice President Mohammad Hatta, for diplomacy as the road to recognition of Indonesia's independence. Sjahrir made it the task of Indonesian foreign policy to mobilize international support to compel the Dutch to recognize Indonesia's sovereignty. Although Sjahrir admitted to a suspicion that the existing imperialist and capitalist international power structure would give Indonesia nothing more than "independence in name only," he believed that Indonesia's weakness left it no choice but to hope that the United States, the new hegemonic power of the Pacific, would live up to its anticolonial rhetoric and press the Dutch to agree to the transfer of sovereignty.

[4] This conflict, of course, antedates the revolution. A principal division in the nationalist movement of the preceding decades had been between those who favored "cooperation" with the colonial authorities and those who insisted on "non-cooperation."

[5] See George McT. Kahin, *Nationalism and Revolution in Indonesia* (Ithaca: Cornell University Press, 1952), pp. 173–174. See also Tan Malaka, "Fighting Diplomacy," in Herbert Feith and Lance Castles, eds., *Indonesian Political Thinking: 1945–1965* (Ithaca: Cornell University Press, 1970), pp. 444–448. An excellent discussion of the struggle-diplomacy conflict is contained in Benedict R. O'G. Anderson, *Java In a Time of Revolution* (Ithaca: Cornell University Press, 1972).

[6] Kahin, *op. cit.*, p. 174.

In the hope of winning American support, Sjahrir urged his countrymen to refrain from anti-foreign actions as he sought to present Indonesia's most "reasonable" face to the outside world.[7]

Both Sjahrir's cooperationist policy and the "100% independence"
demand of his critics served needs imposed by the parliamentary
competition for political power. Sjahrir's support of a policy of reliance on foreign backing reflected his own political skills and his
incumbency in a position of governmental leadership. A course emphasizing negotiation required leaders who could impress favorably
those whose support was solicited. The Sjahrir group included some
of Indonesia's most cosmopolitan, westernized intellectuals, men well-
equipped to deal with foreigners. Their record of opposition to collaboration with the Japanese added to their qualifications for that
task. And as the group already seated in the government, the Sjahrir
Socialists had a vested interest in preserving some measure of stability
and order, rather than following a course of armed struggle that
would invite political and social upheaval, incur great physical costs,
and might well, in the process, threaten their own hold on the government. Though most who opposed Sjahrir's negotiation policy probably
had genuine objections to his policy, it can safely be assumed that, for
many, an important motivation—perhaps for some the most important
one—was the hope that they could use the negotiation issue to un-
seat the Sjahrir government, thereby providing openings for themselves. Moreover, for many of Sjahrir's critics, political leaders with
exhortative political skills and military leaders eager to fight, the self-
reliant road of armed struggle was more appealing because it demanded the kind of leadership they were best suited to give. And
being out of power probably increased their readiness to believe that
the spirit of national struggle would enable them eventually to overcome the technological and logistical weakness that so impressed the
westernized intellectuals who held power.

The importance of those political considerations, and their relationship to the deepening sense of disillusionment about the possibility
that the outside world would aid Indonesia against the Dutch, is ob-
servable in the sequence of events surrounding each of the agreements which marked the progress of the negotiation policy. When
Sjahrir finally succeeded in negotiating an agreement with the Dutch
—the Linggadjati Agreement, signed in March 1947—nearly universal
opposition to the concessions he had made in the agreement and in
subsequent talks on its interpretation led to his resignation as prime

---

[7] Feith and Castles, *op. cit.*, pp. 443–444. For a fuller exposition of Sjahrir's views,
see his *Our Struggle* (translated by Benedict R. O'G. Anderson) (Ithaca: Cornell
Modern Indonesia Project, 1968).

minister. But his successor, left-wing Socialist leader Amir Sjarifuddin, under US pressure coupled with the promise of economic aid,[8] embraced Sjahrir's position. Though he had earlier criticized Sjahrir's concessions, Sjarifuddin, once in power, went even farther than Sjahrir had gone to accommodate the Dutch.

He did not go far enough to satisfy the Dutch, however, and in July 1947 they launched an all-out attack against the Republic. The Indonesian government appealed to the United Nations, but the Security Council, following Washington's lead,[9] refused to back Indonesia's call for arbitration and a Dutch withdrawal from territory taken in the attack. Though Indonesians of all political persuasions were bitter at the unwillingness of the United States to restrain the Dutch, who were dependent on American economic and military aid, Sjarifuddin yielded to "perceptible American pressure"[10] and in January 1948 he accepted Indonesia's second negotiated agreement, the Renville Agreement. In exchange for substantial territorial concessions, the Indonesians got the promise of a plebiscite in the Dutch-controlled areas, with the understanding that the United States would ensure that it was conducted fairly. Sjarifuddin encountered an avalanche of critics, Sjahrir among them, who charged him with having compromised the country's independence. He was replaced as prime minister by Hatta, whose government immediately began carrying out the Republic's part of the Renville Agreement; but when an impasse developed with respect to the plebiscite, Washington failed to provide the promised backing in the United Nations. Sjarifuddin, out of power, now repudiated the Renville Agreement which he himself had negotiated, demanded the cessation of negotiations with the Dutch until all of their troops had left Indonesia, and called for the nationalization of all foreign property without compensation.

At this juncture, two events occurred which altered the nature of political competition for the rest of the revolutionary period. With

---

[8] In an aide memoire issued immediately after Sjahrir's resignation, the United States urged Indonesia to cooperate without delay in the formation of an interim government that would give to the Dutch "sovereignty and ultimate authority" in Indonesia until 1949. See Kahin, *op. cit.*, pp. 208–209. On the promise of aid, see Leslie Palmier, *Indonesia and the Dutch* (London: Oxford University Press, 1962), p. 56. As early as November 1945, Hatta had already spoken of the importance of foreign economic aid. See Hatta's "Haluan Politik Pemerintah" (The Direction of the Government's Policy), in Osman Raliby, *Documenta Historica*, I (Djakarta: Penerbit Bulan Bintang, 1953), pp. 526–527.

[9] Kahin, *op. cit.*, p. 220.

[10] See the comments of a member of the Indonesian delegation, Dr. Johannes Leimena, quoted in Alastair M. Taylor, *Indonesian Independence and the United Nations* (London: Stevens and Sons, 1960), p. 311.

feelings of betrayal by the United States running high, and the Soviet Union having consistently supported Indonesia in the United Nations, many Indonesians began looking to the Indonesian Communist party (PKI) for leadership. But the PKI's growth and the hope that the Soviet Union might prove an effective and reliable supporter came to an end with an unsuccessful Communist rebellion in September 1948. Two months later the Dutch launched their second all-out offensive, beginning with a surprise attack in which the Indonesian leaders were captured. The effect of the Communist rebellion, the capture of the leaders, and the subsequent fighting was to end what had essentially been a relatively weak version of parliamentary competition, in which an important share of decision-making power was held by a president who was not subject to parliamentary sanction. In large measure because of the absence of serious political competition and the direct involvement of the substantial personal prestige of Sukarno and Hatta, the two agreements negotiated in 1949, the Roem-Van Royen Agreement and the Round Table Conference Agreement, unpopular as they were, did not bring down the cabinet. Although the latter agreement did provide for the transfer of sovereignty to Indonesia, it also contained some extremely onerous provisions, the most significant of which were: the Indonesian government's assumption of the debt of the previous Dutch administration, which meant that it would be paying for the operations that had been carried out against the Republic; the retention by the Dutch of West New Guinea (West Irian) pending the outcome of further negotiations to be concluded within one year; and safeguards for Dutch economic interests in Indonesia. The transfer of sovereignty had come partly because Indonesia's resistance to the Dutch military action had proved strong enough to convince the Dutch that the cost of occupying Indonesia would be very great and partly because Washington finally, for a variety of reasons,[11] had begun to exert pressure on the Dutch to compromise. But it was also US pressure that led the Indonesians, who hoped for substantial economic aid from the US after independence, to accept such an unpopular agreement.[12]

[11] Washington, hitherto concerned that any anti-Dutch action on its part might have unfavorable repercussions on European security, now saw that a prolonged Dutch campaign in Indonesia would be equally disastrous. Moreover, a move in the Senate to cut off Marshall Plan aid to the Netherlands was gaining support. The State Department was also believed to fear that the Sukarno-Hatta leadership, now proven anti-Communists by their suppression of the 1948 rebellion, might be totally discredited because of the failure of their cooperationist policy, with the result that leadership of the revolution would fall into the hands of pro-Communist elements. See Kahin, *op. cit.*, p. 417.

[12] Palmier, *op. cit.*, p. 68. The United States promised economic aid to the Indonesians if they were successful in reaching agreement with the Dutch.

What the revolutionary period showed was that where policy-makers had to face a politically competitive situation, a policy of negotiating concessions in the hope of winning outside help carried dangerously high political risks. Those risks grew steeper still as the behavior of both superpowers, especially the United States, which repeatedly pressed Indonesia to accept unpopular agreements, led the Indonesians increasingly to see the outside world as a hostile place. But for the policy-makers, the opposition's accusations of selling out the country had to be balanced against another set of political pressures. All of the incumbents had a vested political interest in a course that would preserve a relatively stable Republic with themselves at the helm, even if it meant less than "100% independence." Obliged to deal with Indonesia's problems from a position of weakness, they were naturally attracted by the promise that foreign support might enable them to overcome that weakness, and in so doing, justify their right to govern. Much as they disliked making such embarrassing concessions, the incumbents felt they had no choice. The importance of incumbency and the political pressures it represents in the making of foreign policy is manifested in the striking conformity between incumbency and the advocacy of negotiations. Sjahrir, a militant anti-cooperationist vis-à-vis Japan, relied on negotiations when in power, but criticized the manner in which all of his successors did so; he opposed every agreement they made with the Dutch up to and including the one which brought about the transfer of sovereignty. Amir Sjarifuddin opposed negotiations both before and after his tenure as prime minister; but in power he made the most sweeping concessions to the Dutch of any government during the revolution. Sukarno and Hatta, in power throughout, supported all of the negotiated agreements; the Tan Malaka group, out of power throughout, opposed all negotiations. The revolutionary period, then, was a time when the needs of political competition led incumbents consistently to opt for an embryonic foreign policy of development, as it induced their opponents to exploit a rising suspicion that Indonesia's independence had been compromised to bring them down.

CONSTITUTIONAL DEMOCRACY (1950–1957)— FROM DEVELOPMENT TO INDEPENDENCE

In the first half of the period of constitutional democracy, the foreign-policy patterns of the revolutionary years persisted. The embryonic foreign policy of development of the revolutionary period became a genuine development-oriented foreign policy, in which the Indonesian government sought above all to project to the outside world an image of reasonableness that would inspire foreign con-

fidence in Indonesia and support for the reconstruction and development of its economy. All four of the early constitutional democracy
cabinets were strongly inclined to rely on the west to help Indonesia
deal with its most pressing problems, and to facilitate that support
they were prepared to tolerate the continuation of political and economic vestiges   of colonial rule. Their dependence on the outside
world was not, however, as severe as it had been during the revolution; to the extent that Indonesia's independence was compromised,
it was more by passivity and inaction than by concession.

Like their predecessors during the revolution, these cabinets were
caught amid the cross-currents of political competition. As incumbents, they incurred the obligation of fulfilling popular expectations
that living conditions would improve, and they saw how difficult
economic progress would be without outside economic assistance.
Lacking either the means or the will to base Indonesia's development
on a mobilization of domestic resources, they saw no alternative to
reliance on outside help. Moreover, these cabinets were dominated
by men whose political skills were those of "administrators,"[13] and
there was a substantial political incentive for them to pursue a foreign
policy of development, since it required precisely the kind of skills
they possessed. But the opposition had an equally strong incentive to
advance its own political position by exploiting popular resentment
of the incumbents' reluctance to attend to the requirements of independence. The foreign policy of development proved politically costly
for its backers, and all four cabinets lost political favor because of
their unwillingness to pursue a foreign policy aimed at removing the
limitations on Indonesia's independence; foreign policy contributed,
directly or indirectly, to the fall of three of those four cabinets.

Indonesia's first cabinet after the transfer of sovereignty was headed
again by Hatta, who launched Indonesia on a course of "pro-western
neutralism," maintaining diplomatic relations exclusively with the
western countries,[14] making strenuous efforts to develop good relations with the Netherlands, and acquiring foreign aid commitments,
including a $100 million loan from the Export-Import Bank. Hatta's
neutralism was expressed primarily through his resistance to pressures

---

[13] See Herbert Feith, *The Decline of Constitutional Democracy in Indonesia*
(Ithaca: Cornell University Press, 1962) on the distinction between "administrators" and "solidarity-makers." Much of the data on which the following analysis
of the constitutional democracy period is based comes from Feith's definitive
study.

[14] The Hatta cabinet did recognize the Communist government in China and the
Chinese sent an ambassador to Indonesia, but no Indonesian representative was
sent to Peking until 1951. See *Ibid.*, p. 87.

to back the United States in the Korean war. He accepted the already clearly established consensus that Indonesia should have an "independent and active" foreign policy, meaning that it should avoid aligning itself with either bloc. But his virtual ignoring of nationalist feelings that Indonesia should press vigorously for the transfer of West Irian to Indonesian sovereignty and his willingness to accept the existing dominance of foreign capital, the continued presence of Dutch troops in Indonesia, and the retention of Dutch nationals in high government positions stirred substantial criticism. This opposition had gained strength considerably during the eight months of Hatta's tenure when he resigned to resume the vice-presidency.

Hatta's successor as prime minister, Mohammad Natsir, followed essentially the same policies and was subject to the same pressures as Hatta, but it was Natsir's fate to be in office when the year's deadline set by the Round Table Conference Agreement for the resolution of West Irian's status passed. As the deadline approached, with West Irian still in Dutch hands and no prospect of a settlement, Natsir sought to avoid arousing domestic emotions, holding to the view that the best way to facilitate negotiations was to demonstrate that Indonesia would honor its international commitments and would safeguard the rights of foreigners. He hoped that either Dutch reasonableness or US pressure on the Dutch would somehow enable Indonesia to realize its West Irian claim.

There was wide dissatisfaction with Natsir's Irian policy, but it was his collision with Sukarno on the issue that was most significant. Since the inception of the constitutional democracy period, Sukarno's political role had undergone a substantial decline. This was a time of genuine parliamentary competition, in which political power was more concentrated in the cabinet than it had been during the time of the revolution. Sukarno, whose agitational or "solidarity-making" political skills made him well-suited for leadership of an emotional antiDutch campaign, had begun, even under the Hatta cabinet, to move away from his former cooperationist stance. The Irian question increasingly became "his" issue, as Sukarno sought to use foreign policy to rebuild his political position. When the deadline had passed, Sukarno urged the abrogation of the Round Table Conference Agreement and the exertion of pressures on Dutch businesses in Indonesia. Natsir's rejection of this proposal considerably embittered the president. When the Natsir cabinet fell several months later, one of the contributing causes was Sukarno's antipathy toward it, and that antipathy owed much to the president's belief that Natsir had been insufficiently vigorous in his handling of the Irian problem.

The cabinet of Sukiman, Natsir's successor, fell because its efforts to get economic aid led it to accept conditions which allegedly compromised the country's independence. There were two critical foreign-policy issues during the Sukiman cabinet's tenure, both involving the extent to which Indonesia should move toward alignment with the United States in order to get aid. The first concerned the government's decision to sign the American-drafted Japanese Peace Treaty, an action which was widely opposed because of a belief that signing it might be interpreted as aligning Indonesia with the United States. Though a majority of parliament disapproved of the action, the Sukiman government managed to survive. The issue over which the cabinet fell was Foreign Minister Subardjo's secret agreement with the US ambassador that in exchange for economic aid, Indonesia would make a contribution to the defense of the "free world." When this commitment became known a month later, a storm of protest erupted. There was undoubtedly much genuine concern that Indonesia's independence was in danger, but there can also be no doubt that the issue was exploited by those who already wished to bring down the Sukiman cabinet. It is noteworthy that the man who made the commitment, Subardjo, had in 1946 been a strong supporter of Tan Malaka, who took the strongest anti-cooperation position, while Sjahrir was then the government leader urging negotiations. In 1952 Subardjo, in power, was making the concessions, while the Sjahrir Socialists were among the leading critics of his policy. The incident also had the effect of reinforcing the fear that the United States would go to considerable lengths to induce Indonesia to commit itself to the "free world" side. But its most important and long-lasting effect was to demonstrate that any course which could be interpreted as leading toward alignment with a bloc would be politically suicidal.

Wilopo, who followed Sukiman as prime minister, fell primarily because he alienated his own party, the Indonesian Nationalist party (PNI), but two key issues involved his unwillingness to antagonize foreign economic interests. By 1952 a sense of disillusionment with life in post-revolutionary Indonesia which had been developing over the previous two years had begun to grow more severe as economic conditions worsened owing to the post-Korean boom decline in raw materials prices. One expression of the growing frustration was an increasing hostility toward foreign economic concerns. Thus, when the Wilopo cabinet agreed to the request of Royal Dutch Shell for the return of its North Sumatran oil wells, opposition was so great that the announced decision was never implemented. Wilopo's downfall came as a result of his handling of squatters on foreign estates in East Sumatra. The rights of foreign landowners were guaranteed in the Round Table Conference Agreement, and Wilopo believed that the return of these lands to their owners would be viewed abroad as a test of Indonesia's willingness and ability to safeguard the rights of the new foreign investment they sought to attract; besides Indonesia needed the foreign exchange the estates could earn. When Wilopo moved to evict the squatters, however, several were killed, and the ensuing furor led to the fall of the cabinet.

During the last four years of the period of constitutional democracy, Indonesian foreign policy accorded greater emphasis to steps seen as perfecting and defending Indonesia's independence than to policies intended to win the confidence of the west and thereby secure foreign aid and investment. An important part of the explanation of the shift lies in the intensification of political competition. The first two years of the period were a time when anticipation of the impending national elections, Indonesia's first, injected an added element of ideological antagonism into political life. The elections were an inducement to seek short-term political advantage, which meant being more responsive to popular desires. Moreover, unlike recent cabinets which had embraced both of the largest parties, the cabinet that initiated the foreign policy shift excluded its major competitors. Political competition thus grew more polarized, and there was a sense that the stakes of competition had been raised. Finally, the cabinets that held office after 1953 had the benefit of the accumulated experience of their predecessors, and the political lesson of that experience was unmistakable. Whereas foreign policy had been a liability for the previous cabinets, by shifting toward an independence policy, those who held power during the 1953–1957 period generally succeeded in deriving political advantage from their conduct of foreign policy. Yet there was a certain ambivalence in their handling of foreign economic matters, which may be taken as evidence that these cabinets were subject to some of the pressures that all incumbents felt to avoid jeopardizing foreign sources of economic support.

Ali Sastroamidjojo, who served as prime minister from July 1953 to July 1955 and again from March 1956 to March 1957, gave a new definition to the "independent and active" foreign policy. Whereas the previous cabinets had followed an essentially pro-western policy while avoiding actions that would constitute a formal commitment to the west, Ali sought to create a balance in Indonesia's relations with the two blocs. In December 1953 he negotiated Indonesia's first trade agreement with the People's Republic of China, followed by a Dual Nationality Treaty in 1955; in March 1954 he established an Indonesian embassy in Moscow. His most spectacular move, however, was the staging of an international conference of Asian and African heads of state at Bandung in April 1955. With respect to the Irian problem, Ali's cabinet was the first to respond to the nationalist impulse to eliminate this symbol of Indonesia's incomplete independence. For the first time, the Irian issue was raised by Indonesia in the United Nations. Although the Indonesians were unsuccessful in gaining UN approval of even a relatively mild resolution, for which they blamed the US[15] and which they took as reconfirmation of the hostility of the outside world, the cabinet managed to convey the impression that it had begun "doing something" to resolve the Irian impasse. Ali associated himself with the mass demonstrations being held in Indonesia; he won the Bandung conference's endorsement of Indonesia's Irian claim; and the first attempts at infiltrating Indonesian troops into West Irian were undertaken, though the government never admitted responsibility for them. Taken together, the Ali cabinet's foreign policy initiatives suggested that the government was working to reduce Indonesia's dependence on the west by cultivating relations with other power groups. The "independent and active" foreign policy was being transformed from the relatively narrow and passive aim of avoiding commitments to an active effort to assure Indonesia's independence of action by placing Djakarta in a position to balance competing power groups against one another.

But where steps directly related to the loosening of foreign economic control in Indonesia were concerned, the Ali cabinets were much more equivocal. Although the first Ali cabinet substantially accelerated the pace of the economy's "Indonesianization" by providing credits, licenses, and a protected position for large numbers of new Indonesian firms, no large-scale nationalization of foreign business was undertaken. Despite its general hostility toward foreign capital, the government issued formal declarations intended to attract new foreign investment, and foreign capital was assigned an important role in the Five Year Plan (1956–1960) approved by the second Ali cabinet. The Ali cabinets also compromised on the issue of squatting on foreign estate lands, ordering a halt to eviction of squatters who had been on the land prior to a particular date but seeking to prohibit further squatting. The pressures of incumbency thus led Ali to move cautiously when it came to jeopardizing foreign aid and investment. But what Ali's foreign policy proved was that if the combination of deep suspicion of the outside world and a politically competitive situation made a foreign policy of development costly, that combination also made it possible to gain political support through largely symbolic measures that conveyed a sense of progress toward a foreign policy of independence.

[15] This judgment is based on personal interviews with Indonesian officials. For the best discussion of the Irian problem, see Robert C. Bone, Jr., *The Dynamics of the Western New Guinea (Irian Barat) Problem* (Ithaca: Cornell Modern Indonesia Project, 1958).

The interlude between the two Ali cabinets was filled by the Bur-hanuddin Harahap cabinet. This cabinet initially represented something of a return to the approach of the earlier years of the period, emphasizing economic stabilization, the search for foreign capital, and the restoration of relatively close cooperation with the west. In the hope that the Dutch would see the wisdom of making concessions that would strengthen the political position of their "friends" in Indonesia, the Burhanuddin cabinet launched an "offensive of reasonableness," in which they refrained from raising the Irian issue at the 1955 session of the United Nations and moved to revive direct negotiations with the Dutch. This return to the path of negotiations and "reasonableness" evoked great hostility in Indonesia, with the government being accused of "begging" from the west. Even Sukiman, whose cabinet had gone farther than any other in committing Indonesia to the west, denounced the negotiations as a "national tragedy."[16] With the cabinet caught between domestic political opposition and the Dutch unwillingness to make concessions, the talks broke down. Then, in a sudden reversal, the Burhanuddin cabinet broke the impasse by announcing the unilateral abrogation of the Netherlands-Indonesian Union, which, when subsequently enacted by parliament, was declared to include all of the other obligations undertaken in the Round Table Conference Agreement.[17] The abrogation, taken in the name of independence and self-reliance, was so enormously popular that it enabled the Burhanuddin cabinet to avert the imminent danger that it would fall before the date already set for its replacement by a cabinet based on the recently held national elections. Once again, the political costs of cooperation and the political benefits of self-reliance had been demonstrated.

THE RISE AND IMPLEMENTATION OF GUIDED DEMOCRACY (1957–1965)—THE FOREIGN POLICY OF INDEPENDENCE

The period from 1957 to 1965 saw the evolution of an increasingly pronounced form of the foreign policy of independence. Faced with what Indonesians viewed as repeated confirmation of the west's hostility toward Indonesia, the policy-makers during this period emphasized the elimination of fetters on their country's independence and the warding off of perceived new pressures intended to restrict their national freedom. At no time, however, did Indonesia completely

---

[16] Feith, *op. cit.*, p. 454.

[17] The formal parliamentary action did not take place until after the second Ali cabinet had assumed office. For details, see Palmier, *op. cit.*, pp. 95–96.

ignore the developmental use of foreign policy, and substantial foreign aid was received during these years. Moreover, it also became clear that there could be political risks in moving too far toward a foreign policy of independence, when it tended to weaken severely the domestic position of those Indonesians with close ties to the aid givers.

Since the end of the revolution, political competition had focused on the cabinet, and foreign policy had essentially been formulated by the ruling political party leaders, with only occasional and relatively insignificant intrusions by President Sukarno and the army. In 1956, however, Sukarno had begun to assume an important foreign-policy role, with two lengthy trips abroad in which he displayed a flamboyant and independent style of diplomacy that posed a threat to Prime Minister Ali's authority in the making of foreign policy.[18] In 1957 the nature of political competition and the foreign policy-making process began to change drastically. Two developments—growing disillusionment with the performance of the political parties in the parliamentary system and a deterioration of relations between Djakarta and the outer islands—opened the way for a dramatic enlargement in the roles of Sukarno and the army in national politics. The declaration of martial law in March 1957 provided a rationale for army involvement, just as it enabled Sukarno to reduce the cabinet's independent decision-making role by personally intervening to form an "emergency, extra-parliamentary business cabinet," as the second Ali cabinet's successor. When rebellions broke out on the islands of Sumatra and Celebes in early 1958, the leading role in the unsuccessful rebellions taken by some of the principal figures of the early constitutional democracy cabinets resulted in the effective elimination of their parties from the political arena. At the same time, the PKI acquired a new importance. Sukarno, who was without an organizational base of support, realized that he needed a force to balance the army's power, if he was to avoid becoming dependent on the army. Having emerged as the strongest party in Java's 1957 elections, the PKI was the only group available that had an effective organization and capacity to mobilize people down to the village level. Thus, Sukarno decided to foster the development of the PKI as a counterweight to the rising power of the army.

The pattern of political competition that grew increasingly prevalent through the guided democracy period, was, therefore, a triangular one, in which Sukarno, the army, and, for most of the period,

---

[18] That challenge was made especially clear when Sukarno advised the foreign minister to sign an Indonesian-Soviet Joint Statement without consulting the prime minister or the cabinet. See Feith, *op. cit.*, p. 514.

a much weaker PKI maneuvered for power. The intense competition of those years was to some extent masked by the authoritarian character of the guided democracy system, in particular the glorification of Sukarno's leadership and the absence of any formal opposition. Sukarno sought to solidify his own role and to prevent an open clash between the army and the PKI by co-opting the competitors into the government and, in a sense, making them all incumbents. Thus, in the day-to-day handling of foreign policy and the formulation of its ideology, Sukarno was given considerable latitude, but in setting the general direction of policy and in making the key decisions he had always to consider the effect of foreign policy on the political balance among the three forces. As a result, though Sukarno clearly dominated the making of guided democracy foreign policy, his real freedom was much less than it seemed. For with the shift from parliamentary competition, in which the stakes were fairly low and defeat did not rule out a subsequent return to power, toward a death-struggle competition between forces fundamentally opposed to one another's existence, risks that could previously be taken were now too dangerous to bear. If a foreign policy of development had been politically dangerous before, the risks were now overwhelming.

The foreign policy of the new period was ushered in by two momentous events in late 1957 and early 1958. In December 1957, following a third failure to gain UN support on the West Irian question and amid rapidly declining national unity, the Indonesians nationalized all Dutch businesses in their country and evicted all Dutch personnel except "experts." Because the United States was held responsible for Indonesia's UN defeat,[19] the PKI was able to enhance its political position by citing the UN vote as proof that the Communist powers, which had supported the Indonesians, were their true friends. But the nationalization also proved extremely beneficial to the army, which was given responsibility for managing former Dutch enterprises, and to Sukarno, who acquired a vast supply of new resources to distribute in a politically advantageous way.

Equally momentous for the course of guided democracy foreign policy were the regional rebellions which erupted in February 1958. They were widely believed to have the backing of the United States and, to a lesser extent, Great Britain,[20] thus making the Indonesians

---

[19] George McT. Kahin, "Indonesia," in Kahin, ed., *Major Governments of Asia* (Ithaca: Cornell University Press, 1963 edition), p. 682.

[20] The shooting down of an American pilot was heralded as proof of United States involvement. There is, in fact, very strong evidence, including statements made by the leaders of the rebellion to the author, that the United States gave some military support to the rebels until it became clear that they would fail.

less receptive than ever to a developmental foreign policy based on aid from the west. Coming on top of the UN vote, the foreign-backed rebellions had a profound impact, convincing many Indonesians that the west was not only an unreliable supporter but a real threat to their national integrity.

Determined not to stake Indonesia's claim to West Irian on hopes for "a gift from the imperialists," Sukarno devised a multi-faceted strategy of confrontation. In mid-1960 he broke diplomatic relations with the Netherlands. He undertook a substantial military buildup, based mainly on Soviet aid, since the United States had refused to sell Indonesia the needed military equipment. His strategy also included limited landings of Indonesian forces in West Irian, mass rallies and calls for volunteers, and a continuation of diplomatic efforts. With the threat of war in West Irian mounting, the United States finally abandoned its "pro-Dutch neutrality" and in August 1962 Washington pressed the Dutch into settling the dispute on terms favorable to Indonesia. Though the United States gained considerable good will by its last minute assistance, most Indonesian leaders felt that Washington had changed its position only because Djakarta had succeeded, through its military buildup, in creating a threat to regional stability. The Irian victory thus was generally seen as a triumph for Sukarno's strategy of confrontation, not as a vindication of reliance on the west, nor, for that matter, on the Soviet Union, whose aid was appreciated but seen as motivated mainly by a desire to lead Indonesia toward Communism.

If the Irian campaign was widely supported as part of the completion of the drive for independence, its political uses were no less significant. Each of the three major competitors supported the campaign strongly, but for different reasons. The army saw it as a basis for the expansion of the military establishment and a vehicle for its modernization. It also provided a pretext for the continuation of martial law and an opportunity for the military to participate heroically in a popular national enterprise. The PKI found the Irian campaign useful as a way of identifying itself with a nationalist issue, thereby helping to rebut the accusation that it was an agent for foreign interests. For President Sukarno, the struggle for West Irian was an ideal issue to justify the kind of exhortative, solidarity-making leadership he could give. Moreover, the sense of crisis created by the confrontation against the Dutch served as a means of helping to keep the lid on domestic conflict, lending support to Sukarno's call for national unity under his leadership and making it more difficult for the PKI's enemies to find some pretext for eliminating the Communists. Clearly, then, there were important incentives for all of the major competitors for power to support strongly the West Irian campaign, while, conversely, the costs of opposing it would have been unacceptable.

In the aftermath of the triumph in West Irian, Sukarno began to speak of improving economic conditions. Partly reflecting the prevailing relative good feelings toward the United States as a result of its role in the Irian settlement, Indonesian technocrats were permitted, in consultation with the International Monetary Fund and the United States, to work out an aid package and an economic stabilization plan to stem Indonesia's rampant inflation. Indonesia's seriousness about the development effort appeared to be borne out in late May 1963 by the promulgation of regulations implementing the stabilization program and by Djakarta's willingness to work out an accommodation with American oil companies, the latter reflecting both Sukarno's awareness of the importance of the foreign exchange earned by oil and the army's dependence on oil for its mobility.[21] For all its suspicion of the outside world, the Sukarno government, like every other incumbent regime since the revolution, seemed to realize that it simply did not command the resources to solve Indonesia's economic problems without aid. Even in the midst of guided democracy, there was pressure to make some effort at a foreign policy of development.

But the stringent anti-inflationary regulations adopted as a precondition for western economic aid were no sooner announced than they encountered a storm of criticism, led by the PKI, but joined in all along the political spectrum. The stabilization plan's foreign sponsorship and the knowledge that the unpleasant regulations had been imposed by the IMF and the United States as preconditions for aid[22] left its backers exceedingly vulnerable to the criticism that Indonesia's independence was being compromised. Though the army undoubtedly was aware that the stabilization plan's implementation would have significantly enhanced its position vis-à-vis the PKI by ensuring that Indonesia maintained close, and to some extent dependent, relations with the United States, the generals had compelling economic and political reasons for withholding support from the plan. They were unwilling to absorb the budget cut required under the plan, just as they could not have relished the prospect of speaking up in defense of a foreign-sponsored plan amid a torrent of hostile criticism on nationalist grounds. The army simply could not afford to run the risk of being labelled deficient in nationalist spirit.

Had the stabilization plan not run aground on domestic political

[21] On the oil crisis, see Frederick P. Bunnell, "The Kennedy Initiatives in Indonesia: 1962–1963" (unpublished Ph.D. dissertation, Cornell University, 1969), pp. 351–373.

[22] *Ibid.*, pp. 311–316.

hostility, it would probably have been abandoned anyway as a consequence of Indonesia's developing confrontation with the proposed Federation of Malaysia. Indonesia had said virtually nothing about the plan to combine the three British Borneo territories of Sarawak, Brunei, and North Borneo with Singapore and Malaya in a new federation until an anti-Malaysia revolt broke out in Brunei in December 1962. Perceiving the revolt as a manifestation, right on Indonesia's doorstep, of the worldwide anti-imperialist struggle which they aspired to lead, the Indonesians backed the rebellion without hesitation. In the succeeding months, support for the rebellion grew into strong opposition to the Malaysia plan on the ground that it was actually a plan for the perpetuation of British influence in the region, imposed on the peoples concerned without their approval, and aimed ultimately at preventing the expansion of Indonesia's influence in the region. Negotiations among Indonesia, Malaya, and the Philippines in the summer of 1963 produced agreement to accept the formation of Malaysia if a UN team decided that this was the desire of the British Borneo peoples. But the British and Malayans, with the UN investigation still in progress, announced that Malaysia would be formed regardless of the outcome of the UN survey. Taking this "premature announcement" as an insult, the Indonesians refused to recognize the federation, broke trade relations, and vowed to "Crush Malaysia." The "premature announcement" was important in inflaming Indonesian passions because many saw it as confirmation of Britain's contempt for the rightful regional position of a truly independent Indonesia. The embargo on trade with Malaysia substantially added to the independence appeal of the Crush Malaysia campaign, for dependence on Singapore as an entrepôt had long been resented bitterly by the Indonesians as a limitation on their independence.

The confrontation against Malaysia, which had begun as a fairly uncomplicated expression of support for a national liberation movement, escalated into something much more substantial because, like the West Irian campaign, it involved the issue of Indonesia's independence and at the same time fulfilled a number of important political functions.[23] It was used by all of the competitors for power to legitimize domestic political goals. For the army, it provided justification for a large military budget and a possible reinstatement of martial law,[24] while the PKI sought to use mobilization against

[23] The political uses of confrontation are discussed in greater detail in Franklin B. Weinstein, *Indonesia Abandons Confrontation: An Inquiry into the Functions of Indonesian Foreign Policy* (Ithaca: Cornell Modern Indonesia Project, 1969), especially pp. 3–11.

[24] Martial law had ended with the transfer of West Irian to Indonesian sovereignty in May 1963.

Malaysia as a pretext for demanding the creation of an armed peasant militia. The confrontation policy served to facilitate the task of conflict management, lending support to Sukarno's pleas that national unity was essential. It also sustained a situation in which the solidarity-making political skills of its backers were in demand. And, more fundamentally, it enabled a basically conservative leadership to convey the impression of revolutionary progress without undergoing the risks and costs of a real domestic revolution.

By 1964, however, the army leadership was beginning to see that the confrontation policy was helping the PKI more than the army. Increasingly, confrontation was being used to isolate the army from its foreign allies. Relations with the United States had deteriorated drastically, while Indonesia was drawing closer to Communist China, which supported the confrontation policy fully. When at the end of 1964 Sukarno, evidently without consulting his principal advisers, decided to announce Indonesia's withdrawal from the United Nations as a protest against the seating of Malaysia in the Security Council, the army became alarmed indeed. In mid-1965 the army initiated a series of peace feelers, apparently without Sukarno's knowledge, aimed minimally at gaining the cooperation of the Malaysians to ensure that confrontation did not weaken the army's political position any further. But an accelerating leftward trend in Indonesia's domestic politics led to the attempted coup of 30 September 1965, an event which set in motion political changes that within a year produced a dramatic reversal in Indonesia's foreign policy.

THE NEW ORDER (1966–1971)—THE FOREIGN POLICY OF DEVELOPMENT

The attempted coup of 30 September 1965 ruptured the fragile consensus which had kept the death-struggle competition of guided democracy manageable. The PKI's implication in the attempted coup, in which six army generals were murdered, was seized by the army as justification for the destruction of the PKI, and in a matter of months hundreds of thousands of alleged Communists, including the party's top leaders, were slaughtered or arrested. Sukarno attempted to keep alive some sort of leftist force as a counter to the army, but he failed. By March 1966, amid student demonstrations and irresistible pressure from the army, Sukarno had no choice but to yield de facto leadership to General Suharto, who had led the army in crushing the attempted coup. With the virtual elimination of both the PKI and Sukarno as political forces, the army now dominated the political process. Moreover, political party leaders who might have criticized some of the army's policies were intimidated by the still tense political atmosphere, in which opposition to the new govern-ment's views could lead to denunciation as a Communist sympathizer or, if one's anti-Communist credentials were unchallengeable, as a dupe. The only political competition which remained was bureau-cratic competition, a continuing rivalry among generals, technocrats, ministers, party leaders, and others for personal or factional gain. In this kind of competition, which had of course always gone on beneath the more significant parliamentary and death-struggle competition of the previous periods, the stakes were very low, with the threat of neither exclusion from the government, as in the case of parliamentary competition, or destruction, as in the case of death-struggle competi-tion.

Indonesia and the World Community

In this new situation, striking changes in Indonesia's foreign policy became possible. The political incentives for carrying out the kind of confrontative policy Sukarno had pursued no longer existed. The political uses which had made confrontation important to all of the chief political forces in the tri-polar competition of the guided democ-racy period were now irrelevant. On the other hand, the army-led government of the New Order was subject to the same pressures to follow a foreign policy of development that had been felt by every previous incumbent regime; in fact, those pressures were somewhat more intense than before because of the disastrous condition of the Indonesian economy in 1966 and the army's evident desire to use the promise of economic development, widely cited as Sukarno's chief failing, as a basis for legitimizing its own rule. Unlike its predecessors, however, the new government was relatively unrestrained by political competition in the implementation of a developmental foreign policy.

Following the transfer of authority in March 1966 the first task of Indonesian foreign policy was the restoration of the confidence of the western creditor nations in Indonesia. Suharto moved cautiously at first, still fearing Sukarno, but by August 1966 the confrontation against Malaysia had been abandoned and an agreement to normalize relations signed. Shortly thereafter Indonesia returned to the United Nations and took a leading role in efforts to foster regional cooperation, lead-ing to the formation of an Association of Southeast Asian Nations (ASEAN). The reorientation of policy also included a curtailment of Indonesia's ties with the Soviet Union and Communist China, culminating in a suspension of relations with the latter in October 1967.

But the key to Indonesia's search for respectability in the eyes of the western powers was its economic policy. When the Indonesians asked the IMF to agree to the postponement of Djakarta's debt, the answer was: "First tell us your plans for improving the economic situation in Indonesia." Indonesia's long-frustrated economists, of course, needed no encouragement from the IMF to formulate the sweeping economic stabilization plan which was adopted in October 1966. A new foreign investment law, containing attractive conditions for investors, was also enacted.

Indonesia's efforts to convince the creditor nations of its devotion to economic development have borne fruit in the form of new aid commitments that have grown progressively to a commitment of $670 million for 1972.[25] The aid-giving countries, grouped together in an Inter-Governmental Group on Indonesia (IGGI), have also co-operated by agreeing to the long-term rescheduling of the Sukarno debts. Pledges of foreign investment by 1972 had already exceeded $1.5 billion, though only an extremely small percentage of those commitments had actually been realized. In 1969 Indonesia was able to launch a Five-Year Development Plan with 81 percent of its financing in the first year derived from foreign sources. But this success in gaining foreign economic aid has meant that Indonesia under the New Order has become more dependent on the outside world than it has been at any other time since the revolution.

Suharto's foreign policy of development has stirred considerable criticism, though it is seldom expressed publicly. There has been a very deep and widespread concern about Indonesia's dependence on foreign aid. Some of the leaders most closely-identified with the developmental foreign policy of the early 1950's, now politically frustrated, have become strong critics of Indonesia's "excessive" dependence on others. Even many of those directly responsible for Indonesia's present foreign policy are clearly ambivalent. They don't like their present dependence on the outside world, but they feel, in essence, that their obligation as incumbents to deal with Indonesia's problems leaves them no choice. Resentment of the IMF's influence in determining Indonesia's fate is intense among political party leaders and intellectuals, but it extends as well to army officers and even to the top levels of the foreign ministry. Particularly humiliating for the Indonesians is the practice of requiring that they meet with the IGGI nations to discuss each year's aid needs and to hear the IMF's report

[25] Aid commitments by the IGGI members have grown as follows: $200 million for 1967; $360 million for 1968; $500 million for 1969; $600 million for 1970; $640 million for 1971; and $670 million for 1972.

on Indonesia's economic performance and the validity of its aid request. The stabilization policies identified with the IMF have been extremely unpopular from the start. The stabilization plan was enacted, according to one of its leading backers, only because the potential opposition, which came from all along the political spectrum, was too intimidated to express itself. Many Indonesian leaders also object to the passivity of their country's foreign policy and its onesidedness in emphasizing warm relations exclusively with the western powers. They embarrassedly conclude that their country's chief posture toward the outside world is one of "begging." It is clear that despite their willingness to follow a foreign policy of development, the Indonesians have by no means abandoned their belief that the outside world is essentially a hostile, exploitative place. As the Indonesian leaders' vehement criticism of the damaging American decision to release its rubber and tin stockpiles confirms, they remain highly suspicious of the intentions of the outside world toward Indonesia. Moreover, the resurgence of Japanese economic power in Southeast Asia, coupled with Indonesia's bitter experiences in negotiations with the Japanese over the last several years, has convinced many Indonesians that their independence is indeed again in jeopardy.

The New Order's freedom to carry out a foreign policy of development in the face of such attitudes reflects the latitude afforded by the absence of serious political competition. There has, of course, been bureaucratic competition, and although personal and factional rivalries do not represent the clash of opposing political forces as such, they have injected a measure of bargaining into the policy-making process. The making of foreign policy under the New Order has been shared by the army, the technocrats, and the foreign ministry, and there have been policy disagreements and personal rivalries within and among those three groups. There is no doubt, however, of the army's supremacy, because the president is a general and the army is the only one of the three with a genuine domestic political base. The foreign ministry and the technocrats are useful to the army not only because of their technical expertise and ability to win aid commitments from the west, but also because they can, and do, absorb a good deal of criticism that might otherwise be directed against the army. Both the foreign minister and the technocrats find that their strongest political card, the enthusiasm they arouse in the aid-giving countries, is at the same time a political liability because their high standing among foreigners arouses suspicions that they are serving foreign interests. The foreign minister's position is further weakened by the president's tendency to rely on generals and technocrats as ad hoc emissaries to handle many of the most sensitive foreign policy matters; on a variety of matters, the foreign minister has found himself overruled in favor of the counsel of generals or technocrats.[26] The technocrats, though they have considerable influence in the determination of policies related to foreign economic matters, are weakened by their fundamental dependence on the army, for they realize that only the army possesses either the inclination or the capacity to give them the influential position they now hold. The army itself, of course, is by no means monolithic. Army factions divide along various lines, but for foreign policy the most important is the continuing rivalry between the "institutional" intelligence generals, particularly those who have dominated the army and defense ministry intelligence establishments, and "free-wheelers," who serve as personal assistants to the president and run the very influential "Special Operations," often referred to as an Indonesian CIA.

This bureaucratic competition, however, has only limited bearing on the general direction of policy. Though particular factions are sometimes identified with different policy approaches—the foreign minister, certain army generals, and certain technocrats are generally thought to be more interested in moving toward an independent foreign policy than are certain other generals and technocrats—policy differences are often obscure and there is often considerable confusion as to which faction has triumphed in a particular decision. The bureaucratic competition for access to the president, personal prestige, and other rewards motivates some of the positions taken by policy-makers, but the fundamental imperatives setting Indonesia's foreign policy course are the pressures which the nature of the Indonesian political system imposes on incumbents to seek outside help and the freedom to do so permitted by the lack of serious political competition.

In 1969 some changes in Indonesia's foreign policy of development became evident. The Indonesians began to seek a restoration of good relations with the Soviet Union, and in 1970 negotiations concerning the long-term rescheduling of Indonesia's debt repayments to the Soviets bore fruit in the form of an agreement similar to that previously reached with the IGGI nations. There has since been some talk of improving relations with China, though the prospects for any substantial changes in Sino-Indonesian relations will depend on the willingness of the Chinese to soften their attitude toward Indonesia. A principal reason for these ventures was the Indonesian leaders' belief in the desirability of reducing Indonesia's dependence on the west by culti-

---

[26] Examples are decisions relating to presidential trips abroad, the terms on which the confrontation against Malaysia was to be ended, the diplomatic handling of the West Irian referendum of 1969, and ambassadorial appointments.

vating alternative sources of economic support. It may be significant, however, that these modest efforts to restore some of the independence to Indonesian foreign policy coincided with a very limited and short-lived restoration of a weak form of parliamentary competition, mainly as a consequence of Suharto's 1969 decision to hold nationwide parliamentary elections in July 1971. Although there was never any expectation that the elections would in any way threaten the army's hold on political power, the easing of the tensions of 1966–67, the increasing boldness of Djakarta's relatively free press, and the political maneuvering in preparation for the elections did produce some serious criticism of the development foreign policy. In the fall of 1970 certain important Djakarta newspapers began running editorials with titles like "How To Sell a Nation/People,"[27] in an apparent attempt to win political support by attacks on the vulnerable technocrats and foreign minister. There have been unconfirmed reports, however, that some of the attacks actually were encouraged by army leaders anxious to remind the technocrats and foreign minister of their dependence on the army and, at the same time, to shift the burden of criticism from the army to the civilians. In any case, the newspapers involved were subsequently pressed by the government to mitigate their attacks, and the army emerged from the 1971 elections with a tightened grip on political power.

Achievements, Failures and Prospects

The foregoing analysis of the foreign policy-making process in Indonesia over the last quarter century suggests that a key problem for the future will remain how to acquire needed foreign aid for economic development without sacrificing the country's independence. The future course of Indonesian foreign policy will depend on the outcome of the continuing trade-off by incumbents between pressures to seek outside help for development and pressures to avoid compromising the country's independence, with political competition playing a crucial role in determining which set of pressures prevails. Barring truly impressive progress in economic development or the creation of political leadership capable of mobilizing Indonesia's domestic resources —both of which seem unlikely in the near future—pressures to seek outside aid for economic development will remain strong.

Suspicion of the outside world, on the other hand, is so endemic, even among the young leaders who led the anti-Sukarno demonstra-

[27] *Merdeka,* 7 December 1970.

tions of 1966, that a foreign policy of development is likely to continue to provoke strong criticism lest Indonesia's independence be sacrificed. Though the present Indonesian elite is more pro-west than pro-Communist, its perception of a hostile outside world is likely to be expressed, as in the past, mainly in anti-western terms. This occurs mainly because Indonesia encounters western political and economic power more directly than that of the Communist powers. The continuing expansion of Japan's international role will almost certainly increase the Indonesians' concern about their independence.

As for political competition, its return as a serious factor, in the form of liaisons between factions of the army and other political groups, is probably only a matter of time. It seems safe, therefore, to speculate that so long as the Indonesian political system remains relatively noncompetitive, with political competition restricted mainly to bureaucratic rivalries, the leadership will have substantial latitude to pursue a foreign policy of development. But to the extent that political competition revives in Djakarta, that freedom will probably narrow, and Indonesia may move once again toward a foreign policy of independence.

PART TWO

The Foreign Policies of the Smaller Asian States

Korea and Vietnam

ROBERT A. SCALAPINO

World War II and its aftermath bequeathed to
posterity a series of "divided states," three of them
in East Asia—China, Korea and Vietnam. Subsequently,
none have had a more troubled history than the two
Koreas and the two Vietnams, both in terms of their
relations with each other and with the outer world.
In some respects, the foreign policy problems of a
divided state are unique, since such a state must
struggle with its primary rival for international
recognition, and since also, it must be continuously
concerned with the unification issue. At the same time,
it must face many of the problems of any emerging
society, including those that relate to independence
versus interdependence, and the relative costs of each.

South Korea: Determinants of Foreign Policy

Let us turn first to the Republic of Korea (South
Korea) and its Communist counterpart in the North.
The Republic of Korea was established in 1948 out of
the failure of American and Soviet efforts to agree
upon a unification formula. Within two years,
the fledgling state was involved in a desperate struggle
for survival, the Communists having elected to
attempt unification by force of arms. The evidence
strongly suggests (but does not definitively prove)
that the Communist decision to launch the
Korean war—which also involved the Russians—
was based upon the assumption that the United States
would not defend the South. This may have

147

occurred because statements by the Secretary of State and others earlier indicated that Korea did not lie within the American defense perimeter.[1]

The Korean war, however, brought not only an American response, but a formal commitment from the United Nations, and at least token aid to the Republic from fifteen nations in addition to the United States. Thus, when this enormously destructive war ended, South Korea was recognized as the sole legal government by the United Nations (the prewar elections covering the South having been observed by UN representatives in contradistinction to those in the North, where no UN involvement was permitted). The Republic also had diplomatic relations with a sizeable majority of the non-Communist states, whereas the Democratic People's Republic of Korea's (DPRK) ties were confined exclusively to the Communist bloc.

Crucial to the survival of the Republic during the past twenty years, however, has been the consistent economic and military support of the United States. In one sense, such support has an interesting historical background. Traditionally, Korea sought a maximum degree of isolation from the outer world as a small nation surrounded by such major societies as Communist China, the Soviet Union and Japan. Indeed, the high quotient of xenophobia and exclusivism present in its political culture caused Korea to be labelled "the Hermit Kingdom." When isolation proved increasingly difficult to maintain, however, in the late nineteenth century, the Korean government turned to the United States for aid, in an effort to preserve its independence in the midst of rising external threats. In part, this was because of the favorable impact of the early American missionaries. A more important factor, however, was the distance of the United States which meant no territorial designs or need for spheres of influence—an ideal benefactor to a small country beset by threats from nearby neighbors. In this period, however, the United States had no desire to become involved in the defense of this remote land, and consequently, its assistance was minimal. Step by step, however, Korea moved toward colonial status, with the final acts of the drama taking place in 1910.[2]

The drama of 1950 was of a very different type. After World War II Korean independence had been guaranteed by the great powers in the Cairo Declaration of December 1, 1943, and reaffirmed at

[1] For a comprehensive discussion of the issues leading up to the Korean war, see Glenn D. Paige, *The Korean Decision—June 24–30, 1950* (New York: The Free Press, 1968), especially pp. 65–76.

[2] Details are given in the major study by Chong-Sik Lee, *The Politics of Korean Nationalism* (Berkeley and Los Angeles: University of California Press, 1963).

Yalta and Potsdam. The circumstances surrounding the end of World War II, however, dictated that Korea would be occupied by the Soviet Union in the North, and by the United States in the South. This dual and wholly diverse occupational pattern probably made inevitable the long-term division of Korea, since the Communist government of the North could not tolerate an open opposition, and the non-Communist leadership of the South was equally determined to prevent the Communists from securing power. When Communist efforts at unification by force failed, and the UN counteroffensive also fell short of attaining its maximum objective of unification as a result of Chinese Communist intervention, the two Koreas were destined to continue as de facto states, sharing a small peninsula under conditions of extreme mutual hostility.

The immediate aftermath of the Korean war brought very limited progress in South Korea, either in domestic or foreign affairs. Throughout the 1950's, the tasks of effectuating an open political system and simultaneously launching a program of major economic development seemed beyond the capacities of this small, battered nation and its leadership. Most observers, including many Americans, despaired of the Korean future despite the massive aid being given. North Korean economic development, under the aegis of a tight, authoritarian regime, was far more successful. Finally, the aged President Syngman Rhee was toppled, and after one year of growing chaos, a military coup was carried out in the spring of 1961. South Korea thereupon began a new era.

The 1961 military coup brought a group of young military officers to power, men for the most part from relatively humble backgrounds and with limited formal education. In general this group represented the most indigenous, the most *Asian* leadership to hold power in the Republic. Few had had western educations, other than short-term military training. Their foreign language capacities were also limited, except for Japanese, the language in which they had been schooled.

However, significant and highly successful changes in economic policies were effectuated under these men which made South Korean economic development one of the most rapid in the current world by the end of the 1960's. In politics, developments were more mixed, but the parliamentary system survived, political opposition was allowed, and competitive elections were conducted. Gradually a broader, more complex foreign policy began to take shape. Before examining the essentials of that policy, however, brief mention should be made of the decision-making structure of the Republic.

From the moment of its inception, the Republic of Korea was marked by a political system in which the premium was upon strong presidential leadership. Under President Pak Chong-hi, that system has not been altered. The Korean "Blue House" is the center of decision-making in foreign as well as domestic policy. The president, moreover, has acquired a substantial personal staff to aid in policy-making. Indeed, it is commonly acknowledged that often presidential secretaries are more important than cabinet officials, although there are individual exceptions. The Ministry of Foreign Affairs has a sizeable number of trained personnel, many of them with good-to-excellent educations. Basic as well as relatively minor policy decisions, however, are made by the president. While the Korean National Assembly, through its Committee on Foreign Relations, plays some role in policy debate, to date, the legislative branch has been largely an instrument of the executive due to the nature of power distribution in the political system.[3]

What are the essential elements of current South Korean foreign policy? Four primary themes are prominently displayed, each of which requires some exploration. First, the cornerstone of the Republic's foreign policy continues to be the alliance with the United States, especially as this relates to security matters. Secondly, relations with Japan, normalized in 1965 after stormy internal struggles, have steadily become more important, particularly in the economic field. Thirdly, South Korea has made a determined effort in recent years to expand its relations with a wide range of states and has even begun to relax the rigidity characterizing its earlier attitude toward all Communist states. Finally, policies toward North Korea remain both strict and minimal, with little expectation that peaceful unification—or even significant contacts—can be accomplished in the near future.

SOUTH KOREA AND THE UNITED STATES

The Mutual Defense Treaty of 1954 is the central document binding the United States and the Republic of Korea. That treaty stipulates that an armed attack upon either country would cause each to "act to meet the common danger in accordance with its constitutional processes." By the beginning of 1970, the United States had provided South Korea with $2.9 billion in military aid, at a steadily declining level, however, with 1969 assistance in this field amounting to $140

---

[3] See C. I. Eugene Kim, ed., A Pattern of Political Development: Korea (The Korea Research and Publication, Inc., 1964), espec. "The Constitutional Development," pp. 158–169; and Pyong-Choon Hahm, The Korean Political Tradition and Law (Seoul, Korea: Royal Asiatic Society Korea Branch, Monograph Series Number 1, Hollym Corporation), 1967.

million.[4] In addition, two divisions of American troops, totalling between 50–60,000 men, had been stationed in Korea since the end of the Korean war, together with more than 100 combat aircraft and appropriate naval units. Expenditures for these amount to about $500 million yearly. Clearly, this is little more than a token force, but it has served as witness to the American commitment.

With the advent of the Nixon Doctrine and the general domestic pressures for a lower American posture in East Asia, however, the United States in the 1969–1970 period made a decision to reduce the troop level in Korea by at least 20,000. This decision, together with other developments on the American scene, created serious repercussions within the Republic. For the first time since the days of Syngman Rhee, the credibility of the American commitment was openly questioned, and strenuous protests, public and private, were voiced. In part, these protests were advanced to bolster demands that the United States provide additional, and more modern military equipment to South Koreans so that they would be in a better position to defend themselves, particularly in the air and at sea. It was argued that the Soviet equipment available to the North Koreans was in many instances superior to the American equipment furnished the South. In part also, the timing of the American withdrawal from Korea was challenged especially while the Vietnam war continued.

The South Koreans are now reconciled to the fact that the American presence will be lowered, whether or not their worst fears are realized, namely, the return of American isolationism. This reconciliation indeed, has begun to have a decided impact upon other aspects of South Korea's foreign policy, as we shall note shortly, and even upon its domestic policies. Meanwhile, the past economic role of the United States has been no less important to Korea than its military one. Approximately $3.6 billion in economic assistance was extended to Korea by the United States between the end of the Korean war and the end of 1969. Much of that, of course, came in the form of straight relief to a war-ravaged people in the years immediately following the Korean war. It involved not merely provisions for food, but also for the rebuilding of communications, housing, schools and similar necessities. Once again, economic aid has tapered off as the Republic has approached self-sufficiency. Without American assistance, however, Korea, like Japan, could not possibly have reached the levels of productivity characteristic of recent years.

[4] *United States Security Agreements and Commitments Abroad—Republic of Korea,* Hearings before the Subcommittee on Foreign Relations, US Senate, 91st Congress, 2nd Session, Part 6, February 24, 25, and 26, 1970 (Washington, D.C.: US Government Printing Office, 1970).

Despite their deep concern with recent trends in American foreign policy the leaders of the Republic hope to maintain a close alliance with the United States throughout the 1970's—given the will of the Americans. They continue to see this alliance as their best guarantee against Communist aggression, and also as an economic-cultural link of vital significance. In 1969, of $702.8 million of exports, $339.3 million (48 percent) went to the United States. At the same time, Korean leaders are increasingly talking about the need for "self-reliance," and more broadly gauged ties with the external world, even as they exhort the United States to adopt a proper (slower) timing in helping its Asian allies to stand on their own feet.

SOUTH KOREA AND JAPAN

Continuing, strong links with the United States are also viewed by many Koreans as a highly desirable counterpoint to the growing ties with Japan. For two decades after World War II, relations between the Republic and Japan remained very bad, symbolized by the deep hatred for Japan held by men like Syngman Rhee. On June 22, 1965, however, a treaty between the two nations was signed in Tokyo which inaugurated a new era in South Korean-Japanese relations. That treaty was not concluded without prolonged, sometimes stormy negotiations, and bitter internal protests within Korea. Nevertheless, in the six years that have passed since 1965, relations with Japan have steadily become more significant for the Republic, particularly in the economic sphere. In 1969, for example, Japan imported Korean products valued at nearly $150 million, with every indication that trade in both directions would expand rapidly in the future. Japanese investment in Korea was one vitally important element in the dramatic economic spurt taking place in the Republic in recent years.

Meanwhile, the Japanese government, together with a significant element of informed Japanese opinion, has indicated that the Republic and its future are of more than economic interest. Premier Sato and others have stated explicitly that the security of South Korea bears a direct relation to the security of Japan. Hence, bases in Japan proper will be available for American use should the security of the Republic be threatened by external aggression. Despite the oft-repeated Communist assertion that a Northeast Asian Treaty Organization is in the making, however, concrete military links between South Korea and Japan are far from established. Japanese constitutional restrictions, the mutual prejudices of these two peoples, and the strong reluctance of the Japanese public currently to support any external military commitment all serve as barriers. The Japanese government has thus ruled out, at least for the present, any direct military aid to the Republic, and President Pak has stated that Korea desires no such pledge from Japan—only economic interaction.

For the foreseeable future, the security of northeast Asia will hinge primarily upon a series of bilateral arrangements, with the United States situated as the central spoke of the system. Each nation will be expected to assume the primary responsibility for its own defense, with the American nuclear umbrella serving as a shield against superpower assault. Such a system is not completely satisfactory to South Korea, and despite their reservations about Japan, many Korean leaders talk of the need for a meaningful *Asian* collective security system. Japan may come to play a more active collective security role, possibly even starting to furnish the Republic of Korea with advanced military equipment and specialized military training. Any full-fledged military alliance between the Republic and Japan would appear to be precluded for the near future, however, with general trends in the Pacific-Asia region determining events beyond 1975. Meanwhile, concern over American credibility has produced a decided uneasiness among South Korea's leaders, with one repercussion being a significant political tightening on the domestic front.

FOREIGN POLICY INNOVATIONS

The Republic of Korea has sought to expand its international contacts, both political and economic, substantially in the past decade. First, it should be noted that despite Communist bloc protests and opposition from some of the Afro-Asian group, the United Nations continues to maintain an official presence in Korea. Technically, the Korean war has not been concluded, and the UN Commission continues to operate in South Korea. The UN presence, however, is essentially a token one apart from the American element, and the practice of submitting the Korean reunification issue automatically to the United Nations each year has finally been discarded.

At present, the Republic of Korea is recognized by 92 nations, and by 1969, the Republic traded with no less than 98 countries. For many reasons, as we have noted, relations are closest with the United States and Japan, but some 50,000 South Korean troops were dispatched to South Vietnam. In addition, some 35–40,000 Korean technicians have been dispatched abroad, adding substantially to South Korean foreign exchange earnings in the 1965–1970 period. In late 1970, the Republic even established its own technical assistance agency, with a hospital and technical assistance in irrigation having previously been given to South Vietnam, and a ceramics factory built for the African state of Niger. Indeed, the South and North have consciously vied in recent years for the approval of "the newly emerging world," with good will missions and small aid programs being advanced by both governments. Moreover, the Republic has recently indicated that it was prepared to apply the so-called Halstein Principle "flexibly" (originally a principle advanced by the Federal Republic of Germany that it would not accept diplomatic relations with states granting formal recognition to East Germany).

Indeed, at present, South Korea officially classifies Communist nations into two categories: hostile and non-hostile. The former category includes North Korea, North Vietnam, Communist China and the Soviet Union at present. All other Communist states (including Cuba) are classified as non-hostile, and the new Republic trade law permits economic intercourse with them.

POLICY TOWARD NORTH KOREA

South Korean diplomatic missions have greatly expanded, and foreign policies have clearly become more flexible since the Rhee era. Relations with the North, however, remain much the same despite the recent initiation of talks between the Southern and Northern Red Cross representatives. The 17th parallel between North and South Korea is probably the tightest boundary in the world today. Contacts of any type with the North have been banned since 1948 under the National Security Law. The only physical connection between South and North Korea consists of two strands of telephone wire. These connect the North Korean Armistice Commission office with the United Nations Armistice Commission in Panmunjom. The UN Command contacts the Communists by using its line, and gets the response from the Communists on their line!

Is progress toward peaceful unification possible? The Republic of Korea has long supported the position that unification should be accomplished under UN aegis, and in accordance with the original UN proposals for supervised, free elections in both Koreas. In recent years, President Pak has on several occasions asserted that the prerequisites for any change in South-North relations are for the North Korean Communists to desist from all types of military provocation, including the dispatch of armed agents to the South, and to make a public announcement that they will henceforth renounce their policies of seeking to Communize the whole of Korea by force. When this happens, and "is verified by the United Nations," Pak has stated, the Republic would propose various concrete measures for South-North relations, presumably involving exchange of communications and other forms of contact. Moreover, according to Pak, *when* the North Koreans are prepared to recognize UN authority and competence with respect to the unification issue, "we would not be opposed to the North Korean Communists' presence at the UN deliberations on the Korean question."[5]

Republic leaders couple the demand that the North desist from its efforts at "liberation" by subversion and war with a strong public commitment to ultimate unification. Both South and North insist that in the end, there can be only one Korea. Southern leaders have now begun to call for peaceful competition—in development, construction and creativity. In recent years, they have permitted various academic conferences to be held in the South on the unification issue. Indeed, in comparison with earlier years, the present leadership has shown a greater willingness to have public discussion of the issue, as well as advancing certain concrete proposals. As might be expected, however, southern proposals are dismissed as "preposterous" by Kim Il-sŏng, who takes a hard line of a very different sort on the unification issue, as we shall soon note.

Thus, the prospects for quick or easy progress seem slim. The Red Cross talks, initiated in the summer of 1971, by the end of the year, had made virtually no progress. The North clearly hoped to initiate people-to-people contacts in the South, taking advantage of its much tighter police-state structure, and the South was as clearly reluctant to let this happen. The two Koreas are currently light-years away from the level of contact and degree of accommodation which now characterize the two Germanys. The background governing the two situations, of course, is also radically different. Enormous enmity was built up as a result of the Korean war, and huge casualties were suffered on both sides. Until recently, moreover, economic development in the authoritarian North was more rapid than in the quasi-open South, and southern leaders frankly admitted that this was a strongly inhibiting factor since the South wished to enter unification discussions "from strength—both economic and politico-military." In this respect, perhaps, the South was analogous to East Germany.

Despite the difficulties, however, both South and North are now talking publicly about the issue, and it is conceivable that within this decade, the first solid steps toward contact will be taken. Unquestion-

---

[5] B. C. Koh, "Dilemmas of Korean Reunification," *Asian Survey*, Vol. XI, No. 5 (May 1971), p. 491. For additional evidence of official Republic positions, see *Text of Government Memorandum to U.N.* (1), in *The D. R. P. Bulletin*, November 1, 1970, pp. 5–7, and Shin Tai-whan (Minister of The National Unification Board), "Prospect for Territorial Unification," *Ibid.*, January 1, 1970, pp. 6–9.

ably, such a movement would be facilitated if the North, even as an unannounced, informal act, would give up its commitment to unification by force. The replacement of Kim Il-sŏng might also provide an opportunity for new, more constructive approaches since Kim has long proclaimed the "liberation" of the South on Communist terms his primary objective, and all North Korean organs refer to him as the "Great Leader of the *Forty Million* [i.e., all] Korean People."[6]

For the South, therefore, the decade of the 1970's will continue to be a dangerous one, necessitating heavy military expenditures and requiring constant vigilance, with the risk always that these requirements will damage the prospects for political openness and/or economic development. Indeed, recent political trends are very worrisome. At this point, nonetheless, the Republic of Korea enjoys a better international reputation than at any time since its creation, and clearly, without abandoning its basic ties with the United States, it hopes to create and maintain a broader, more flexible foreign policy that does not preclude relations with neutrals and even Communists. Recognizing that its immediate future is closely tied to the policies of the United States and Japan, the Republic of Korea nevertheless hopes to advance its international legitimacy and underwrite its security by having the widest possible range of economic and political contacts—with a corresponding reduction in the ideological quotient in its international relations.

North Korea: Determinants of Foreign Policy

Such a policy, if successful, will mean a more independent, nationalist Republic of Korea, albeit, one still closely interactive with the key non-Communist nations of the Pacific-Asian region. How does such a position compare with that of North Korea, or—to use its official designation—the Democratic People's Republic of Korea? The DPRK was a product of the Soviet occupation as much as the Republic was a product of the American occupation. Indeed, as one of the most conservative societies of the 20th century, Korea was one of the least likely candidates for Communist success. North Korean Communism was fathered by the Soviet Army, not by an indigenous

[6] For example, at the outset of the 5th Party Congress in November 1970, Kim was hailed in the P'yŏngyang press and radio as "Comrade Kim Il-sŏng, the great leader of the 40 million people, peerless patriot, national hero, ever-victorious, iron-willed brilliant commander, one of the outstanding leaders of the international Communist movement and working-class movement, and General Secretary of the Central Committee of our Party." P'yŏngyang Radio, November 2, 1970.

revolution. Moreover, Kim Il-sŏng owes his initial success strictly to Soviet support. He was practically unknown in Korea in 1945, and had no public support.[7]

Today, the DPRK is one of the purest examples of a monocracy—a government by one man—that exists in the contemporary world. This society of fourteen million (less than one-half of the population of the South) is under the Stalinist rule of Kim Il-sŏng who appears to be in absolute control of party, state and army. Naturally, one man cannot make all decisions. More importantly, he cannot guarantee that his orders will not be frustrated by a subordinate bureaucracy, or by a populace which, however loyal, cannot perform miracles. There can be no question, however, that decision-making on critical matters, domestic and foreign, rests with Kim who combines in his personage the offices of Secretary-General of the Korean Workers' Party, Premier of the DPRK, and Marshal and Commander-in-Chief of the Korean People's Army.

RELATIONS WITH COMMUNIST STATES

The foreign policy, like all other aspects of policy of the DPRK, is proclaimed to rest upon *chuch'e*, or self-reliance. Indeed, an extreme nationalism together with a high quotient of isolation, have governed North Korean attitudes and policies for more than a decade. Interestingly, the North Korean leaders found Communist internationalism largely bogus, at least as it was visited upon them. As a client state of the Soviet Union in its initial years, the DPRK was so thoroughly controlled that Kim Il-sŏng himself admitted in later years that they were even told by Soviet authorities what to print in their newspapers and what to study in their schools.

Naturally, the Korean war heightened North Korean dependence upon both the Soviet Union and Communist China. Virtually all military equipment had to be obtained from abroad, and some three-fourths of it came from the Soviet Union. Understandably, therefore, the decision to strike against the South had to be cleared with Stalin, and Soviet military advisors were with Kim throughout the conflict. The Chinese were less influential in the initial period but when their troops were required to save the North Korean regime from obliteration, they came in force, and remained until 1958. In postwar rehabilitation also, the Communist bloc was as indispensable to the

[7] For details, see Dai-sook Suh, *The Korean Communist Movement—1918–1948* (Princeton, New Jersey: Princeton University Press, 1967), espec. Part V, pp. 253–329. Also, *Communism in Korea* by this author and Chong-Sik Lee, Chapters III and V (Berkeley and Los Angeles: University of California Press, 1972).

North as were the United States and other allies to the South. Precise figures are impossible to obtain, but it is estimated that external aid amounting to over $1 billion was extended to P'yŏngyang in the years immediately following the Korean war. Entire factories were set up by Russians, Czechs, and Poles. The Chinese and others provided the essential foodstuffs to keep the North Korean people alive in the terrible years immediately after the war.

By the mid-1950's, however, the involvement of Russia and China in Korean affairs threatened serious internal repercussions. The Korean Communist movement had always been composed of very heterogeneous elements—"domestic" Communists who had remained in Korea, underground; the "Kapsan" or Manchurian guerrilla forces centering upon Kim; men who had intimate connections with the Chinese Communists at Yenan and elsewhere; and Soviet-Koreans, the group most closely attached to the Soviet Union. Kim had eliminated his key rivals from the domestic faction during the Korean war, having the leaders executed on charges of treason that were almost certainly fictitious in the main. In 1956, however, another internal struggle boiled up, and on this occasion, both the Soviet Union and Chinese People's Republic attempted intervention in an effort to save certain Korean comrades close to them from being purged. The effort was ultimately unsuccessful, but it clearly posed a major threat to Kim Il-sŏng, and remains an episode which he has never forgotten.

From this point, chuch'e was given steadily increased emphasis, both as a weapon against internal rivals who were accused of being sycophants of foreign powers, and as a weapon against those powers. Perhaps such a policy succeeded largely because the two Communist giants were soon to be engaged in a progressively more bitter quarrel, making the type of collaboration undertaken in 1956 impossible. In any case, the basic lines of DPRK foreign policy for the past decade can be discerned as follows: an effort to maintain an independent position within the Communist world, while at the same time standing firm on an international "revolutionary" line; close relations with various small Communist parties and revolutionary groups, especially groups in a strategic position to take action against such governments as those of Japan and the United States; staunch maintenance of economic as well as political nationalism, but a gradual increase of efforts to achieve international recognition, with special emphasis upon the Asian-African arena, and a modest expansion of trade with the non-Communist world; and finally, a dedication to the "liberation" of the South under Communist aegis, with Vietnam currently considered the appropriate model.

Let us examine each of these central North Korean policy commitments briefly. When the Sino-Soviet cleavage first broke into the open, North Korea like many small Communist states and parties, sought to maintain neutrality, and from time-to-time, in conjunction with others, to act as mediator. Ultimately, this policy failed, because it was impossible to convince Moscow that "neutrality" was possible. At the end of the Khrushchev era, P'yŏngyang-Moscow relations were extremely bad, and as one result, Soviet military and economic aid to North Korea was severely reduced, helping to produce some of the same problems in the DPRK that the People's Republic of China had encountered when Russian assistance was abruptly cancelled in 1959. Meanwhile, on such substantive issues as de-Stalinization, Albania, Cuba, the Indian-Chinese border controversy, and the nuclear proliferation ban treaty, the positions of North Korea and China were almost indistinguishable by the 1963–1964 period. P'yŏngyang authorities now began to issue bitter philippics against the iniquities of "modern revisionism," with specific references to Soviet policies that were barely veiled.[8]

In these years, the concerns of the North Korean leaders were similar to those of Peking: Soviet "big power chauvinism," including its interference in the internal affairs of fraternal states and parties, and the stern retaliatory measures which it took against those who challenged Soviet policy; and the fear of Soviet-American rapprochement, seen as involving superpower manipulation of international politics in such a fashion as to disadvantage revolutionary movements and causes.

As indicated, however, the costs of estrangement from the Soviet Union proved to be extremely high. North Korean factories and military equipment had to have parts and replacements. Hence, when the Brezhnev-Kosygin era came into being, Kim Il-sŏng accepted "normalization" of Soviet-DPRK relations as a necessary economic-military measure. North Korean leaders, however, including Kim, continued to attack "revisionism," and to indicate substantial policy differences with Moscow. From all appearances, "normalization" was an act of necessity, but not of great warmth.

Shortly, problems emerged on the other side of the ledger. In the spring of 1966, efforts were made by certain "small" Asian Communists (the Japanese Communist party taking the lead) to bring Peking and Moscow into some measure of accord so that more effective aid could be given to the hard-pressed North Vietnamese.[9] This effort failed, and the blame was placed upon the intransigence of Mao Tse-tung

[8] See the remarkable article, "Let Us Defend the Socialist Camp," *Nodong Sinmun* (The Workers' News), October 28, 1963, pp. 1–2.

[9] For certain details, see Robert A. Scalapino, *The Japanese Communist Movement, 1920–1966*, pp. 266–272 (Berkeley and Los Angeles: University of California Press, 1967).

himself. Relations between Peking and P'yŏngyang grew worse, and at the height of the so-called Great Proletarian Cultural Revolution, various Red Guard posters sprang up in Peking and elsewhere, attacking Kim Il-sŏng personally, and criticizing North Korea's efforts to "sit on two stools." Certain prominent leaders close to Mao including K'ang Sheng, moreover, privately warned party cadres to beware of the "subversive activities" of the Soviet and Korean Communists in Manchuria.[10] With the end of the Cultural Revolution, however, relations with China were quickly mended, no doubt as a result of an assessment of mutual national interests. Thus, when Chou En-lai visited P'yŏngyang in April 1970, he spoke as of old, proclaiming China and Korea as being neighbors as closely related as lips and teeth, and standing together as comrades-in-arms against Japanese and American imperialism.[11]

By a process of weaving and feinting, first to one side and then to the other, Kim and his party—sandwiched between two quarreling Communist giants—have managed to survive, and maintain a certain independence. Nevertheless, the breakdown of Communist internationalism has brought serious problems to North Korea for nearly two decades. For Russian, Chinese and Korean comrades, this has been a most uncomradely era, and if relations today are correct—with the Chinese, even seemingly cordial once more—it is very doubtful whether Kim Il-sŏng will ever fully trust either Peking or Moscow again. Nor is it certain that one of the major Communist states will not attempt at some future point to intervene once more in North Korea's internal politics, particularly when Kim is replaced.

At the same time, Kim knows that North Korea is heavily dependent upon both major Communist states, and particularly the Soviet Union, for survival and growth. Since 1961, the DPRK has had a Treaty of Friendship, Cooperation and Mutual Assistance with both the Soviet Union and the Chinese People's Republic, providing for basically the same type of assistance afforded the Republic of Korea in its treaty with the United States. Under the provisions of this treaty and supplemental agreements, moreover, the Russians have furnished the North Koreans with such highly-modern military equipment as PT-75 tanks,

---

[10] For excerpts of a K'ang Sheng speech reportedly made on February 8, 1968 to party and military personnel in Kirin Province containing the attack on "the enemy agent activities of the Korean revisionists," see *Ch'ing-li Chieh-chi Tui-wu* (Purification of Class Ranks), compiled by the Pao-shan (Yunnan) Revolutionary Committee Political Work Section, January 1969, contained in Joint Publications Research Service, *Translations on Communist China*, No. 140, March 18, 1971, pp. 34–38 (pp. 36–37).

[11] See *Peking Review*, April 10, 1970, pp. 3–24 (p. 22).

surface-to-air missiles, missile patrol boats, and MIG-21 fighter air-craft. Moreover, despite some changes of potential significance in the 1960's, close to 85 percent of North Korean foreign trade as of 1968 was still conducted with the Communist states, the great bulk of it with the Soviet Union.[12] Thus, *chuch'e* has its limits as well as its costs.

We can assume that as long as Communist internationalism works so badly, and the Sino-Soviet cleavage continues, the DPRK will continue to seek "normalized" relations with its two big Communist neighbors to protect its independence, fully aware of the impossibility of a truly unified Communist bloc. For the lifetime of Kim Il-sŏng at least, North Korea will also be counted among the more "militant" elements in the Communist world, strongly resisting "revisionism," Soviet-style.

The character of international relations within the Communist bloc in recent years has led to circumstances not too dissimilar from those governing historic relations among western states: alliance, enmity, and "neutralism" have all emerged *within* the Communist arena. Thus, in the 1960's, when confronted with Communist "big power chauvin-ism," North Korea drew closer to some of the small Asian Communist parties that faced similar problems, notably the Japanese, Indonesian, and Vietnamese parties. With them, it formed an alliance of sorts, involving frequent consultations, common political positions, the proffering of mediator services, and—in the case of the Japanese, at least—probably some financial aid from P'yŏngyang, particularly after the JCP's troubles with Peking.

The alliance of "the small Asian Communists" faced a rocky road, with the Indonesians soon to be decimated in the backlash to the abortive coup of 1965 in which they participated; the Vietnamese forced to be extremely cautious as a result of their growing depen-dence upon both the Soviet Union and China; and the relative impotence of the Japanese Communists. Nevertheless, in some mea-sure, the alliance has continued, with ties between P'yŏngyang and the JCP being especially close. Meanwhile, North Korea has also sought to cultivate other revolutionary forces, and according to certain reports, it set up in 1966 a guerrilla warfare training center for foreign youths to which more than 2,000 youths from between 25–30 countries came. Subsequently, revolutionary bands in such countries as Mexico and Ceylon have been connected with these

[12] See also Premier Chou En-lai's speech of June 24, 1970 in Peking welcoming a DPRK delegation headed by Pak Sung-ch'ol, Peking Radio, June 24, 1970, in *Survey of China Mainland Press,* July 1970, pp. 23–25.

activities.[13] A few American groups, notably the Black Panthers via Eldridge Cleaver, and some of their white auxiliaries, have also come back from North Korean visits as state guests filled with praise for Kim's revolutionary ardor.

NORTH KOREA AND NON-COMMUNIST STATES

Every Communist state today seeks to conduct foreign policy on at least three levels, more or less simultaneously: government to government; people to people; and comrade to comrade. Since the policies pursued at these various levels are frequently incompatible, hard choices must sometimes be made, with the mix being altered from time-to-time, depending upon the character of immediate goals and the "objective" international situation. Thus, while the DPRK has recently sought to create an image of itself throughout the Communist (and revolutionary) world as the foremost exponent of the armed struggle for power and the unstinting supporter of global revolution, it has also sought to expand its contacts with various non-Communist governments, both for political and economic reasons.

By the end of 1970, the DPRK had diplomatic relations with 36 "nations." Of these, 13 were in the Communist bloc (including Yugoslavia), and the "Provisional Revolutionary Government of Vietnam"; 18 were African and Middle Eastern states; 3 non-Communist Asian states; 1 was Latin American (Cuba), and 1 was the Maldives. While this represents far less international recognition than that accorded the Republic of Korea, the DPRK has made diplomatic gains in recent years, especially within Africa. At the same time, trade relations have been established with other states, notably Japan, with lesser economic exchange being conducted with the Netherlands, West Germany, Australia, Great Britain and Greece. Trade with non-Communist countries remains small, scarcely 15 percent of total trade. Moreover, as indicated earlier, the goals remain strongly those of economic nationalism. At the 5th Party Congress in November 1970, Kim and others announced an effort to achieve 65–70 percent self-sufficiency in the raw materials needed for industrial production.[14]

---

[13] Ceylon broke its recently established relations with the DPRK in the aftermath of evidence that the rebellion of 1971 by young Ceylonese dissidents had received some North Korean support. For a report on this and the involvement of P'yŏngyang with Mexican radicals, see "North Korea—An International Guerrilla Training Center," *Journal of Korean Affairs*, Vol. I, No. 1, April 1971, pp. 35–36.

[14] See *Nodong Sinmun*, November 3, 1970, pp. 107, for Kim's report.

Nevertheless, like the Chinese People's Republic, the DPRK has shown that it can separate politics from economics when the needs are sufficiently great.

NORTH KOREA: POLICY TOWARD THE SOUTH

In the final analysis, however, most aspects of DPRK foreign policy have been subordinated to or oriented toward the goal of "liberating" South Korea. For many years, the basic proposals of Kim Il-sŏng regarding unification have remained the same: first, the United States must withdraw all of its forces from the South, and in effect, the Mutual Defense Treaty between the United States and the Republic of Korea must be dismantled; second, discussions must be conducted between "democratic personages" from both states, looking toward the reduction of armed forces on both sides to 100,000 men or less. At this point, various exchanges, economic and cultural, can commence, and a political consultative conference attended by all bona fide political parties and organizations (to be read those considered "democratic" by the Communists) will be held. Subsequently, unification is to be accomplished either by general North-South elections, or if a transitional step is necessary, through a confederation of the North and South.

This proposal, most recently put forward in slightly revised language by North Korean Foreign Minister Ho Tam (the husband of Kim Il-sŏng's cousin) on April 13, 1971,[15] is based upon three underlying positions: that the Pak Chong-hi government must be toppled; that all external commitments to the Republic must be ended; and that unification must, in the final analysis, take place under Communist aegis.

Despite earlier indications that it would enter into no agreements with the Pak regime, however, the DPRK accepted with alacrity the proposal for South-North Red Cross talks in mid-1971. Why? While violently anti-Pak, Kim Il-sŏng has long wanted greater access to the people of South Korea, and the use of the unification issue as a polit-

[15] For Ho Tam's unification proposal, see *New York Times*, April 14, 1971. For additional official expressions of the view on unification and the South Korean "liberation" movement, see "Let Us Overthrow the Pak Chong-hui Clique, Which is Going on the Rampage to Implement Its Wild Ambition for Long-Term Office by Resorting to Oppression, Political Tricks, Swindle, and Frauds," Editorial, *Nodong Sinmun*, April 26, 1971, p. 1; and Yi P'il-su, "A Mass Struggle is Needed for the South Korean Revolutionary Forces," *Kulloja*, March 1, 1971, pp. 57–64. A general survey of the North Korean position is contained in *Kulloja*, The Worker, December 1, 1970, pp. 37–43. See also Benjamin H. Min, "North Korea's Foreign Policy: A Survey," *Journal of Korean Affairs, op. cit.*, pp. 3–13.

ical weapon against ROK leaders. Kim counts upon his superior political organization, and the police-state controls over dissidence which he has perfected, minimizing the impact of such contacts in the North, while they are fully exploited in the South. (Recent developments would suggest that Pak has similar worries.)

Changes in Chinese foreign policy, particularly with respect to Sino-American relations, may also have influenced Kim. Following Peking's lead, P'yŏngyang now gives some indication of hoping to enter the world, including the UN—on its own terms—while at the same time, going onto the political offensive with respect to unification, exploiting such elements of openness in the South as exist. With respect to Japan also, Kim has signalled his interest in expanded "people-to-people" relations, without abandoning his attacks upon the government.

Kim Il-sŏng has asserted on numerous occasions that the liberation of the South will require an armed struggle, and it is a struggle in which the North expects to participate. Since 1962, a major military effort has been underway in North Korea, with approximately one-third of the total budget going for military expenditures. On a per capita basis, the DPRK is one of the most highly militarized states in the world today, with 470,000 out of its 14 million citizens in the regular armed forces, and a people's militia of 1,400,000. Beginning in the late 1960's, moreover, the infiltration of agents and armed bands from North to South was stepped up—a climax was reached in 1968.

The model, however, is not Korea—1950, but Vietnam—1960 and thereafter. Kim does not presently contemplate another effort to march with a major force across the DMZ. Rather, he hopes to direct a major political campaign against the South, establishing an underground branch of the party there; furnishing it with funds, supplies, and training and moving it toward guerrilla warfare and terrorist activities of a disruptive nature. Meanwhile he hopes the North will serve as "the impregnable revolutionary base," providing all assistance necessary as the advanced stages are reached, including manpower.

Kim and his followers have made no secret of these plans. Their basic outline had been presented at various party gatherings, and in the media. Naturally, party leaders have referred to such events as the attempt of 31 North Korean commandos to assassinate President Pak in January 1968, and the sizeable infiltration activities of the fall of that year as efforts undertaken by "heroic South Korean patriots." They have also proclaimed that the Revolutionary Party for Reunification (the Communist branch that they have attempted to establish in the South), is purely an indigenous effort—despite the fact that when it was uncovered in 1968, its leaders admitted that funds, training and support came directly from the North and that they had made numerous secret trips to P'yŏngyang via high-powered speed boats.

To date, progress in "liberating" the South has been extremely disappointing to Kim, and very costly. Unquestionably, the high military expenditures of the 1960's had a depressing effect upon economic growth and living standards. As a result, there has been some retreat from the adventurism of the 1967–1968 period, and Kim has promised a heavier concentration upon economic growth in the period immediately ahead. However, there is absolutely no indication that the idea of "liberation" has been abandoned. On the contrary, all party conferences continue to emphasize the critical importance of helping to free the southern brethren from their bondage. Thus relations between the Republic and the DPRK remain those of belligerents, with violence always close to the surface on the Korean Peninsula.

South Vietnam

In Vietnam violence is not merely close to the surface but omnipresent. The Republic of Vietnam (South Vietnam) was officially born on October 26, 1955, more than a year after Ngo Dinh Diem had achieved virtually absolute power as South Vietnam's first effective indigenous leader in its modern history. The Constitution of 1956,[16] provided for a republican form of government under a presidential system. The National Assembly had vested in it the power to approve of all laws, and of all international treaties and convocations as well. Moreover, the declaration of war or conclusion of peace had to have the agreement of at least one-half of the National Assembly. However, the 1956 Constitution also provided that "The President is vested with the leadership of the nation," and in the tumultuous years of its precarious existence, the Republic's policies—foreign and domestic— have been concentrated primarily in the hands of the president—be he Diem or Nguyen van Thieu. At the height of his powers, Diem was without challenge in basic decision-making, with the Cabinet his personal instrument, and the Assembly totally controlled by him. Now, the Republic is officially under a new Constitution, enacted in 1967.[17] At present, the representative branch of government composed of two

[16] For an informed, detailed analysis of the 1956 Constitution, see J. A. C. Grant, "The Vietnam Constitution of 1956," *American Political Science Review*, June, 1958, p. 440.

[17] For an analysis of the Constitution of 1967, and the processes involved in enactment of the new fundamental law, see Robert Devereux, "South Vietnam's New Constitutional Structure," *Asian Survey*, Vol. VIII, No. 8, August 1968, pp. 627–645.

Houses, has a fairly wide range of membership, including some individuals strongly opposed to the President and prepared to advance alternate policies. Nevertheless, the executive branch towers over the legislative in real power, and in the final analysis, the basic policies are those of the president. A strong presidential system continues—both as a product of law and, more importantly, of the political circumstances presently governing this society.

Throughout the fifteen years of its existence, the Republic of Vietnam has been engaged in a desperate struggle for survival. Its foreign policies, inextricably connected with the domestic situation, betoken this fact. When it came into being the Republic was quickly recognized by 35 nations—15 of them western—11 Latin American, 6 Asian, and 3 African (including the Union of South Africa).[18] As might have been expected, those recognizing the Republic of Vietnam at this point were the more vitriolic anti-Communist states. In the years between 1956 and 1968, however, a large number of additional countries recognized the South Vietnamese government, including almost all states not currently either Communist or in the "non-aligned" bloc. By the end of 1968, some 98 nations had recognized the Republic at one point or another, although that recognition was subsequently withdrawn or allowed to lapse in some cases either as a result of political changes within the state concerned or due to other circumstances. Diplomatic relations between France and the Republic, for example, were broken as a result of deep hostility between de Gaulle and Saigon; Sweden turned away from the Republic, and gave permission for the National Liberation Front to establish offices in Stockholm. In other cases—such as Cuba and the Congo (Brazzaville)—moves to the left produced a rupture. Nevertheless, the Republic has retained recognition from well over one-half of the nations of the world, although its diplomatic missions abroad are very limited at present.

To date, four factors have dominated the foreign policies of South Vietnam: near-total dependence upon the United States for survival; a deep antagonism at the governmental level toward France, the ex-colonial power, and toward the Communist states; limited external relations, except with certain neighboring Asian states and with Japan; and a dedication to the principle of maintaining a separate, independent status vis-à-vis the Democratic People's Republic of Vietnam (DPRV) the Communist regime of the north.

---

[18] The lists of states officially recognizing the Republic of Vietnam, having trade relations with it, or engaged in cultural exchange were furnished the author by the Vietnamese Consulate, San Francisco.

At this point, the future of the Republic appears to hinge heavily upon three interrelated factors: internal political and socio-economic developments; the policies and attitudes of Hanoi; and those of Washington. For the moment, let us center our attention on the question of American involvement and policies.[19] In one way or another, the United States has been involved in Indochina since Ho Chi Minh and his guerrilla forces were first given some logistical support in their drive to penetrate Japanese-controlled Vietnam near the close of World War II. As is well-known, that involvement increased significantly with the Eisenhower decision to provide a full range of aid and support to the Diem administration; the Kennedy decision to prevent the Communists from taking South Vietnam by force of arms; and the Johnson decision to prevent a South Vietnamese collapse by sending a major American military force to that country. This is not the place to review those decisions or others connected with them. For the Republic of Vietnam today, the issue is future American policy. The Nixon Doctrine has its most critical test here. The aim of that policy is to make it possible for South Vietnam to defend itself against the North Vietnamese (and their southern Communist allies) while gradually withdrawing American military forces.

This policy is under considerable attack at home and abroad. The Vietnam war has been even more divisive than the Korean war for the American public, and a number of Americans, including some in high political office, are arguing for the immediate, total withdrawal of American forces, an abandonment of South Vietnam, and an acceptance of Communist control of Indochina. Others are not as extreme but are nevertheless inclined to support a rapid withdrawal policy—their patience exhausted by one of the longest wars in American history and by the rise of a multitude of internal problems and needs. The currents of isolationism are now running strong once again on the American scene: for reasons not dissimilar to those that advanced isolationism after World War I.

Nor is there any guarantee that the Nixon Doctrine will work in Vietnam, even if domestic political conditions permit it to be applied.

---

[19] For four serious works presenting the background of the Vietnam war in different perspectives, see Ellen J. Hammer, *The Struggle for Indochina—1940–1955*, 1966 edition (Stanford, California: Stanford University Press, 1966); Joseph Buttinger, *Vietnam: A Political History* (New York: Praeger, 1968); Chester A. Bain, *Vietnam—The Roots of Conflict* (Englewood Cliffs, New Jersey: Prentice-Hall, 1967); and John T. McAlister, Jr., *Vietnam—The Origins of Revolution* (New York: Alfred Knopf, 1969).

It is generally recognized that the optimum opportunity for its success in military terms demands the continued use of American air power and American military advisors for a substantial period after American ground forces have been withdrawn—unless a political settlement is reached which would provide for the mutual withdrawal of all external forces, including those of North Vietnam. It is also conceded that substantial American economic and technical assistance, as was granted to the Republic of Korea, will be necessary, even if the Republic of Vietnam survives militarily.

The assumption that because South Vietnam is heavily dependent upon American support, its leaders are "puppets" avidly responding to every American suggestion and/or command is one of those doctrines that survives in non-Communist as well as in Communist circles despite all of the evidence to the contrary. "My-Diem" or "American-Diem" was a couplet ceaselessly advanced by the Communists in an effort to show that Ngo Dinh Diem was merely a tool of American imperialism.[20] Yet even at this point, with the documentary evidence far from complete, we know that relations between the United States and the Diem administration were never completely smooth, and that the most serious differences over policies periodically erupted, with Diem frequently rejecting American advice. So it has been in the post-Diem era.

It would be a fascinating study to analyze the relations between the "superpowers" and their small allies or, as some would prefer to call them, their client states, taking such examples as American-South Korean, American-South Vietnamese, Soviet-East German, and Soviet-Rumanian relations as case studies. Almost certainly, relations between the United States and its small allies would be seen as taking a freer form because of the ambivalence and uncertainty with which the United States has applied its power in such instances. Domestic critics, indeed, have often argued that the United States in point of fact is victimized by its allies, and should be far more insistent upon a quid pro quo relation with such states.

In any case, the present leaders of South Vietnam—like their predecessors—are pro-Vietnamese, not pro-American, and they would

[20] For an account of the Diem years, including issues of foreign policy, see Robert Scigliano, *South Vietnam: Nation Under Stress* (Boston: Houghton-Mifflin, 1963), and Bernard B. Fall, *The Two Vietnams—A Political and Military Analysis*, Revised Edition (New York and London: Praeger, 1962). These two sources, the first from an American participant-scholar perspective, the second from a French observer-scholar point of view, taken together, provide the most objective overview of the Diem era in English yet available, although both works are naturally affected by the period during which they were written.

strongly prefer a situation where dependence upon America could be substantially reduced. Inevitably, heavy, long-sustained dependence breeds resentment. It also encourages the development of a wide range of techniques—some of them exceedingly subtle—whereby to increase one's independence, flexibility and leverage. All of these factors are present in current American-South Vietnamese relations. Moreover, whoever leads the Republic of Vietnam in the future— assuming that that Republic survives—can be expected to seek a movement in foreign policy similar in its broad direction to that taken recently by the Republic of Korea.

RELATIONS WITH OTHER STATES

Meanwhile, the present South Vietnamese leaders betray an understandable schizophrenia toward France, a country under whose political aegis most of them were reared.[21] Like their North Vietnamese Communist counterparts, many of the non-Communist leaders are far more at home with the French language, French culture, *and* French administrative-legal precedents than with those of any other foreign nation. It has often been remarked, indeed, that the particular mixture of French and traditional political practices existing in Vietnam has constituted the worst possible combination from the standpoint of breaking through the layers of the past, and inaugurating the reforms and changes so necessary to improve the political health of South Vietnam.

If French influence is still substantial, however, circumstances have combined to cause a major deterioration in the political relation between the governments of France and South Vietnam in recent years, especially in the de Gaulle era. Many French leaders—and de Gaulle was prominent among them—would never forgive the United States for what they regarded as an undermining of the French position in Southeast Asia. In the trauma of their defeat and withdrawal, they blamed the United States, and naturally, some of the bitterness was transferred to those indigenous forces that allied themselves with America. With de Gaulle gone, and one of the last totally French-oriented leaders of the region—Sihanouk—ousted from power at least temporarily, new political relations between the French and the various leaders of the old Indochina may gradually be forged. The historic French role in this region, however, will never

[21] For one French perspective, see Jean Lacouture, *Vietnam: Between Two Truces,* with an introduction by Joseph Kraft, translated from the French by Konrad Kellen and Joel Carmichael (New York: Vintage Books, 1966).

be restored irrespective of the precise political future in store for it, and it is likely that even French cultural influence will gradually be diluted, mixed with other influences. Perhaps, with the colonial era irretrievably past, a healthier relationship can be established by all of the parties concerned—but for the near future, the elements of pain, anger and estrangement will be strong.

As might be expected, the Republic of Vietnam is currently shunned completely by the Communist states, with almost all of them according recognition in some form to the so-called Revolutionary Government of the National Liberation Front (RGNLF). This situation is likely to continue, at least until it becomes clear whether the Republic will survive and in what form. Apart from her relations with the United States, South Vietnam's most important relations have naturally been with the other states of Indochina, namely, Cambodia, Laos, and North Vietnam. Of almost equal importance, however, have been her relations with certain other Asian states facing similar Communist threats: the Republic of Korea, the Republic of China on Taiwan, and Thailand. Let us note both sets of relations briefly.

Under Sihanouk, relations between Cambodia and the Republic of Vietnam were extremely bad.[22] Sihanouk, firmly-committed to the belief that the Communists would win the war in South Vietnam, and angered by Saigon's support of certain anti-Sihanouk Cambodians, not only recognized the DRV and the RGNLF of South Vietnam as the legitimate governments of North and South, but also allowed the Communists to use eastern Cambodia as a privileged sanctuary, storage depot and staging ground for military campaigns.[23] With Sihanouk's overthrow, Cambodian-South Vietnamese relations at the official level changed radically. The government headed by Lon Nol not only reopened relations with the Republic, but solicited Saigon's military support in challenging the 50–70,000 North Vietnamese soldiers reportedly in Cambodian territory. Despite the very strong ethnic animosities between Cambodians and Vietnamese (of all political persuasions) at the grass-roots level, the two governments now conduct regular discussions on military and political matters of mutual

---

[22] For several works on Cambodian foreign policy and Sihanouk's views, see Roger M. Smith, *Cambodia's Foreign Policy* (Ithaca, New York: Cornell University Press, 1965); Michael Leifer, *Cambodia: The Search for Security* (New York: Praeger, 1967); and John P. Armstrong, *Sihanouk Speaks* (New York: Walker and Co., 1964).

[23] For two recent perspectives on the Cambodian situation, see Peter A. Poole, *Cambodia's Quest for Survival*, American-Asian Educational Exchange, 1969; and Douglas Pike, "Cambodia's War," *Southeast Asian Perspectives*, March 1971, pp. 1–48.

concern. Thus, the future of relations here presumably depends upon trends in domestic Cambodian politics—a matter of grave concern to all of the non-Communists, since it is recognized that the political-military situation in Cambodia is extremely fragile.

The Laotian government headed by Prince Souvannaphouma has consistently maintained an official neutrality toward North and South Vietnam, and Vientiane, the capital of Laos, hosts representatives of both Hanoi and Saigon.[24] Hanoi's consistent violation of the Laotian Agreement of 1962, however, has embittered Souvannaphouma and his government, causing it to take an increasingly anti-Communist stance during the past decade. The Laotians are aware of the fact that North Vietnam has at least 40–50,000 troops in Laos, and controls much of the southeastern section of the country; that it constitutes the backbone of the Pathet Lao, and controls their activities, even disciplining their leaders when they object to Hanoi decisions. Thus, Souvannaphouma clearly hopes for the survival of non-Communist governments in both Cambodia and South Vietnam, and recognizes, indeed, that his own survival depends upon this.

Within the last several years, therefore, the officially recognized governments of Laos and Cambodia have veered from neutrality or hostility toward the Republic of Vietnam to a position of interaction and/or support. However, the non-Communists of Indochina have not fashioned the same type of open alliance that was recently created under the aegis of Peking and Hanoi. The ouster of Sihanouk served as the background for the convening of a "conference of the Indochina people," with the Chinese prominently involved, and subsequently, Communist statements have indicated a pledge to "liberate" the whole of Indochina by overthrowing the governments currently in power. The Communists have thus officially proclaimed as policy something which shrewd external observers always maintained: the struggle now going on involves not merely Vietnam, but the whole of the old Indochina as well, and in all probability, other parts of continental Southeast Asia.

Apart from American assistance, South Vietnam has received its greatest external support militarily from the Republic of Korea, a state that had experienced its own "liberation" threat. Some 50,000 South Korean soldiers have been stationed in South Vietnam since 1968, operating in the northern sector. A small Thai detachment has also fought in Vietnam. It is these states, together with the

[24] The role of the North Vietnamese in Laos and their relation with the Pathet Lao is covered in excellent fashion in P. F. Langer and J. J. Zasloff, *Revolution in Laos: The North Vietnamese and the Pathet Lao* (Santa Monica, California: The Rand Corporation, 1969).

Nationalist government on Taiwan that share most closely the concern with Saigon over Communist efforts to subvert and overthrow non-Communist governments, since each faces a similar challenge.

The role of other non-Communist Asian states has varied from open friendship and assistance to open coolness and skepticism concerning the Republic's survival prospects. Malaysia and Singapore, deeply-troubled by the implications of a Communist victory in Indo-china, have espoused support for the Republic, and the former state has provided minor assistance such as the training of police units. Japan, the most powerful economic force in Asia and a nation with a significant stake in the future of this entire region, has also made no effort to disguise its hope that a non-Communist South Vietnam survives, and has given small amounts of economic assistance to the Republic. At the same time, faithful to its policy of separating politics from economics, the Japanese government does not prohibit trade between Japan and North Vietnam. Under propitious conditions, it would no doubt be prepared to undertake major investment and technical assistance in South Vietnam, while still pursuing "normal" relations—economic and quite possibly political as well—with North Vietnam.

Indonesia under Sukarno was completely hostile to the Republic, and had established full diplomatic relations with the North. Those relations continue under the Suharto government, but the attitude toward Communism has changed dramatically, and correspondingly, the South is now treated with a friendly neutrality. The Indonesian government, moreover, provided direct assistance in the form of military training to the Lon Nol government of Cambodia in its effort to fend off the North Vietnamese. India, on the other hand, while maintaining an official neutrality as a member of the International Control Commission which still moves between Saigon and Hanoi, has in fact shown a number of signs of favoring the Communists and their front, the National Liberation Front (NLF). In 1970, for instance, Madame Binh, RGNLF "Foreign Minister" and Paris negotiator, was received officially by Prime Minister Indira Gandhi. In the aftermath of its alliance with the USSR and the incursion into East Pakistan, moreover, India announced its intention to establish full diplomatic relations with Hanoi, whereupon Saigon demanded the reconstitution of the I.C.C.

On balance, however, the Republic of Vietnam has improved its position with its neighbors in Southeast Asia substantially in the past five years, primarily as a result of internal changes in some of the governments concerned, but partly as a result of new evaluations of Communist objectives in the region. Even among non-Communist states, however, there remains considerable skepticism as to whether a non-Communist South Vietnam (or Indochina) can survive, hence, a caution with respect to economic and political relations. Only as and if the Republic shows a capacity to sustain its existence during the coming, difficult years will relations with the key nations of the region become deeper and more meaningful.

Thus, in the final analysis, the most important issue currently for Republic foreign policy is also a domestic issue in part: how shall the war be ended, and what are appropriate policies with respect to the National Liberation Front and Hanoi? The present policy of the Thieu government on these matters is as follows: While the Constitution outlaws Communism in South Vietnam, the NLF (which as a front is not officially a Communist organization) can participate in Republic elections providing it is willing to give up its efforts to overthrow the government by force of arms. (In de facto terms, the NLF and its Communist leadership have been participating in recent South Vietnamese elections in a variety of ways, including the running and endorsing of candidates, especially at local levels—in addition to conducting their own "underground" elections.) However, the Communists insist upon a full range of legal and illegal tactics at this point, and have shown no interest in confining themselves to elections, or in seeking the legalization of the NLF and its pale companion, the Alliance of National, Democratic and Peace Forces. Naturally, distrust on both sides is enormous, and this fact alone makes a reliance upon legal procedures extremely difficult.

POLICY TOWARD NORTH VIETNAM

The agreement to allow NLF participation in elections while at the same time strongly opposing any coalition government with the Communists, or the establishment of any interim, "neutral" government for negotiatory or election purposes represents some change in the position of the Thieu government, a change influenced by American attitudes. With respect to relations with Hanoi also, recent developments indicate a somewhat greater element of flexibility, but a position far from that of the Communists. The South Vietnamese government, cognizant that the issue of Vietnam is seemingly inseparable from the broader issue of the fate of Indochina as a whole, has taken the following official position: the South Vietnamese people should have the right to determine their own future without having a political system imposed upon them by external force; the independence, sovereignty, territorial integrity and neutrality of Laos and Cambodia should be accepted by all parties; all external military forces should be withdrawn from South Vietnam, and from Laos and Cambodia as well (including the forces of North Vietnam); and a timetable for such withdrawal should have a high priority in international negotiations. Meanwhile, a cease-fire in place throughout the whole of Indochina would be acceptable if some international mechanism could serve to insure that all parties correctly observed the provisions of that cease-fire; all prisoners-of-war—Communist and non-Communist—should be immediately and unconditionally released; and an international conference should be convened to settle the entire Indochina conflict.

With respect to future relations with the North, the South Vietnamese government has asserted that it would be prepared to undertake certain economic exchanges, recognizing the need of the North for additional foodstuffs, and also to discuss such issues as private communications, cultural exchange, and eventual reunification.[25] It is clear, however, that the current Republic leaders do not envisage peaceful unification as a realistic prospect in the near future, and they are not willing to experiment with Communist, non-Communist political integration at any level.

North Vietnam

In contrast to the uncertain future of the Republic of Vietnam, the Democratic Republic of Vietnam (DRV) seems relatively stable despite the enormous costs of the war. It faces no serious threat of invasion from without, and internal opposition was eliminated long ago. Organized in the typical fashion of a Communist state, the DRV brooks no dissent from the decisions of the party Politburo. Even before the establishment of the present state, the Communists had skillfully and ruthlessly eliminated the leading non-Communist elements within the Viet Minh, guaranteeing them control of that movement, hence, leadership of the anti-French campaign. The preamble of the Constitution of 1960 begins with the statement that Vietnam is a single entity from Langson to Camau, and makes it emphatically clear that "the Indochinese Communist party—now the Dang Lao Dong (Vietnam Workers' Party)" is destined to govern that entity.

[25] For the official position of the Republic on reunification in the Diem era, see *The Reunification of Viet-Nam,* Ministry of Information of the Republic of Viet-Nam, Saigon, 1960. For a recent position, see the Statement by Ambassador Pham-Dang-Lam, Chief of the Delegation of the Republic of Viet-Nam at the 97th Plenary Session of the Paris Meetings on Viet-Nam, December 30, 1970, Release by the Delegation of the Republic of Viet-Nam.

It proclaims the founding of the Democratic Republic of Vietnam on September 2, 1945 as a result of the August Revolution, and bases the legitimacy of the state upon the elections of January 6, 1946, in which "the entire Vietnamese people, from north to south, enthusiastically took part." Thus within the Constitution itself, the major claims of the Communists are set forth: Vietnam is a single entity and the Workers' party is the only legitimate governing force.

The Communist interpretation of the 1954 Geneva Agreements is that after Dienbienphu, "the French imperialists and American interventionists" were defeated, and peace was restored on the basis of the recognition of the independence, sovereignty, unity and territorial integrity of Vietnam. However, only the North was completely liberated; hence, the Vietnamese revolution has entered a new phase, with the North moving toward Socialism via a "national people's democratic revolution," and the South carrying out the struggle for "the peaceful reunification of the Fatherland."

The Constitution of 1960[26] thus makes it clear that the Democratic Republic of Vietnam is the only legitimate government of the Vietnamese people, and that that government is firmly committed to Marxist-Leninist principles. It also outlines the role of the citizenry, and the structure and functions of state institutions in a manner similar to that of other Communist constitutions. It is interesting to note, however, that the powers granted to the president are as substantial as those in the Republic's Constitution, providing him with far more than a mere ceremonial role. Among other powers, he is the Supreme Commander of the Armed Forces and the President of the National Defense Council. Moreover, in addition to having the right to appoint the Premier, Vice Premiers, and all members of the Council of Ministers, he has the right to conclude treaties (with the concurrence of the National Assembly or its Standing Committee) and appoint representatives to foreign states.[27]

Such provisions, however, ought not to obscure the likelihood that the head of the party, whatever his titular position in the state, will hold the foremost power in the system. During his lifetime, Ho Chi Minh was evidently the fountainhead of all critical decision-making, although his role may frequently have been that of mediator within

[26] For the text of the DRV Constitution of 1960, see Fall, *op. cit.* (Appendix I), pp. 409–441.

[27] In addition to the sources cited, see P. J. Honey, ed., *North Vietnam Today —Profile of a Communist Satellite* (New York: Praeger, 1962), and P. J. Honey, *Communism in North Vietnam* (Cambridge, Massachusetts: MIT Press, 1963), and for invaluable materials emanating from the North Vietnamese media, see JPRS, *op. cit. Translations on North Vietnam.*

the Politburo where all major decisions were made. Despite a vast amount of speculation, we know almost nothing about the operations of the Vietnam Workers' Party Politburo. It has long been rumored that various differences of opinion have existed more or less continuously within that body, some of them pertaining to ties with, or predilections for foreign Communist parties—specifically, those of Moscow and Peking. Ho Chi Minh,[28] it has been surmised, served during his lifetime as arbitrator of those differences and final authority, although he himself evidently took responsibility for some of the most difficult (and unpopular) decisions, particularly those relating to relations between the Viet Minh and France. The data, however, is insufficient at present to ascertain with confidence either the general decision-making process as it has operated in North Vietnam since 1945, or the precise views of the key political actors. It can only be asserted with some confidence that Ho, around whom a cult of personality was progressively created, played a decisive role; that the Politburo of the Vietnam Workers' party is the context in which basic decision-making takes place both with respect to foreign and domestic policies; and that divisions involving heated debates have existed at this level from time-to-time, although rarely have these surfaced in such a fashion as to be discernible to the North Vietnamese public or to external observers. Rarely has any government— even a Communist government—operated behind such a complete cloak of secrecy.

As might be suspected, the foreign policy of the DRV shows a remarkable similarity to that of North Korea as set forth earlier. North Vietnam like the DPRK aims at the following basic goals: independence within the Communist world, and non-alignment between the Soviet Union and the Chinese People's Republic, with the hope that greater unity between these two can be achieved; meantime, the insistence upon a firm "revolutionary" line on the international front; close relations with various small Communist parties and revolutionary groups, especially those in East Asia, the maintenance of a strong nationalist line containing elements of aloofness and xenophobia—but continued heavy dependence upon both the Soviet

[28] Note the following statement of Ho Chi Minh, made in the fall of 1965, concerning the independence of South Vietnam: "The contention that the southern part of our fatherland is 'a neighbour country' separate from the North is a misleading one. It is just like saying that the southern states of the United States constitute a country separate from the northern states." Official transcript approved by the DRV of an interview with journalist Felix Greene, November 18, 1965, in Ho Chi Minh, *Against U.S. Aggression—For National Salvation* (Hanoi: Foreign Languages Publishing House, 1967), p. 104.

Union and Communist China for survival; and strenuous efforts to achieve international recognition and support. Finally, it has emphasized a rigid insistence upon "total victory" in the war to "liberate" South Vietnam.

RELATIONS WITH COMMUNIST STATES

In ideological terms, and also with respect to concrete international policies, Hanoi is closer to Peking than to Moscow, and that has been true for more than a decade, Ho's supposed "pro-western Communist proclivities" notwithstanding. In its position on such issues as Albania, Yugoslavia, the Sino-Indian border dispute and the nuclear test-ban treaty, the DRV gave ample evidence of its unhappiness with Khrushchevian policies. In recent times, moreover, in its participation in the Indochinese People's Conference and particularly in its recognition of the Sihanouk government-in-exile, Hanoi has indicated divergencies from Moscow of potential significance. At the same time, the Soviets remain supremely important to the North Vietnamese war effort, supplying as they do extensive military and economic aid, including all of their sophisticated equipment.

Moreover, there can be little doubt that whatever its current ideological-political proclivities for a hard line—hence, for policy positions frequently close to those of Peking—Hanoi's leaders hope to preserve their independence from Chinese and other foreign influences. Unlike North Korea, however, North Vietnam has no common border with the Soviet Union. Indeed, should the United States withdraw militarily from this area—and unless Russia or some other power establishes a presence in the vicinity, the only near power will be the Chinese People's Republic. Thus, the maintenance of full independence in the longer run may be exceedingly difficult, irrespective of the outcome of the Vietnam war. Indeed, there are signs that Hanoi was more displeased than P'yŏngyang with Chinese "irrationality" during the Cultural Revolution, and particularly with the difficulties created by the Chinese for both the Soviet Union and North Vietnam with respect to such issues as the passage of Soviet goods across China; more recently, Hanoi was clearly perturbed by Peking's new American policy. Publicly, however, the North Vietnamese have avoided any but the most oblique criticism of either major ally, and they have striven manfully behind the scenes to prevent the Sino-Soviet dispute from affecting them too adversely, insisting to both parties that they must remain "neutral," given the serious struggle in which they are engaged.

The Democratic People's Republic of Vietnam, however, currently belongs to those Communist states taking a hard line internationally. As in the case of North Korea, moreover, its leaders proclaim that Vietnam and Communist China are close neighbors, like lips and teeth, and Chou En-lai reciprocates by asserting that Communist China and its 700 million people remain the great revolutionary rear area for the Vietnamese revolution, and that Communist China will shrink from no sacrifice in order to ensure the success of Hanoi's efforts.

RELATIONS WITH OTHER STATES

The intense isolation that characterized North Vietnamese attitudes and policies in the 1950's has given way to some extent, as Hanoi solicits international friends and allies. Once again, it is useful to recall the tripartite character of the foreign policies of Asian Communist states in general: government to government; people to people; comrade to comrade. Diplomatic recognition on a government-to-government basis of the DRV is still confined largely to the Communist, and a portion of the "non-aligned" states. Only a few western governments, notably Sweden, have established full diplomatic relations with the DRV. The North Vietnamese message now extends to almost every society, however, via "people to people diplomacy." The American people, for understandable reasons, have been an especially important target, as were the French people in the period before 1954. Hanoi has long believed that the struggle with the United States will have "a French ending," with the United States forced to abandon the conflict not primarily because of military defeat but because of a combination of domestic and international political pressures. Hence, it has been as crucial to exert efforts on the political front within the United States—and in the world at large—as upon the military front in Indochina. And for these purposes, all sorts of individuals and groups can be utilized: pacifists and various religious leaders; media personnel; student radicals of assorted varieties; "progressive bourgeois" elements; and, naturally, committed Communists. This is a situation calling for united front tactics.

In the final analysis, to be sure, most of the above elements are not to be trusted. The leaders of the DRV, indeed, appear to trust few individuals or groups outside of their own inner circle—and perhaps even within that circle, trust is a precious commodity. Vietnamese political culture has combined with the years of bitter political-military struggle to produce a Communist movement and leadership wedded to clandestine, conspiratorial techniques, and as noted earlier, enfolded in layers of secrecy, intrigue, and complexity. Almost every prominent Vietnamese Communist leader has used countless aliases in the course of his career, making a reconstruction of the history of this movement extremely difficult. All of these factors affect comrade-to-comrade relations, especially in an international setting. Nevertheless, the DRV leaders are quite capable of making distinctions between "comrades" and "people" notwithstanding the great emphasis currently being put upon united front policies. That fact is clearly illustrated by the manner in which the NLF and its various leaders are treated, and the inner organizational structure of that body. Likewise, it is illustrated by the relations with Asian comrades, particularly those with similar problems.

POLICY TOWARD THE SOUTH

At present, however, DRV policies—foreign and domestic—all center upon the quest for southern "liberation" and the eventual unification of Vietnam. What are the basic ingredients of Vietnamese Communist policy with respect to these issues? First, the Communists have consistently told their own people—and in slightly less positive terms, the world—that they intend to settle for nothing short of total victory. Indeed, they have insisted for some years that the Americans and their Vietnamese allies have already been defeated and are simply stubbornly unwilling to recognize that fact, hence prolonging the agonies, but that the end result is certain. Coupled with the insistence upon total victory is a commitment to protracted war. Ho Chi Minh was fond of saying that the Vietnamese under his command would fight another twenty years if necessary, and were prepared to make any sacrifices, expending as many lives and as much equipment (theirs and their enemies) as necessary to achieve the party's purpose.

From these basic principles, no one on the Communist side is allowed to diverge, even in the face of adversities. However, "protracted war" is a vague concept, susceptible to many interpretations. It is even possible that a political compromise with the Republic might be reached within the structure of the Communist position, justified as a temporary expedient. In any case, there have evidently been serious, even bitter debates over tactical matters connected with the war within top Communist circles.[29] These may well continue. It would take a major upheaval in DRV policies, however, to obtain an acceptance of the permanent, or quasi-permanent existence of a non-

[29] For one analysis of Vietnamese Communist military writings, see Patrick J. McGarvey, *Visions of Victory—Selected Vietnamese Communist Military Writings, 1964–1968* (Hoover Institution, Stanford University, Stanford, California, 1969).

Communist South Vietnam, or the idea of a truly unified, neutral Laos and Cambodia. The leaders of the DRV (and the Vietnam Workers' party) have never forgotten that theirs was once the Indochinese Communist party. They have long provided the backbone for such groups as the Pathet Lao and the Khmer Rouge. Without Hanoi's aid and guidance, indeed, these groups would be of no significance. North Vietnamese forces, as is well-known, have been in both Laos and in Cambodia in force for many years, and they give every evidence of intending to remain, at least until the forces allied with them can seize power.

It is in this context that the Vietnamese Communist position on unification should be seen. First, it would be well to dispose of the fiction that on this and related matters, the NLF,[30] or the more recent Alliance have had, or can have an independent position. Given the control over both of these organizations by the VWP (in some respects, via the People's Revolutionary party of South Vietnam, the southern branch of the VWP) an organizational position divergent from that of the party would be inconceivable. This does not, of course, rule out the possibility of differences over this issue within the party, or between the party and certain non-Communist front figures. As yet, however, no significant differences have surfaced, once Politburo-level decisions have been made. Hence, while there are some differences in wording and style between Hanoi and NLF proposals regarding an end to the war and post-war policies, there are no differences of substance, as all parties acknowledge.

Naturally, the Communists entrust the official formulation of terms for ending the conflict in South Vietnam to the NLF and the "Provisional Revolutionary Government of the Republic of South Vietnam," since there has never been a public admission by Hanoi of the presence of DRV forces in the South. However, Hanoi has put forth at various times its own proposals for a solution of the Vietnam issue, proposals entirely consistent with the latest NLF eight-point program.

That program includes the following basic points: a cease-fire between the South Vietnamese People's Liberation Armed Forces and the forces of the United States and other foreign countries immediately after the US has pledged to withdraw all foreign troops under its command from South Vietnam (the original date stipulated

---

[30] The most authoritative studies of the NLF are those of Douglas Pike, *Viet Cong: The Organization and Techniques of the National Liberation Front of South Vietnam* (Cambridge, Massachusetts: MIT Press, 1966), and *War, Peace and the Viet Cong* (Cambridge, Massachusetts: MIT Press, 1969). See also the important article by Jeffrey Race, "The Origins of the Second Indochina War," *Asian Survey*, Vol. X, No. 5, May 1970, pp. 359–382.

was June 30, 1971); upon that US pledge, a promise to immediately discuss measures to insure the safety of such troops and the release of captured military personnel; a cease-fire between the South Vietnamese PLAF and the "armed forces of the Saigon administration" immediately after the Provisional Revolutionary Government and a Saigon administration *without* Thieu, and one "that adheres to peace, independence, neutrality and democracy" have come to terms on the formation of a provisional triangular coalition government (involving the Provisional Government, personalities from organizations upholding "peace, independence, democracy and neutrality," and the Saigon administration sans its current leader) to organize general elections; a pledge by these parties to work out measures to honor the above agreements, including the creation of a constitution "representative of the South Vietnamese people's will for peace, independence, democracy, national concord and neutrality," and also for "truly free elections;" a policy of "militant solidarity and mutual support and assistance to Laos and Cambodia on the basis of respect for each other's independence, sovereignty, and territorial integrity; the establishment of diplomatic relations with all countries, irrespective of their political systems, including the United States, "on the basis of the five principles of peaceful coexistence;" the acceptance of economic and technical aid from all countries, providing no political strings are attached; and a step by step approach to unification, "based upon the respect by each of the two zones for each other's equality, policies, and political structure."[31]

This program, clearly fashioned so as to have maximum appeal to the non-Communists of South Vietnam and of other countries as well, should be read with its full context in mind: Hanoi's pledge of total victory to the Vietnamese people; the personalities involved in the so-called NLF and Alliance; and the meaning of terms like "independence," "democracy," "neutrality," and "free elections" in Communist parlance. The President of the "Provisional Revolutionary Government of the Republic of South Vietnam" is Huynh Tan Phat, widely regarded as one of the leading Communists currently attached to the South. Nguyen Huu Tho, President of the NLF, is a relatively unknown, second-rate lawyer without any personal following or power, the perfect front type for the party. Both the NLF and the so-called

[31] The following literature sets forth the NLF position on reunification and other matters: *The NFL of South Vietnam—the only genuine and legal representative of the South Vietnam people,* Liberation Editions—South Vietnam, 1965; *South Viet Nam National Front for Liberation—Documents* (South Vietnam: Giai Phong Publishing House, December 1968); and the "Central Organ of the South Viet Nam National Front for Liberation," *The Struggle* (in English), Hanoi.

Provisional Revolutionary Government have always acknowledged Ho Chi Minh as leader of the nation, and both have always accepted the policies of Hanoi as set forth by the Vietnamese Workers' party. Since all elements in South Vietnam know that the party will brook no interference from anyone in the North, the thesis that any government in the South under Communist control could, or would wish to remain independent of Hanoi is a fiction difficult to maintain, even to the most naive.

The current Communist and non-Communist positions on the unification issue, and related questions are so far apart that it is difficult to see the emergence of a complete, negotiated political settlement. It would be more logical to expect these issues to be "settled" by the tide of military events, or to drag on "unsettled" for an indefinite period. It is always conceivable, however, that decisive developments on the military or political front could produce a breakthrough on a "temporary" basis, or that certain partial political agreements might be reached without any over-all settlement. Perhaps the critical question is this: Given the serious military setbacks suffered by the Communists in recent years, *could* a military respite be sufficiently attractive to cause an acceptance of a non-Communist South Vietnam for the present, looking toward its eventual collapse under combined political and guerrilla assault?

Prospects for the Future

As we have seen, the divided states of Korea and Vietnam have much in common with respect to foreign policies, despite their cultural and geopolitical differences. In both cases, profound ideological-structural cleavages inhibit union on the basis of power-sharing, or political competition in the western parliamentary sense. Both parties, moreover, share the deepest internal enmities as a result of costly military struggles that have exacted high sacrifices in human lives and physical damage. There is no mutual trust among the rival elites, and more importantly, no basis for such trust. Hence, the grounds for compromise are extremely limited—and yet, ultimate unification remains a broadly based nationalist goal and hope.

Meanwhile, both the non-Communist and Communist states that have emerged in these two territories inevitably seek to create for themselves greater security on the one hand, and greater independence on the other. The former objective involves them in a range of policies: alliance with those superpowers that can serve as benefactors; extensive military expenditures; and socio-economic and political policies designed to appeal at home and abroad, together with an effort to use such devices as people-to-people diplomacy to garner more international support. The latter objective causes them to seek a broader international base, while at the same time exhorting their people to be more self-reliant and less dependent upon external sources of support. In the case of the Communists, as previously noted, this involves the special effort to achieve a non-aligned position between the Soviet Union and the People's Republic of China while cultivating other sources of economic and political contact, particularly in the non-western world. In the case of the non-Communists, it involves the gradual movement away from almost sole dependence upon the United States as conditions permit, with such states as Japan and other neighboring Asian states playing increasing roles in sustaining economic growth and possibly in underwriting security needs.

The shadow of war still hangs heavily over these East Asian states, and in the final analysis, they may not be masters of their own fate, irrespective of the outcome of the conflicts immediately at hand. All of them live in the near vicinity of continental-mass societies which are themselves in great transition and mutual conflict. To date, however, it is precisely the breakdown of Communist monolithism and the extensive commitments of the non-Communists, and particularly the United States, to a broad political-military equilibrium in the Pacific-Asian region that have preserved such independence as these states possess. Will such conditions—or adequate substitutes for them—prevail in the future?

Thailand, Laos and Cambodia

DAVID A. WILSON

The three Southeast Asian countries of Thailand,
Laos and Cambodia have been involved in the Vietnam
war to different degrees for the past 20 or more years.
They have been dependent, in varying ways, on
economic and military aid from the United States.
Thailand, the most powerful and viable of these three
countries, has pursued a foreign policy over the years
which has combined its needs for outside aid for
internal development and international recognition
with its desires for regional influence and cooperation.
The foreign affairs of Laos and Cambodia have
consisted mainly of tactics and internal strategies,
since both these countries are fighting for survival
amidst contending internal factions. For these two
nations, the possibilities for foreign policy are dictated
substantially by the surrounding big powers.

Thailand: The Strategic Setting

Geographically, Thailand is in the center of the Southeast
Asian peninsula bordering on Cambodia, Laos,
Burma and Malaysia, with an extended sea coast
on the Gulf of Siam as well as on the Indian Ocean.
The principal port, and only deep-sea commercial
port, is Bangkok, the capital city, 25 miles up-stream
from the mouth of the Chao Phraya River.
Thailand is a nation of about 35,000,000 people
who produce an annual GNP of between US
5½ and 6 billion dollars.
Thailand's economy is basically agricultural in terms of

employment although the agricultural sector accounts for only about 30 percent of the value of production. The rate of growth of the entire economy has been strong in recent years, averaging 6–7 percent. The rate of population growth is about 3 percent and the per capita income per annum is about US $140. Thailand has a relatively well-developed system of transportation—waterways, railways, roads, etc.—as well as communications, banking and credit facilities. For all this, Thailand is a relatively unmobilized society with important constraints on its capacity to deploy people and resources for public development. The political system has included an elected national assembly and provincial and municipal assemblies but is still dominated by an elite which originated and is institutionalized largely by the central government bureaucracy. Political leadership originates, for the most part, in the armed forces, particularly in the army. The character of this elite, like so many other aspects of Thailand's social and economic structure, is becoming increasingly complicated by the appearance of new subgroups. Each of these tends to have its institutional base, some of which—most notably the banking, commercial and industrial leadership—are not strictly governmental.

In the political system, the capacity to draw upon the population for participation in or support of politics is limited by social discontinuities, such as the rural-urban gap, and the number of non-Thai minority communities in the north and northeast as well as non-Buddhist minorities on the southern border with Malaysia. This characteristic weakens or at least limits the ability of the government to embark on certain kinds of activities. This social gap, while quite significant, should not be exaggerated. The government of Thailand is well-developed in organization, in communication with the population, and has deployed trained officials for general administration and specific programmatic and organizational purposes. Within the class of bureaucratic governments, it is relatively effective and responsive to its society.

Thailand: Determinants of Foreign Policy

The United States has been a key element in the foreign policy of Thailand since 1950. The relationship between these two countries has displayed a strong tendency, in spite of various ups and downs, to become closer, more complex and more mutually committed. At present this relationship is practically, if not formally, a bilateral alliance oriented toward the war in Vietnam, Laos and Cambodia; an alliance which has resulted in substantial commitments of human, material and political resources, on both sides. By 1971, however, this alliance was undergoing stress which can hardly be without consequence, and which we shall examine shortly.

The history of Thailand's foreign policy is not infrequently adumbrated by such phrases as "bending with the wind," "reinsurance," or "playing both sides." There is sufficient evidence to support such interpretations in events and policies of the latter half of the last century and of the period of the East Asian war of 1941–45, although other interpretations are possible.

Thailand is in a curious position because the country is at the same time a major regional force and a minor power in the area of great power politics. Since the 1850's, Thailand has consistently sought, through diplomacy, to establish a position in the world at large rather than to insulate itself or to resist external influence—a policy which was successful in the early history of contact with the expansion of European imperialism. Thus, the foreign policy of the kingdom has tended to reflect a self-confidence, if not boldness, rather than a passivity. Nevertheless, with limited resources and limited capacity to mobilize and deploy these resources, the foreign policy of Thailand has necessarily been constrained.

The political space within which Thailand's foreign policy has operated in the past 20 years has been to a great extent shaped by influences that originated with the great powers of the Pacific area, particularly the People's Republic of China, the United States and increasingly Japan. At the same time, Thailand has had a considerable self-originating influence in the regional politics of Southeast Asia.

Southeast Asian regional-international politics has in these past 20 years had two more or less autonomous configurations of activity in which Thailand has played a considerable part. The first is in Indochina (Laos, Cambodia and Vietnam) where the efforts of Vietnamese, both Communist and non-Communist, to establish control over Vietnam have been forceful. These efforts have impinged heavily on the territory of Laos and Cambodia. The second area of Thai involvement has been in the Malay lands—Malaysia, Indonesia and the Philippines together with the multi-racial city-state of Singapore —where a quest for some basis for political order has been actively pursued by the leadership of all of the nations. This quest has been full of conflict although international warfare has so far been avoided.

A third area of Thailand's foreign policy is defined by characteristics of the kingdom's internationally open economy. As a part of the policy of dealing openly with the world by diplomacy, Thailand has engaged actively but conservatively in international trade. In the period up to

World War II Thailand experienced substantial economic growth associated largely with increased production of rice and later rubber and tin for export. In the past 20 years this fundamental economic pattern has continued with considerable effort directed toward certain other exportable commodities as well as toward attracting foreign economic assistance and investment. This economic activity has constituted a major foreign policy arena in dealing with customers, with donors of foreign grants and loans, and with the circumstances and terms of foreign investment, which include a complex of activities with centers of activity in Japan, the United States and western Europe—extending as well to eastern Europe, the Soviet Union and Africa.

One of the imperatives determining foreign policy for the government of Thailand at present, is the protection of the territory of the kingdom. This imperative is a recent development historically because it is only in the past century that Thailand, as well as other states of Southeast Asia, have acquired a clear, distinct and definable territorial character. In the system—which can be called the traditional mode of inter-state politics and which prevailed until the emergence of European territorial colonies and protectorates—monarchies extended dominion in varying degrees of directness and intensity. Boundaries were loosely-defined—more frontiers or marches than boundaries—and governmental power diminished with distance. Kings, kinglets and princes ruled over towns and related to each other by tribute. Some of these relationships were direct, straightforward and virtually permanent while others were indirect, ambivalent and shifting. Therefore, much of the politico-military activity affected the shifts of allegiances and resulted in what would appear to be transfers of territory. This apparatus has been dismantled for the most part although it may be in a process of rediscovery in Laos and Cambodia.

The kingdom of Thailand, however, is now clearly defined territorially, and the kingdom exhibits a consequent nationalism. The political rhetoric of fifty years disseminated through a nationwide school system and all other means has established the value of king and country for several generations of Thai of all classes.

The king symbolizes and embodies for the Thai the second imperative of foreign policy, e.g., the protection of the social structure. It is, of course, axiomatic that the foreign policy of a government is predicated on the maintenance of the social and political structure of which the government is a part—Thailand is no exception. The fundamental elements of the structure are the monarchical-bureaucratic government with army leadership based on a peasant-agrarian society of generally passive and deferential citizens. For this reason, if no other, the foreign policy of Thailand expresses considerable skepticism, even hostility, to the extension of the influence of Communist governments in Asia.

The third imperative of Thailand's foreign policy is its dependence on other countries—particularly the great powers—for security and economic assistance. Throughout modern times, Thailand has assumed the character of a small country that needs the cooperation, assistance or support of other nations to assure its security and integrity. Thailand's foreign policy has quite consistently followed directions of alliances and collective arrangements in pursuit of its objectives, a pattern which has been implemented in various ways—ranging from the solicitation or acceptance of foreign advisors to membership in international organizations and alliances. And it has been the discontinuities in these contingent aspects that have generated the opportunism of Thailand's foreign policy.

PROBLEMS IN THAILAND'S DEFENSE

Thailand generally exhibits an anti-Communist attitude, which is reflected in its foreign policy in Indochina. Since the establishment of the People's Republic of China in 1949, the governments of Thailand have been preoccupied with resisting the expansion of Chinese power or influence into Southeast Asia—specifically into Thailand. This has manifested itself in a general regional policy orientation based on the assumption of Chinese hostility and reaction to specific events. For example, *inter alia*, the Sino-Soviet backed peace movement of the early 1950's, the establishment of a Thai autonomous area of Yunnan in 1953, the position of Communist China at the Geneva Conference of 1954 and the Bandung Conference of 1955, Chinese support for Thai neutralists in 1957–8, Cambodian recognition of Communist China in 1958, Communist China's position at the Geneva Conference of 1962, Chinese support of the Thailand Patriotic Front in 1964–67, Chinese desultory building of roads in northern and western Laos from the middle of the 1960's have all distressed the Thais.

Thailand's policy toward Communist China has been compounded by two closely-related questions throughout the past 20 years. These are the activities of Communist regimes in Vietnam and the position of the Chinese community in Thailand. In comparison to other nations of Southeast Asia, the degree of assimilation and integration of the overseas Chinese in Thai society has been high. This success can be attributed to a combination of policies that encourage assimilation and support an assimilated and integrationist leadership in a generally well-organized Chinese community.

In modern times, Thailand resisted diplomatic relations with any Chinese government until 1946, when relations were established with the Nationalist government of China. This was part of a series of events connected with China and Chinese politics that tended to politicize the Chinese community in Thailand. These Chinese politics involved Nationalist and Communist competition for control, with the Chinese embassy, the Chinese Chamber of Commerce of Bangkok, as well as party organizations all playing important roles. In the course of this struggle the Communist elements came very close to gaining control over the principal community organizations. The Thai government was able to prevent this in 1951–2, however, at least in part because China was diplomatically represented by the enfeebled Nationalist government. The community leadership that emerged was substantially integrated with the leadership of the Thai government, both politically and economically. The success of this integration was partially dependent upon continued refusal to recognize the Peking regime, the persistent opposition to its seating in the United Nations, and ultimately to a total embargo on trade with the Chinese mainland. In this fashion Thailand's China policy is closely linked to a long-standing issue of domestic politics. Capacity to sustain the policy is, of course, reliant on confidence in continued US support.

The second compound in Thailand's China policy is Vietnam. The rhetoric and the concept of Thailand's China policy makes little differentiation between Communism in Vietnam and in China. Thanat Khoman, Foreign Minister for the past decade, has a fancy for the term "Asian Marxists" to cover this issue. In any case Communist China is seen generally as a participant in the militancy and aggressiveness of the Vietminh, the North Vietnamese and the Viet Cong. Communist governments are viewed as colonialists of previous eras and thus are seen as a persistent threat to Thailand's independence.

Since 1950 Thailand has consistently supported the governments of South Vietnam on the grounds that Communist-dominated regimes have been the principal threat to Thailand's independence. Thailand's policy in Laos and Cambodia has been similar for this period. A policy of distrust or even antagonism toward "neutralist" governments in either Laos or Cambodia expresses Thailand's concern for weakness in the face of hostile expansion, particularly in the critical Mekong Valley.

Defense of this crucial and unsettled frontier is, of course, Thailand's fundamental defense problem. The instability of governments in Laos and the volatile character of Cambodian foreign policy under the Sihanouk regime and after have been constant factors in Thailand's politico-military foreign policy for twenty years.

This policy has been based on the development of an alliance with the United States. As the French involvement in the Vietnam war was ending in 1954 the United States started exploring the possibilities of a treaty for collective defense in Southeast Asia. Thailand eagerly responded. The Manila Pact and the South East Asian Treaty Organization (SEATO) were the results.

Thailand sought to include South Vietnam, Cambodia, and Laos in the SEATO area. And although the Thai government wanted a strong clause on subversion, they felt that the final draft of the pact was too equivocal. Also, Thailand's satisfaction with the commitment of the United States to the defense of Thailand against Communist aggression was somewhat lessened by American reluctance to commit troops or to establish a military command structure in the organization.

The relationship between the United States and Thailand since the establishment of SEATO has been troubled by recurring crises of skepticism about the mutual firmness of commitment, which, until recently, were resolved by an increasing level of involvement. A brief look at the history of these crises should cast some light on the character of the US-Thai relationship.

SEATO was established as one of various responses to the 1954 settlement of the war between France and the Vietminh in Vietnam.[1] Two other responses—the quasi organization of neutralism by India and Indonesia, and Communist China's acceptance of the policy of "peaceful coexistence" focused on the slogans of Afro-Asian solidarity and "peaceful coexistence"—resulted in a potentially antiAmerican environment in Asia. Under these banners Communist China sought to oust American influence from Southeast Asia largely by enticement rather than threat. Communist China's policy was intended to disprove the assumption of Communist aggression upon which SEATO was based, while providing an incentive to small Asian countries, including Thailand, to reduce their involvement with the United States.

Peking's conciliatory policy worked in Thailand and also in the United States. In its first years there were serious doubts about the utility of SEATO in a world in which conciliation and détente seemed to be creating a new international ambiance. These doubts were enhanced by the variety and inconsistency of interests represented in SEATO as well as the ambivalent character of the SEATO treaty's position on "indirect aggression." This broad and undefined term referred to a range of hostile activities that might be subversive

[1] In addition to the United States and Thailand, the members of SEATO are the Philippines, Pakistan, Australia, New Zealand, Britain and France.

of Thailand's central values and which were, even at that time, seen as more likely than a clear-cut invasion. Although these doubts were somewhat resolved in subsequent years Thailand's principal ambition through SEATO—to be assured of US support in case of threat—remained uncertain until 1962.

During 1958, tension between Thailand and Cambodia exploded when Cambodia extended de jure recognition to Communist China. Unprecedented public demonstrations in Bangkok and some alarm in the government followed the communiqué of Communist China and Cambodia that included hostile allusions to Thailand. These regional events, combined with a minor financial crisis and continuing neutralist and even Maoist criticism of the government's foreign policy, resulted in a coup, led by the late Field Marshal Sarit Thanarat, which suppressed Thailand's constitutional government in October 1958. After taking power, the new regime reaffirmed its commitment to the United States.

A crisis in Laos that began in 1959 and was not settled until 1962 was a direct challenge to the validity of SEATO as a basis for US-Thailand relations. Both of these countries had, during 1957 and 1958, been encouraging the government of Laos toward a more forthright, rigorously anti-Communist stance. The fragility of the Lao government's position was revealed in 1959 when it was suddenly overthrown by a relatively obscure army officer. This coup d'état plunged the Lao political factions into civil war, a situation that quickly attracted the intervention of North Vietnam, Thailand, Communist China, the Soviet Union and the United States.

The Thai government backed the so-called "right wing" faction in this war, fearing a replication of the hostile neutrality of Cambodia. Moreover, Thailand sought the intervention of SEATO to prevent any expansion of Communist influence in the Lao kingdom. SEATO proved incapable of combined action beyond verbal protestations and in the end only certain members—the United States, Britain, Australia and New Zealand—were able to respond. SEATO's internal disunity alarmed and disillusioned Thailand. Prime Minister Sarit said to the SEATO Ministers in 1961, "Instead of setting about our work in complete unison we have before us a sad spectacle of filibustering, contention and working at cross purposes."

The United States, faced with the distasteful prospect of a confrontation with Communist China and the Soviet Union in the remote jungle-covered mountains of Laos, was short on enthusiasm. The Kennedy administration finally rejected the possibility, and set about negotiating an international agreement to neutralize Laos. This put Thailand in a dilemma. On one hand, SEATO seemed ineffectual, but on the other hand, the treaty embodied a commitment from the United States to defend the kingdom. What was the value of this commitment? How could it be made to work?

Thailand's solution to the problem was ingenious. Foreign Minister Thanat Khoman and Secretary of State Dean Rusk announced in 1962 that "the United States regards the preservation of the independence and integrity of Thailand as vital to the national interest of the United States and to world peace." In addition it was declared that "the United States intends to give full effect to its obligations under the [SEATO] Treaty to act to meet the common danger in accordance with its constitutional processes." The Secretary of State reaffirmed that "this obligation of the United States does not depend upon the prior agreement of all other parties to the Treaty, since this Treaty obligation is individual as well as collective."

By this declaration the interests of Thailand and of the United States converged on the matter of the defense of Thailand's independence and integrity including subversion by Communists. In the years after 1962 these two countries worked closely on strategy, plans and programs regarding the Mekong Valley frontier.

With the US decision to use airpower against North Vietnam, and the establishment of US air bases in Thailand, the relationship between the two countries was significantly changed. Six major air bases were constructed by the United States, and eventually about 50,000 American military personnel were stationed in Thailand. It is reported that most of the sorties against North Vietnam in 1966, 1967 and 1968 were flown from these bases in Thailand. Bombing of North Vietnamese facilities in Laos as well as attacks in South Vietnam also originate in Thailand.

In 1967 this commitment of bases was supplemented by Thailand's agreement to send a ground force contingent to South Vietnam. These troops began arriving in 1968 and reached a total of 12,000 infantry and support troops. At least from the point of view of the Thai, these are more than a mere token of their earnestness in the defense of their kingdom from Communist-led power.

Thus, in the 1960's, Thailand and the United States have become involved in a strong mutual alliance. Both allies have devoted their country's resources and lives to the anti-Communist cause, and the character of the relationship has changed to a deeper and more complex set of problems.

In both the Thai government and public, there is anxiety about having moved so close to the fire. While the investment of the United States in Southeast Asian defense is much greater than before, Thailand has also laid more on the line. The ability of the United

States to pursue the effort to a satisfactory conclusion—ability measured by both political will and capability to actually implement such an end—is of much greater importance. On the other hand, the US government has been alarmed by events in remote parts of Thailand that could be interpreted as an incipient rural rebellion. Washington is haunted by a spectre of Thailand, the base area and ally, crumbling into a state of chaos and violence; becoming another expensive and frustrating liability comparable to South Vietnam. So the alliance continues to be tense and anxious.

Thailand is now faced with the problem of anticipating the development of the US position in this alliance as the interplay of the Nixon Doctrine and Congressional limitations proceed. The difficulty is to assess, even in 1972, the extent to which the United States will withdraw its forces from Southeast Asia and thus remove a fundamental and major basis of Thailand's present policy. In spite of assurances from the Washington government that what is underway is a substantial withdrawal of forces but not an abandonment of position, it appears that at least on a contingency basis a more gloomy prospect (from the Thai point of view) must be admitted.

Thailand's policy continues to stand on a world conception of great powers with great responsibilities. For example, Thanat Khoman said to the UN General Assembly on September 23, 1970:

Since a military stalemate is not realizable in Southeast Asia one may have to look for a political stalemate, a modest step toward which was started with the Asian and Pacific nations congregating in Djakarta a few months ago. It was regrettable that such an assemblage was not strong enough to produce tangible results because it lacked the necessary ingredient of power, even a political power, which could create the kind of stalemate that would ultimately lead to negotiations or a possible political modus vivendi for peaceful co-existence. To have any chance of success, there must be an accruement of more weighty states to restore the balance. The participation of the four major powers, or failing that, the two great powers on the same side will more certainly ensure success and make possible a prospect of meaningful negotiations and eventual settlement (emphasis added). This undoubtedly is the optimum. How can it be brought about is perhaps the greatest and most difficult problem of our time which no person of goodwill should brush aside without giving a thought to it and even a try.[2]

[2] Thanat Khoman, "Address to the General Assembly of the United Nations, September 23, 1970," Press Release No. 58 (New York: Permanent Mission of Thailand to the United Nations, September 23, 1970).

The press has made a great deal of various statements by the Foreign Minister of Thailand that are interpreted as more conciliatory toward the People's Republic of China, and more open toward the possibility of a more active relationship between Thailand and the Soviet Union. Similar interest has been taken in renewed talks through the agency of the Red Cross, between North Vietnam and Thailand on the subject of repatriating Vietnamese living in Thailand. These activities certainly seem to be symptomatic of an emerging crisis of confidence on the part of the Thai government concerning the commitment of the United States to Thailand. How this crisis will be resolved is impossible to forecast as it is contingent on so many imponderables.

PROBLEMS IN REGIONAL DEFENSE

While the alarms and explosions in the Mekong Valley and Indochina properly attract the greatest share of interest and resources, another major element of Thailand's foreign policy is a long-standing and, apparently long-run, devotion to the development of regionalism. Instability in Southeast Asia is a general threat to the integrity of Thailand. The conflicts and confrontations among peoples and states of the region whether in Indochina or within the Malay area (Malaysia, Indonesia and the Philippines), all work to Thailand's disadvantage both politically and economically. Consequently, Thailand has sought a role in easing tensions and developing organizations to cope with these conflicts.

The quest for regional cooperation in Southeast Asia entered its present phase in 1961 with the formation of the Association of Southeast Asia (ASA) by three smaller nations—Thailand, the Philippines, and Malaya. The launching of ASA marked the first effort since the abortive Southeast Asia League in 1946–47 to find a basis of power in the cooperation of states solely within the region of Southeast Asia. The Foreign Minister of Thailand has played a leading role in this effort.

ASA in its early years worked for cooperation at a low level of technical problems and demonstrated a capacity for agreement commensurate with the limited capacities of its member states. It inevitably and properly became involved not only in the disputes between its members—the Philippines and Malaya—over North Borneo, but also in the almost catastrophic death throes of Sukarno's Indonesia. The burden of these problems rested on traditional diplomacy in which Thailand participated actively, rather than on ASA as an organization. The notion behind ASA revealed a striking resilience in the face of these conflicts and survived the break of relations between the two members and also the confrontation between Indonesia and Malaysia. When the confrontation was ended and Indonesia entered a new foreign policy course, the idea of a limited regional organization became the focus of a wider cooperation.

In 1966 and 1967, again with Thailand taking a leading role, a new, expanded organization was developed. Although efforts to attract the participation of Burma and Cambodia were fruitless, a conference in Bangkok in 1967 announced the formation of the Association of Southeast Asian Nations (ASEAN). The members were the three ASA nations plus Singapore and Indonesia. Subsequently ASA and ASEAN were merged.

Of course this enlarged arena of regional organization increased potential difficulties. The tremendous size and diversity of Indonesia with its complex and contentious political life may be at least equal to the three original ASA states as a potential source of conflict. At the same time the concentration of urban Chinese in Singapore, which could not be assimilated into the Federation of Malaysia, is a challenge to the effectiveness of ASEAN or any other Southeast Asian regional arrangement—especially since Britain is reducing its defense presence in Singapore.

The government of Thailand has also joined in several arrangements other than SEATO that extend outside of Southeast Asia, the most notable of which is the Asian and Pacific Council (ASPAC). Other economic and specialized institutions such as the Asian Development Bank (ADB), the Southeast Asian Ministers of Education Organization (SEAMES), and the Mekong River Development Project have been joined by Thailand.

Thailand's tendency to reinforce regional security and its hope that this regional stability will bring concomitant security from external (i.e., great power) invasion is increasing. Thailand foresees that its ultimate protection may lie in combination with other states whose interests are similar and whose mutual dependence is greater. The Ministry of Foreign Affairs expressed this view in 1961 at the time of the establishment of ASA.

Closer cooperation among the countries of this region in the form of regional grouping is . . . of vital importance. It is a question of bare survival for these nations because it will not be possible for them to compete with economically advanced countries on an equal footing so long as they do not unite with a view to restoring some sort of balance of power.

These rudimentary ideas expressed in 1961 have evolved into a doctrine of regionalism that is strikingly realistic in its assessment of potentialities.

The doctrine contains two elements both of which have been repeated frequently by the Foreign Minister of Thailand. The first theme is national strength: "each and every nation in Southeast Asia should do their utmost to consolidate and promote their own national strength, their political structure, their economy, their human and material resources. They should do so individually and they can do better by working together in joint endeavours through regional and sub-regional cooperation."[3]

The second element is an ingenious solution to the small and poorly based military capacity of the nations of Southeast Asia. This is:

that regional security can best be maintained through close cooperation among Asian Countries forming a kind of 'collective political defense.' The term 'political' is used here in its widest sense to encompass cooperation in economic, social and cultural fields as well, leaving outside of the scope the military activities. . . . Such a grouping will also serve to strengthen the hands of its member countries in dealing more adequately with external powers and will reduce the likelihood of outside interference.[4]

Such statements are an unequivocal expression of the aspirations of the leadership of Thailand for greater autonomy in the world and a realistic recognition on their part that any further enlargement depends upon cooperative stability within the region. The leaders of Thailand know from experience that power is generated by settled cooperation within a state and among states. Consequently, they seek to encourage by their participation the growth of cooperation and the diminution of conflict in Southeast Asia.

ECONOMIC POLICY

The other major element of Thailand's foreign policy besides its regionalism is economic. The government remains committed to an open economy and depends very heavily on foreign trade to sustain economic activity and growth as well as to provide revenue. Moreover, the government encourages, and in some cases subsidizes,

[3] Thailand, Ministry of Foreign Affairs, *Foreign Affairs Bulletin*, August-September 1961, p. 34.

[4] Thanat Khoman, "Answers to Questions Posed by Yomiuri Shimbun," Press Release No. 24 (New York: Permanent Mission of Thailand to the United Nations, June 23, 1969).

foreign investment. Much of the configuration of domestic economic policy, particularly conservative fiscal policies, are influenced by foreign economic relations. Thailand has sought economic assistance with considerable success not only from the United States, but also from other nations and multilateral institutions such as the Colombo Plan, World Bank and Asian Development Bank (ADB).

Thailand has shared the general world disappointment over the failure of the UN Conferences on Trade and Development to modify a world trade system dominated by industrialized nations. As a country whose principal productive capacity is devoted to primary products of agriculture, fishing and mining, Thailand's foreign economic position is determined by the markets for such commodities, which are notoriously difficult to influence. Another consideration is Thailand's need to import capital and consumption goods. Thus the crucial indicator of success (or lack of success) in foreign economic policy is the balance of payments and the foreign exchange reserves.

Thailand consistently has had a deficit in its trade balance for the past ten years although until 1970 the balance of payments has been favorable—the difference being a result of their investment in terms of foreign aid and military spending on the Vietnam war. This changing balance resulted from declining invisibles, particularly U.S. military spending, somewhat compensated for by increased exports. But since 1970 the very substantial reserves which had been increasing for the previous five years have shown a decline.

In the decade of the 1960's Thailand's foreign economic policy had three basic aspects. The first and weakest aspect is exports—which the government has generally left to the private sector. The second aspect has been the solicitation of foreign economic assistance from other nations and international organizations. Most of this assistance has been invested in infrastructure for production and commerce—water control, transportation, communications and electric power. The third aspect has been an effort to attract foreign investment. Much of it has been oriented toward import substitution although some has gone into development of exportable commodities.

In the late 1960's the character of this foreign economic policy has been shifting, with the emphasis moving toward the export side. Programs designed to ameliorate the trade deficit are now being discussed if not formulated. Export promotion activities, trade agreements (particularly with Japan, Thailand's principal trading partner), negotiation with competitors (e.g., the US), investment in export oriented enterprises, and attention to invisibles (tourists, shipping, insurance) are all parts of the emerging policy. While there is also a developing pressure for protection in the form of import taxes both general and specific, the dominant government position appears to be opposed to this kind of solution to the balance of payments problem. Like all economically underdeveloped countries, Thailand has severe limits on what can be accomplished in dealing with powerful industrial nations. The continuation of Thailand's considerable economic success of the 1960's is therefore very dependent on the aid of the great powers.

Laos: Determinants of Foreign Policy

There is a certain absurdity in speaking of the foreign policy of tiny countries ravaged and divided by invasion, foreign-supported rebellions and civil war. The problems faced by their governments are matters of strategy and tactics rather than of policy. These are problems of survival, neither more nor less; and the rules of the game are immediately established by others. The distinction between foreign and domestic politics is hopelessly blurred.

Both Laos and Cambodia profess "policies" of neutralism but the principal and immediate difficulty of both countries is to discover a basis of unity, and the leaders of both seek this basis by efforts to disentangle the affairs of their people from the war in Vietnam. So far, this search has proved fruitless; in fact ground is being lost in both a literal and a metaphoric sense.

The rules of the Laos game were established in Laos and Switzerland in the years 1961 and 1962. Leaders of Laos agreed (Zurich, 1961) on the governmental basis of the neutrality of Laos, and on the structure of government and division of offices (Khang Khay, 1962). These several agreements were endorsed and guaranteed by a conference of governments of interested powers under the co-chairmanship of Britain and the Soviet Union (Geneva, 1962) in a Declaration on the Neutrality of Laos. The government of Laos became the most "neutral" in Asia in that it was recognized and dealt with by governments of all persuasions; it foreswore military alliances (including SEATO protection), foreign military bases, and the use of force which might impair international peace; and was guaranteed neutrality by fourteen nations of the world including the United States, Soviet Union, Britain, France, India, and Communist China as well as all its neighbors, Thailand, Burma, North and South Vietnam, and Cambodia. Other than on paper, the agreement lasted a mere nine months —from July 9, 1962 (when the government of Laos signed the Declaration of Neutrality), to March 31, 1963 (when fighting broke out between different factions of the "neutralist" element of the tripartite army of Laos).

As far as Laos is concerned "internal" politics is of more significance to international relations than foreign policy because there is no effective state in Laos—only contending localized factions. Each of these factions has its foreign connection and supporters. The degree to which each faction is dependent upon or captured by its foreign supporters is functionally related to the degree of cooperation among factions as a government of Laos. In the past decade the increasingly desperate imperatives of the war in Vietnam working upon and among these factions have forestalled, undermined and, perhaps, forever demolished the possibility of such cooperation.

Nevertheless, there are two reasons to believe that the situation is not hopeless. The first is that each of the factions aspires to a greater degree of autonomy from its supporters, which might be found through cooperation among Lao politicians. The second is that the interests of foreign supporters in the affairs of Laos are largely either matters of defense, or for interests of using Laos as a route to other people or places. As such indirect interest diminishes, the possibility that these factions may break free and cooperate with each other increases as the control of the external supporting powers diminishes.

By the late 1960's the factions of Laos were clustered into two elements—the Royal Lao Government (RLG) of Prince Souvannaphouma in Vientiane and the Lao Patriotic Front (NLHS)—Pathet Lao headed by Prince Souphanouvong and based in Sam Neua. The RLG is heavily dependent upon the assistance of the United States and its allies both to maintain economic stability and to sustain the Lao army. The RLG since 1964 has acquiesced in various forms of US air operations over Laos including reconnaissance and bombing in Laos and North Vietnam. It is not at all unlikely that the RLG cooperates in other ways with the United States in the prosecution of the Vietnam war particularly in the area of Laos through which the Ho Chi Minh trail passes.

The NLHS depends upon North Vietnam, Communist China and the Soviet Union for assistance, including the support of North Vietnamese troops. The NLHS acquiesces in the construction and operation of the Ho Chi Minh supply routes in southeastern Laos and cooperates in training and staging insurgent cadres aimed at Thailand. The RLG and NLHS have engaged in a seesaw war with each other in northern Laos with control over the Plain of Jars being the principal issue.

In this period 1965–70 the role of the Soviet Union was mainly diplomatic. The Soviet Union has managed to maintain a position that recognizes the legitimacy of both sides. At the same time it had the least at stake directly since its principal concern is to avoid a direct confrontation with the United States in Southeast Asia. Therefore, considerable effort has been made by both sides to influence the Soviet Union to lend support to their efforts.

In 1970, the relationship between the two factions, which had never been completely broken off, turned to exchange of terms for negotiation of a new national government. From an international point of view, the key considerations have to do with US bombing in Laos on the one hand and the presence of North Vietnamese troops in Laos on the other. In the long run it appears that both sides are engaged in a complex maneuver to prepare positions for a possible international conference to settle the war.

Cambodia: Determinants of Foreign Policy

The problems of foreign relations in Cambodia have, since the fall of Prince Norodom Sihanouk in 1970, become increasingly like those of Laos. The Pnom Penh government is confronted by a Cambodian National Liberation Front headed by Prince Sihanouk in Peking. Both profess a continuation of neutralist policies but each is heavily dependent upon support from foreign sources. Meanwhile the country is ravaged by fighting that combines in some indeterminate way elements of civil and international warfare. Unlike Laos, however, there is no international agreement that purports to govern the situation.

In the period from 1954 when Cambodia acquired its complete independence on the basis of neutrality until his downfall in March 1970, Prince Sihanouk was one of the most avid and imaginative practitioners of the policy of neutrality. He perceived his purpose as maintaining the territorial integrity and independence of the small, agricultural kingdom of Cambodia (population: 6.5 million, area: 70,000 sq. miles, GNP: $850 million) against threats he detected from his immediate neighbors, Vietnam and Thailand, as well as from expansionist great powers, particularly China and the United States. He sought to accomplish this end by a volatile manipulation of diplomatic relations with the world powers, the solicitation of assistance, and a quest for international guarantees of Cambodia's borders.

But the pressures of the war in Vietnam overtook him in the period since 1965 when he acquiesced to logistical operations of the armies of North Vietnam and the National Liberation Front of South

Vietnam on Cambodian territory. The pressures generated by this situation within Cambodian politics were such that Sihanouk tried both by direct demand to the North Vietnamese and, apparently, by appeal to the Soviet Union and Communist China to have the scale of the operation reduced, if not eliminated. These pressures arose principally from anti-Communist factions particularly in the army of which General Lon Nol was the commander. At the same time, disaffection with Prince Sihanouk had also increased as a result of spreading internal disorder and economic difficulties. These pressures provided a sufficient basis for ousting the Prince—who was abroad—from his position as Head of State in March 1970.

This action was accompanied by a number of vigorous public demonstrations against the presence of North Vietnamese and NLFSV forces in the country. These led to an ultimatum from the Cambodian government demanding the instantaneous withdrawal of all Vietnamese forces. Subsequent widespread demonstrations—both pro-Sihanouk and anti-Vietnamese—led to a serious disruption of internal peace and the extension of North Vietnamese military operations in Cambodia. Meanwhile, Prince Sihanouk proceeded to Peking where he established a government-in-exile—known as the National United Front of Kampuchea, Cambodia.

As fighting developed, the two sides of the Cambodian political scene became more clearly reliant upon external support. The Lon Nol government sought military assistance "from all sources" and received it from the United States and South Vietnam. Prince Sihanouk joined in a declaration proclaiming a "common front" with North Vietnam, NLFSV and NLHS (Laos) to "struggle against the common enemy."

As the struggle in Cambodia has developed it has become increasingly bitter and absolute. No suggestion of a basis for a resolution of the conflicts internal to the country has emerged. Unlike Laos there is no indication of maneuvering in anticipation of an international settlement. Both countries share the misfortune of seeing international conflict overwhelm internal politics.

Cambodia's fate is closely tied to that of South Vietnam, for whichever side emerges as the dominant force in that country following the withdrawal of American military power is likely to be in a position to determine the course of events in Cambodia as well.

Malaysia, Singapore and the Philippines

ROBERT O. TILMAN

Malaysia: The Strategic Setting

Malaysia, Singapore, and the Philippines share many common characteristics and they face many common problems. They share geography; each broke peacefully with its colonial master and was spared the burdens of a bloody revolution; the elites of each are English-speaking; each practices democracy with varying degrees of restraint; each feels a basic commitment to the free-enterprise model of economic development; each is open to foreign visitors and capital; each has been ideologically western in political outlook despite symbolic gestures toward non-alignment; each is prosperous by southern Asian standards; and each of the three countries has been relatively stable. Each of the three has also been plagued with internal problems in the past, and for two of the three these continue today. None of the three is sufficiently large to have a major impact on events in Asia on its own, but all three have found it possible to work together only in organizations with limited goals. The leaders of each state are concerned about the emergence of China in Asia, but there is little agreement, or even consultation, among them on how best to guarantee their own security. Many of the problems are similar, but each of the three countries is groping for its own solutions within the framework of its particular national idiom. These problems, solutions, and idioms constitute the subject of the present essay.

Malaysia

When Malaya[1] gained independence from Britain in 1957 her leaders still assumed that Britain was destined to remain a major power in Asia indefinitely. Britain had quit India, Burma, Ceylon, and then Malaya, but there were still the important outposts of Singapore and Hong Kong, the newly acquired colonies of Sarawak and North Borneo,[2] and the oil-rich protectorate of Brunei. Perhaps some leaders were aware that Singapore could not remain a colony forever, but the British presence in Hong Kong seemed much more permanent, and, given the state of development of the Bornean colonies, it would probably be a number of years before Britain could consider setting them free. The British could be expected to remain in Southeast Asia for many years, and thus the cornerstone of Malaysian foreign policy —the Malaya-United Kingdom Mutual Defense Treaty—seemed reasonable and rational to most of Malaya's British educated political leaders.

Given these expectations, the Labour party decision in the late 1960's to disengage east of Suez should have shaken the very foundations of Malaysian foreign policy, but instead it was received in Kuala Lumpur with relative equanimity. In the decade after independence subtle but significant changes had taken place in Malaysia, and these changes had an impact on the course of Malaysian foreign policy.

THE FOREIGN POLICY SETTING

Unhappily, almost any discussion of internal and external politics in Malaysia must still begin with a discussion of the country's racial base. The British encouraged the immigration of Chinese labor from the treaty ports of southern China and, while few remained in the mines and on the rubber estates, many gravitated to Malayan cities rather than returning to their less hospitable homeland. The Malays at one time found themselves a minority in their own country, though today, because of higher birth rates and slight manipulations of census categories, they can again claim majority status.[3] In Malaysia as a whole the Chinese constitute about 35 percent of the population,

[1] The Federation of Malaya (the nine states of the colonial Federated Malay States and the Unfederated Malay States, plus two of the three components of the old Crown Colony of the Straits Settlements—Penang and Malacca) existed from 1957 to 1963. In 1963 Malaya was absorbed into the larger Federation of Malaysia (Malaya, plus semi-autonomous Singapore and the colonies of Sarawak and North Borneo). Singapore left Malaysia in 1965.

[2] Both Sarawak and North Borneo (now Sabah) had been protectorates prior to the close of the Second World War, when they were taken over as colonies.

[3] The higher fertility rates among the Malays are well-documented. The official

while the Malays and other *bumiputras*, "sons of the soil," account for about 53 percent. For years the two major races worked harmoniously, though it was apparent that integration had not proceeded much beyond this functional level of "working together." The bitter race riots in Kuala Lumpur on May 13, 1969, which brought down the constitutional government and ushered in a two-year period of extraparliamentary rule, reminded all of the precariousness of the social base in Malaysia. All policies, foreign and domestic, must take into account possible racial ramifications.

Malaysia's economy has been strong, in part because of nature, and in part because of the British. Nature endowed the Malayan Peninsula with vast deposits of easily accessible tin ore, and Britain encouraged the development of extensive plantation agriculture of cultivated rubber and oil palm. After post-war reconstruction Malaysia has produced between a third and a half of the world's supply of tin ore concentrate and natural rubber. However, Malaysia's economic achievements are also its major points of vulnerability. Rubber accounts for approximately half of Malaysia's foreign trade, and rubber and tin together, more than 80 percent. Perhaps the most important trade fact so far as foreign policy is concerned is that Malaysia's traditional customers (Britain and the United States) are declining in importance, while the importance of trade with the USSR (and most recently, China) is rapidly increasing. In 1966 Russia for the first time emerged as the major importer of Malaysia's natural rubber, and its importance seems likely to increase.[4]

---

policy is to group all natives together into a single census category. This is defensible in West Malaysia where there are few aborigines and where recent Javanese and Sumatran immigrants have been almost totally assimilated into the Malay community. However, it is doubtful that all of the Natives of Sabah and Sarawak, who considerably outnumber the Malay minority and who have not always enjoyed good relations with Malays, would appreciate this statistical procedure. Conversion to Islam is taking place rapidly however, particularly in Sabah, where official pressure is not uncommon, and traditionally Muslim Natives have been regarded more as Malays than aboriginal tribesmen. Thus, in time, the official census categories may more accurately reflect the actual situation.

[4] The decline in British consumption is associated with the country's worsening position in the world market. The United States has increasingly turned toward synthetics and various other substitutes for natural rubber. The manufacture of synthetics in the United States received great impetus when the country was cut off from its major source of natural rubber in the Second World War, and manufacturers have built on a foundation that was financed largely by the government. The development of synthetics has proceeded slowly in Russia, largely because it is much more economical to use natural rubber and avoid tying up scarce capital in an undertaking as expensive as synthetics. China can be expected to follow the same pattern, and thus the time may come when the Malaysian economy will be heavily dependent on these two Communist powers.

The historical experience of the Malayan Emergency[5] also left its mark on the course of Malaysian foreign policy. Although the guerrillas in the jungles possibly received considerably less outside support from Communist states than is popularly accepted, they are nevertheless identified closely in the minds of Malaysian politicians with the People's Republic of China. Even had Malayan political leaders personally desired closer relations with China at the time of independence in 1957, the fact of the Emergency would have made this impossible, and these memories have lingered until very recently. Indeed, they have not yet been totally erased even today.

Until the end of the 1960's relations with Britain, the former colonial power, were very cordial. The first Prime Minister of Malaya, Tunku Abdul Rahman, in his speech on the occasion of independence, spoke glowingly of the contributions Britain had made and described his country as one of Britain's "best friends." The Tunku, like most of the members of his cabinet and most of the higher officers of the senior civil service, was British educated, and apparently the prime minister enjoyed his British experience considerably.[6] Certainly he was at ease among British politicians (more so than among many Asian leaders), and apparently the feeling was mutual. During most of the first decade of independence Tunku Abdul Rahman formulated much of Malaysia's foreign policy almost single-handedly, and these policies usually included a close association with his British friends and cronies. The colonial history of Malaysia is now undergoing revision, but in the era of the Tunku, Britain and the other members of the "old Commonwealth" were among Malaysia's best and most trusted friends.

[5] The Emergency (the official term) extended from 1948 to 1960 and claimed some 11,000 lives. Two characteristics of the Emergency stand out in the memories of most Malaysian politicians: the guerrillas were Chinese, and the Chinese were Communists. The first is almost an objective fact (there was a façade pan-racial support, but the Malayan Races Liberation Army was overwhelmingly Chinese). The ideology and motivations of the Army are not so certain, however. There is no doubt that the leadership and the cadres were Communist, but the commitment of the ranks is less certain. Even in the case of the leadership there was probably more racial and anti-colonial motivation than official accounts admit. Remnants of the Malayan Races Liberation Army still operate on the Thai-Malaysian border, and reliable reports indicate that new recruits joined following the May 13, 1969, riots in Kuala Lumpur. It has been reported that the guerrillas, estimated at 500 before May 1969, now number some 1,500. (Radio Australia, Overseas Service, August 12, 1971, 1145 hrs. G.M.T.)

[6] For a brief summary of the life of the Tunku see my "Malaysian Foreign Policy: The Dilemmas of a Committed Neutral," in John D. Montgomery and Albert O. Hirschman, eds., Public Policy, XVI (Cambridge, 1967), pp. 118–20.

Internal Determinants of Malaysia's Foreign Policy

Malaysian foreign policy of the Tunku Abdul Rahman era has been characterized previously as "the dilemmas of a committed neutral."[7] Malaysia (and particularly the parent state of Malaya) aspired to function as a broker or arbiter between the colonies and the former colonial powers and between the ideological poles of east and west. However, it was not altogether successful in this attempt. Malaysia consistently found itself steering a course far closer to the western than to the eastern shore on all issues related to the cold war, and in colonial-anti-colonial debates her image and actions were contradictory. Among many Afro-Asian states Malaysia had an image of being "soft on colonialism," or as was sometimes alleged by her more volatile neighbors, she seemed to be a lackey of the imperialists. Malaya probably did not deserve this image, and indeed her conduct in the United Nations was as "correct" as that of her hostile and avowedly anti-colonial neighbor, Indonesia, on the eve of the creation of Malaysia and in the early stages of "confrontation."[8] Nevertheless, Malaysia consistently found it difficult to gain acceptance in the councils of the non-aligned, and it is still trying to live down this image of the late 1950's and early 1960's.

The last years of the reign of Tunku Abdul Rahman were not as pleasant as the first decade. The creation of Malaysia in 1963, in perspective, seems to have been a catalyst that accelerated changes in Malaysian society that were probably inevitable. The composition of Malaysia was based on racial calculations, and thus it is not surprising that it proved impossible to avoid increasingly heated discussions of issues that were manifestly economic or social, but were latently racial. The climax, and probably the nadir of the Tunku's popularity, came in the post-election rioting of May 13, 1969.

Tunku Abdul Rahman held on to the prime minister's post through much of the extra-constitutional period, but he was frequently eclipsed by the Head of the National Operations Council, and his long-time Deputy Prime Minister, Tun Abdul Razak. In August 1970 the Tunku announced his resignation, and the following month the Tunku's nephew, the new Yang di-Pertuan Agong (King), appointed

[7] *Ibid.*

[8] *Konfrontasi* against Malaya was declared by President Sukarno in 1962. Confrontation died with the GESTAPU Affair in 1965 and was officially buried in the treaty of August 11, 1966 "normalizing relations." For a discussion of relations between the two countries see my *Malaysian Foreign Policy* (McLean, Va., 1969), pp. 50–52 and sources cited therein. On Malaya's stance in the UNO, see *Ibid.*, Table 1, p. 9.

Tun Razak the second Prime Minister of Malaysia. There is evidence that Razak was never in complete agreement with the foreign policies of his predecessor,[9] but he was also a dedicated and well trained civil servant who had learned not to question the policies of his superiors in public. Even had he been in complete agreement with his prime minister, however, it is apparent that the international and domestic situation faced in 1970 differed considerably from that of the Tunku's time. New situations called for new policies, and as a new prime minister he was in a good position to lead Malaysia in a somewhat different direction.

In his brief tenure as Prime Minister, Razak has considerably increased contacts with the eastern bloc, taken part in the Summit Conference of Non-Aligned Nations at Lusaka, Zambia, reversed Malaysian policy toward the seating of the People's Republic of China in the United Nations, and announced the existence of a Malaysian scheme for the neutralization of Southeast Asia. While all of this represented departures from the policy of Tunku Abdul Rahman, Razak has also continued some of his predecessor's policies. The most notable of the latter was the decision to replace the decaying Malaysia-United Kingdom Mutual Defense Treaty with a five-power defense agreement, which again brought Malaysia into concert with her old Commonwealth friends and protectors, Great Britain, Australia, and New Zealand (in addition to Singapore). However, even here there were some significant differences between this agreement and the one previously negotiated by Tunku Abdul Rahman.

CONTACTS WITH THE COMMUNIST BLOC

Malaysia began increased contacts with Communist countries in 1967 with the recognition of the USSR, but in the succeeding several years she maintained a cool, though correct, posture toward the states of eastern Europe. Later, however, these relations grew more intimate and more frequent. Aeroflot now operates flights between Kuala Lumpur and Moscow, trade agreements have been signed with Poland and Hungary, Tun Razak has visited Yugoslavia and Rumania, and with the latter Malaysia has signed her first agreement with a Communist state for economic and technical cooperation.[10]

[9] For a discussion of some possible differences between the two Malay leaders based on observations made up to July 1967, see *Malaysian Foreign Policy*, pp. 56, 57.

[10] These and other evidences of the thaw between Malaysia and the Communist bloc are summarized in Marvin Rogers, "Malaysia/Singapore: Problems and Challenges of the Seventies," *Asian Survey*, XI (February 1971), 127–28.

At the Lusaka Summit Conference and again at the Commonwealth Prime Ministers' Conference in Singapore in January 1971 Razak stated in explicit terms that Malaysia had "no wish to be made a pawn in any game big powers play." At the same time that Malaysia has been making overtures to the non-aligned states of Africa and Asia it has been subtly but significantly reinterpreting the history of the colonial period in a manner that places it much more in the ideological mainstream of the non-aligned states. Chief spokesman of this revisionist history has been a powerful new figure in the Razak cabinet, Tan Sri Ghazali bin Shafie, formerly a senior civil servant but now one of the major architects of domestic and foreign policies.[11] Speaking on behalf of the government following the introduction of a bill to amend the Constitution to limit the freedom of speech, Ghazali spoke of classic British policies of "divide and rule," of "colonial greed," of colonial opposition to plans to encourage Javanese immigration because "Javanese immigrants were easily assimilable," of "the infamous education policy of the colonial government," of Malaya being caught in "the feverish current of national independence," and of "holier-than-thou British journalists" with their "fractured reporting."[12] Apparently the post-colonial honeymoon is finally over, and Malaysia, somewhat belatedly, is attempting to establish its anti-colonial credentials.

COMMUNIST CHINA AND THE UNITED NATIONS

Malaya, and later Malaysia, consistently voiced support for Peking's admission to the United Nations provided adequate safeguards could be introduced to guarantee the continuing membership of Taipei: neither capital in the Malaysian view represented all of the people of China. However, until 1970 each year Malaysia joined with the United States to designate the China question an "important issue" (requiring

[11] Ghazali holds the titles of Minister with Special Functions, Head of National Unity and General Planning Unit, and Minister of Information and Broadcasting. Ghazali, who was Permanent Secretary of the Ministry of External Affairs under the Tunku, has long been regarded as an important figure, but his rise under Razak was nevertheless dramatic. He resigned his civil service appointment, was immediately appointed to the Senate, and immediately thereafter entered the Cabinet in a senior position.

[12] Parliament, March 5, 1971, text issued apparently in full in Malaysia Information Service, "Democracy: The Realities Malaysia Must Face," March 15, 1971, 10 pp.

a two-thirds majority in the General Assembly) an act that in effect contradicted their professed stand. After abstaining in 1970 Malaysia announced that in 1971 she would vote to seat the People's Republic, though she still would not vote for the ouster of Taiwan.[13] While the prime minister has denied that this constitutes a "two-China policy," it seems difficult to describe it in any other way.[14]

THE NEUTRALIZATION OF SOUTHEAST ASIA

Shortly after assuming the mantle of the Prime Ministership Tun Razak called for the neutralization of Southeast Asia. Though little substantive information has been added to explain the scheme, Razak has spoken of tripartite guarantees (USSR, China, and the United States) to insure the neutrality of the region, and the plan was apparently explained in greater detail to other Southeast Asian leaders at various international conferences. However, the skeleton has yet to grow any flesh and muscle, and little can be said about it at the present time. Of course, much will depend upon the possibility of a rapprochement between the United States and China, and thus Razak may necessarily be waiting until this can be assessed.

THE FIVE-POWER DEFENSE AGREEMENT

Malaysia seems to regard the newly established five-power defense agreement as a pact of considerably less importance than the treaty it replaced, and from at least two perspectives this seems to be an accurate appraisal. There are no teeth in the present pact, for the countries have agreed only to "consult" in the event of an actual or perceived threat. Moreover, the forces readily available to repel an attack will be minimal, unless the two countries being protected (Malaysia and Singapore) supply the manpower and equipment themselves. From another perspective the five-power agreement is of diminished importance. Since the 1969 riots Malaysia seems to have come to realize that the major threat to the country derives from internal more than external sources. One British senior official has been quoted anonymously as remarking that since the 1969 riots Malaysia has "come of age," for they "have come to realize the

---

[13] *New York Times*, May 26, 1971, p. 5.

[14] Speech before Parliament, March 12, 1971, reported in *Malaysian Digest*, March 15, 1971, p. 7. The argument seems to be that this is not a "two-China" policy because Taiwan is not recognized and thus does not constitute a "China" in Malaysia's eyes.

British rundown [the term commonly used to describe the British withdrawal from Malaysia-Singapore] is not going to bring their house down, and a British presence is not going to solve their problems." As the official concluded, "May 13 showed how irrelevant the British were."[15]

Malaysia: Achievements, Failures, Prospects

Malaysia will continue to face several old problems, but myriad new ones of far greater complexity are also appearing. To the north there are still guerrillas on the Thai-Malaysian border, and to control these Malaysia must maintain good relations with her northern neighbor. To the south Singapore continues occasionally to provoke irritation, though relations have improved considerably as the wounds of Singapore's Malaysia period healed on both sets of leaders. Relations with Indonesia improved dramatically under the Suharto regime, and the two countries are again able to talk in earnest about solidarity among the members of the great Malay arc. Relations with the Philippines are occasionally strained by the troublesome Philippine claim to Sabah, but this claim usually resurfaces only when the issue becomes entangled in domestic Philippine politics, and it disappears from the international arena as soon as the pressure is removed at home.

Malaysia's new problems, however, are likely to be far more complex and certainly more difficult to resolve. The major international question involves relations with China. Thus far Malaysia's preferred friendship and China's hints of an impending thaw have drawn mixed reactions from each side. Malaysia was reported to have made contact with Peking through a trade delegation in Peking, and it was even reported that a lesser official of the Chinese Ministry of Foreign Affairs had described the guerrillas in Perak as not Communists but "brigands."[16] Yet Peking continues to permit *Suari Revolusi Malaya* (Malayan Voice of Revolution) to operate within its territory, and the radio station regularly broadcasts virulent propaganda as well

[15] Quoted in Anthony Polsky, "A Twilight Gathering," *Far Eastern Economic Review* (May 1, 1971), p. 51. It should also be noted that on several occasions the Australian Prime Minister has assured Parliament that the country's forces would not be used under the five-power defense agreement to quell internal disturbances. If the circumstances of the 1948 Emergency were to be repeated one wonders if it would now be defined as an "internal disturbance."

[16] *New York Times*, May 26, 1971, p. 5.

as detailed instructions to Malaysian guerrillas.[17] In all of his planning Razak must also keep in mind the social base of his constituency, particularly at a time when the new Five-Year Plan has as one of its major goals the redistribution of resources to correct the imbalance existing between Chinese and Malays. China must be taken into account in Southeast Asia, as Razak and many other Southeast Asian leaders well realize, but if it is given too much freedom of movement, or if it receives particularly good public relations, then the task of making Malaysian Chinese into permanent Malaysians in fact as well as name may become doubly difficult. Political deculturation is not an irreversible process.

Razak's strategy for survival, though it has never been actually described as such, seems to involve a big-power guarantee of the neutrality and inviolability of Southeast Asia, while Malaysia concentrates on nation-building at home. However, neutralization has been correctly, but not warmly, received, either by the large powers of the world or the small states of Southeast Asia. Even the USSR failed to give Malaysia its support, despite the fact that the Russian proposal for a Southeast Asia collective security arrangement seemed to have much in common with the Razak plan. Perhaps eventually the Razak scheme will be accepted, and ASEAN seems to be moving tentatively in this direction. Of course, much depends upon the future role of the United States in Southeast Asia. If America opts out of Asia completely Razak will probably have to reformulate his neutralization scheme drastically. A Southeast Asia watched over by Russia and China, whether hostile or friendly toward each other, would constitute a world unlike the triply guaranteed Southeast Asia which Razak now envisages.

Singapore: The Strategic Setting

An island republic of only 225 square miles with a population of slightly more than two million[18] cannot forge a truly independent

---

[17] Speech of the Malaysian Prime Minister before the Commonwealth Prime Ministers' Conference, Singapore, January 15, 1971.

[18] The official estimate for 1970 was 2.07 million. Thanks to a well organized family planning program the annual growth rate of the population has dropped from 4.1 in 1959 to 1.7 in 1970. Wags sometimes point out that the area of Singapore is 226 miles at low tide.

foreign policy, but Singapore has achieved a remarkable degree of foreign policy autonomy despite these constraints. In part this can be attributed to the quality of its political leadership, but the vitality of its population, its strategic location, and historical luck must not be totally discounted.

Singapore: Internal Determinants of Foreign Policy

The population of Singapore is overwhelmingly of ethnic Chinese origin,[19] most of whom migrated to the island from southern Chinese ports in the latter half of the nineteenth and the early part of the twentieth centuries. The extent to which de-Sinicization ("de-tribalization" is the term often used by Prime Minister Lee Kuan Yew) of these ethnic Chinese has taken place is a much debated question, and ample evidence can be gathered to support almost any position. Spoken Chinese (usually Hokkien) is very much the language of the street and of the lower and middle levels of commerce. The predominant cuisine is Chinese (though the food of almost any nationality can be found somewhere), and Chinese-language signs are to be found throughout the city. Although minority groups are involved in almost all major areas of social and economic activity, most residents are quite obviously of Chinese ethnic origin. While the tropical versions of colonial and modern architecture predominate, there are many of the old-style Chinese shop-houses and a few new ersatz-Chinese buildings. Thus, Singapore may look and sound very much like a Chinese city, but appearances and sounds are deceiving. Primary and secondary education is offered in any of the major local languages (English, Chinese, Malay, and Tamil), but the English stream has proved to have the greatest attraction for most races. English is the language of higher education, high-level commerce, much of government, and is popular in many segments of Singapore social life. But, similarly, Singapore is not a transplanted British (or American) city-state, just as it is not a third China. Singapore, in the end, is—diverse, heterogeneous, and often contradictory, but it remains unique. Thus, it is not surprising that Singapore has often aspired to an independent foreign policy, even while realizing that complete independence is unattainable.

The Singapore economy can only be described as booming. In the decade 1961–70 the gross domestic product grew by more than 10

---

[19] Some 75 percent of the population is Chinese; Malays account for about 14 percent; Indians, 8 percent; and others, 2 percent.

percent in six of the ten years; only once (1964) did it fall below 5.9 percent; and twice the GDP growth rate reached 15 percent (1968, 1970).[20] The climate for foreign investment has proved to be attractive in Singapore, largely because of economically-motivated government policies that have encouraged investment, fostered internal stability, minimized corruption, and virtually eliminated threats of major strikes. In the minds of most of Singapore's leaders, economics and politics—both foreign and domestic—are so intimately interrelated that it is virtually impossible to separate the various strands of the woven fabric. As an island city-state without a natural hinterland, Singapore must also trade to survive.

The British granted a large measure of internal self-government to Singapore in 1959, and the party that assumed the leadership at the time was the same in name as the party that rules today. However, the composition and, even more pronounced, the image of the party has changed considerably. In 1959 the People's Action party (PAP) was viewed by many as a party of the far left, but after numerous internal struggles and one major factional split the moderate wing under the leadership of the prime minister emerged victorious, and today the PAP rules with a broad base of popular support.[21] PAP leaders still take pains to describe the party as "democratic socialist," and the prime minister frequently acknowledges his fraternity with Socialist parties elsewhere in the world (particularly with the British Labour party), but, despite these symbolic gestures, the development of the Singapore economy owes more to Adam Smith than to Karl Marx. While the spirit of free enterprise is strong in Singapore, critics have also been quick to point out the authoritarian aspects of PAP rule. These certainly exist, but at the same time it cannot be denied that the PAP leadership has provided the island republic with stability, efficient government, dramatic development, and international respect. This is no small accomplishment.

[20] "Annual Budget Statement of the Minister of Finance," presented to Parliament, March 8, 1971, Table IIA, mimeographed.

[21] The troubled history of the PAP is well chronicled in Thomas J. Bellows, *The People's Action Party of Singapore: Emergence of a Dominant Party System* (New Haven, 1970), chaps. 2–5. The PAP rules today without an opposition in Parliament, though this somewhat overstates the extent of its popular support. The extreme left of the PAP broke away to form the Barisan Sosialis (Socialist Front) in 1961 and in the 1963 general elections the Barisan won 13 of 51 seats (after breaking with the PAP it had held 14). In 1968 the Barisan boycotted the elections and permitted the PAP to capture the entire house of 58 seats. Only seven seats were in fact contested. Had the Barisan chosen to run it would certainly have taken some seats, but it is doubtful that it would have approached its 1963 level.

The top leadership of Singapore realistically recognizes its own limitations in influencing the course of international affairs. In the words of a Chinese proverb, which Prime Minister Lee Kuan Yew often quotes, "big fish eat small fish and small fish eat shrimps."[22] In the prime minister's eyes the world is presently dominated by two very large fish with a third slowly growing to major proportions, and the little shrimp of Singapore is surrounded by many small fish. Singapore's task is to prove the Chinese proverb to be false, or at least to render the Singapore shrimp indigestible, and the country's strategy for survival must achieve this end.

Singapore leaders begin with the assumption that the two superpowers are interested in Asia because of the area's size and resources, both natural and human.[23] Perhaps neither power actually harbors imperialistic ambitions, but each is sometimes compelled to behave in an imperialistic manner in order to deprive the opponent of Asia's resources. In this environment a small state might pursue one of several alternative strategies for survival. A small state might attach itself to one of the superpowers, but this is a winner-take-all game, and it is difficult to hedge one's bets. Small states might enter into regional associations to overcome some of the disadvantages of being small, but there are serious difficulties inherent in international groupings of underdeveloped states, and in Southeast Asia strong regional associations are even more unlikely because of the heterogeneity of the area. The third alternative is to become so important to all powers —super, medium, and small—that the threat of interference on the part of any nation will provoke a deterring reaction on the part of others.

THE SINGAPORE STRATEGY

Singapore leaders have apparently opted for the third alternative, though occasionally they seem to waver between this strategy and attachment to one of the two major blocs.[24] This strategy is demand-

[22] Lee has often quoted the proverb. He also used it to illustrate some of the problems facing Singapore in an address to the Democratic Socialist Club, University of Singapore, June 15, 1966.

[23] This paragraph (and much of this section on Singapore) is based on press conferences, and public statements of the Prime Minister and the Foreign Minister (Rajaratnam) during the period 1965–70. All material (some 800 pages of typescript) is on the public record, though much of it has not received wide circulation.

[24] Of course, Lee has gone out of his way on many occasions to deny that he is

ing, there have been numerous complications, and the Republic is learning to live with short-range stability but long-range uncertainty.[25]

The British decision to disengage east of Suez probably came as no surprise to Singapore, but the haste with which it was eventually to be done must have been a shock. As late as March 1966 the prime minister was speaking confidently of having ten or fifteen years before Singapore would have to assume responsibility for its own defense,[26] and after the Secretary of State for Commonwealth Affairs, George Thomson, toured the Asian members of the Commonwealth in early 1968 informing leaders that the withdrawal would be completed by the end of 1971 a new sense of urgency could be seen in Singapore. The British rundown was to be accelerated, and Singapore's chosen strategy for survival had to be pursued as diligently as possible.

When the British decision to withdraw from Singapore was announced it was presumed by some that the United States might move in to fill the vacuum, but Singapore leaders quickly quashed such rumors. In part, this was consistent with Singapore's strategy for survival, for an invitation to the United States would have committed the Republic to a win-or-lose game, and there is considerable evidence that the prime minister expects the United States eventually to lose in Asia, not by defeat, but by default.[27] In part, however, this

---

associated with a bloc in any way. It might, however, be difficult to convince a Communist diplomat of this.

[25] An essential and early ingredient of the strategy, though not particularly relevant to the study here, was the development of a "rugged society" (the popular term) able to live and work under conditions of stress and occasional uncertainty. Lee sought to copy many aspects of the Israeli model, and Israeli advisors actually helped in the creation of mobilization and training schemes for Singapore defense forces. However, probably because of the hostility of Singapore's Muslim neighbors toward Israel, these advisors entered as "Mexicans," though their true identity was admitted later. The prime minister revealed that the choice of the Israeli model was not accidental. He has commented that after Singapore's expulsion from Malaysia his government made a thorough study of many small countries surrounded by larger neighbors. Eventually their attention narrowed to three (Switzerland, Finland, and Israel), and "in the end, we opted for the Israeli fashion." (Address to the Council of the Socialist International, Zurich, October 1967.)

[26] Speech at the Peking Restaurant, Singapore, March 12, 1966. As late as November 1967 Dennis Healey had assured Singapore and Malaysia that Britain would not withdraw its forces before the middle of the 1970's.

[27] On many occasions the prime minister has voiced fears that the United States, particularly the American people, lack the determination to carry through the adventure upon which the country had embarked in Asia. For understandable diplomatic reasons Lee has refused publicly to commit himself in regard to the wisdom of the initial movement into Vietnam, but he has made it clear several

also reflects the discomfort many Singaporeans feel when Americans are present. As Singaporeans have often remarked, including the prime minister who has repeated such sentiments many times, one can understand and "get along" with the British, who have been on the island for 150 years, but "the Americans are a different breed."

Singapore has found it difficult to chart a consistent and logical policy toward China. Although China cannot yet be regarded as a superpower, or perhaps even as a major power, it is apparent that she must be entered into any Southeast Asian equation. There is a feeling that China will eventually emerge as a modern, powerful, wealthy nation, and there seems to be the suggestion that when this happens the major threat posed by China will disappear.[28] In the meantime, however, China encourages and even assists revolutionaries throughout Southeast Asia, and her style of interference does not precisely fit the Singapore strategy. Singapore has found that she cannot deal with China in the same manner that she deals with Russia and the United States. Singapore's strategy for survival in the international arena has been designed to cope with thrusts and counter-thrusts from national entities, but the China of the past two decades has often played a qualitatively different political game.[29]

---

times that any attempt to achieve quick victory, or to get out "on the cheap," will deal a heavy blow to those who have strongly committed themselves to the American efforts. When the prime minister visited the United States in 1967 he was widely quoted for his staunch support of President Johnson's hard-line policies in Vietnam, and, indeed, the prime minister has his own version of the domino theory, though he steadfastly refuses to describe it in such terms. However, in fairness it should also be pointed out that his support for American policies has always included the caveat that increased firepower is no substitute for patience, determination, and sympathetic understanding. (The prime minister's "domino theory" has been clearly stated in several public speeches. In particular, see his address before Singapore and Malaysian Students, International Students House, London, April 22, 1966; his television interviews with foreign correspondents, TV Singapura, November 5 and 8, 1967; and his address to the American Association of Singapore, November 10, 1967. The prime minister's misgivings about the constancy of American policy came out in his interview taped at the studios of TV Singapura on November 5, 1967; in the address to the American Association cited previously; and in a television interview held in the Peninsula Hotel, Hong Kong, October 14, 1968.)

[28] "They are determined, as a people, to unify and build a modern, powerful, wealthy Chinese nation, and I say good luck to them. And I think the moment they get prosperous, good luck to me, because I will be much safer." (Lee Kuan Yew, "Meet the Press," New York, October 22, 1967.) Some two weeks later in Singapore the prime minister suggested that China might begin to emerge in such a condition "in the 1980's." (Interview with foreign journalists, TV Singapura studios, November 8, 1967.)

[29] To add to the difficulties, there is always the danger that Singaporeans may

A developed, powerful China may be welcomed, but a struggling China seeking to enhance her position in Asia must be feared. Moreover, even a fully developed China may be dangerous in the Singapore strategy for survival unless there are counter-balances to her power in Asia.

At least to the present generation of Singapore leaders Japan cannot play the role of a major power without provoking great resentment. For the record most Singaporeans probably regard the past as "forgotten if not forgiven,"[30] but the clear implication on the record, which is often more explicit off the record, is that the Japanese have not yet proved that they can again be trusted. This reluctance to trust the Japanese is by no means confined to Singapore, though it is probably more pronounced there than in most countries of Southeast Asia. However, it cannot be dismissed as insignificant in most of the countries of the region.

Singapore: Achievements, Failures, Prospects

The possibility of détente between the United States and China certainly comes as no surprise to some in Singapore, though the suddenness of the announced visit by President Nixon probably caught many off guard.[31] If a new era of overt tri-power politics in Asia

---

rediscover their Chinese origins and reverse the process of nationalization into a Singapore identity. While this seems unlikely under present circumstances, there are many "Chinese chauvinists" who only recently have been eclipsed and who wait in the wings for an opportunity to resume their positions of leadership.

[30] Lee Kuan Yew, interviewed by Professor Shinkichi Eto, NHK-TV, Tokyo, October 16, 1968.

[31] In response to a comment that perhaps the security of Singapore might be guaranteed by the major powers, the interviewer asked the prime minister: "Can you realistically hope to see a joint guarantee—I mean to suggest, that it should be a joint guarantee by China and America seems absurd." To this Lee replied: "I will not rule that out. . . . I can envisage that in the 1980's . . . a new generation will emerge in the People's Republic of China that has had quite a lot of trials and tribulations of building up a great industrial society from nothing and is not very anxious to see it all go back to the stone age [because of nuclear conflict]. When a pragmatic, realistic, and hard-headed younger generation emerges as it must, whether it is in the late 1970's or in the 1980's, I can well imagine such a group of men saying, 'All right, let us keep what we have and build on it.'" (Interview with foreign journalists, TV Singapura, November 8, 1967.) Note, however, that again the concept of the standoff enters in. China will not interfere with Singapore because of the threat of retaliation on the part of other major powers.

is in the offing, then Singapore's strategy of survival has probably been well chosen. If, on the other hand, the visit marks the first major step in the American withdrawal into "fortress America," then the Singapore strategy may prove a failure.[32] The success of Singapore's strategy for survival may depend upon the cooperation—wittingly or unwittingly—of all the major powers. If one power opts out it may be an entirely different game.

The Philippines: The Strategic Setting

Until recently, and in many ways even today, the Philippines has not expressed interest in pursuing foreign policies independent of those of the United States. The Philippines was one of only two Southeast Asian members of the Southeast Asia Treaty Organization (SEATO, the accepted but not official name), and indeed the pact had its birth in Manila in September 1954; the Philippines was one of the few Asian states to make a contribution to the American effort in Vietnam; and the Philippines has strongly, if not always enthusiastically, supported other manifestations of the general American effort to "contain Communism," including support for the Nationalist Chinese, exclusion of Peking from the United Nations, and non-intercourse with Communist states. Much of Philippine foreign policy has been a mirror image of American policy, and, in fact, in some policy areas it can best be interpreted as American policy with a lag-time of five to ten years. Thus, our task here is less to examine the substance of Philippine foreign policy and more to analyze the factors contributing to this parallelism. Moreover, in view of recent shifts in American policy and the growing anti-American sentiment in the Philippines it will be necessary to speculate on the future of the Philippine-American "special relationship."

The Philippines: Internal Determinants of Foreign Policy

American colonialism is probably not viewed by most Filipinos as a national catastrophe, or even as an unpleasant experience. In fact, many Filipinos, particularly among the older and middle-aged generations, probably look back on the period as a time of moderniza-

---

[32] In the thinking of the prime minister a powerful China will probably find common cause with a powerful Russia, particularly if there is no third power around to disrupt the entente. If this is not the case, and it is not self-evident that it should be, then Singapore's strategy may still prove to be appropriate.

tion, development, and national consolidation, and a minority may even regard it almost as the "golden age" of the Philippines. There were numerous irritations that arose, of course, but in perspective the American colonial period was marked by close cooperation and sometimes genuine affection between Americans and Filipinos. Philippine nationalism mounted steadily in the period between the two world wars, but, unlike many nationalist movements occurring after the Second World War, the element of xenophobia was largely missing. When the Philippines gained independence in 1946 Filipino leaders regarded it purely as a political and administrative act. No nationalist leader of the time seriously suggested that the Philippines should sever its cultural and emotional ties with the former colonial master.[33]

Almost to the last many Filipinos thought that the United States would protect them from the invading Japanese armies in World War II, just as America had clearly implied, even if it had not explicitly promised. That America placed a higher priority on Europe might have been expected to have produced mass disillusionment, but it did not. Many Filipinos actively worked with their Japanese conquerors with varying degrees of enthusiasm, but many fought valiantly beside Americans at Bataan and Corregidor, and many retreated to the mountains of central Luzon to maintain a Filipino-American presence in the country throughout the Japanese occupation. Perhaps if the Japanese had pursued more enlightened and humane colonial policies the Philippines might have developed politically in a considerably different manner,[34] but they did not, and the Americans returned to the Philippines more as liberators than conquerors.

Educational and cultural ties between the Philippines and the United States have been, and remain, strong. The educational system is patterned on the American model, and the medium of instruction in all but the first two years is English. Graduates from the better Philippine universities continue their studies at American institutions with less emotional and academic adjustment than is necessary for most foreign students, and Philippine-trained professionals can move into their fields in the United States with comparative ease, just as American-trained Filipinos can return to practice with almost no bureaucratic formalities. Admittedly these close ties have produced the

[33] It should be noted that nineteenth-century Filipino nationalists regarded Spain in the same manner. Their goal was to cut political and administrative ties, not to renounce Spanish culture.

[34] This observation need not be applied exclusively to the Philippines. Most Southeast Asians found to their disappointment that the Japanese were more harsh and insensitive than their European colonial masters.

problem of a "brain drain" from the Philippines to the United States,[35] but for our purposes the important point is that these exchanges take place with great frequency.

The Philippine mass media is also closely linked to its counterparts in the United States. The Manila press, which is predominantly English, reports much American news; American movies enjoy great popularity; and many American television series are shown regularly throughout the Philippines. It would be an exaggeration to say that the communications media has been totally Americanized, but the effect of the Philippine-American colonial relationship is clearly evident.

Economic ties between the United States and the Philippines have been as close as the cultural and educational links. Although all percentages have declined in the past decade the United States remains a major source of manufactured imports, a major consumer of Philippine raw material, and an important source of foreign investment.[36] The Philippines is particularly linked to the United States in the export of sugar. Philippine sugar enjoys preferential tariff treatment (of declining proportions, and preference will disappear completely in 1974), large quotas, and guaranteed prices somewhat above world market prices. Although there is no unanimity on this, some economists have in fact argued that the Philippine sugar industry, which remains the major foreign exchange earner, cannot survive without the subsidies provided by the American market.[37] Perhaps this overstates the problem, but the importance of the American sugar market cannot be ignored even by the most ardent Filipino nationalist.

Finally, there are several factors affecting the nature of Philippine foreign policy that are not directly related to the history of Philippine-American relations. The ongoing Huk[38] rebellion in central Luzon serves as a constant reminder to Filipino leaders in nearby Manila

[35] I have briefly discussed the brain drain and Filipino migration to the United States in another context in my *Ethnicity and Politics: The Changing Political World of Philippine-Chinese Youth*, Chapter 1, in press.

[36] See Frank H. Golay, ed., *Philippine-American Relations* (prepared for the American Assembly, Englewood Cliffs, 1966), esp. the various tables contained in the statistical appendix.

[37] For a recent discussion of the various aspects of the sugar problem, see *Solidarity*, VI (May 1971). This issue is devoted almost exclusively to the role of sugar in Philippine-American relations.

[38] "Huk" is a contraction of "Hukbalahap," which is an acronym derived from Hukbo ng Bayan Laban sa Hapon (Tagalog for People's Anti-Japanese Army), the name taken by Communist resistance fighters in the Second World War. Huk activity continues intermittently in Luzon, though much of it has now degenerated into common banditry.

that some indigenous Communists are unfriendly to the government. It is not clear to what extent the description "Communist" is applicable in the case of the present-day Huks, but they are nevertheless regarded officially and popularly as followers of Marx, Lenin, and Mao.[39]

The Chinese minority of the Philippines also has played a part in defining the parameters of Philippine foreign policy. Although the minority is small (perhaps no more than two percent), its economic influence is great, and its political orientations are both suspected and feared. That these fears are probably groundless is immaterial for they are firmly implanted in the minds of many Filipino politicians, and policies toward China and Taiwan have been affected by these lingering suspicions.

In the south another minority, long neglected by Manila, has created new problems for the government. Mindanao is the last great frontier for expansion in the Philippines, and, as Christian settlers and land speculators have pushed inland, the Muslim lowlanders and hill tribes have resisted. The resulting upheaval has not had a significant impact on Philippine foreign policy, but the political implications of the proximity of Mindanao to Sulu and Sabah—both seats of Muslim irredentism—cannot be ignored.

Mention must also be made of the *laissez-faire* economic and political environment of the Philippines. In both politics and economics Filipinos strongly resist the imposition of any overriding centralized authority. In many aspects of life the typical Filipino holds a deep commitment to individualism. He expects to be able to say almost anything he wishes (true, false, irresponsible, or even libelous—it often makes little difference); he will go to almost any lengths to beat the system, sometimes for personal gain, but often more as a matter of principle; and he lives day-to-day with little sympathy for anyone who tries to arrange his life for him, either long- or short-range. Rightly or wrongly, most Filipinos who philosophize on such subjects equate "freedom and individualism" to the west and "discipline, planning, and sacrifice," to the Communists. These impressions may be oversimplified, or even inaccurate in some cases, but they have influenced some foreign policy choices.

The Philippines: Achievements, Failures, Prospects

Since President Nixon enunciated the "Guam Doctrine" Filipino leaders have increasingly voiced concern about the readiness of the

---

[39] One wing of the Huks under Commander Danté seems to be ideologically motivated, but the relative size of this faction is difficult to ascertain.

United States to guarantee the security of the Philippines. However, the alternatives of an alliance with the United States are by no means apparent. The Philippines is a member of the Association of Southeast Asian Nations and the Asia and Pacific Council, both of which are regional groupings of East and Southeast Asian nations.[40] However, neither has demonstrated the ability, or interest, to transform itself into a regional security arrangement, though ASPAC is admittedly composed of many of the most anti-Communist (particularly anti-Chinese Communist) states of Asia, and ASEAN is showing signs of trying to transform itself into the organizational manifestation of the Malaysian neutralization scheme. For its part, the Philippines will probably not find it easy to work within the framework of any regional association where serious purposes demand mutual trust and respect. Because of its Christianization and its adoption of many of the ways of the west the Philippines is often suspect in the eyes of fellow Southeast Asian states. Filipinos are not westerners, but many fellow Asians harbor grave doubts that they are truly Asian. The shift from bilateral arrangements with the United States to multilateral associations with her Southeast Asian neighbors may prove to be a painful and difficult experience for the Philippines.

The possibility of a détente between the United States and the People's Republic of China is obviously causing considerable soul-searching in Manila. Until very recently few politicians have ever advocated recognition and, fewer still, a continuing relationship with Communist China. For most Filipino political leaders mainland China was Communist, and mainland China was an enemy of a friend. It therefore followed that any Communist enemy of a friend must also be an enemy of the Philippines. Moreover, the Philippines did not even recognize Russia, and, many felt, China was a far more dangerous enemy than the USSR.[41]

Another fear of Communist China stems from Filipino doubts

[40] ASPAC was created in 1966 (Japan, South Korea, the Republic of China, South Vietnam, Thailand, Malaysia, Australia, New Zealand, and the Philippines); ASEAN, in 1967 (Indonesia, Singapore, Malaysia, Thailand, and the Philippines).

[41] One of the strongest advocates of better relations with the People's Republic of China is the presidential possibility, Senator Benigno Aquino of the opposition Liberal party. However, even Aquino's position is of relatively recent origin. In November 1970 President Ferdinand Marcos dispatched the Executive Secretary of his Cabinet, Alejandro Melchor, to Moscow to discuss recognition and loans, and it is reported that Melchor returned enthusiastic. However, many Filipino politicians remained skeptical about the wisdom of "giving Communism an entering wedge," and no further action has been taken.

about the political loyalties of the Philippine-Chinese minority. Most of these are now Philippine-born, but few politicians feel that their hearts are really in the Philippines. In an effort to make certain that the minority is untainted by Marx and Mao the Philippine government enlisted the assistance of the Kuomintang in supervising the curriculum and the staff of the Chinese-language schools.[42] This supervision is established in a treaty between the Philippines and the Republic of China, and a rapprochement with the People's Republic, which would probably entail a simultaneous rupture of relations with Taiwan, would, of course, jeopardize this arrangement. In the eyes of many Filipinos this would invite a surge of Communist influence in the schools, and if the schools were closed it might actually increase the susceptibility of the disgruntled minority to Communist overtures. The argument may be a fallacious one, but it is accepted by many Filipinos, and it makes many leaders reluctant to risk upsetting the present arrangement.

A very difficult period in Philippine-American relations is also approaching. The Laurel-Langley Act of 1954 (which replaced the original Trade Act of 1946) ends in 1974, and at that time American imports into the Philippines, and Philippine imports into the United States, will be taxed at full tariff. In addition, there is the difficult problem of dealing with American individuals and corporations in the Philippines, which since independence have been treated as Filipino for legal purposes. Finally, most of the military base agreements must soon be renegotiated, and, in fact, preliminary discussions are reported already to have begun.[43] This renegotiation process is likely to be difficult and perhaps painful. These discussions will necessarily entail a larger review of American military commitments in the area, and after the PHILCAG disclosures of 1970[44] the bases

[42] Chinese-language education in the Philippines is optional, while the English language curriculum is required. Usually the two curricula are offered by different staffs teaching in the same buildings, with each curriculum offered for half a day. Today there are some 150 Chinese schools throughout the Philippines with an enrollment of about 70,000. School principals are usually recruited from Taiwan, and the Nationalist Chinese Embassy, working through an association of Chinese schools, has responsibility for reviewing the qualifications of the teachers, the selection of textbooks, and the planning of the curricula. (*Ethnicity and Politics: The Changing Political World of Philippine-Chinese Youth*, chapter 3.)

[43] See my "The Philippines in 1970: A Difficult Decade Begins," *Asian Survey*, XI (February 1971), 147.

[44] The Philippine Civil Action Group (PHILCAG) was dispatched to Vietnam at the urging of President Lyndon Johnson, who wanted to demonstrate that the Vietnam effort had the support of America's Asian allies. The amount of pressure

have become for demonstrating students symbols of American manipulation of Filipino politicians for imperialistic purposes. Thus, it
is almost certain that any agreement that does not include the total
withdrawal of American forces can be expected to trigger massive,
and possibly violent, student reaction. On the other hand, few Filipino
politicians think that this drastic action would be in the best interests
of the Philippines, or in the best interests of many of the politicians
themselves. Students and political leaders seem to be set on another
collision course.

The Philippines convened a Constitutional Convention in mid-1971,
charged with the responsibility of amending, or completely rewriting,
the present basic law of the nation. The impact this Convention may
have on Philippine foreign policy is uncertain, but in many of the
demands for abandoning the present Constitution (heard more often
outside than inside the Convention) there is an implied and sometimes
explicit anti-American tenor. If this should become the mood of the
Convention there is little doubt that the President would be affected
in his coming negotiations with the United States.

The Philippines has not yet devised its "strategy for survival."
In the past it has been content to let the United States lead the way,
and, if the United States ceases to lead, the Philippines will find
itself with no one to follow. The experience of the Second World
War should have taught the Philippines that in a crisis the United
States can be expected to place its priorities in North America and
Europe and that America's Asian allies will pay dearly if they fail
to recognize this unfortunate but harsh fact. However, at the present
time there is little evidence that the Philippines is prepared to come
to terms with the realities of the international environment in the
seventies.

Malaysia, Singapore, and the Philippines are facing a difficult period
of readjustment. At no time since the Second World War has the
future seemed so uncertain. Britain was forced by economic necessity
to withdraw virtually to her home islands, and the United States,

---

applied to President Marcos is not certain, but it was probably considerable, since
Marcos had vehemently opposed the scheme as a presidential candidate. In early
1970 the Symington Committee revealed that $3.6 million had been paid to the
Philippines in quarterly installments between 1966 and 1969, and Senator Symington labelled the Filipino contingent "mercenaries." An indignant denial was
promptly made by President Marcos, but these denials were qualified once the
Committee released a photocopy of one of the cancelled checks. See "The Philippines in 1970: A Difficult Decade Begins," p. 147, and Michael P. Onorato, "The
Philippine Decision to Send Troops to Vietnam," paper presented at the annual
meeting of the Association for Asian Studies, Washington, D.C., March 31, 1971,
mimeographed.

disillusioned over Vietnam and faced with mounting domestic problems, shows signs of making a similar decampment. At the same time China is evincing an interest in reentering the diplomatic arena after an absence of more than a decade, and the China of today has the potential to be a far more powerful force in international politics than was the China that attended the Bandung Conference in 1955.

The Malaysian neutralization scheme, Singapore's strategy for survival, and the Philippine-American alliance all depend in varying degrees upon an American presence in Southeast Asia. Under any circumstances some adjustments are necessary, particularly in the area of Philippine-American relations, but these are likely to be considerably more drastic and probably more painful if the only major powers left with an interest in the future of Southeast Asia are the Soviet Union and the People's Republic of China.

Perhaps it is asking too much of Americans to be unobtrusive, but there is an excellent opportunity for the United States to correct some of the mistakes it committed in Vietnam by maintaining a constructive, low-profile presence in insular Southeast Asia in the 1970's. If America can accomplish this feat there is probably greater hope for long-term stability in the region than at any time since the countries gained independence. If America chooses total disengagement, or if by any chance it should again opt for massive involvement (which seems unlikely), then the foreign-policy alternatives for Malaysia, Singapore, and the Philippines will be severely restricted, and, in fact, almost non-existent. Difficult times may be ahead for the countries of insular Southeast Asia. The problems of readjustment they are likely to face will severely test the intuition, flexibility, and diplomatic skills of their leaders.

Nepal, Burma and Ceylon

LEO E. ROSE

The three southern Asian states of Nepal, Burma and Ceylon do not form any natural regional, cultural or political conglomerate, and cannot be analyzed within a single conceptual framework. Indeed, the contrasts are more striking than the similarities both in their political style and the repertory of responses to their geopolitical situations. Nepal, a Hindu monarchy in which traditional cultural and political forms are still in an early stage of transformation, was never absorbed into the British Indian empire and maintained an autonomous identity throughout the colonial period. Burma and Ceylon were both British colonies with a Theravada Buddhist culture-base, but with widely varying colonial experiences and degrees of political and economic development. In the post-independence period (i.e., after 1948), both states have traveled quite distinct political paths—Ceylon maintaining a British-style parliamentary democracy; Burma adopting a political system under which a radicalized military elite has assumed a dominant role.

There are some similarities between the three states, however, that do lend plausibility to their inclusion in this chapter. They are all small states in southern Asia exposed to a variety of external pressures, particularly economic manipulation. In defining the fundamental principles of their foreign policy, these states have adopted the same rhetoric if not necessarily the same strategy of implementation, providing an excellent example of how the same words can have very different meanings in different settings. All three countries also have long histories in which resistance to foreign aggression, with varying degrees of success, plays a prominent role in their cultural consciousness, shaping to some extent the framework within which they view the contemporary world.

The Strategic Setting

Nepal: This Hindu kingdom in the central Himalayan area to the south of the crest of the world's highest mountain range has a formidable, but not impassable northern border which has been a decisive factor in the determination of its regional affiliations. Nepal's southern border with India, in contrast, lies on the Gangetic plain, from which numerous routes lead into the hill areas which form 80 percent of the territory of the state. The southern rim at the foot of the hills, called the terai, is the focus of most of Nepal's agricultural and industrial production and provides the government with approximately 75 percent of its revenue. The hill areas are formed by three east-west ranges: the Siwalik in the south; the Mahabharat in the center; and the Himalayas in the north. The Mahabharat range, Nepal's principal defense line against invasion from the south, is also India's line of defense against aggression from the north in this and other sections of the frontier with Chinese-controlled Tibet.

Nepal has had extensive trans-Himalayan contacts with Tibet for at least 1500 years, but in the total social context these have not proven particularly crucial. The central Himalayan area's relations with the Gangetic plain, on the other hand, have been definitive for at least 2500 years, and Nepal is in many ways an extension of northern India culturally, intellectually and politically. The real challenge to Nepal's *national* existence, thus, has usually come from the south, and it is only in the past two decades that the north has figured prominently in Nepali security considerations. Situated between Asia's two largest, and in recent years increasingly hostile countries, India and China, Nepal is vulnerable to both; its foreign policy is largely an exercise in minimizing the effects of external intrusions while maximizing the potential benefits of a balance of power policy. Nepal's borders are well-demarcated in most areas and delimited in international agreements, and there are no significant border disputes complicating relations with either neighbor.

While Nepal's geography has been a major factor in preserving its national independence, it has also intensified the problems of national integration within the country. Nepal is divided into distinct geographical regions defined primarily by the three major north-south river systems that bisect the east-west ranges. Communications in an east-west direction from the capital, Kathmandu, have always been difficult and have complicated the task of establishing an effective centralized administrative system. The natural lines of communication in much of the hill area run in a north-south direction—that is either to India or Tibet—and this is of considerable political and economic significance.

Burma: While independent kingdoms had existed within the territory now comprising the Union of Burma for several centuries prior to the British conquest in the late 19th century, their boundaries had fluctuated widely in periods of comparative strength vis-à-vis various neighbors—particularly the Chinese and Thais. The British formally demarcated the border between India and Burma (which formed a single colony until 1936) as well as those to the east with French-dominated Laos and independent Thailand. Burma's northern border with China, however, was never formally delimited during the British period except in certain sections through treaties with the Tibetan and Chinese governments.

Independent Burma, thus, inherited a potentially serious border problem with China. The physical boundaries in the western section of this frontier are an extension of the Himalayan range and are nearly as imposing as those which separate Nepal and Tibet. Communications with Yunnan province in China in the northeastern section, however, are not as difficult, and the memory of Chinese invasions via these routes is still a vivid part of the Burmese historical consciousness. Unlike Nepal, Burma is not a buffer zone between China and India and thus is not in a position to play "balance of power" politics. China is the only neighbor that threatens Burma's national existence, and apprehension toward China is very much a part of the present regime's foreign policy. A formal boundary agreement was signed with Peking in 1961 in which China made several minor territorial concessions and recognized Burma's independence. But the Chinese Communists have continued to support rebel political movements in Burma through the provision of arms, training and financial support, raising uncertainties in Rangoon, Burma's capital, about Peking's ultimate objectives.

Burma's western borders with Pakistan and India are marked by well-defined river or mountain boundaries. Land communications in this frontier region are difficult, and even the British conquerors entered Burma from India via the sea route.[1] The Burmese, thus, have

---

[1] The Japanese conquest of Burma in World War II intersected the only Allied land communications with China. The Burma campaign conducted by the Allies in order to open up the "Ledo Road" to China demonstrated the great topographical and climatic problems faced by any military operation in Burma from the Indian side.

no historically-based perception of India as a potential aggressor—or, on the other hand, as a possible source of support in the event of aggression from other directions. Border agreements have been signed with both Pakistan and India and joint demarcation on the ground is underway. The only potential source of trouble in this frontier region is the various tribal communities that straddle the border, which have not been fully absorbed into any of the dominant political systems and which are susceptible to political manipulation.

Access from the east (Laos and Thailand) is comparatively easy, and most of Burma's wars have been fought with the Thais for control of this intermediate tribal region. There are no serious border or political problems between Burma and its two eastern neighbors, and indeed the three governments have been broadly supportive of each other.[2] A North Vietnamese-dominated Laos, of course, would be another matter, as it would constitute a potential source of support for the various ethnic and leftist political groups in Burma that contest the authority of Rangoon in this eastern region.

Ceylon: This island's strategic location at the tip of the subcontinent on the principal lines of communication in the Indian Ocean has exposed Ceylon to external dangers, both past and present. The Muslims, Portuguese, Dutch and British have all invaded Ceylon at different times in the past few centuries, primarily to protect the coastal trade entrepôts established there to facilitate commerce with Southeast and East Asia. Only the British conquered the entire island and established a full-fledged colonial system, but the impact of the other invasions is still apparent in the country's social and cultural structure.

The dominant external factor for contemporary Ceylon, politically and economically, is its northern neighbor, India. Sinhali resistance against Dravidian (Tamil) invaders from south India forms an important aspect of Ceylonese history. Even more significant, however, is Ceylon's subordinate economic relationship to India which developed during the British colonial period and has continued, somewhat modified, in the post-independence era as well. Ceylon's strategic location makes the island an important potential factor in the Indian Ocean *if* big power rivalry should become activated in this region. The situation would be even more critical for Ceylon if China should gain hegemony over Southeast Asia, and become one of the contenders

[2] The Ne Win regime in Burma was unhappy when Thailand allowed the opposition Burmese political leader, U Nu, to settle in Bangkok in 1970. Rangoon was even more disturbed when, according to reports, he was not prevented from crossing the border into rebel-held territory in eastern Burma, but no formal, public protest has been made on this issue.

in this littoral area. These are, however, all potential and distant dangers which by no means presently dominate councils in Ceylon's capital, Colombo.

Social Factors in Foreign Policy

Nepal: The political elite in this kingdom consists primarily of high-caste Indoaryan Hindus who migrated to Nepal during the Muslim invasions of India (12th–16th c.) and gradually assumed a dominant role throughout the sub-Himalayan hill area as far east as Sikkim. The present royal family, for instance, traces its descent from a prestigious Rajput (warrior/ruler caste) family from Rajasthan, and like most other Nepali elite families has intermarried extensively in India. The social and cultural ties between the elites in both countries, thus, are deeply-based.

While approximately 75 percent of the hill area population of Nepal are from non-Indoaryan ethnic communities, a large proportion of these have been "Hinduized" (that is, brought within the Hindu social/cultural system) to varying extents. The result has been a distinct hill political culture characterized by the dominance of high-caste Hindu groups and a well-defined hierarchical relationship between the elite and the subordinate ethnic communities. There are, however, two groups in Nepal that defy easy integration into this hill culture and continue to pose a serious problem to national integration. The first consists of communities of relatively recent Tibetan origin inhabiting the northern border area. These communities are not very numerous but occupy a highly strategic section of the country. Far more perplexing for Kathmandu, however, are the people of recent Indian origin (25 percent of the total population of Nepal) in the terai, most of whom have migrated to Nepal in the last century and have retained close familial, caste and economic ties with India.

Burma: The Burmans, whose social-political culture is strongly influenced by Theravada Buddhism, form the majority of the country's population but occupy only the central plains area that constitutes less than 50 percent of Burma's territory. The extensive hill areas on the frontier regions are largely inhabited by non-Burman ethnic communities, some of which have never been absorbed into the Burman socio-political system. The Karens and Shans in the east and northeast and the Nagas in the west, for instance, include a large Christian component that has strongly opposed Burman Buddhist "cultural imperialism."[3] Some of the Kachins in northern Burma have adopted Buddhism, but are equally resentful of Burman programs aimed at political/cultural integration. Among all these ethnic groups there is a long tradition of resistance to Burman, Chinese and Thai dominance at different periods in the past.

A different kind of problem for the Rangoon government is that of the large Chinese and Indian minorities, most of whom have settled in the central plains area in the past century, but who often have familial-based economic ties with the hill areas as well. Neither of these minorities has directly challenged the political authority of the Burmese government as have the hill tribes, but their dominant role in the economy led Rangoon to impose drastic economic policies directed at the Indian and Chinese Burmese. A substantial proportion of the Indian community was "induced" to return to India by this discriminatory legislation; few Chinese followed their example, choosing instead to make the best accommodation possible with the Burmese government.

Ceylon: The large majority (65 percent) of the Ceylonese are Sinhalese, claiming descent from Indoaryan migrants and speaking a Sanskrit-derived language. Most of them are Theravada Buddhists, but with the influence of the Hindu caste system also readily apparent. They occupy the central hill areas, and provide the labor force in the southern coastal metropolitan areas. A large Tamil minority (20 percent) from South India is divided about equally into two distinct groups: (1) the Ceylon Tamils, who have resided in the island for several centuries, are Ceylon citizens, and are well-represented in commerce, the professions, academia and government service; and (2) the Indian Tamils, mostly descendents of migrants brought to Ceylon as plantation workers during the British period, who do not hold Ceylonese citizenship. The former group is important both politically and economically; the latter lacks the political prerogatives of citizenship but is organized into labor unions that wield considerable influence. Both speak Tamil, a non-Indoaryan Indian language as their mother tongue, and are Hindus, which distinguishes them from their Sinhali neighbors. Northern Ceylon is a virtual Tamil preserve, but many members of this community are also found in the coastal metropolitan centers.

---

[3] Burma, thus, provides a case study for a plains culture which is attempting to integrate contentious hill minorities, while Nepal is a hill culture trying to integrate a pliable but resistant plains minority. This hills/plains conflict is also an aspect of Ceylon politics, but the pattern of domination/resistance is not as well defined there as in Nepal and Burma.

There are several other small minorities, of which the Christians and the Muslims are the most important. The Christians have virtually dominated the civil and military establishments and are well-represented in intellectual, commercial and public media enterprises as well. The Muslims are mostly the descendants of a once-prosperous trading community. Sinhali resentment of the superior position of these minority communities underlies much of the political dissidence in contemporary Ceylon, even though a Sinhali-dominated political party has held power for most of the period since 1956.

STRATEGIES OF NATIONAL INTEGRATION

All three states are multi-ethnic societies in which "nation-building" is a problem of epic importance to the dominant political elite. The policies of the three governments are broadly similar in objective—that is, the imposition of the majority political culture on deviant minorities—but the strategies employed have differed in important respects.

In Nepal, the emphasis on the "Hinduization" of the non-Indoaryan hill tribes continues, reinforced now by the encouragement of a nationalist consciousness defined as loyalty to the high-caste Hindu hill political culture. The monarchy is used as a unifying symbolism and great importance is attached to the development of a national language (Nepali) and a common set of political institutions. The terai Hindus of Indian descent probably constitute the greatest obstacle to the achievement of these goals as they are the only large minority with a plausible alternative focus of political loyalty (India) and a viable alternative language (Hindi). The Nepal government has moved slowly in its program aimed at integrating the terai people into the "national" culture, but the effort is being made. So far, there has not been any official Indian opposition to this "Nepalization" process, but the attraction of the Indian political, economic and intellectual environment is, in itself, a barrier to Nepal's national integration.

The Burmese government faces a more difficult and dangerous situation than Nepal as the hill minorities are both more distinct in cultural terms and more intransigent in their opposition to "Burmanization." Rangoon's national integration policies have varied from attempts at enforced Burmanization to the acceptance of an accommodation based on a limited autonomy concept. The present military regime appears to be opposed to any significant concessions to the ethnic minorities, and has adopted a highly centrist model.

The political dominance of the Sinhali community in Ceylon is not seriously challenged, as the minorities have usually avoided direct confrontations in favor of accommodations with the Sinhali political leaders that preserve their established privileged position in the economy and government service. This had been partially achieved, at least tacitly, by 1970; indeed, the main problem for the government is not dissidence within the minority community but rather within the majority community which led to the Sinhali-based "Che Guevarist" uprising in 1971 against the minority-dominated Establishment.

The role of distinct and, in some instances, rebellious minorities in these three countries has had a considerable significance on their relations with neighboring states. The existence of the "Indian" minority in the Nepali terai, for instance, has provided New Delhi with a handy instrument for political intervention which it has employed in various ways on several occasions—to good effect. The hill tribes in Burma, and particularly some elements of the Kachins, Shans and Karens, have made it clear that they are prepared to accept support from external sources in their struggle against the Burmans. China has on one occasion intervened in support of the Chinese minority which, according to Peking, was being maltreated by the Burmese; the Indian government, in contrast, accepted without public protest the stringent Burmese government regulations aimed at the Indian and Chinese commercial interests in Burma. Similarly, New Delhi has taken a moderate position on the Indian Tamil community in Ceylon, and agreed to Colombo's insistence that a large proportion of them be repatriated to India.

Foreign Policy: The Domestic Determinants

Decision-making authority in Nepal resides with the monarch, King Mahendra, and his personal secretariat, who constitute the principal power center in Nepal's political system. All important decisions are made in the palace. The bureaucracy, including the army, provides some technical competence and is essential to policy implementation, but its subordinate relationship to the palace is unquestioned. Members of the Council of Ministers, responsible solely to the Crown, will on occasion play a peripheral role in decision-making, but through their status as advisors to the King rather than as a prerogative of the office they hold.[4] Finally, the national "parliament" (Rashtriya Pan-

---

[4] Frequently, one of the ministers will serve as a spokesman for the government on foreign policy issues, gaining personal political merit with the public when the policy has positive results or providing a convenient scapegoat should one be required. In all cases, however, it can be presumed that statements of any importance had received prior clearance from the palace.

chayat), which is selected on a "non-party" basis and holds its sessions *in camera,* is also more a consultative than a legislative body.

The palace, of course, is not completely unhindered by internal political and economic constraints on foreign policy issues. The hill-dominated political elite concentrated in Kathmandu valley, which the King adroitly manipulates but upon which he depends for support, is very sensitive on national identity questions, particularly when these concern relations with India. All policies to this group should be at least implicitly directed toward minimizing the impact of Indian political, cultural and economic influence in the country. This is not always possible, as the government must frequently compromise this basic objective for practical reasons. Disguising concessions to New Delhi in acceptable nationalist rhetoric is a well-developed skill in Kathmandu, but the attraction for assuming an anti-Indian pose has also proved irresistible to some political leaders, including at times even the King—usually with deleterious consequences for Nepal.

There are, moreover, counter-elites among the "excluded" ethnic communities in Nepal that do not share the worldview of the dominant hill culture elite. Some of the more important local leaders of Indian descent in the terai, for instance, have been isolated from the power center in the capital to such an extent that they depend upon New Delhi for the protection of their economic and political interests.[5] Other ethnic communities in both the eastern and western hills are also heavily dependent upon India for the necessities of life and as an alternative source of employment. Land pressure in some areas of the hills is so intensive that survival is possible for many Nepali families only if one or more sons is sent down to the plains for work or service in the Indian army. The Kathmandu-based political elite decry the "colonial" status implied in the system under which Nepali "mercenaries" serve in the Indian and British armies. But, as the government knows, to end such recruitment at this time for "nationalist" reasons or to pacify China and Pakistan (against whom the Nepali units have been used) would have disastrous economic consequences in the hills. The King and his political protéges, thus, have had to use the nationalist theme carefully, directing different kinds of appeals to different audiences, both foreign and domestic.

Burma, like Nepal, has a small, easily-identified political elite which controls the decision-making process. In the Burmese case, however,

[5] The 1964 land reform program, for instance, was directed primarily at terai landowners of Indian origin. It was New Delhi's warning against the implementation of this policy along blatantly anti-Indian lines that deterred Kathmandu.

it is the army headed by the President, General Ne Win, and its political wing, the Lanzan party, whose authority is virtually unchallenged at the governmental level. A number of bureaucratic technicians serve as advisors to Ne Win and the small coterie of military officers who make up his inner circle, but the bureaucracy as an institution is no more influential than that of Nepal.

The only legal non-official body within the country that has the potential capacity to influence the government's domestic and foreign policy is the Buddhist Sangha, the institutional vehicle for the numerous influential Buddhist monks who played such an important role in the nationalist movement during the British period and in the politics of the 1950's. Through the skillful use of both the carrot and the stick, the Ne Win regime has managed to neutralize the Sangha as a political force but has by no means either eliminated or absorbed it into the governing elite. The Sangha would seem to have no strongly-held views on foreign policy, but it does tend to be narrowly nationalist and even xenophobic in perspective. On foreign policy issues, its influence has been exerted primarily through its insistence on measures aimed at curbing the influence of the Indian and Chinese minorities, complicating Burma's relations with both these states in the process.

Burma's pluralistic social structure is another important factor in the government's calculations on relations with foreign powers. Some of the non-Burman ethnic groups are eager to obtain foreign aid in support of their anti-government activities, and Rangoon's foreign policy has been devised to minimize their capacity to do so, particularly with respect to China. Unlike Thailand, the Chinese community in Burma has not been largely "nationalized" and it is assumed in Rangoon that the Chinese Burmese are a potentially subversive element in the polity. Peking's crude attempt to interfere in support of the Chinese minority in 1967 and the revelations in 1969–70 that China was directing and assisting pro-Maoist rebel groups in Burma on a substantial scale was, of course, very disturbing to the Burmese authorities. Some minor restrictions have been placed upon the operations of the Chinese Communists in Burma in retaliation, but it would have been politically dangerous to break relations with Peking which might then extend greater assistance to Burmese rebel groups. However, the government has felt compelled to modify its isolation policy and has opened up the country again to the western powers on a very limited basis, in part as a counterbalance to China.

Ceylon's democratic political system, based on representative multi-party politics, provides a clear contrast to Nepal and Burma in the way in which domestic factors impinge upon foreign policy formulation. Participation in the decision-making process in Ceylon is very broad, with diverse political, economic and ethnic interests playing prominent roles. In formal structural terms, foreign policy is the responsibility of the prime minister and cabinet, with the parliament exercizing an ultimate control through its power to remove a government by a no-confidence vote. The bureaucracy, which is the most stable element within a rather volatile political system, has a strong influence in decision-making as well as in the implementation of policy.

The party system in Ceylon is remarkably comprehensive. On the left are three parties, and an avowedly Maoist revolutionary organization, the Janatha Vimukti Peramuna (JVP), that led the abortive "Che Guevarist" uprising in 1971. The Communists are divided into three factions—the pro-Moscow CP(M), the pro-China CP(C), and a Trotskyist party, the Lanka Sama Samaja party (LSSP). All three compete for the same constituency—the large, well-organized union movement and the student community in the coastal metropolitan area. There are wide differences between them on ideological and tactical questions, but in fact they are all part of the Establishment; indeed, the CP(M) and the LSSP are junior partners in the United Front (UF) ministry formed after the 1970 elections. The JVP, in contrast, is largely rural-based, with the newly emergent Sinhali educated class as its main source of support.

The main partner in the UF ministry, the Sri Lanka Freedom party (SLFP) led by Prime Minister Mrs. Bandaranaike, has its support base in the Sinhali rural areas in central and southern Ceylon. The SLFP affects a radical posture on foreign policy issues, but in fact is more flexible than either of its UF partners. The other major party in Ceylon, the United National party (UNP), is moderately conservative, representing primarily rural and urban middle-class interests throughout the country except the Tamil-majority areas where two ethnic-based parties contend for the support of this community.

Since independence, Ceylon's cabinets have been dominated by either the UNP (1948–56, 1965–70) or the SLFP (1956–65, 1970–). The foreign policy platforms of the two parties differ in substance, with the SLFP having a perceptible pro-Communist bloc flavor while the UNP is mildly pro-west. In practice, however, their foreign policies have fluctuated within rather narrowly-prescribed parameters and have varied much less than their rhetoric. Both parties have accepted nonalignment as a basic principle, and would pay a high price, both internally and externally, for extreme deviations from this policy. The UF government came close to this in 1970 when it broke diplomatic relations with Israel, established relations with East Germany, North Korea, North Vietnam and the Viet Cong, and demanded the withdrawal of the US Peace Corps and the Asia Foundation. But this imbalance was corrected to some extent in 1971 when the government renewed the "Voice of America" agreement under which the US uses broadcasting facilities in Ceylon for its Asian radio programs.

Coalition politics have also had a significant impact on the foreign policy of both UNP and SLFP governments.[6] The SLFP, for instance, has had to assume positions on certain issues which it might well have moderated except under pressure from the leftist partners in the coalition cabinet. Similarly, during the 1965–70 period, the UNP government depended upon the support of Tamil members of parliament for its majority, and this influenced the cabinet to take a comparatively liberal position in negotiations with India over the repatriation of Indian Tamils. In any case, foreign policy decision-making in Ceylon is obviously an extremely complex process, and one in which virtually all elements of the population have identifiable interests, well-defined positions and the capacity to exert a degree of influence.

Relations with Foreign Governments

Nepal, Burma and Ceylon are all in the process of economic transformation and are ill-equipped to resist external economic and political manipulation, whatever the source. Their traditional subsistence agrarian economies have been largely monetized over the past century but are not yet self-supporting, while their small industrial infrastructures are still heavily dependent upon inputs of capital and technical skills (either through aid or private investment) from outside.

Nepal, Burma and Ceylon, however, have devised quite different tactics to meet this situation. Nepal has adopted what might be called an "everybody's invited" policy with the expectation that the various participating powers will counterbalance each other and that foreign aid will be maximized. Burmese policy has been the exact reverse, at least since 1962 under the present military regime. Rangoon has chosen the "exclusivist" road under which the country has been isolated to the fullest extent possible from foreign political and economic forces. Some foreign aid is still accepted, but with so many restrictive stipulations that it could not possibly be effective. Ceylon lies somewhere

---

[6] It was reported, for instance, that the SLFP ministers proposed that India be asked to provide military assistance during the JVP uprising in 1971, but that some of the CP(M) and LSSP ministers objected.

in-between; not as inclusivist as Nepal but not as exclusivist as Burma. Both SLFP and UNP cabinets have sought the selective involvement of foreign economic interests, governmental and private, on terms that are considered compatible with Ceylon's economic and political interests and policies. It rarely works out quite that way, however.

All three countries have adopted nonalignment as the fundamental principle of their foreign policies, although with differing interpretations. For Nepal, situated precariously between India and China, nonalignment means essentially noninvolvement in the Sino-Indian rivalry in the Himalayan area without, however, breaking existing ties between New Delhi and Kathmandu. Burma interprets nonalignment on the Swiss model, and seeks to isolate the country from either global or regional disputes as far as possible. Ceylon, meanwhile, continues to think of nonalignment in Nehruian terms as a "positive" policy which allows the lesser powers to play an active part in world affairs, even at times as an intermediary in the settlement of big power disputes—a role both Nepal and Burma would prefer to shun.[7]

In the immediate post-independence period, these states had stable, if vulnerable economies. Nepal was virtually undeveloped because of the strict isolationist policy followed by Kathmandu up to 1945. Burma and Ceylon both had relatively prosperous economies, with promising prospects for rapid development. All three adopted a "politics to the fore" approach at some point which assigned higher priorities to political factors (particularly nation-building and regime preservation) than to economic development when these were not compatible. The results have been predictable in terms of a low rate of economic development, but probably less so in Nepal which has a more flexible ideological component in its political infrastructure. Rangoon, with its "Burmese Path to Socialism," and Colombo with its social welfare state ideology, are both more inhibited by political factors in policy formulation.

Moreover, despite their strong *verbal* attachment to the principle of "self-reliance," all three countries are probably more dependent than ever on external economic assistance. Nepal continues to be a virtual adjunct of the Indian economy, with approximately 95 percent of its foreign trade and 60 percent of foreign aid from this source. India also provides the only alternative employment market for thousands of Nepalis, thus reducing the pressure placed upon Kathmandu in

[7] During the 1962 Sino-Indian war, for instance, Ceylon summoned a meeting at Colombo of the major nonaligned powers and played a prominent role in the formulation of proposals intended to serve as the basis for a settlement. Nepal declined the invitation in order to avoid having to take sides, while Burma attended but functioned more like an interested observer than a participant.

this respect. Nepal's "politics first" approach seriously complicated the vital negotiations with India on the revision of the 1960 trade treaty in 1970–71. The result is that Nepal continues to suffer from most of the disadvantages of a common market with India but has gained few of the advantages, and political considerations have deterred Kathmandu from correcting this situation on the basis of a realistic appraisal of the country's economic interests.

Burma's economy in 1948 was comparatively autonomous (i.e., foreign economic interests were not particularly prominent) for an ex-colonial state. While important segments of the economy were controlled by the Indian or Chinese minorities, these did not provide either India or China with the capacity to intervene economically as neither minority had maintained structural economic ties with their home countries. The Burmese government, however, decided on an expropriation policy that has had disastrous domestic economic consequences without in any way improving Burma's position vis-à-vis its two large neighbors.

By 1970, the "Burmese Path to Socialism" had transformed the country's once-substantially favorable balance-of-trade into a chronic deficit, imposing additional sacrifices on the Burmese people. Foreign aid to supplement declining earnings from exports is, thus, more necessary than ever, but is increasingly unavailable. Aid from the US and the west was reduced to insignificant levels with the introduction of the "Burmese Path to Socialism" in the 1962–65 period. A 1967 dispute with China terminated Burma's profitable aid-trade arrangement with that country. Soviet aid had also been reduced in the aftermath of the failure of the expensive Russian-sponsored farm mechanization program. The government finally liberalized its policy on trade and aid, but probably too late to be effective in the context of the rapidly-changing situation in Southeast Asia.

Ceylon finds itself in a similar situation to Burma, though for quite different reasons. Ceylon also began its independence with a favorable trade balance, which was used to finance the most ambitious social welfare program in southern Asia. The trade situation gradually deteriorated, however, while social welfare demands and expectations expanded, imposing irresistible pressures upon the popularly-elected governments.

The ensuing economic crisis was worsened by the 1971 JVP uprising which drastically reduced Ceylon's earnings from trade and tourism and increased expenditures on the military and the police. Even more important, it deterred the UF government from taking some of the hard economic decisions which were essential but were bound to be unpopular. The heavily-subsidized rice price, for instance, is a major economic burden but a political "sacred cow." The program is possible only because of the rice/rubber exchange agreement with China, under which Peking sells rice to Ceylon at lower than world prices while buying Ceylonese rubber on favorable terms. This arrangement, however, discourages Colombo from adopting a more rational rice-marketing policy that would enable it to sell the rubber on the international market for hard currency, which could then be used to finance industrialization or infrastructure projects. Moreover, it enhances Ceylon's dependence upon China and inhibits its freedom in foreign policy decision-making.[8]

Ceylon's deteriorating international economic situation is also, ironically, one of the main obstacles to the implementation of the UF government's radical economic reform program. It was necessary, for instance, to postpone the nationalization of Ceylonese banks handling foreign exchange as their services were required to float badly-needed loans from foreign commercial banks. Even more critical were the negotiations with the World Bank over three essential development projects, including the Mahaveli River diversion. The World Bank's terms, reportedly, ran counter to some aspects of the UF's internal and external economic program, but the need for aid from the Bank was so great that Ceylon's bargaining position was virtually nil. Here again, policies introduced to meet domestic political requirements have been counterproductive in the long run. Ceylon, like Burma and Nepal, has found that there is no easy path to economic independence, and that policies that ignore economic facts of life are no solution— even in political terms. But they face a dilemma in that unpopular economic policies can threaten the very existence of the regime.

SECURITY AND DEFENSE FACTORS

These three regimes contend with a variety of external security problems as well as serious internal threats which have assumed increasing importance in the past decade. The policies adopted by the three states have varied on this, as on other questions, although a broadly similar response pattern may now be emerging.

From the mid-19th century, Nepal had been a "semi-satellite" of British India, and after 1947 New Delhi sought to maintain this rela-

---

[8] This was evident during the 1971 JVP uprising. China was officially exempted from any responsibility for these events, but the North Korean diplomatic mission was declared persona non grata. There is no evidence that the North Koreans were any more active than the Chinese in providing ideological guidance and inspiration to the JVP, much less material support. The North Koreans were expendable, however, while the Chinese were not.

tionship to the extent that changing circumstances and its own value system permitted. Nepal continued to constitute a vital component in the Indian security system on the northern border. The 1950 Indo-Nepali treaty amounted to a virtual military alliance. An Indian military mission supervised the reorganization and training of the Nepal Army, and Indian army personnel manned the border posts between Nepal and Chinese-controlled Tibet for intelligence-collecting purposes. The Nepal Army obtained its arms and equipment from India, and Nepali army officers received their training in India. Finally, there was the system under which Nepalis were recruited into the Indian Army, providing a vital defense link between the two countries.

This relationship began to change in the 1960's, particularly after India's embarrassing defeat in the 1962 border war with China. For a time, Nepal obtained some arms from the US and UK, and in 1970 the Indian military mission and border post personnel were withdrawn at Kathmandu's insistence. While these steps modified Nepal's involvement in India's security system, they did not end it. An agreement was reached between the two governments in 1965 under which India obtained exclusive responsibility (with certain exceptions) for the provision of arms and equipment. The military mission has reappeared in different guise, and the exchange of intelligence data between the two governments continues. The 1950 treaty, moreover, is still in force, and Nepal has informed China and Pakistan that it does not intend to restrict the recruitment of Nepalis into the Indian Army or to limit their utilization by New Delhi.

Thus, defense in the Nepali context means defense against China —the only possible external threat—or Chinese-supported internal subversion or rebellion. Indeed, this is implicit in Kathmandu's China policy which is based upon the assumption that Chinese aggression, either direct or indirect, would bring massive Indian assistance. Nepalis also believe that a major change in China's present policy, which is generally supportive of the present regime, is remote as long as India is a functioning political system with a credible military capacity. Kathmandu's view that China now poses no direct threat to Nepal is based, thus, upon the assumption that Peking would be extremely unlikely to challenge India militarily on this section of the frontier and that the Chinese will continue to find it more profitable to maintain friendly relations with King Mahendra's "reactionary, feudalistic" regime.

Kathmandu has no such guarantee, of course, against Indian intervention, direct or indirect, for it is understood in Nepal that China lacks the capacity—and probably the will—to contend directly with

India south of the Himalayan crest on anything but a short-term basis—such as in the 1962 border war. If King Mahendra acts with some degree of confidence in his relations with India, it is not because he is backed by the Chinese but rather because he assumes that New Delhi has a major stake in political stability throughout the Himalayan area and has nothing to gain by a change in regimes in Nepal.

Burma, on achieving independence, opted against membership in the Commonwealth, and thus lost the degree of security provided at that time by British military support and assistance. Rangoon adopted a nonalignment policy and renounced military assistance from either the east or west bloc. But from the very beginning of its existence, Burma faced severe security problems, primarily but not exclusively internal, and placed heavy emphasis upon building up its army. In this early period, India provided much of the military aid that enabled the embattled Burmese government to survive and eventually to surmount the various dissident forces in the country.

This virtually exclusive preoccupation with internal rebellions has influenced the character of the Burmese military, which has long been primarily involved in "counterinsurgency" operations. As a result, the army has developed only a limited capacity to meet direct external aggression. Under present conditions, China constitutes the major potential external threat to Burma, and Rangoon has adopted a number of policies intended to minimize this danger. The nonalignment and isolation policies are, in part at least, intended to alleviate any apprehension in Peking that Burmese territory might be used against China, thus inviting preemptory retaliation. Since 1967, when relations with China deteriorated, Rangoon has actively sought direct assurances of support from India and tacit assurances from the US and the USSR in the event of massive Chinese intervention in the country. Rangoon has also sought to neutralize the Chinese minority as a potential fifth column by depoliticizing it to the greatest extent possible, primarily by adding to the cost paid by the Chinese community for political activity.

These policies have not provided Burma with the sense of security enjoyed by Nepal, for it depends upon a variety of uncertain factors including the willingness and capacity of India, the US and the USSR to counteract China in this area. However, despite the serious border clashes between Burmese and Chinese forces in 1970, in which several hundred men were killed according to reports, Rangoon would still seem to operate on the assumption that China is not expansionist—at least in its direction at this time. This confidence is reinforced by what is perceived to be a broader balance of power in Asia that raises the price of expansionism to prohibitive levels. Burma's security, it is believed, can be best preserved by avoiding direct involvement in this balance of power system, but also by doing nothing to upset it in any way.[9]

Having achieved independence under less traumatic conditions than Burma, Ceylon voted for membership in the Commonwealth and continued its dependence upon the British for its minimal security requirements. This stance eventually came into conflict with Ceylon's nonalignment policy, and the first SLFP government was constrained to eliminate the defense ties with the UK. No other powers were brought in to replace the British, however, as Colombo placed a very low priority on defense and security questions in that period.

Colombo's attitude subsequently has not changed substantially as, in contrast to Nepal and Burma, Ceylon presently does not face even a potential external enemy. The Ceylon government's concern on security questions is limited almost exclusively to internal subversion, possibly assisted by outside forces. The 1971 JVP uprising, of course, aroused serious apprehensions and resulted in some modifications in the UF government's perspectives on defense and foreign policy.

During the uprising, Ceylon desperately sought to maintain the façade of nonalignment by invoking aid from a variety of sources. But it was apparent that even the leftist UF regime placed its main reliance upon India, the US, and the UK, and that the USSR, UAR, and assorted non-western powers were brought in almost as an afterthought. China was not even approached, although its financial aid offer of $25 million (which was made only after the uprising had obviously failed) was gratefully accepted. Colombo has learned that political relations with the Communist bloc, or at least the Asian Communist states that advocate "national wars of liberation," can pose serious security problems. The UF ministry is disinclined to break relations with these states for a wide variety of reasons, both domestic and foreign,[10] but presumably greater attention has been paid subsequently to their operations within the country.

It is now apparent to Colombo that India is the only relatively "safe" and effective source of support against external aggression or internal subversion, unpalatable as this is to some political groups in Ceylon. At the early stage of the 1971 uprising, when the results were still in doubt, the UF cabinet considered asking New Delhi for the loan of a large military force, and if the situation had deteriorated

[9] The moderate position taken by Burma on US involvement in the Vietnam war, for instance, may reflect Rangoon's reluctance to encourage a general US disinvolvement in southern Asia.

[10] Diplomatic relations were not broken with North Korea in 1971 when the latter's diplomatic mission was ordered out of Ceylon.

seriously there is little doubt that massive Indian military intervention would have been invited—and granted.[11]

Ceylon also shares India's concern over recent developments in the Indian Ocean area that would turn it into another arena for big power rivalry. Despite rumors to the contrary, Colombo is no more likely than New Delhi to offer naval base facilities to *any* of the big powers since this would only aggravate tension in the area. Thus, Ceylon, unlike the other South Asian states, is prepared to accept Indian hegemony in the region as a lesser evil which does not run counter to any basic Ceylonese foreign policy objectives or pose a threat to the country's existence. Economic and national minority (Tamil) questions still belabor relations between the two states, but broad agreement has been achieved between them on political issues vital to the southern Asian area.

Achievements, Failures and Prospects

Nepal, Burma and Ceylon would probably consider their survival as independent political entities as their most significant achievement in the past quarter century. Each state has managed to establish a distinctive national identity in the international community and now plays an active role in international organizations such as the UN and UNCTAD, and in regional groupings such as the conferences of nonaligned states. Moreover, they have refused to be completely overawed by their giant neighbors, India and China, or by the US and USSR. The rather narrow parameters imposed on them by geopolitical and economic factors have already been discussed, but there have been occasions when each of these states has flouted political reality in the face of strong external pressure.

On the positive side can also be added the fact that these states have not been turned into arenas of direct confrontation in big power politics. Their own determination to avoid becoming "another Vietnam" is part of the story, of course, but no doubt the major factor has been the evident disinclination of the major powers to extend their conflicts into these areas. Neither China nor India, for instance, is interested in expanding their military confrontation in the Himalayas to Nepal or Burma, as this would both strain their resources and have

---

[11] India sent a 150-man unit to guard Colombo's international airport and five naval vessels to guard Ceylon's coast against the smuggling of arms to the rebels. India is also assisting in the arming and training of the expanding Ceylonese army, particularly in counterinsurgency. Aid from other foreign powers took the form of arms, ammunition and equipment.

uncertain international repercussions. Kathmandu and Rangoon understand that their actions and policies have only a peripheral effect upon developments in this region as the critical decisions are made elsewhere. They therefore seek the maximum noninvolvement possible, propitiating the gods—and their big neighbors—when this seems necessary.

Nepal, Burma and Ceylon set impossible goals for their foreign policies in the early post-colonial period, so it is probably inappropriate to speak of their non-achievements as failures. Their tendency to ignore geopolitical power and economic realities in defining foreign policy goals has been a bit quixotic at times, but not particularly damaging. Their persistence in pursuing certain unattainable objectives, such as economic autonomy, reflects more the compulsions of a domestic "nationalist" factor in decision-making than naiveté about the real world. The leadership in these states has a basic concern with survival, not only as "states" but as "political systems" as well. This occasionally leads them to adopt foreign policy positions that can be comprehended only from the narrow perspective of internal intra-élite competition. The fact that their foreign policy decisions are seldom decisive in determining results encourages this particular variety of ethnocentrism.

What of the future? The prospects would seem to be for more of the same, at least as long as the delicate balance of power throughout the Euro-Asian and Pacific areas is not overturned. Their low (in Burma's case, negative) GNP growth rate prevents any substantial improvement in their international economic position, and makes their call for "economic independence" meaningless. Politically, they are dependent upon but not part of the balance of power in southern Asia except in the broadest terms, and this will continue to serve them well as a protective device as long as the balance lasts. All three states have a basic interest in a political settlement that brings peace and stability to the region. But the terms must be such that the balance of power is not irretrievably upset, as this would be viewed as more dangerous than the continuation of conflict and confrontation.

PART THREE

Superpower Interaction in Asia

The US and Asia

WAYNE WILCOX

The Strategic Setting

In the early years of the American Republic, Asia meant Cathay—the rich trading world centered on China, immensely difficult to reach from Boston and New York. China's first American visitors were, therefore, Yankee traders—and they came for profit. However, percentage-wise, Europe was more important to the Americans trade-wise than China and later Japan. Several private fortunes, including the basic endowment of Yale University, stemmed from Asian trade, but early America was a Euro-centered country.

In the age of continental expansion, the foreign policy of President Washington's successors might have been described by the Emperor of China as that of the "Hermit Republic." From Jefferson's embargo through most of the 19th century, the United States was colonizing the west and pursuing a foreign policy designed to free the western hemisphere from European influence while Washington consolidated a national space of continental proportions. Once California, the Northwest Pacific Territories, Alaska and Hawaii were added to the national community, America became a *Pacific* power, and began exploring the coasts that lay on the other side of its new national frontier.

Theodore Roosevelt's naval diplomacy, Admiral Dewey's exploits in Manila, a renewed interest in a decreasingly viable Chinese empire and its trade and the external manifestations of a "manifest destiny" ethos prepared America for its coming of age in an imperial epoch. The Spanish-American war established America's independent hegemony in the Caribbean and, because of an active naval policy, attracted the Philippines as a colony. By 1900, America was an Asian power and had begun work on bases to support a naval diplomacy in the Far East.

Continental Asia in 1900 allowed little room for American colonialism. India was the "brightest jewel in the British Empire," securely ruled by the greatest of the European great powers. On either side of India, Britain was supreme from Suez to Malacca and a set of imperial preferences and tariffs made American trade expansion difficult if not impossible. The Netherlands ruled the Dutch East Indies, and France was establishing dominion over Indochina. Japan had begun to surprise the world with its technological growth, its coherent government and society, and its ability to maintain a distance from prying foreigners. It was China that provoked competition among the great powers—the great prize, sought alike by the Europeans, Czarist Russia and, later in the opening decades of the century, Japan as well. As America was establishing itself as a Pacific, or perhaps as an Asian power, it too joined the China "sweepstakes," pursuing a policy entitled "The Open Door Policy." In effect, this policy was primarily a late-comer's bid to avoid exclusion and the foreclosure of trade opportunities.

For the first half of the twentieth century, almost all of the instability and violence of Asia centered on, or was intimately associated with China's inability to rule itself. Once the vigor of the western European imperial onslaught weakened in the precariously balanced intra-European-American understandings about China, Russia and Japan redoubled their efforts. Japan conquered Taiwan, Korea, Manchuria and large areas of coastal China in the era of the 30's and early 40's before World War II's fortunes witnessed Japan's imperial collapse. Russia's weakness after the Communist Revolution was more than compensated for by its strength after World War II when the Chinese Communist army, with Russian support, won the Chinese civil war and brought China under effective government for the first time in the century. Russia exploited its position with Peking's brotherly Communists until the Sino-Soviet dispute erupted visibly in 1959. By 1971, a distinctly Chinese national Communist regime had established itself, dependent upon no foreign power nor subject to any domestic strife capable of being exploited by foreign powers. China's relations with all of the great powers of the 1970's are those of near-equality. China is understood to have regained a position of national sovereignty and an international influence commensurate with its size and demonstrated power. Thus the condition that propelled America, Japan, Russia and the Europeans into competition on the Asian mainland throughout most of the century has ended.

While the agony of civil and world war left the Chinese weak but united, the rest of Asia lay in confusion. The Japanese armies had been strong enough to destroy European rule but not strong enough to establish their own. Nationalists were weak almost everywhere except India, where British policy had skillfully favored moderate elements by decentralizing the decision-making process and establishing parliamentary institutions and procedures. Moreover, India had not been invaded by the Japanese, and the colonial writ still had sting.

In the Dutch East Indies, called by the nationalists Indonesia, Dutch rule had been a thin veneer in the archipelago and its sole aim was to serve commercial interests. Since it had not gone deep into the life of the various societies, but had successfully frustrated an alternative government from arising, the effect of Japanese conquest was to destroy almost all authority. When, at war's end, Holland attempted to restore its rule, there were no foundations on which to build, and force alone could justify governance. One effect of war, and especially of Japanese policy during the war, was to disseminate arms and military training to the Indonesian peoples. There were, therefore, three armies or types of military forces awaiting the Dutch—Dutch trained regulars, who might or might not share an allegiance to the Dutch crown; Japanese trained regulars, who would most surely be seen by the Dutch as the enemy, and guerrilla forces, self-trained and largely nationalist and Communist in orientation. The Dutch simply did not have the military power, will or international support necessary to rule by force. Their legacy, and the legacy of war, was to leave the new government of independent Indonesia little more than sentiment on which to base government. The establishment of a strong independent Indonesia was to be inherently uncertain and incredibly difficult. And Indonesia's weakness and disunity presented many of the same conditions that propelled the great powers into competition in China.

Like Indonesia, French Indochina had witnessed the destruction of French authority which in any case had been established only in the first decade of the century. French rule went deeper than that of Holland, in part because the French brought the Church with their imperial venture. At war's end, the re-establishment of French rule faced many of the problems witnessed in Indonesia, but France was a more powerful country than Holland, its leaders entertained the imperial notion with more conviction, and, for high European cold war political reasons, the United States was willing to lend support to France's efforts even though it disagreed with them in the Asian context of the late 1940's. Moreover, there was a base on which to rebuild French rule, or so it appeared.

In Korea, the Japanese had ruled long enough to establish public authority, but it was one of the most harsh and hated forms of colonial enslavement in Asia. Literally millions of Koreans had been externed to Japan and Manchuria for manual labor, and such nationalist leaders as existed had fled either to the west or to the USSR. In the aftermath of Japan's defeat in World War II. there was a government to be claimed, but by whom? The nationalists, the collaborators and the victorious allies were all part of the post-war scene, but there was no clear victor among the competing parties.

Taiwan, or Formosa, presented another complicated case. Taiwan had been conquered by the Japanese and transformed into a relatively efficient producer of cane sugar for the home islands. Taiwan had been won by aggression, however, and the allies had included it in the post-war restoration of Chinese territory. The problem was that there was no one Chinese government at the end of the war, yet Japan was decisively vanquished. Again, the question was: who should assume control of the existing public authority? The Chinese civil war gave the answer. As nationalist Chinese forces were beaten back from their last city strongholds, the government of Chiang Kai-shek retired to the island and brutally claimed what the Japanese had brutally established. The Taiwanese nationalist movement had been decimated by the mass execution of thousands of politically active young Taiwanese in 1947, and although this act was condemned by Chiang Kai-shek who laid responsibility at the feet of the offending general, the act was done. Nationalist China grasped the last straw of authority. An army of refugees provided a constituency, as did the remnants of the Republican army.

Farther west, the British were also abandoning their "jewels." India became independent in 1947, but out of British India came two states; one Muslim—Pakistan—and one Hindu—India. And in the division of the British Indian empire came a wave of killings claiming perhaps one million persons in a bloody exchange of populations. A year later, Ceylon became independent and Burma, always a nettle in the British lion's mane, became free as well. Compared to political transitions elsewhere in Asia, these nationalisms were triumphant with little bloodshed in the process of decolonization. But as the India-Pakistan communal riots of late summer and fall 1947 showed, the evacuation of the British merely reduced one of the elements of political instability in the region—others lay embedded in centuries-old rivalries of caste, religion and social group.

The European empires in Asia had very complex political effects on the changing strategic and security relationships in the region. By bringing western technology, agriculture and capitalism with them, they profoundly smashed the basis of the old order whatever it might have been. Karl Marx wrote that British imperialism had done more to "modernize" India than any force in history because it introduced new ideas of production and human management to a centuries old tradition that could not establish the basis for progressive improvements in material welfare. The colonials themselves would have agreed with Marx, and saw their splendid engineering works, famine control schemes and plantations as "progress," the lifting of Asian society into a higher level of human achievement.

The colonial empires also brought a new set of ideas to challenge Asian notions of legitimacy, human purpose and human worth. Christianity was only one of the banners so proudly borne; there was also democracy, humanism, socialism, communism and fascism. Asia, like Europe, was swept up in a global search for an ideology to accompany industrial, urban society. And because it shared European's needs and problems increasingly as development proceeded, European debates and solutions became more relevant. Mankind, at least in Asia, was joining with Europe and America in a universalization of symbols, notions, ideas and philosophical systems.

For as long as Europe was technologically superior, organizationally dominant and psychologically confident, its rule in Asia was assured. A few gunboats could coerce the Chinese emperor, regardless of the fact that the Chinese probably outnumbered all of the European colonial nation populations. In India, railways, adequate communications and social discipline gave immense striking force to a very small army, especially since it was pitted against competing prices, scattered forces and a primitive logistics system. The Dutch could rule the islands of Indonesia because they controlled the seas, and the Indonesians saw themselves as Javanese, Sumatrans and others, rather than as a nation.

But Europe taught Asia by example as well as by precept. The nationalists almost immediately understood that organization—mass social organization—was a prerequisite to a successful national independence movement. Almost all of the nationalists championed industrial development, and all of them selectively searched through their history for a set of examples like epics and heroes from which a new sense of confidence could be communicated. It was called "revivalism," but it was something entirely new.

For as long as Europeans ruled, Asian violence was a pale reflection of European rivalries. The British Indian army served in the Middle East in World War I, not because of Indian interests in the war, but because of British interests. Mercenary troops also fought for France and the Netherlands. Once colonial territories were "staked," however, the parallel interests of the colonialists were in maintaining law and order and title to control. America fulminated about the "redcoats" and the wickedness of colonialism, justifying its Asian interests in terms of simple trade or Asian freedom. Russia, and subsequently the USSR, challenged colonialism as part of capitalism, fighting a European struggle in the Asian periphery. It was Japan, the counter-imperialist, whose interests could not be incorporated in a European Asia that finally set imperialist against imperialist.

A balanced assessment of European imperialism in Asia is yet to be written, and perhaps never will be written. In the balance of trade within the relationship, the Asians were subordinated politically and their cultures were impacted with extraordinary force by the combined weight of the industrial, democratic and technological revolutions of the 19th and 20th centuries in Europe. The legacy of imperialism was psychologically destructive and socially stimulating. It was economically contradictory, for while roads, power, ports and railroads were developed, the second stage industrial revolution was frustrated by metropolitan country dominance in complex technology. Educationally and procedurally, Europe gave much more than it took, especially in the case of England and France. Colonial Asia bore a much lighter burden of war and social turbulence than did the European societies of the imperial countries. As Japan seems to show, however, industrialization and social discipline tend to be most effectively internalized in a country managed by its own nationals. The accommodation of new ideas, and their interpretation with regard to existing values, is best done in a highly distinctive, nationalistic way. Imperialism denied Asians the chance to make their own hard choices, and allowed them to indulge in the luxury of transferring blame to outsiders who were, in fact, responsible for decision-making. Most of all, the imperialists asked too little of the populations they governed. Far more rigorous demands were made of the European peoples, and because of those demands, the European peoples demanded more and more control over their own governments. It is no accident that the strong Asian governments of the post-war period are those that came to power in war, and in bitterly contested social struggles that forced sacrifice, choice and discipline.

After its brief colonial adventures at the turn of the century, America attempted to manage its expanded political responsibilities in the world. The Marines attempted to keep the peace in the Caribbean, while paternalistic American governments attempted to bring some benefit to the Philippine population. World War I redirected American efforts to Europe, and the failure of the Wilson administration to carry the Congress and the country for a European America, committed to permanent great power status in the European balance of power, led the United States quite as rapidly to abandon European concerns. The interwar period was one of perpetual crisis; the Communist revolution in Russia seemed to threaten established order throughout Europe, and reparation difficulties constantly embroiled American governments in thankless, unsuccessful efforts at economic diplomacy. In the mid-1920's, world trade was convulsed and began to weaken, and the Great World Depression signalled the opening of the third decade of the century. It was not just America that was isolationist; the entire world economic system had appeared to collapse, setting regime against regime, and allowing tyrants promising the millennia to rise in Italy and Germany. In Asia, the Japanese had begun their fateful attack on China. Whatever restraints on convulsive change in world politics might have been in play in the period, they were overwhelmed by conflict-producing crises that followed, one after another, in awesome sequence. Washington had its hands full, its leaders realistically noted, and European and Asian developments were of less moment than bread lines at home.

World War II was both a crisis and cathartic. The scale, duration and terrible costs of the violence need no repeating. It was, truly, a world war with almost every major society, European and Asian, subjected to violence. Because it was fought with so much ferocity and on such a grand scale, it bankrupted the middle powers and left standing only those societies lucky enough to have been on the periphery of direct battle, like the United States, or so directly involved that total mobilization was accomplished, like the USSR. The catharsis lay in the exhaustion of all but the two superpowers who then organized, by default as much as by design, the peace.

The United States was not, by 1945, an innocent among nations, but neither was it accustomed to global security management. The USSR, labelled a pariah among nations and ruled by a vicious and erratic Joseph Stalin, was also unaccustomed to global power and influence. And those states whose leaders had imperial experience were anemic and worse, prostrate at war's end.

And so it was that the government of the United States undertook to recreate and universalize the European state system based on national sovereignty, free trade and a modicum of diplomatic and political procedures favorable to collective security. The United Nations was an innovation of some importance, but the logic of its design required that the superpowers agree before it could act in security matters, and the logic of history was that they were unlikely to do so. The United States was willing to support the UN, subject to the fact that it be allowed a veto in the Security Council, because the membership of the body was overwhelmingly pro-American or allied with America. The Russians were reluctantly willing to enter the UN because it established their parity of great power status with the United States, ended the threat of post-war isolation by another "cordon sanitaire" and offered some diplomatic opportunities that might not be present in bilateral diplomatic dealings.

The American task, as seen by the decision-makers of the period, was to restore the vitality of the war-shattered European states, restrict the advance of Communist countries by force of arms, facilitate the orderly decolonization of the Asian and African "holdings" of the Europeans, prevent Japanese and German rearmament and establish instrumentalities for world trade and fiscal order. This was, in short, a plan of restoration of the pre-World War I European system, and the integration of the colonies, as free nations, into such a world. It was a monumental task.

After World War II, the defeat of Japan and the establishment of the United Nations, the United States began to involve itself intimately in decolonization issues, and hence in Asia. During the war, President Roosevelt had antagonized Churchill by gently suggesting that India should be made independent; after the war, the Attlee government needed no prodding. The American role in forcing the Dutch to quit Indonesia was also crucial. The recommendation to Washington that the US back the Indochinese rebels led by Ho Chi Minh was not accepted because of the delicacy of American-French relationships, and France's crucial role in the rearmament of Europe in the early days of the cold war. Therefore, the US acted against its general principles and supported France in a vain colonial war. The Truman administration specially noted that US forces would not involve themselves in the Chinese civil war in the Formosa Straits, a decision which was reversed only because of the outbreak of the Korean war—that watershed in American policy in modern Asia. In Korea, both the Secretary of State (Dean Acheson) and the Joint Chiefs of Staff specifically excluded Korea from the free world defensive perimeter, hoping that various nationalist factions might resolve the issue short of war. When the North Koreans attacked with great force, a policy was reversed and American troops were committed, not because the US had assigned a high priority to a non-Communist Korea, but because of the military means which Kim Il-sŏng and the Russians adopted. The Korean war hardened the US attitude against the Viet Minh, the North Koreans, and the Chinese. It extended the cold war to Asia, and involved the United States directly in a number of civil wars.

In the early 1950's, European recovery was underway and the fathers of the Marshall Plan had reason to congratulate themselves. The Truman Doctrine had extended a strategic protection to the far states of Eastern Europe—Greece and Turkey—after the gross destruction of Czechoslovakian freedom in 1948. Decolonization was proceeding without too much bitterness, except with France. The Stalinist regime seemed to be more and more tyrannical, and at least verbally aggressive, and the Chinese Communists had won the civil war. Thus containment appeared to have been successful in Europe, but was tenuous in Asia.

Events in a number of states heightened this concern. In Korea, Kim Il-sŏng, who had spent the war years as a refugee in the USSR, had returned home with Russian patronage and with Russian military equipment. He was contested by a Princeton Ph.D., Syngman Rhee, whom almost every American found more difficult than the Communists. Nonetheless, both sides were resorting to violence and the North Koreans were pressing with very superior armed forces. In the Philippines, the Huk rebellion testified to the potency of guerrilla Communism, as it did with much more force in Vietnam where Ho Chi Minh's forces, supported by both Russia and China, inflicted heavy casualties on the French until they were forced to concede defeat in 1954. In Malaya, a Chinese-supported insurgency tore at the British-supported government. In Burma, "White Flag" Communist terrorists machine-gunned the leadership of the government, decimating national leadership and presenting a formidable guerrilla challenge to an already weak government in Rangoon. In Indonesia, the strongest and best led political party was the Indonesia Communist party (PKI), and there appeared to be no central nationalist figure capable of leading the government.

While it was American public policy to facilitate nationalism's success everywhere in Asia, it was not a policy that aimed at handing the new governments over to the Communists, especially in light of the emergence of the Sino-Soviet bloc which had shown in eastern Europe that it was bent upon world hegemony. In order to stiffen non-Communist nationalism in an era of European withdrawal and Japanese defeat, it became necessary to transfer American resources and forces to Asia and to enter competition with indigenous and foreign Communists in a large number of countries. In some cases, this support could be entirely indirect, as with economic assistance to India. In other cases, support could be offered in collaboration with the European power which was vacating its position gradually, as with the British in Malaya or the French in Indochina. But in a significant number of cases, ranging in intensity between Korea and the Philippines, the United States was forced to directly involve itself with nationalist forces and sometimes, as in Korea, take the country over until the fighting had stopped. Where there was vigorous nationalist leadership, as with Magsaysay in the Philippines and Nehru in India, American policy could be relaxed, relatively consistent, and conducted with a minimum of visibility. In more internally chaotic countries just the reverse was often the case.

This policy of intervention on the part of both the US and the USSR has been condemned as neo-imperialism. In the sense that both governments applied their power and resources to produce results attractive to them, and that dependent elites found in such support critical margins in their own domestic struggles, the charge is correct. What is at issue is the purpose to which the power was put. Western leaders consistently argued that their actions were in support of nationalism, the freedom of choice of new governments, and orderly processes of political change. The United States government also argued that it would not permit changes to take place which compromised its security or that of its allies, and it championed as well the integration of competitive national economies in world trade in the convertible currency area.

The USSR also justified its actions as support of nationalism—but a nationalism in which governments were led by groups friendly with the USSR, and hence governments organized by the Communist party of these countries. Moscow has charged that American support for nationalist leaders who were not Communists was inconsistent with free choice (although the same charge was returned with equal vigor) and that orderly processes of change could not take place in a competitive, capitalist, world system. Russian governments, like those in America, also saw their own security interests as vital, and looked for trade opportunities within a Socialist commonwealth of nations rather than the convertible currency world. The differences between Moscow and Washington were, therefore, more than simple misunderstandings and mutual suspicions—they went to the core of the organization of the post-World War II world system.

Every Asian country has now entered the turbulent path toward national development and economic change. New cities are being built, and new life styles are emerging. A new work ethic is being imposed, and consequent new social problems are emerging. With so much change at work in the family, the economy, the state and, especially, the individual person, social turbulence is inevitable. Asian governments must keep order, provide a sense of direction and morale for their populations, and represent the values and aspirations of a people.

Under such conditions, it appears inevitable that men will have different ideas about how best to proceed, and where first to quest.

Politics is the process with which the competition between such leaders can take place, and representative government or democratic centralism the procedures by which the winning group of leaders finds the support for pursuing a particular course in the population. Throughout Asia, there are Communists, democrats and an extraordinarily wide variety of eclectic and unique types of leaders, all convinced of their prudence, wisdom and vision. In their struggles with one another, it is natural enough to call upon foreign as well as domestic support, especially if the stakes are high and the costs of failure death, imprisonment or exile.

Thus the cleavages of the cold war superpower visions of the world meet and reinforce the differences between political leaders in modernizing countries. The result has been violence everywhere except in those countries where nationalist leadership occupied such a strong position that the extreme fringes were too far from power to attract much foreign support.

In sum, the post-war period brought the US global responsibilities concerning the management of security relationships not simply between Moscow and Washington, or between NATO and the Warsaw Pact countries, but between various elites in uncertain and rapidly changing political systems emergent from colonial rule. In Asia, the management of such relationships involved the US in extremely burdensome and violent conflicts.

The US and the Asian Community

THE CHINESE CIVIL WAR

The general outlines of the Chinese civil war appear clear, although volumes are still to be written about the certain aspects of the war which are particularly complex and confusing. The progressive nationalist movement of Dr. Sun Yat Sen had two cores—Communist and Nationalist. Upon his death, Chiang Kai-shek, representing or at least having the following of the Nationalists, assumed control and the Communists, led by Mao Tse-tung, went into opposition which, in increasingly bitter fighting, took on the attributes of a civil war. At that time, China was under siege from Japan, and Chiang Kai-shek's dilemma arose from two enemies, one the more potent militarily and the other the more salient politically. As the war widened, Nationalist forces bore the main brunt of Japanese attack, while after Japan's surrender in 1945 the Nationalists and the Communists both benefitted from war supplies captured from the Japanese. The Communist forces, suitably strengthened and well led, then laid siege to the Nationalist armies which were more battle worn and less well led. The United States attempted to mediate the dispute. Chiang Kai-shek expected more American support than was forthcoming, and the Red armies swept everything in their path. The *fall* of China became, in the American public debate, the *loss* of China, and as anti-Communism had become an important theme in domestic politics with the rise of the cold war, the *loss* of China became the *betrayal* of China. Officials who had observed the Chinese civil war in less than strident anti-Communist tones were given short shrift by the Secretary of State (John Foster Dulles) and the Congress (led by Senator Joseph McCarthy), and they also suffered in the absence of support from the intellectual community.

If public opinion needed any pushing toward a more virulent anti-China position, that push came during the Korean war as Chinese "volunteers" crossed the Yalu river after General MacArthur's forces had nearly crushed the North Korean armies which had been abandoned by the USSR. It was at this time that the 7th US fleet was positioned in the Formosa Straits, and the "containment" doctrine was applied to China. After the Korean war, the US kept the 7th Fleet in position as a constant reminder to Peking that Washington was not prepared to allow the Communists to end the nationalist regime on Taiwan. The positioning of American strategic weapons, and the apparent nuclear threat used at the termination of the Korean war and at the Quemoy-Matsu crisis of 1958, left China to ponder the consequences of nuclear war with the United States should it attempt to "end" its civil war by force.

American opinion toward the Chinese Communist regime has always been mixed. As long as Americans were fighting the Chinese in Korea and struggling with them as part of the Sino-Soviet bloc, Peking was obviously the enemy. In the brief period after the Korea war and before Quemoy and Matsu, however, Chinese governments had allowed "a thousand flowers to bloom;" they had proven polite and moderate at Bandung with the non-aligned nations in 1955 and had facilitated the Geneva Settlement of 1954 concerning Vietnam. It was not until the Sino-Soviet rift emerged in 1959, however, that the threatening image of a "bloc" started to dissipate and the Chinese experiment came to be looked upon with curiosity and interest. Chinese nuclear explosions and progress in rocketry made a détente with Peking acceptable and desirable even to Washington's Hawks. It was the Ussuri River clashes between Russian and Chinese troops in 1970, however, which showed that the rift between Peking and Moscow was more than ideological rhetoric. The time had come for

America to take advantage of the division between its enemies, and to remove its presence from the now-cold civil war battlefront in China. In July 1971 Presidential Advisor Kissinger sneaked into Peking for an agenda setting meeting with Chou En-lai, and upon his return President Richard Nixon announced that he would go to China in early 1972. The Chinese would note that the invitation was from Chou En-lai, not Mao Tse-tung, and that Richard Nixon was traveling to Peking. And a 19th century diplomat would be shocked to think that states which had not even recognized each other's government would be involved in heads of state official visits!

The Chinese civil war is not yet over, and hard choices remain but American involvement in one Asian civil war appears to be rapidly declining; and since that civil war is the centerpiece of the new Asian politics, this change assumes fundamental importance for the future.

THE KOREAN CIVIL WAR

The end of World War II came too fast and too completely for the diplomats. For all the parlaying at Teheran and Yalta, and all the cables exchanged between the allies, there was no clear plan about the post-war disposition either of Japanese colonies or of European colonies in Asia. Neither the French nor the Dutch had any forces to assume occupation duties in their Asian colonies, and American public policy toward Indochina and Indonesia was at best vague. The Japanese, once they had surrendered, refused to govern. As a result, the British accepted the Japanese surrender in a number of countries remote to their experience or, for that matter, interest.

Korea did not appear to be a special problem. The Russians and Americans agreed that a provisional military government, Russian in the north and American in the south, should serve until a national Korean government could be installed. After a short period, the Russians announced that their military government would be wound up and removed, since a nationalist regime headed by Kim Il-sŏng had been elected. The United States Army stayed in South Korea somewhat longer, and there was less unanimity about a nationalist leader in the south than in the north. Syngman Rhee emerged as the leader by a skillful if not always appreciated ability to appear to be America's hand-chosen leader. The Acheson speech that depreciated Korea's strategic worth in the cold war came at a time when both Rhee and Kim Il-sŏng were claiming to be the sole national government of Korea. It is unclear whether the Russians counselled the North Koreans to attack—they privately and with considerable passion deny it—but it is much less unclear that Kim Il-sŏng had every reason to attack for his own Korean civil war reasons. His army was well-equipped and ready for war; he knew Rhee's support in the US was weak and his army weaker still. The Acheson speech had appeared to withdraw American support for a South Korea. Rhee was daily consolidating his political strength in the south, and in time the division of Korea would be accepted. No nationalist Korean wanted that unhappy condition, be he Communist or not.

The North Korean *blitzkrieg* demonstrated for the world which side had prepared for war. President Truman's unexpected commitment of American forces, and the curious situation at the UN (the Russians having walked out previously) that allowed the "Uniting for Peace" General Assembly resolution making US action equivalent to UN action both caught the North Koreans and the Russians by surprise. They were to pay for it dearly, and later ruefully wonder whether they had been entrapped by a calculated American policy. The Russians were in no condition to go to war with the United States/United Nations, and North Korea was simply no match for the forces deployed against it. It was left to China to intervene, or Korea would have been united under Rhee—the militant anti-Communist. China would have then found its sensitive Manchurian frontier bordered by an enemy government, and no Chinese could forget that Manchuria had been conquered by Japan *through* Korea.

Although there is considerable evidence that the Chinese were attempting to warn the United States not to push to the Yalu and to respect China's frontier concerns, these "signals" were missed, ignored or misunderstood. Even had they been properly received, the United States/United Nations forces might have continued north under the formula of supporting nationalism, establishing national unity in Korea, and denying the Communists the successful use of their military forces in civil wars. The Chinese did intervene, the war became a costly stalemate—costly to the United States because it appeared "unwinnable" without nuclear weapons, and costly to China because General Ridgeway's forces took an immense toll of Chinese troops—a total, indeed, that would be reported during the great Sino-Soviet debate as larger still than that estimated by allied commanders.

Thus, a new president and two exhausted countries arranged a peace over the heads of warring Korean factions, delivering a verdict that both dreaded—partition, and a truce guaranteed by China and the United States. The violence of the small encounters between North and South Koreans, and between North Koreans and Americans, demonstrates the frustrations of a denied national identity, and the dangers of a "frozen civil war" opposed by the warriors themselves.

While the United States has maintained a large garrison in Korea since the war, and has been generous in developmental and rehabilitational aid, it seeks to extricate itself from this Asian civil war. The Nixon Doctrine enunciated at Guam in 1969 calls for a mitigation of the American military role in Asia. To that end, reductions in the Korean garrison have been ordered, while Korea's request for first line aircraft and other new military equipment has been given a sympathetic hearing in Washington. There is a genuine danger in such a policy, since it might appear to recreate the conditions of 1950. Moreover, South Korea's splendid economic development might have to be sacrificed to ever higher levels of arms expenditures as American protection is withdrawn and as the North Koreans continue to maintain a very high level of military preparedness. Whatever the result, if there is to be a second Korean civil war, it seems clear that it will be even more destructive than the first although great power involvement may be less direct.

THE VIETNAMESE CIVIL WAR

The most costly, violent and tragic civil war in which America has involved itself in Asia is in Vietnam. Since the late 1930's, the Vietnamese have not known peace, suffering first the Japanese invasion in 1941, then the French-Indochinese war (1945–54), then the North-South war (1955–65) and then the American Vietnamese war (1965–present).

The wartime history of Vietnam is similar to that of Korea. A military administration by Japan effectively destroyed French authority while nationalist leaders lucky enough to escape went either to France/Britain or to the USSR/China. Those leaders who went to France found that they were not the group patronized by the French, but rather were expected to patronize the French. The remaining non-Communist nationalists, therefore, were set against the French and driven into a united front with the Communist nationalists, led by the very gifted Ho Chi Minh. As the war intensified, the Communist party effectively dominated the United Front by reason of its access to support from and sanctuary in China as well as by the popular support that effective nationalism received against the French.

When the United States backed the colonialists the war simply intensified. The French military establishment, with access to American funds and equipment, thought that they could win a military victory in Vietnam. In every pitched battle, they won; yet their control over the countryside was continuously eroding and their base of support in the countryside vanishing. When, in 1953, Pierre Mendes-France talked with Chou En-lai in Geneva, promising support for a settlement should he be premier, the French were in serious military difficulty in Vietnam. The United States very nearly intervened to save Dienbienphu, but Secretary of State Dulles was apparently overridden by President Eisenhower, and the French sued for peace.

At Geneva in 1954, the diplomatic balance was extremely complex. The USSR was willing to aid France in a settlement if the French would not support the US-sponsored European Defense Community (EDC). At Geneva the United States was reluctant to see France settle on weak terms, and therefore played a hard-line in forcing the Communists into *territorial* concessions to a South Vietnamese authority of some form. The Chinese cooperated in the treaty, both in conformity with Soviet policy and also in the hope of general international recognition of China's importance in the world. The British attempted to stage-manage the very complicated negotiations.

The United States wanted from the Geneva conference a nationalist Vietnamese government which was free of the French and which it could support against Vietnamese Communists. This was a tardy return to the general American policy line of support for the nationalists. The Russians and Chinese were willing to assure the presence of the North Vietnamese at the settlement for their own, non-Asian or at least non-Vietnamese reasons. The French government, in the face of strong public opinion, wanted out without losing the confidence of the army. The Vietnamese representatives at the conference found that the great powers dictated the terms, and the result was predictable—partition, guaranteed this time by the USSR and Great Britain (fronting for the US). The result within Vietnam was also predictable—enormous bitterness and barely restrained war. Ho Chi Minh may have thought that South Vietnam, which had not been accepted as a country but rather as a provisional region for organizing national elections, would fall of its own anarchy. But a Rhee figure emerged from France in the person of Ngo Dien Diem. As he took over the reins of government, he showed extraordinary skill, breaking the power of various religious-military sects, building an army based on refugee Catholics who had fled from the north in 1954, and establishing effective police and taxation instruments. Like Rhee, he did so with a large measure of high-handedness, but he did so under enormous pressure and against great odds. By 1956, it appeared that South Vietnam was not only on the map to stay, but was in fact beginning to show signs of confidence, development and coherence. This left Ho Chi Minh with no choice but to attempt to bring him down and unify Vietnam.

Ho Chi Minh had learned from the Korean war that although the North Vietnamese Army could easily have conquered South Vietnam by conventional attack, such an attack would have produced precisely the same American response as it had in Korea. Moreover, the Russian guarantors of the Geneva settlement of 1954 would have been greatly displeased, especially since Khrushchev was pursuing a policy of normalization with the United States. It was therefore necessary to adopt a strategy of guerrilla siege upon the government at Saigon, and to do so with ever-escalating pressure but with as little North Vietnamese presence as possible.

Just as many northern Vietnamese Catholics and non-Communists had gone south, many southerners had gone north. They were, therefore, returning "home" as they began going south in 1958. The Chinese, abruptly shifting to a hard line following their lack of success in winning a détente with the west and increasingly isolated from the USSR which was successful in such a course, appeared to support Ho Chi Minh's efforts to eliminate the American stronghold in Saigon.

Diem's consolidation of power had not come without the making of many enemies, Communist and non-Communist. His heavy reliance upon the Catholics alienated the politicized Buddhist monks and their followers, and the religious sect leaders whom Diem had broken also bore him a grudge. The American presence and the Francophile tastes of the court both tainted the Diem regime with a colonialist, non-nationalist image. The cost of fashioning an effective public authority was the expansion of an opposition, and that opposition became a prime ally of the Communist cadres who had been activated in the south, or sent "home." The new name of the United Front was the National Liberation Front (NLF), and as before, it contained a good number of the sorts of men which the United States had consistently sought to back against the Communists.

After the outbreak of the Sino-Soviet dispute, Hanoi reasonably concluded that it could play Moscow off against Peking to follow that policy which it thought most appropriate, and as long as no frontal attack embarrassing the Soviets was made, it was unlikely that they would sanction Hanoi. The new American President, John Kennedy, appeared not to be a convinced anti-Communist. The next step was to open communication and supply lines to South Vietnam from North Vietnam through Laos—the Ho Chi Minh trails—and to begin a low level attack on the real root of Saigon's authority—strong village headmen loyal to Diem. Political terror directed against officials, organized effectively and conducted efficiently, is one of the most potent forms of political action.

By 1961, Laos, the figment of the imagination of the Geneva diplomats of 1954 had collapsed, and a US-USSR parley led Averell Harriman to conclude a settlement for the "reneutralization" of Laos which in fact legitimized its partition and signalled the fact that the USSR could no longer guarantee the Geneva accords. President Kennedy understood the significance of these actions, and the assassination campaign against local officials in South Vietnam, and sent the fated observer-training force of 1,500. It had been decided—the civil war would be fought in the south on the enemy's terms and with his means.

Diem's regime was structurally and politically weak—that it worked at all had always amazed foreign observers. When put under sustained assault of the most effective kind, it collapsed from want of a following with any real capacity. Either American resources—especially human resources—had to be committed, or the cause declared lost. President Kennedy increased the American force level, and President Johnson increased it still more. President Johnson, more than President Kennedy, saw that the only real chance to win even a stalemate in Vietnam lay in converting the war into a type of Korean war—make the North the visible enemy, make the American force a multilateral United Nations-like force, and produce a settlement over the heads of the Vietnamese by dealing with the USSR and China. No matter how provoked, however, the North Vietnamese would not evidence their interest in the battles of the South. They committed their regular troops modestly, carefully and as invisibly as possible; they actively played Soviets against Chinese; and they conducted a brilliant public diplomacy aimed at American public opinion.

For Washington the battle was lost because a nationalist leader could not be found, and Diem's strengths were too narrow to build a nation under siege. If American public opinion did not allow all-out war against North Vietnam, and it did not, and if the President did not believe American security interests in Asia rose or fell on this issue alone, which he did not, and if the North Vietnamese were able to hang on against the killing power of the American military forces, which they could, then victory would go to Hanoi unless Moscow or Peking betrayed them in a most unthinkable manner.

The Vietnamese civil war is not over, but like the Korean war, it has become an indigenous matter with external powers exercising much less influence in decisive political outcomes. South Vietnam may have hidden strengths of resistance, or it may adopt and accommodate to a national Communism which preserves the tradition of cultural pluralism of the region. In any case, the Vietnam war is mainly a civil war, and not a reinforced international conflict pitting superpowers and clients against one another.

In the struggle for independence against the Dutch, the united forces of Indonesian nationalism were as diverse as the island archipelago. The Communist party was strong, as were the parties of the religious conservatives. Because of population concentrations, the islands of Java and Sumatra were of key importance—the other regions becoming much less important and much less integrated into the Indonesian national life. Various islands did have local party leaders of considerable strength, however. There was also the Indonesian army, or rather armies, that from the beginning of the nationalist struggle had been a significant political force. The key task for political leaders in the new state was somehow to build a coalition that included all of these groups. Politics had to be an exercise in national integration, with or without national economic development.

The course of political life so worried the United States in the early 1950's that it involved itself in a covert attempt to topple the government by backing separatist forces, led by the Muslim parties, in Java. This rebellion was abortive, and in its aftermath Sukarno's policies showed a continuing distrust and antipathy toward the United States, as well they might. The strength of the PKI also worried Sukarno, however, and although it was necessary for him to include Communists in his grand national coalition, there is no evidence that he was their handmaiden.

Sukarno, the nationalist, was one of Asia's most successful leaders. The Indonesian government he inherited was one of the most tenuous and ill-established in Asia. The political coalition required to maintain even minimum levels of political order was perhaps the broadest in any Asian state. The distance between various parts of the country, and between various groups in the country, presents "federal" problems unmatched in Asia except perhaps in Pakistan. The Americans, the Russians and the Chinese all have made large-scale commitments to their clients in the country to attempt to "win," and Sukarno parried every thrust, turned away every challenge and managed to survive until the abortive PKI coup d'état in 1965.

Sukarno's strategy was as complex as the situation. In essence, it was politically inclusive, heavily focused on the building of a set of semi-mythical symbols that both right and left could accept (such as New Emerging Forces [NEFO] which presumably were being led by Indonesia, etc.) and with public policy directed toward social rather than economic investments. The costly Djakarta stadium is often cited as an example of a spendthrift and irrational leadership; less often are the literacy statistics of Indonesia cited, but they show the greatest growth of any Asian state in the 1950's and 1960's. At the end of Sukarno's rule, Indonesia was still politically divided, as the army-PKI struggle showed, and Indonesia was still a divided and poor country. But it had managed to maintain its political unity in the face of great power challenges, and it had invested heavily in the morale and confidence of the society. Until the PKI violated the "inclusiveness" rule of the Sukarno political system by attempting to kill top army leadership, the costs of losing in the Indonesian political system were not too high. The government was perhaps inefficient more than humane, but the various sections of the elite treated each other with the minimum civility necessary for organized competitive politics. By monopolizing the middle of the nationalist spectrum and including all groups in the government, Sukarno kept foreign interference to a minimum and avoided successful, protracted, civil war.

When, finally, the army and PKI fought the battle for succession to Sukarno's position in the society, no foreign power played a decisive role. Once the army had proven successful, however, it had removed the left from the national coalition and needed compensatory support from outside the country. The non-Communist world's economic assistance represented one such resource transfer; the USSR's policy of claiming that the PKI was under Chinese adventurist direction, and that its own policy was favorable to the army government was another such external prop.

As elsewhere in Asia, the Indonesian civil war is not over. Thousands of Communists and their supporters were killed in the aftermath of the coup attempt, and the viciousness with which army officers were killed by Communists has poisoned army-PKI relations for a generation. There is no reason to believe that economic development will reduce social tension in Indonesia, or that a firm national patriotism has yet emerged. On the other hand, the superpowers have both learned a lesson in Indonesia. Their attempts to build decisive influence have proven abortive, as the United States learned in rebellion-stimulation in the early 1950's, and as the Soviets learned in attempting to use their military assistance to build political influence in the mid 1960's. China too has learned that influence in Indonesia is as uncertain a product of involvement as in any country in Asia, having been forced to send a ship to evacuate Chinese merchants and traders from the country at a time when external observers believed Sukarno and Chou En-lai were in intimate embrace. Whatever Indonesian politics may be, they are not quick in responding to tugs on the helm by external powers, no matter how "powerful." Moscow, Washington, Peking and Tokyo all appear to share this view, and have adjusted their diplomatic goals accordingly.

Burma is little noted nor reported extensively in the world press, although its governments since 1948 have been under continuous violent assault by a formidable combination of guerrilla Communist movements (The Red Flag and The White Flag groups) and tribal-ethnic separatist movements. Burma's position is unenviable in other ways as well—one of Asia's longest frontiers with China, immediate proximity in the west to the Naga and Mizo insurgencies in India and to the Bangla Desh insurgency in East Pakistan. In the East, only Thailand stands between the Indochinese zone of war and precarious Burma.

The Burmese had never adjusted themselves to British rule, and the British were continuously forced to mount expeditions against would be insurrectionists. World War II destroyed what British authority there was in Burma, and the allies, to weaken Japan, systematically politicized and armed ethnic groups like the Kachins and Shans who harassed Japanese forces. When peace came between the allies and Japan, the Kachins and Shans did not disarm, or forget about their training. Indeed, they attempted to exert pressure on Rangoon for independence.

The only type of government that had a chance to work in Burma was an Indonesian-style grand coalition that excluded no major group in the country, and was committed to national integration before any other goal. The White Flag Communists' assassination of Aung San and the other members of the government in the first years of independence left Burma without experienced and skillful managers. U Nu alternated between Buddhist monasticism and political leadership, and in the late 1950's found his country under great pressure from the Chinese along the northern frontier. Burma subsequently normalized relations with Peking by signing a subordinate frontier treaty and by withdrawing from close contact with China's enemies. U Nu's indecisive leadership fell once to an army coup d'état led by General Ne Win, who later restored parliamentary government under U Nu, and fell once again, for good, to General Ne Win in a second coup d'état.

The Ne Win government, although based on army support, is no stronger than predecessor governments. The tribal insurgencies have continued, and most of northern Burma is beyond the control of Rangoon. The White Flag and Red Flag Communists are at bay, perhaps because of Russian and Chinese policy but more likely because their capacities are also weak, although they continue to pose significant threats to a weak government. Ne Win's own ability to act is severely limited by his need to ensure complete consensus within the army which is as divided as other groups in Burmese society. And Burmese foreign policy was once well summarized to a foreign visitor by a high official: "We wish Burma could be towed, like an island, into the sea and left alone." The economy exhibits negative growth, and there is no great natural resource lode, as in Indonesia, that promises future growth.

The lessons of the continuing Burmese civil war are not easy to perceive. Its condition and location are unique. But Burma appears to represent the situation of a political system having accommodated itself to endemic violent opposition, and its public policies appear to be examples of attempted moderation of opposition violence, while maintaining a core authority. Burma has been able to do this only by isolating itself from the contest between the superpowers and China. No matter what the resource transfers, and Rangoon is realistic enough to know that no great power can highly prize such a country as Burma, government authority would be insufficient to manage the effects of resource transfers to enemies of Rangoon, either Communist or ethnic groups. An increase in the level of conflict, in short, destroys Rangoon regardless of the battlefield outcome. Burma's policy of "hermit diplomacy" is likely to continue, therefore, and the great powers are unlikely to be drawn into the contest even if China should choose to play a much greater role in the country.

THE PAKISTAN CIVIL WAR

East and West Pakistan were separated by 1000 miles of Indian territory, and by their highly unique and distinctive cultures, religions, languages and social organization. When Pakistan was created in 1947, it was the product of a Hindu versus Muslim controversy, with Pakistan being created as a homeland for the Muslims. At the time, religious identity was the most significant political factor in Indian politics. Once Pakistan was created, that identity was a "given" and the new state had to create new bonds of identification between such diverse and distant peoples.

West Pakistan contained the capital, much of the industrial resources of the country, and the largest number of trained soldiers and managers. In the 1950's, the United States became a close ally of Pakistan, transferring military supplies and large amounts of economic assistance to Pakistan, most of which was deployed in the west wing. When, in 1958, General Ayub Khan seized control of the state from faltering democratic forces, East Pakistan's voice in public affairs grew even more weak, and political alienation grew. As in Burma and Indonesia, a wide popular base was essential in such a divided and diverse country as Pakistan if the state was to survive; instead, the military government appeared to narrow the base to the northern sections of West Pakistan alone.

In 1969 after much agitation, the Ayub Khan government fell and was replaced by another military government led by General Yayha Khan. This government proclaimed itself a caretaker regime, promising the transfer of power to popularly elected representatives who would frame a constitution. Elections were held in 1970, but it immediately became apparent that East Pakistan's vote had gone overwhelmingly to a party that was committed to regional autonomy of the broadest kind, bordering on provincial confederation. West Pakistan results seemed to show both interwing regional disputes and class conflicts, generated out of the considerable economic and social changes produced by a decade of development.

The army caretakers found themselves arbitrating between competing political men, but were themselves not disinterested. A free East Pakistan would so weaken the national budget of the country that it could not bear the defense costs which the army felt were vital to a credible defense posture against India. East Pakistan leadership believed that defense expenditures were inflated, benefited the west wing almost entirely, and were more involved with the Kashmir issue than with national defense. However, the Awami League leadership knew that some step toward meeting army concerns was necessary if East Pakistan's autonomy was to be gained.

In 1971, in the final stages of constitutional negotiations, civil war broke out. The extreme wing of provincial autonomists claimed independence for East Pakistan, and attempted to force the Awami League leadership into a "Bangla Desh" position. The army found itself divided, and West Pakistan political forces militated against acceptance of high amounts of provincial autonomy for East Pakistan. Events outran their control, as violence spread in the eastern wing, and as the army reasserted political control with a level of violence and destruction that shocked the world. At this juncture, India entered the dispute by providing support and sanctuary for the rebels and by involuntarily becoming the host of several million refugees fleeing the violence of the civil war.

The policies of the great powers concerning Pakistan have been highly restrained. Both the US and USSR have made humanitarian appeals and called for a political settlement, while Peking has loyally supported the national government's efforts to put down the insurrection.

When one attempts to generalize from these conditions of civil strife in which the United States has played a role since 1945, it becomes increasingly clear that foreign influence in Asia, never the most important variable in political events, is diminishing. Partially by choice but more significantly by the scale of Asian developments themselves, the foreign powers find themselves less and less influential in managing security relationships within, and between, the Asian powers. Nationalism has emerged triumphant in Asia, although such a development has not yielded peace or order. Civil war appears to be an endemic rather than a unique condition in many of the modernizing countries of Asia, and the United States increasingly shuns involvement as the scale, costs and benefits of involvement become increasingly unfavorable.

The US: Achievements, Failures, and Prospects

The thrust of American diplomacy seems to be toward a reduced role in security management throughout the world, and especially in those areas of civil strife and national conflict far removed from vital American security and economic interests. On the strategic level this requires deterrence on the part of the nuclear powers, and between the United States and its principal allies in West Europe and Japan. On the political level, this policy requires a reduced posture of commitment to regimes and frontiers throughout the Third World, with fewer resources available for highly political transfer, and more resources committed to multilateral assistance efforts. On the economic level, it requires little but permits a wide range of postures including increased trade with Communist regimes, bilateral and multilateral economic assistance, concessional trade practices, the promotion of foreign private investment and so forth.

The "fall" of a particular small Asian country is unlikely to be considered a "loss," much less a "betrayal" as the Communist world continues to develop variety and dissonance in its evolution and as a worldwide revolution in world politics takes the nation-state out of its monopolistic position as the sole significant actor in international relations. The new environment of American foreign policy allows a wider range of foreign outcomes to be "satisfactory" as long as they do not involve major countries like India and Japan, or result from "rule changes" such as the use of direct military force by another superpower. In short, the new world order which the United States sought to establish at the end of World War II has been largely established, and a more conventional diplomacy of balance, maneuver and trade can be followed without widespread systemic disruption.

Viewed in global perspective, Asia has become part of the universalized state system. China's inclusion in the international system completes the globalization of the European state system, and while Asia remains one of the most turbulent world segments, it is nonetheless a part of a system of managed conflict for which the European state system has procedures and means of resolution. The uniqueness of Asia, in American foreign policy, is therefore fast eroding and should, by the middle 1970's, be a memory more than a reality.

International organization, on the other hand, has been rapidly developing—with new international actors such as the global corporation. Trends such as the worldwide mobility of skill groups, enhanced communication and transportation facilities and the universality of industrial-urban modernization needs are knitting together aspects of the human experience at a rapid rate. There is no reason to believe that this integration will necessarily produce peace or order, but it does signal global interdependence and the erosion of previous forms of national patriotism and autarky. America's role in this world is as the pioneer, and its future association with Asia and with the rest of the world will be the result of its ability to transform its social and organizational creativity into international purposes that sustain the new globalism of ideas, resource exchanges and human empathy.

The ability of *governments*, American and Asian, to control international relations is weakening. Individuals have more autonomy in their choice of allegiance and life style than ever before, and the revolutions of transportation and communication make the retreat behind curtains, iron, bamboo, or oceanic, less and less possible. The new actors in world politics are supranational and transnational, and owe their allegiances more to groups than to nations. The global corporation serves stockholders, regardless of nationality, just as international organizations serve their functional goals, not those interests of their "member" states. This kind of world is wholly new to world history, and all diplomats are now pioneers. It would be a grave mistake to overestimate the ability of Washington to control the emerging world order, or even to significantly effect discreet outcomes in its development. But it would not be unrealistic to expect American policy to fundamentally affect the shape of the emerging structures of world politics. The superpower societies tend to lead in research and development, and tend to be both rich and forceful. Their lead, if it meets more broad needs, will be followed even if their lead, if counter to national aspirations, can be frustrated.

The future influence of the United States in Asia, therefore, depends upon its ability to associate its goals and preferences with those of the Asians at the *international* level. The era of great power influence in a pre-nationalist Asia is over, and with it, the opportunities for *domestic* influence-gathering. New forms of functional cooperation, organized by international organizations, global corporations, regional groupings and other transnational actors will have potent domestic effects, but they are remote from national government controls. The shaping of international forms of exchange, and the control of transnational economic actors, however, is a shared international concern and US policy is important in its shaping.

The future, as always, is contingent upon choices, outcomes, behavior and chance. Policy must be mindful of behavior patterns, and must base choices in calculations about their likely outcomes. Chance induces humility, and rightly so. America's future in Asia rests with its decision-makers, and with choices made in the new seats of power both in Asian states and in transnational "capitals." But no policy will succeed that does not understand the fundamental transition in Asia and in the global system itself, that have produced the revolution in which we now live.

The USSR and Asia

THOMAS P. THORNTON

The Strategic Setting

A nation's international relations reflect its view of
the world. Despite perhaps more ideological overlays
than most other countries have, Soviet policy in Asia
is determined from a distinctly Russian viewpoint.
Russians see the USSR as part of "Asia"—although most
Asians would not agree with them. Indeed, a substantial
portion of the USSR is occupied by the Central Asian
Republics. These republics form a sort of cultural and
ethnic bridge between Asia and the USSR proper. For
example, there are Turks in the USSR as well as in
Turkey; Tadjiks are closely related to Afghans; and
Kazakhs have ties across the border to China's Sinkiang
province. Mongols stretch from the USSR, across
Mongolia, into China. Islamic culture has some of its
finest monuments in the USSR and over ten percent
of the USSR's population is of Islamic background.

Yet as the process of Russification develops and the
barbed wire along the USSR's border frustrates natural
relationships, these cultural ties atrophy increasingly,
so that each new generation perceives less of a cultural
continuum stretching outward. Also, these ties are
primarily to the south. There is little in Russian history
that would contribute to building bridges between
Russians and the two most important Asian cultures—the
Chinese and Japanese.

Historically, "Asia" to the Russians means invading hordes
from the east—still very much a part of the Russian's
heritage. Russians also view themselves as the west's

first line of defense against the uncultured barbarians from the east. Typical are two poems by two of the Soviet Union's best-known writers, Voznesensky and Yevtushenko, written in 1967 and 1969.[1] Each poem is bitterly critical of the Maoist leadership in China and portrays its threat to both Communism and western civilization in vivid colors, referring to the new dangers of Genghis Khanism and the like. Although both poets seek to distinguish between the Maoist leadership and the Chinese people, they portray the new yellow menace with blatantly racist symbols. Because of a history of struggles against invading hordes from the east and a series of wars with Japan and China, the undercurrent of distrust, contempt and fear of "Asiatics" runs very near the surface in Russia.

A Russian standing in Moscow and looking eastward is, first of all, looking away from the sources of Russian—and Soviet—culture. Since at least the time of Peter the Great, Russia's principal cultural orientation has been to the west, and Europe has also been the source of its principal security concerns. Over the intervening centuries, these have grown to be much more pressing than the residual concerns with the east that linger on in the Russian subconsciousness. The three great onslaughts against Russia in modern times have come across the plains to the west; the current nuclear threat may in fact be across the Arctic, but it is seen as coming from "the west."

For Communism also, Europe is the traditional prime concern. Rationalizations aside, the advanced countries of Europe and North America should be the sources of revolution. Soviet attempts to cast them in this role have consistently been rebuffed, but hope springs eternal in Marxist breasts. The prospects of red flags flying in Saigon or Colombo may excite the Soviets; it cannot, however, compensate for their absence over Brussels or Ottawa. Even a Communist China is under the best of circumstances poor consolation for the Communists' inability to do more than foist a puppet regime on the lesser half of a defeated Germany.

Unlike an American, a Russian in Moscow does not look at Asia from across the Pacific—which has proved to be a better access route than the land route across Siberia. Unlike a European, he does not see the Far East as something to be approached via the Suez Canal or around Africa. The Indian sub-continent is his backyard and his Tsarist forebears had hopes of controlling at least part of it as late

---

[1] Yevgeniy Yevtushenko, "On the Red Snows of the Ussuri," translated in the *Washington Post*, April 13, 1969; and Andrey Voznesensky, "Prologue to a Poem," in *Literaturnaya Rossiya*, March 24, 1967.

as the end of the last century. The land route from Central Asia is a familiar one to conquerers. Even though Lenin did not talk of conquering Paris by way of Calcutta, it is a proposition that would have made sense to him both as a Russian and a Marxist.

At the other extreme, across Siberia, lies Japan and the Pacific. The Russians pressed across their continent much as Americans did. Unlike Americans, however, they found no California at the end of their quest and few Iowas or Kansases in between. Rather, fulfillment of Russia's "manifest destiny" found another growing power center to the East—Japan.

Between Japan and India looms the great Asian "fact" for Russia—China. Historically, the Chinese frontier posed less of a problem for Russia than did the Japanese and (British) Indian sectors. In the nineteenth and early twentieth centuries China was too weak to offer a challenge to Russia and the restraints on Russian expansion into China were posed by Japan and the European powers rather than by China itself. In the first decade of Communist rule in Peking as well, China seemed to offer more opportunities than problems. In a sense, Communism seemed to have accomplished what the Tsars had been unable to do. Soviet influence became dominant in China and the vast stretch of border between the two countries was secure.

Now, however, the situation has changed drastically. China presents an immense problem, as well as a threat, to Soviet security. This hostility with China, and competition for Communist leadership has forced the Soviet Union into triangular competition rather than the two-way conflict between Communists and non-Communists that Moscow had expected. Simply by being there, China blocks direct Soviet access to Southeast Asia.

The Russian perspective on Asia can be summarized as follows: the Indian sub-continent is relatively close and in some ways a cultural extension of Soviet Central Asia; Japan is distant across Siberia, but directly on the borders of the USSR and thus a potential threat; China is threatening to be the source of another invasion from the east such as Russians experienced throughout their early history; Southeast Asia is barely discernible beyond China, accessible only by the long route through Suez (when open) or again by sea after the long land journey across Siberia.

To be sure, airplanes reduce travel time, communications are virtually instantaneous and the Soviet Union's new position as a global power ensures it political access regardless of its geography. Yet the facts of history and geopolitics remain important determinants of Soviet policy towards Asia.

Internal Determinants of the USSR's Foreign Policy

A nation's foreign policy can profit from skill, luck or improvisation, but as the French have discovered, it depends most heavily on resources and their application. The USSR has abundant human and natural resources, and, as of the middle of the 20th century, a strong industrial base and most of the various other elements that constitute the wherewithal of "power." The USSR is incomparably better endowed than any other nation of Eurasia—perhaps better than any grouping of nations. Similarly, the USSR has an outstanding military capacity, the *ultima ratio* of foreign policy. By traditional standards it is fully equipped to play the leading role in Asia; even an imperial role should it desire to do so.

However, the resources of the USSR have been increasingly subjected to a host of competing claims, the most important of which has been domestic requirements. Consumer demands have become increasingly forceful in the USSR in the past decade, and the Soviet leadership has paid increasing attention to them. Also, the USSR's complex and modern economy and its military machine require large inputs of resources simply to keep them going and to keep their managers satisfied.

The greatest restraint placed on the optimum employment of Soviet resources in Asia is the role of the US in the region, which tends to bid the stakes up much higher. Particularly in the years immediately following World War II, more abundant resources provided the US with an important head start vis-à-vis the Soviets in Asia.

Another approach to the resources question is that of profitability —i.e., where will invested resources bring the best return? The Soviets, as the US, lack computers that will tell them exactly whether one fleet visit to Havana is worth two to Bombay or a North Atlantic fleet exercise; or whether $100 million invested in a Pakistani steel mill is worth more than twenty $5 million programs scattered through Black Africa. They do know, however, that there are many areas of the world which offer investment opportunities that promise at least as great a return as those available in Asia. The profitability of direct military involvement (a special kind of resource expenditure) in Asia presumably appears extremely low unless in answer to the Chinese threat, and certainly nowhere in Asia is there any region—least of all Vietnam—that is as profitable for Soviet military efforts as is the Middle East.

Another special kind of resource can perhaps be best described as attention span. No matter how large the bureaucracy, the most crucial questions must ultimately be decided by a few men at the top who can efficiently handle only a limited number of problems at one time. The US, western Europe, China and the Middle East provide the Soviet leaders with a plethora of problems. Since Asian affairs (China aside) have relatively little effect on Soviet security concerns they must struggle for both attention and resources in making their claims felt. Asia as a whole certainly receives more attention than do Africa and Latin America, and individual parts of Asia—notably India and Japan—are often the objects of special concern. On the whole, however, Asia probably ranks only in the lower middle of the scale of claimants for Soviet attention and resources.

THE RANGE OF GOALS

Describing another foreign country's policy goals is difficult. It is particularly difficult for the Soviet Union, since its pronouncements on foreign policy seldom go beyond the vaguest banalities. We can at least, however, infer the Soviets' maximum and minimum objectives. At the high end of the scale must inevitably be the desire to exert hegemony over Asia—either as an expression of Russian power or of Communist ideology. Hegemony can be thought of in various ways: a total communization of Asia along the Soviet model is the extreme case and is quite unlikely of attainment. More within the realm of possibility would be a situation in which the other Asian states have no strong and reliable external support and none of them—including China—is strong enough to resist Soviet domination.

But the USSR and Tsarist Russia before it, have never been in a position to pursue hegemony in Asia. In fact, the question could not have arisen until very recently. Since World War II, Soviet aspirations in Asia have been thwarted, for American power has been placed continuously on the western Pacific island chain, sporadically in Southeast Asia, and temporarily and tenuously in Pakistan. China has been an independent and increasingly strong rival since the late 1950's, and in the 1960's Japan developed into an economically independent power center with considerable military potential. In addition, the large and potentially significant countries of India, Pakistan and Indonesia have staked out independent international roles for themselves. Thus, hegemony remains an unrealistic, though enticing, objective for Soviet policy in Asia and will remain so for the foreseeable future.

If hegemony is considered to be the maximum goal in Asia, the minimum objective of the Soviet Union in Asia must be security. As the Soviets view Asia, the only present threats to their security come from the United States and China. This is a determining factor of the US-Soviet-Chinese triangular relationship that in turn determines the course of Soviet policy throughout Asia, and the world.

The perceived threat from the United States is the dominant factor affecting the Soviet international posture throughout the world, hence also in Asia. The US is nuclear-armed and could inflict unacceptable damage on the USSR in case of war. The primacy that the Soviets attach to their strategic relationship with the US is evident in numerous ways—in Asia the most obvious manifestation is Soviet unwillingness to allow the Vietnam problem to interfere with current nuclear arms limitation negotiations.

Yet the focus of the US-Soviet competition is really in Europe, not in Asia. The Bering Straits hardly figure heavily in the strategic planning of either the US or USSR; a potential threat based on Japan is not an immediate concern, and US forces in Southeast Asia are not directly relevant to Soviet-American relations. Moscow recognizes that the US has no vital interest of its own at stake in Asia; that it is not irrevocably committed to deep involvement in the affairs of Asia; that it cannot realistically aspire to hegemony in Asia; and that it is not attempting to organize Asia against the USSR.

The Chinese, on the other hand, are very much a part of Asia. Their vital interests are there and they must remain involved. China can and does aspire to both ideological and political hegemony, and it is seeking to organize Asia against the USSR. Since the reverse of each of these propositions is also true for the Soviet Union, the Sino-Soviet competition in Asia is a matter of deep and abiding concern to Russians. This concern is fueled still more by Russian perceptions of the great masses of Chinese pressing on the Siberian border and the irredentist claims of China to large parts of Siberia and Central Asia. Counterbalancing this to some degree, however, is the fact that the Chinese threat to the USSR is much less cataclysmic in the short run than is that posed by the US. With its minimal nuclear capability, China poses no present threat to the existence of the USSR.

The asymmetry of the Soviet relationship to China and the US is also reflected in its ideology. The Soviets naturally maintain an ideological posture of hostility towards the capitalist world and piously reiterate that the final battle with the west will be along classic Marxist-Leninist lines. Especially in Asia, however, this posturing has little operational significance. The competition with the west (especially the US) is political rather than ideological, thus permitting considerable flexibility and possibilities for tacit compromise.

The struggle with China, which is ideological as well as political, permits much less flexibility or even tolerance of the other side's role.

The Sino-Soviet competition, unlike the US-Soviet game, is essentially zero-sum. This means that in certain circumstances, Chinese setbacks in Asia could be profitable for both the US and the USSR (and, indeed, Soviet losses might profit both the US and China—a point that occupies the Soviets more than the US). US losses, on the other hand, would in general redound to the benefit of the USSR *or* China, not to both of them.

Thus *within the specifically Asian context* China, without question, presents the USSR with the greatest challenge. *At the global level,* the US-Soviet relationship is of equal importance. The challenge to Soviet policy-making in Asia is thus to develop policies that take account of both sets of problems in this triangle, interrelate them, and produce solutions that achieve optimum outcomes—i.e., ones that maximize benefits and minimize losses within and between each set of relationships.

THE AVAILABLE TACTICS

Between the necessary minimum and unattainable maximum objectives of Soviet policy lies the realm of the possible—the proverbial sphere of policy and diplomacy. No less proverbially, policy and diplomacy can be defined as choosing the best alternative, avoiding making choices, or choosing the least bad alternative. The conflicting asymmetrical relationships among the USSR, China and the United States are the primary factors that make choices difficult. The Soviets, probably to a greater degree than the Americans or the Chinese, find it difficult to make policy moves in Asia with any reasonable assurance that they will derive more profit than will their rivals. This problem is only partially ameliorated by the fact that the Soviets are generally playing for relatively smaller stakes in Asia.

The triangle between the USSR-US-China makes choices of policy and diplomacy in Asia difficult. Many of these difficult choices relate to the "ideology vs. national interest" tension that underlies so much of Soviet policy. The Soviets know from experience that unrest and disorder provide fertile ground for the growth of Communism but their influence over events in most of Asia is so slight that they would not have much control over the outcome, and if the disorder escalated their global posture might be jeopardized. Furthermore, the Soviets feel morally bound to promote a myth of social order that is rejected by states with whom Moscow wants to maintain good relations.

Not surprisingly, the ideological component sometimes gets short shrift in Soviet policy-making towards Asia. Of much more importance is the problem of participating in a structure of international relations that protects immediate Soviet interests while providing scope for a dynamic growth of Soviet influence.

The relative Soviet weakness in Asia that continues to frustrate aspirations of hegemony excluded the USSR for many years from any meaningful participation in an Asian balance of power. Furthermore, the tendency of Stalin and Khrushchev to see the world in bi-polar terms made balance of power concepts anachronistic from their points of view. Now, however, the Soviets are for the first time in a position to play balance of power politics.[2] They possess the minimum resources required, the depolarized situation in Asia makes a balance of power feasible, and the more pragmatic post-Khrushchev leadership has a view of the world that (a) makes it an acceptable player, and (b) permits it to deal with other states as potential players.

Not only are balance of power tactics possible now for the Soviets, the situation in Asia makes them mandatory. The "game" in Asia comprises four groups of players: (1) the USSR itself; (2) China and its sometime Korean and Vietnamese supporters; (3) the US and its allies (including also those outside of Asia such as the UK), and (4) the various Third World countries. While the Soviets are encouraged by ideology to hope that the Chinese will someday return to the true faith, their historical experience teaches them to assume that a strong Asian power must be hostile.

The role of the US is not as certain. The most casual observer can see that US interest in Asia is waning. Also, the US alliance systems are not monolithic; the British have retrenched sharply, Japan is becoming increasingly independent, both politically and economically, and the Soviets see US ties with its smaller allies loosening, if not withering completely. The several Third World countries are generally free agents, but not worth the cost that any of the principal players would have to pay to secure them as reliable allies. They can, however, play important subsidiary roles and some, especially India, can be useful adjuncts to Soviet policy.

Given this pattern of existing power relationships, what must the

---

[2] It is interesting to note that two monographs prepared in 1967 and 1968 on the Asian balance of power for the Institute of Strategic Studies (London) devoted a total of less than one page to the role of the USSR. (Adelphi Papers Nos. 35 and 44 by William Chapin and Coral Bell.) A somewhat more recent study, on the other hand, gives the USSR substantial attention. (Wayne Wilcox, "The Prospective Politics of Insecurity and Strategic Asymmetry in Asia", *International Journal* Vol. XXIV No. 1 [Winter 1968–69] pp. 13–34.) This difference reflects the change in perceptions of the Soviet role that took place over a very short period of time.

Soviet strategy for the future entail? The first requirement is to avoid a conjunction of the US and China, for this would present an intolerable threat to Soviet security. Loud protests of US-Chinese collusion—often on the flimsiest of evidence—bear eloquent testimony to Soviet concerns on this score. A corollary of this strategy is the need to ensure that neither the US nor China gain hegemony over the rest of Asia, since this would pose an intolerable threat or at least lead to unstable bi-polarity. The continued existence in force of the Sino-Soviet treaty is in part at least a signal to the US that the USSR would not permit China to pass under American influence. Moscow probably sees this contingency as remote; more pressing are its fears that the US might decamp prematurely from Asia, abandoning the mainland and ultimately the offshore island chain to Chinese influence. The Third World countries need only be kept out of the control or influence of either the US or China.

To sum up, Soviet policy in Asia at the present stage can mainly be comprehended in balance of power terms, although the term "balance of power" is disdained by the Soviets and used only in a pejorative sense. The United States, too, has traditionally followed a balance of power policy in Asia although with some critical differences. The American objective is simply the establishment of power relationships in Asia that prevent the predominance of any single power; Americans need not be a constituent of the balance. The Soviet Union, an Asian power, must participate in the balance. Furthermore, the US cannot realistically aspire to hegemony while the Soviets, as we have seen, can and probably do harbor such long-range aspirations.

For the time being these differences are not critical. The US is in the Asian balance and is likely to stay for some time; the USSR's visions of hegemony have little operational significance. The differences must be kept in mind, however, if Soviet policy in Asia is to be seen in proper perspective. Simply stated, the USSR's ultimate goals are not symmetrical with ours. We cannot and do not aspire to exclude the USSR from Asia while the possibility of evicting the US from Asia always lurks at the back of Soviet minds.

Domestic Politics and Foreign Policy Alternatives

The story of Soviet involvement in Asia (and, for that matter, the entire Third World) falls rather conveniently into ten-year periods. I have no desire to plunge into history here; there is a growing literature on the subject, and I have offered my views elsewhere at some length.[3] In summary, the picture is somewhat like this—give or take a few years on some of the earlier dates:

To 1925—World War I and the Bolshevik revolution: the Soviets exhibited a sympathetic concern with Asia and, following failures in Europe, active involvement in China. Generally, an outward-looking period of Soviet history, especially after the civil war.

1925–1935—The USSR withdraws into its shell, "building Socialism in one country" with little concern for anything beyond its borders and no interest whatsoever in Asia following the collapse of the Kuomintang-Communist alliance in China.

1935–1945—This was the period of the Popular Front and World War I. Everything, including Asian policy, was ruthlessly subordinated to the struggle against Nazi Germany.

1945–1955—Another period of withdrawal and reconstruction after the war. Soviet attention abroad is centered on Europe. Mao presents China as a windfall and Communist revolutions flare briefly in Southeast Asia. Resources are extremely short, however, and Stalin's policy is unimaginative. Asia is regarded with near hostility and left to its own devices.

1955–1965, and 1965–Present—The eras of Khrushchev and his successors warrant a more detailed survey to illuminate the development of Soviet policy to its current stage:

The USSR under Stalin was concerned with Asia—it had to adjust to the existence of a Communist regime in China and had to take a position vis-à-vis the rash of Communist revolts in Southeast Asia at the end of the 1940's. It also sought maximum advantage from its belated entry into the war against Japan. But the effort applied in Asia was extremely small. The Soviets had only limited resources and these were overwhelmingly committed to Europe, where the Soviets perceived the greater danger and more hopeful prospects.

By the beginning of the Khrushchev era, the basis of a change in policy was evident. The situation in Europe had stabilized; the likelihood of a threat had diminished and contained the prospect of Communists coming to power. China had made clear that it was not going to become another Soviet satellite like Mongolia; if Soviet influence was to be projected into Asia, it would not be through a Chinese proxy. The period of extreme resource shortages following World War II had been weathered. A modest surplus was now available as risk capital for investment in areas farther afield.

A whole new sphere of activity opened up as new nations became

[3] See C. E. Black and T. P. Thornton, eds., *Communism and Revolution* (Princeton, 1964), chapters 2, 9, and 10.

independent and free to pursue their own foreign policies. Most of them did not perceive the cold war as the most salient international issue in terms of their own interests, which were mainly developmental. The Soviet leadership correctly perceived a change in the international situation in Asia at a time when the US was making some unfortunate misjudgments. The ill-starred American attempt to extend the ring of containment around the entire Communist bloc à la NATO was not sufficient to contain the Soviets but was sufficiently menacing to spur them to react. The US alliance system even facilitated the Soviet move into areas where the Americans became involved in regional disputes (India-Pakistan) or simply projected more power than some Asians (e.g., Indonesians) found comfortable.

The assumption of a major role on the Asian scene after the mid 1950's marked the first time in this century that Russia had seriously sought to assert itself in Asia, and the scope of the Soviet effort far exceeded anything that the Tsars had attempted. Russians now appeared, seldom empty-handed, as far afield as Ceylon and Indonesia. Soviet scholars and others were encouraged to spread themselves across Asia, see the world first-hand rather than through western writings or their own polemical tracts, and bring back a better understanding of conditions that would provide a sounder base for policy-making.[4]

The results of all this endeavor were mixed. Containment did, in fact, work along the western Pacific island chain. Most importantly it provided an atmosphere in which Japan could develop. However, much of the Soviet impact was ephemeral, resulting more from its novelty than from actual achievement. The more optimistic expectations of the Khrushchev era wilted quickly when it became clear that Asians regarded the Soviets not as messiahs but, at best, as gift-bearing strangers from distant lands. And, or course, the absence of any relevant Soviet military capability deprived the USSR of the ultimate persuasive weapon for its policy. Because of both its strategic nuclear inferiority and the absence of a capability for distant operations, the USSR was clearly a second-rate power in southern Asia.

The last years of the Khrushchev regime were years of bitter disappointment across the whole range of Soviet foreign policy—most notably, of course, in Sino-Soviet relations. No Asian country joined the "Socialist Commonwealth" or became a "national democracy," and as Chinese diplomacy and appeal reached their zenith, Khrushchev simply lost interest in Asia. In pursuit of a détente with

[4] A discussion of this development, together with a number of representative scholarly studies, can be found in T. P. Thornton, *Third World in Soviet Perspective* (Princeton, 1964).

Washington he allowed the US a virtually free hand in Vietnam and his ideological efforts were increasingly directed towards Africa and Cuba. Judged in its own terms, Khrushchev's policy in Asia was nearly a total failure.

Yet for the first time, Moscow approached Asia not as a target for Communist revolutionary activity but as a collection of nations with whom it was possible and often profitable to deal on a state-to-state basis. Since many Asian states were glad to reciprocate the relationship, the USSR became an acceptable player in the Asian balance-of-power game. Khrushchev may not have fully comprehended what was happening. His flamboyant style was geared more to gambling for the quick ruble than to cultivating long-term political investments. Also, his policies were heavily laden with a pseudo-ideological overlay that obscured the reality of events. But in Asia, as elsewhere, he left behind a structure for his successors to build on.

HISTORICAL APPROACHES: THE MATURING OF POLICY

Khrushchev can best be comprehended as an element of the dialectic. In domestic affairs he served as an antithesis to Stalinism, leaving his successors to find a synthesis—a task on which they are still engaged with little success.[5] On the international scene too, he burst through the bounds of policy imposed by the two-camp theory by broadening the ambit of Soviet policy to almost the entire world. Yet Khrushchev was unable to transcend the bi-polar worldview of his predecessors. He only substituted the peaceloving/warlike dichotomy for the Socialist/capitalist dichotomy of Stalin. Nations such as Pakistan and Thailand that participated in the American security system were still beyond the pale. In addition, he overextended himself, on occasion, so that his successors had to cope with more than a few "hare-brained schemes" abroad before they could proceed with further, more orderly expansion.

Khrushchev's personal tragedy was to pass from the political scene when the climate for a further redefinition of Soviet foreign policy was favorable. His successors soon had much greater resources available; the strategic imbalance gradually improved to the Soviets' benefit; Soviet military capabilities for distant operations improved somewhat; China's position declined as a result of the Indonesian coup and the excesses of the Cultural Revolution; and growing American involvement in Vietnam, coupled with shifts in opinion and priorities within the US, provided greater scope for Soviet activity in Asia.

[5] This is, of course, an antithesis only in Hegelian terms and by Soviet Russian standards.

With these advantages in hand and the excesses of Khrushchev's naive ideologizing behind them, Brezhnev and Kosygin have concentrated on a reasonably rational program of relating interests and resources to their policy. There have been no triumphal processions through South Asia and no politicking on Iowa farms, but also no Cuban or Indonesian fiascos, the latter of which we shall discuss presently. Their foreign policy has been marked by the dull but competent professionalism so highly prized by practitioners of the diplomatic art. Kosygin and Brezhnev have been accorded membership in the elite of that society—the wielders of the balance of power. By accepting the fact that countries nominally aligned with the west can be dealt with, they have gone beyond Khrushchev's bi-polarism and made possible the development of meaningful balance of power relations.

In Asia, this confident and more mature style of diplomacy has manifested itself in a policy towards China that has sought to eschew shrillness while showing itself firm and unyielding on points of substance. After some uneasy years, a degree of stability seems to have been established in the relationship. Farther afield, it has entailed developing businesslike, if not intimate, state-to-state relations and avoiding disruptive actions in areas where the USSR stands to gain little from any likely outcome.

The Soviet leadership has of course had to accept limitations on its policy; it has been unable to assert primacy in Asia vis-à-vis the US or China and it has set more modest goals than Khrushchev. It has, however, set about establishing a broad and credible "interest" in Asian affairs. Soviet leaders have repeatedly asserted in recent years that the interests of the USSR must be taken into consideration in one or another area (the Mediterranean is the most forcefully asserted case) and, increasingly, these claims are being accepted. In the Asian context, two Soviet moves are particularly important as symbolic actions designed to underline the Soviet right to be regarded as a full member of the Asian balance.

In the spring of 1968, Soviet naval units appeared in the Indian Ocean, marking the first time that Russian combatants had plied these waters since the Tsarist era. To a considerable extent, the initial appearance of these ships and the steady stream that has followed, can be explained as space-support missions and by the simple fact that the USSR now has some surplus naval capability and has decided to use it. In a more important sense, however, their presence is intended as a signal that the USSR has the capability to project its power into areas far afield just as other maritime powers do and that its influence is no longer limited by total inability to mount distant operations and by dependence on proxies such as Indonesia or the UAR.

The Soviet Indian Ocean squadron is not meant to fight battles; it generally consists of less than a half-dozen ships at any one time. It has shown the flag systematically all around the Indian Ocean littoral, however, and there is little doubt that its message has been read by the states of the region. The Soviet presence in the Indian Ocean will doubtless remain, and although much further expansion is unlikely, once the Vietnam war tapers off similar operations with similar objectives will probably become common in waters farther east.

An even more direct assertion of Soviet determination to claim a "rightful" role in Asian affairs was Brezhnev's June 1969 call for an Asian security arrangement. Brezhnev's statement was cryptic in the extreme. While discussing the possibility of a European security system he said: "We are of the opinion that the course of events is also putting on the agenda the task of creating a system of collective security in Asia." No attempt was made at a further definition of this statement and attempts to elicit details were unavailing, but the proposal was no flash in the pan. Repeated references to it have appeared in the Soviet press, the Soviets have prodded Asian governments to react, and it has become a standard element of Foreign Minister Gromyko's annual policy statement to the UN General Assembly.

For the most part Asians greeted the proposal with embarrassed silence. China of course interpreted it as distinctly antiChinese and much of the reluctance of other Asians to respond favorably reflected their unwillingness to become involved in what they, too, interpreted as an anti-Chinese maneuver. Others, of course, hesitated to take a position until the American attitude became clear. There was undoubtedly a strong antiChinese element in the proposal, although in theory China would have been invited to participate. A security system organized to contain China would greatly benefit the Soviet position—especially in the eyes of Russians who set great store by formalized security arrangements.

The relationship of the Brezhnev proposal to the European security system which the Soviets have long promoted provides some interesting perspectives. A European system would presumably limit Germany just as an Asian system would limit China. A principal goal of any European system would be to freeze the territorial status quo; an Asian system would have the same effect, reducing the danger that territorial revisionism might bring about chaos and jeopardize the course of Soviet policy in Asia. In effect, it would broaden the efforts that the USSR had been making in South Asia to defuse the Indo-Pakistani territorial disputes, and it matters little to Moscow that the other most prominent territorial revisionists in Asia are Communist states.

The proposal is also designed to benefit the USSR in other ways. By its terms, it would ensure that the USSR is accorded a place in the Asian system, and that attempts to exclude it on essentially racial grounds (as was done at the 1955 Bandung Conference) would be unsuccessful. Beyond this, it was in effect a declaration that the USSR is not only one of the constituents of the Asian power balance but one that has a strong voice in determining its structure.

The lack of specificity in the proposal was probably designed to stimulate the Asians to come forth with their own ideas, which could then be fitted into an overall mosaic of Soviet design. Also, it avoided Soviet identification with any specific course of action that might turn out to be repugnant. The Soviets hardly expected that their proposal would be universally acclaimed (although they were evidently disappointed at the little enthusiasm that it generated). They have waited many years to set up a European security system and are probably prepared to wait to see their plans for Asia come to fruition. The proposal was, rather like the fleet operations, a flag-showing maneuver or—to shift the metaphor—the staking out of a claim. The time is not yet ripe to activate the claim fully but all are aware of its existence and, except for China, no voice has been raised to dispute Moscow's right to make this claim.

The USSR and the World Community

REGIONAL APPROACHES: SOUTH ASIA

However, Asian considerations still represent a small part of the Soviet foreign policy effort. Moscow still approaches Asia in terms of individual countries and regions. Traditional perceptions remain important for Soviet policy formulation and Moscow's first great effort in the post-Stalin era was, not surprisingly, directed towards India. Khrushchev was hardly seeking to re-live the Tsarist past; the opportunities offered by Nehru's espousal of non-alignment and a host of other factors were the main determinants. Nonetheless, while discussing South Asia before the Supreme Soviet on July 10, 1969, Gromyko noted that despite the telescoping of distances by technology, ". . . this does not diminish the cardinal importance of establishing friendship and cooperation with those living side-by-side."

While factors of geography and politics would have in any event justified intensive Soviet concern with India, the growing involvement of China made India even more important in Soviet calculations. The emergence of a creative Soviet policy towards India predated the major fissures in Sino-Soviet relations, but as the Sino-Soviet dispute began to develop, Peking could not have appreciated Soviet willingness to contribute resources to capitalist India at a time when its own needs were being met in a niggardly fashion. China also deeply resented Soviet suggestions that India was moving along some ill-defined road to Socialism. Liu Shao-ch'i had made clear as early as 1949 that other Asians were to follow the Chinese path to Socialism and alternate suggestions by Stalin's epigones were scarcely acceptable to China. The ultimate affront came in 1958, when Khrushchev suggested that India (but not China) be invited to join the Big Four powers in a meeting to calm the troubled Middle East situation. Taken together, these various Soviet gestures toward India contributed significantly to the precipitous decline in Sino-Soviet relations.

These costs were balanced, however, by certain benefits. There was much talk in those days—in Washington as well as in Moscow—that the future of Asia would be determined by the competition between India and China. As long as this competition remained peaceful and Sino-Soviet differences were submerged, Soviet policy towards India could be portrayed solely in terms of weakening the west. In 1959, however, the Sino-Indian competition took on a new aspect as the two countries fell apart publicly over Tibet and border disputes; at about the same time the Sino-Soviet dispute too became a matter of public record. Thus the Soviets had both the opportunity and the need to make a public choice in favor of India and capitalize on their investment there. In 1962, Moscow refused to support the "Chinese comrades" when they came to blows with the "Indian brothers" in a brief but fierce border war. Thereafter, Soviet preferences were made even clearer as Moscow moved to build up Indian military capabilities, in part as a means of cementing ties with New Delhi, but also to strengthen India as a counterweight to China.

The nature of the Soviet interest was emphasized by the shift in the USSR's ideological appraisal of India. The enthusiastic and optimistic assessment of Indian Socialism that had prevailed in the mid-1950's began to wither as early as 1958. By 1960 it had become quite bleak and following the discrediting of Nehru's non-alignment policy in 1962, the principal Soviet concern was to forestall a swing to the right in India. Thus even in Khrushchev's time, Soviet interest in India was increasingly predicated on *raison d'état*. This orientation has been even clearer under Kosygin.

The Soviets have not lost sight of other possibilities in India while seeking to turn it against China. They also have worked assiduously to undercut western, especially American, influence and there has been no public Soviet recognition of parallel US and Soviet interests in the sub-continent. In fact, their confidence emboldened them to try a major diplomatic coup. Recognizing the growing Chinese role in Pakistan and the declining American influence there, Kosygin decided to risk making a play for India's principal foe. In the disputes that led to the September 1965 Indo-Pakistani war, Moscow muted its traditional partisanship for India in favor of a neutral role, urging peaceful settlement. Indians had little alternative but to swallow this bitter pill rather than risk losing a major source of military supply, while the Pakistanis were delighted to add a prop to their "triangular tightrope" foreign policy. Kosygin was thus able to emerge as a mediator in the Indo-Pakistani conflict. While his diplomatic feat in bringing about an agreement at Tashkent (February 1966) hardly solved the problems of the sub-continent, it lowered the temperature of the dispute, contributed to stability, and clearly established that the USSR's position in South Asia is second to none. Henceforth, Moscow would have a major voice in the affairs of the region.

As the US found out nearly a decade before, however, having a voice in South Asia affairs can be a harrowing experience. A series of events in early 1971 put Soviet policy to some difficult tests. The least troublesome of these was Mrs. Gandhi's smashing victory in the Indian general elections. Moscow in fact welcomed the success of a leader who was "progressive" and well disposed to the USSR. The dimensions of the victory were such, however, that there was virtually no role left for the pro-Moscow Indian Communists. Not only must Moscow put away any hopes of rapid movement towards Communism in India but it will also have to buy its voice in Indian affairs with real political and economic resources, rather than with the cheap currency of involvement in domestic Indian politics.

Another event demonstrated that Moscow has few qualms about supporting wholeheartedly a "progressive" leader. Soviet reaction to the uprising of a left-extremist Ceylonese group against the "progressive" coalition of Mrs. Bandaranaike apparently caused little debate in Soviet councils. The USSR, along with the US, UK, India, China, Pakistan and just about everybody else, quickly came to Mrs. Bandaranaike's aid—even sending MIGs that presumably were supposed to shoot up bands of young leftist insurgents hidden in the jungles. The Soviet response was logical enough: the rebels belonged to the revolutionary fringe (they were reportedly aided by North Korea), the Ceylonese government included pro-Moscow Communists, and there was deep Soviet concern that Mrs. Bandaranaike might be frightened into shifting the base of her government to the right. Despite the logic of the situation, however, there was something almost poignant in the spectacle of the workers' state rushing in to help a basically moderate government crush genuine leftist revolutionaries. But the USSR is the land of Lenin, not of Rosa Luxemburg.

The tragic events that began in East Pakistan, in March 1971, and led to the Indo-Pakistani war in December confronted the Soviet leadership with the most challenging problems. A relatively even-handed policy became almost impossible to maintain, thus calling into question the last five years of Soviet efforts in the subcontinent. But striking opportunities were offered by India's resentment of US policy which was seen in New Delhi as pro-Pakistani. The logic of choice was clear and after very little vacillation, the Soviets apparently decided that the gains to be made by supporting India well outweighed the likely losses that such a policy would incur with Pakistan—especially in view of the questionable future of Pakistan as a unified state.

The tone of the Soviet government's position was moderate, leaving the door open for the maintenance of a constructive Indo-Pakistani relationship. Throughout the nine month crisis Moscow was careful not to espouse the breakup of Pakistan, and even after Bangla Desh came into existence, Moscow delayed extending recognition. Offensive Soviet commentary was mainly left to "unofficial" statements in resolutions passed by trade unions, "spontaneous" citizens' demonstrations and the like. There was no doubt, however, where Moscow's sentiments lay. Official statements emphasized the need for Pakistan to solve its problems by political rather than by military means and voiced strong support for India's role. It was also widely assumed that Moscow had reassured New Delhi on the subject of military supplies and Indo-Soviet cooperation was seen as restraining the Chinese from any plans that they might have had to help Pakistan.

Throughout the spring and summer of 1971 there was a flurry of diplomatic activity between Moscow and New Delhi. Visits were exchanged at the highest level, and in August the two countries signed a 20-year friendship pact. Although the treaty broke no new ground, and actually formalized the already existing relationship, it was a highly significant benchmark of the extent to which India and the Soviet Union had developed their ties. The Soviets saw the treaty as an opportunity to consolidate their position in India and to probably take a first step towards the formation of a broader Asian security system such as Brezhnev had proposed. In addition, however, the treaty was probably intended as a means of restraining the Indians from taking military action against Pakistan. Throughout the crisis the Soviets apparently sought to dissuade India from steps that would upset stability and possibly trigger American or Chinese intervention. When Indian patience finally snapped in December, the Soviets voiced no criticism and rendered full support to the Indians in the UN Security Council. It is likely, however, that they counselled a rapid end to the hostilities, and they were visibly relieved when the Indians accepted a cease-fire as soon as their objectives were attained in East Bengal.

In the aftermath of victory public opinion in India was strongly pro-Soviet and the government had every reason to be deeply grateful to Moscow. Soviet stock had never been higher in any Asian country. The American and Chinese stars shone more brightly over West Pakistan, but this was a price that the Soviets were willing to pay for their success in India. But Moscow retained some hope of salvaging part of the gains that had been made between 1965 and 1971 in West Pakistan. Bridges between the two countries had never been burned and the USSR still had much to offer as Pakistan sought to make a fresh start. The new Pakistani president, Z.A. Bhutto had been the original architect of Soviet-Pakistani rapprochement and continued to recognize Pakistan's need for a broad diversity of foreign support. Soviet ties with the new nation of Bangla Desh would certainly be close and the other smaller states of South Asia—even if concerned over the new extent of Soviet influence—would draw the conclusion that such a powerful neighbor needed to be placated.

The USSR is probably now entering into a period of consolidation, for further advances may be difficult and hard to justify in terms of cost-benefit analysis, barring another windfall like that of 1971. The USSR cannot supplant the World Bank Consortium as an aid donor. Loan repayments from India are probably just around the corner. India desperately hopes to salvage its non-alignment and this will require an improvement of ties with the United States. The same resistance to deep foreign involvement that has worked against the US role in South Asia will also come increasingly into play against the Soviets. Finally, while Moscow can be pleased with its substantial veto power over events in South Asia it still lacks the positive ability to control developments. The ideologically tinged aspirations of the 1950's have not been fulfilled; the benefits that have accrued to Soviet policy because of its power-political approach have necessarily entailed the limitations inherent in such an approach.

But overall, Soviet policy in South Asia has been a great success. No threat to Soviet security can be mounted from there; even the small US military presence at Peshawar in West Pakistan was terminated in 1969. The Soviets maneuvered successfully in the exceedingly complex interplay of the US-Sino-Soviet triangle and the Indo-Pakistani rivalry.[6] The US position in South Asia as a whole reached new depths in 1971, albeit for reasons not directly related to Soviet activities, and the Chinese have been restricted to West Pakistan. The USSR was by 1972 without question the strongest external influence in the region and Moscow had gained a critically important entree on the Asian scene.

REGIONAL APPROACHES: EAST ASIA

Japan overshadows the other East Asian countries even more than India does its sub-continental neighbors. Yet the Soviets have done little to establish a position of influence in Japan and have made no progress elsewhere in the region except—very unsatisfyingly—in North Korea. The reasons for this are obvious. First, for the first post-war years, Japan was under the firm control of the US and the Soviets to all intents and purposes lacked access to it. Second, South Korea and Taiwan are even less accessible to Moscow; not only are they rabidly anti-Communist, the Soviets' relationships with Pyŏngyang and Peking make it extremely difficult for them to deal with Seoul and Taipei. Finally, Russian stock in the region has never been high; the East Asian countries are strongly ethnocentric. Japan has looked abroad but has found its political and economic models in western Europe and America. Psychologically, the influence of China is more important throughout the region than that of Russia, and even Marxism is more welcome through a Chinese filter.

As we have mentioned, to the extent that Khrushchev singled out one Asian country to be the target of Soviet attentions it was not Japan but India. By Khrushchev's standards, the prospects were much better for a "Socialist" India that would capitalize on its size and the charisma of Nehru to lead the newly independent countries of Asia and Africa. Japan was still something of an international pariah, its economic potential was still unrealized, and it was allied with the US.

Khrushchev was of course a child of his age. Many American and European theorists were equally myopic in their faulty estimates of Japan and India. In the past decade, however, it has become increasingly clear that if any one Asian country has the potential to balance China in Asia it is Japan. Khrushchev's successors undoubtedly recognize this fact. The growing area of friction between the US and Japan and the latter's decision to adopt a posture more commensurate with

---

[6] I have dealt with these developments at length in "South Asia and the Great Powers," *World Affairs,* Vol. 132, No. 4 (March 1970), pp. 345–358.

its capabilities must certainly tempt Moscow to try and separate Tokyo from Washington, and any attempt to organize an Asian security system must include Japan as a major element. Thus a solid working relationship with Tokyo would seem to be at least as much an imperative of Soviet Asian policies as are close ties with New Delhi.

Yet the Soviet leadership that has been able to deal with such US allies as Pakistan, Thailand and even Germany, has been able to muster only a bare minimum amount of flexibility towards Japan. Their dogged insistence on maintaining possession of the small islands of Shikotan and Habomai, for instance, is resented by all Japanese. When Japan is mentioned in the Soviet press, it is almost always as a threat to the security of Asia rather than as a potential contributor. Particularly in the past year or two, dire predictions about resurgent Japanese militarism and a resurrection of the East Asian Co-Prosperity Sphere have been daily fare for Soviet readers and those Asians who are reached by Soviet propaganda. Constant propaganda against alleged Japanese "revanchism" and militarism is more likely, however, to inspire such settlements rather than strike a responsive chord in the breasts of the Japanese who, after all, have been something of a model of peacefulness in the past generation.

But we must remember that Russians regard Japan with genuine misgivings in terms of their own security. Memories of the Russo-Japanese war, the Japanese intervention in Siberia during the Russian Civil War, the undeclared war of the 1930's and World War II all fuel Soviet fears of Japan. Tokyo's continuing close alliance with the US of course makes these fears all the more vivid.

Some of the Soviet blundering also probably results from a false ideological preconception of how to deal with an "advanced" country. The Soviets claim that resurgent Japanese imperialism is—in the classic Leninist sense—an attempt to divert the Japanese masses from their presumed misery. This view of imperialism was faulty when first promulgated and has minimum relevance to contemporary Japan. By seeking to divide the Japanese workers from the government and seeking unsuccessfully to manipulate the divided and ineffective Japanese left wing, the Soviets have further mortgaged their chance to develop a satisfactory relationship with the Japanese government.

The only significant program that the USSR has mounted vis-à-vis Japan has related to the prospective joint exploitation of Siberia. There is a compelling logic to this concept since the Japanese need Siberian raw materials while the Soviets lack the capital and technological capabilities to develop the region. The Soviets, however, have handled the program ineptly. They have whetted the appetites of Japanese businessmen but discussions have repeatedly foundered when the Soviets sought to introduce political conditions. The modest joint programs that have been agreed to will continue and will ultimately have a cumulative effect in drawing the USSR and Japan closer together. Moscow will, however, have frittered away much of the political gains it might have made.

Soviet activities elsewhere in East Asia have been no more distinguished. South Korea is strictly enemy territory, left to the care of Pyŏngyang. North Korea itself, however, has been unrewarding for the Soviets. Kim Il-sŏng and most of the present North Korean leadership were originally creatures of the Soviet Union but the Chinese gradually whittled away at Soviet influence until by 1960, North Korea was a solid supporter of China. A Soviet aid cutoff from 1962 to 1965 had little impact on the Kim government, and since the post-Khrushchev resumption of assistance the Soviets have had to be content with a relationship that is no longer openly hostile but which offers them no control over North Korea. A situation in which North Korea remains free of either Soviet or Chinese domination is about the best that Moscow can expect. The Soviets cannot win in direct competition with China for Korean allegiance because of the political preoccupations of the North Koreans, who understandably accord dominant priority to acquiring control of South Korea. The measures that Pyŏngyang is prepared to take—including direct attacks on American ships and planes—frighten the Soviets who are equally understandably unwilling to risk war with the US over what seems to them to be an inconsequential matter. Restrained Soviet behavior at the time of the Pueblo incident and when an American reconnaissance plane was shot down over North Korea have shown the North Koreans the limits of Moscow's commitment to their prime national concern. Although the Chinese may also have some sleepless nights when they contemplate what Kim may do next, they support him strongly at the rhetorical level and, in the last analysis, share with him an aversion to a status quo that leaves both countries with irredentist claims on areas within the American security system.

The Soviets undoubtedly view the anti-Communist Chiang Kai-shek government with genuine distaste and have no illusions about Chiang's attitude toward them. There is hardly a government anywhere that stands lower in the Soviet books than Taipei. It is therefore a sign of the depths to which Sino-Soviet relations have fallen and of the intensity of the Soviet desire to isolate China that Moscow launched a modest program of informal contacts with Taiwan in 1968—a Soviet journalist visited Taiwan, a Chinese resident of the US went to Moscow and a Chinese Nationalist delegation attended a meeting in Sofia. It is not clear what the Soviets hope to gain from this strategy which has not been pursued consistently. It reflects, however, not only Soviet concern over China but also the pragmatic approach of the post-Khrushchev leadership who probably feel that since Taiwan exists as an international fact, some account should be taken of it.

REGIONAL APPROACHES: SOUTHEAST ASIA

The Soviet position in Southeast Asia differs again from that of either South Asia or East Asia. The Soviets have direct access to the latter but they can reach Southeast Asia only via a hostile China or over sea routes that they do not control. Conversely, no threat can be mounted against the USSR from Southeast Asia. In East Asia Japan provides a clear focus for Soviet activity that is lacking in Southeast Asia; and in South Asia, the USSR has an established position especially in India that it has achieved nowhere in Southeast Asia except perhaps North Vietnam. In sum, the dynamics of the US-Sino-Soviet relationship are markedly different in Southeast Asia where the USSR runs a very poor fourth if Japan is included.

Since the Soviets are unable to dominate Southeast Asia, participate effectively in a bi-polar relationship, or leave the area completely alone, they must turn to a skillful brand of balance of power politics to ensure that they are not excluded completely from the affairs of the region. Specifically, Moscow must promote a situation in which the US and China balance each other, leaving the Soviets some room to maneuver. The USSR is thus concerned with the maintenance of something approximating the status quo in the region—at least as regards inter-state relationships, if not always those of a purely intra-state nature. Soviet writers have often held up the pre-1971 situation in India-Pakistan as a model for Southeast Asia and there is much to recommend such a view of the area to Moscow. The Soviets stand to make no dramatic gains in stable situations but there is some prospect for modest advances on the governmental level and the alternatives of chaos are much less promising.

Destabilizing situations in Southeast Asia tend to work against Soviet interests. The fall of Sihanouk, which resulted from North Vietnamese pressure, brought a pro-western government to power in Cambodia and in Laos, the activities of the Pathet Lao have driven Souvannaphouma steadily closer to the west. Nowhere in the region, except to some extent in Hanoi, does the USSR have any significant influence among local Communist parties. In no case in Southeast Asia can one construct a very credible scenario by which a victorious revolutionary movement or an alteration of international relationships would play into Soviet hands.

Vietnam is of course the principal issue facing the USSR in Southeast Asia. The US involvement there has brought the Soviets many benefits by draining American power and resources into a subsidiary area of the global rivalry, by causing problems for US international position, and by creating an issue around which the Soviet government can rally opinion, both domestically and within the Communist movement. Yet the difficulties that Vietnam presents to the USSR appear small only when compared to those of the US. It is painful for the Soviets to see the DRV, a fellow Communist state, under attack from the US and its allies while Moscow lacks the capability to support it directly. The American incursion into Cambodia in 1970 and the Vietnamese operations in Laos in 1971 served to underline Soviet impotence in the area and to point up the restraints on Soviet policy.

For over two decades, Soviet involvement in Vietnam has been hesitant and tortuous. Khrushchev apparently saw little point in devoting scarce resources to a conflict that he could not decisively influence and from which the USSR stood to gain little. Under his successors the pattern shifted considerably as a result of the change in complexion of the Vietnam war after 1965 and the decline in China's policy effectiveness during the Cultural Revolution. In addition, the escalation of the fighting probably prompted the Soviets to believe that the need for more action on their part was urgent in order to offset growing US and Chinese influence. Even then, however, the substantial quantities of Soviet military assistance to the DRV have not been matched by any offer of direct support. Even the Soviets' political positions have been hedged with qualifications and geared as much to bringing about a negotiated settlement as to support for a DRV victory in the south.

Elsewhere in Indochina the Soviets have also moved with circumspection. Their most dramatic involvement in Laos—the 1962 airlift—was not in support of Laotian Communists but of the neutralist regime. Since then Moscow has given little aid to the Communists while maintaining relatively good relations with Souvannaphouma despite his increasing estrangement from the Communists. In Cambodia, too, following the fall of Sihanouk the Soviets have manifested at least as much interest in keeping their options open with the Lon Nol government as in supporting Sihanouk, the Cambodian Communists or the North Vietnamese operations.

This record points up clearly the fact that the Soviets see their role in Indochina not ideologically determined as much as in terms of power politics—although at a fairly modest level. Aside from the obvious problems of distance and resources, there are important political constraints on Moscow's Indochina policy.

The first of these is the Soviet relationship with the DRV. Hanoi must above all maintain a tolerable relationship with China. Also, the DRV shares with China and North Korea—but not the USSR—the belief that the status quo in Asia should be forcibly altered. Second, the Soviets would have reservations about the DRV even if China did not exist. The North Vietnamese see themselves as an independent power center in Southeast Asia and a strong Hanoi regime would be able to play at least as independent a role as Tito's. The DRV is thus not a completely comfortable ally for Moscow. As long as the Sino-Soviet split persists, Hanoi will remain the focal point of Soviet activity in Southeast Asia for reasons of ideology and power politics. Moscow will continue to build its strength, but with only limited expectations of gaining positive benefits.

Third, Moscow has conflicting interests in the continuation of the Vietnam war. As noted earlier, US involvement in Vietnam is advantageous to the USSR in several respects, yet there is the small, nagging danger that the conflict could expand and draw the USSR into direct confrontation with America. More immediately, the US role in Vietnam has cast a pall over the entire US-Soviet relationship and makes it difficult for the Soviets to pursue their bi-lateral relations with the US in furtherance of a détente and other objectives that are intrinsically of much greater importance than the outcome in Vietnam.

Finally, Moscow is ambivalent about the outcome of the war. It would of course relish seeing an ignominious US withdrawal and probably has little doubt that right and virtue are on the DRV side and should be rewarded. But, as we have mentioned, expulsion of the US would remove from Indochina the principal force offsetting Chinese influence and leave the Southeast Asian power balance shattered. Should an American defeat presage a complete US withdrawal from Asia, Soviet policy would be faced with a disaster.

The other major issue with which the USSR has been involved in Southeast Asia—Indonesia—was rendered considerably less pressing by the ouster of Sukarno in 1965 but the history of Soviet activities there is instructive. Khrushchev saw Indonesia as one of his principal target countries. He provided it with lavish (if often not very useful) economic assistance; he suggested that it was entitled to great power status; Sukarno was eulogized as a progressive; and huge quantities of military equipment were poured into the Indonesian armed forces in the expectation, *inter alia,* that they would serve as a proxy in furthering Soviet interests in Southeast Asia. All of this transpired against a backdrop of rapid growth of the Communist party of Indonesia (PKI) into the country's strongest political force.

The outcome of all of this effort was doubly disappointing. Both the PKI and Sukarno turned to China, not the USSR, for their political and ideological inspiration. When the debacle came, it was the Soviet-equipped army that ousted Sukarno, slaughtered Communists and formed a government that has followed a westward-oriented foreign policy.

The reaction of the USSR to the events in Indonesia has been illustrative of the post-Khrushchev leadership's approach to Southeast Asian affairs. The wholesale massacre of the PKI was perhaps the most severe blow to Communism in the post-war era, but the Soviet response was extremely mild, notable principally for the blame that it heaped on China and its Indonesian followers. The Soviets have never warmed up to the Suharto regime and in their propaganda frequently castigate its anti-Communist and allegedly anti-democratic policies. Nonetheless, Moscow has been careful to maintain correct state-to-state relations with Djakarta, probably recognizing that there is nothing to be gained by driving the Indonesians still more towards the west. The Soviets still have a considerable economic stake in Indonesia—a debt of some $800 million that they would like to collect—and no doubt also want to keep their political options open against the day when a successor to Suharto, perhaps even one drawn from the military, might take a more positive view of the USSR.

Among the other nations of Southeast Asia, Thailand, Malaysia, Singapore and the Philippines have only recently begun to develop contacts with the USSR. Diplomatic relations with Malaysia and Singapore were only established in the late 1960's and are still lacking between Moscow and Manila. The closest tie with any of them is the fact that the USSR is the largest consumer of Malayan rubber. This has had no demonstrable political impact, but of the four nations, Malaysia is probably the best disposed towards the USSR and receives quite favorable treatment in the Soviet press. Perhaps because of its concern over China and its own large Chinese population, Malaysia appears to welcome increased Soviet involvement in Southeast Asian affairs. Indeed, of all the responses to Brezhnev's Asian security proposal, Malaysia's was perhaps the most positive.

There is no doubt that Moscow hopes to develop its relations with Thailand, Singapore and the Philippines, as well as Malaysia. All share the latter's concern over China and the mainland states particularly are anxious to hedge against a possible reduction of the US presence. Thailand has evinced special interest in improving its ties with Moscow—trade and civil air agreements were concluded in

1970—and probably sees this as an extension of its traditional policy of maintaining maximum international flexibility.[7] The Southeast Asian governments no doubt sense that a shift in their region is developing, at least with regard to the involvement of outside powers, and will increasingly seek to adapt to change in the most advantageous way. Even though Soviet capabilities will remain limited, their possible contribution to the Southeast Asian power balance will be considered with interest.

The Soviets must, of course, deal differently with Thailand, Malaysia, Singapore and the Philippines. Thailand and the Philippines are SEATO members and involved in the Vietnam war. Singapore and Malaysia are less aligned and the Soviets are only mildly critical of their involvement with the UK, Australia and New Zealand in the Five Power Defense Agreement. But in all cases, the Soviets have approached these questions with considerable flexibility. Moscow has let it be known, for instance, that it would like to use Singapore's facilities for ship repair and might perhaps someday envision using that port as a "non-base" for naval ships operating in the Indian Ocean. Singapore cannot but be attracted by the economic benefits that would accrue to it and the Soviets have used the lure of trade as an element of their approaches to the Philippines and Malaysia as well.

Southeast Asia has also been the focus of incipient developments towards Asian regional organization. The USSR has taken a very cautious approach to regionalism for several reasons. First, of course, is the relatively small role that it can play in Southeast Asia. Second, the principal manifestations of regionalism are made up mainly of countries that have been traditionally close to the west and are suspicious of Moscow. Most important, however, has been the fact that Japan has played a strong role in these organizations that are mainly economic and developmental in their orientation.

The Soviets see Japanese participation in the Asian Development Bank (ADB), for instance, as a manifestation of Japanese economic imperialism and an attempt to shore up "reactionary" regimes. They cannot quite make up their minds whether Japan is acting as an American cat's paw in these endeavors but in any case find a strong Japanese role inimical to Soviet interests. The situation is made all the worse by the inability of the USSR's best friend in Asia—India—to play a leading role because of its weak economic position.

[7] It is perhaps more than a historical curiosity that Thailand (then Siam) sought in 1882 and 1891 to establish ties with Tsarist Russia as a means of securing support at a comfortable distance against the close-in pressures of Britain and France. See A. Lobanov-Rostovsky, *Russia and Asia* (Ann Arbor, 1951), p. 208.

Yet the Soviets recognize that regional organizations make sense for Asian nations that are faced with political and economic problems that few can solve individually. Moscow sought to bring India, Pakistan and Afghanistan together in a regional economic arrangement and has made numerous statements stressing the general desirability of less developed countries working together. Their inability to forge an arrangement in South Asia, where their influence is strongest, has probably discouraged them from taking any initiatives in other parts of Asia.

Thus far the Economic Commission for Asia and the Far East (ECAFE) has been the only regional organization to receive Soviet blessings. Since ECAFE is an organ of the UN, the Soviets' participation in it is guaranteed. Also, its one-nation-one-vote procedures permit the USSR a maximum of influence with a minimum of expenditure. In contrast, the power relationships within the ADB reflect the size of each donor's input so that Japan's role is the strongest. (Significantly, India shares Soviet enthusiasm for ECAFE on much the same grounds.) Even the Soviets must realize, however, that ECAFE's potential is limited.

In the longer run, the USSR will probably adopt a more positive attitude towards regional groupings. The constituent states are gradually developing working relationships with Moscow, and as Soviet involvement in Southeast Asia grows, Russians will feel more confident in working with the regional organizations. A reduction of the US posture in Southeast Asia after Vietnam will also serve to remove some of the political overtones that the Soviets perceive in ASPAC and ASEAN. Finally, as the USSR becomes more directly involved in competition with China in Southeast Asia, it will probably come to see relatively strong regional forces as helpful elements in the Asian power equation.

The USSR: Achievements, Failures and Prospects

An assessment of Soviet successes and failures in Asia (China aside) can now yield only a tentative trial balance. The new management's policy reorientation is just beginning to pay off; many of the debts of its predecessors remain to be liquidated.

In terms of money, several billions of rubles have been put into various parts of Asia in the past 15 years—a sum that could certainly have been put to good use at home, but does not loom overly large by the standards of modern economic and military diplomacy. Aside probably from a few unsung volunteers in Korea and Indochina, no Russian soldiers have died fighting Asian wars and no costly overseas campaigns have been mounted. Although the sunk costs of Khrushchev's adventure in Indonesia must be recorded, only in South Asia have extensive amounts of political capital been expended.

The most substantial profits of Soviet policy have come from this area of greatest investment. The Soviet leadership—already under Khrushchev—recognized South Asia both as critical to Soviet interests and as an attractive investment opportunity. The skill and resources devoted to the area have been well rewarded and illustrate what Soviet diplomacy at its best can accomplish.

The other great Soviet success in the past years has been the effective articulation of a legitimate interest in Asian affairs and a general acceptance of the Soviet presence by all concerned. By the early 1970's, the USSR had acquired a limited veto power and laid the groundwork for a still stronger position—in South and Southeast Asia, if not further east. Diplomatic skill played a role in achieving this position, but the principal impetus came from the Soviet Union's domestic power base rather than from programs targeted at Asia—an illustration of the homely truth that power, like charity, begins at home. Additional important contributions were of course made by fortuitous set-backs to the USSR's principal competition in Asia—the US' costly embroilment in Indochina and Chinese excesses in the Cultural Revolution.

Yet seen in overall perspective, the USSR's accomplishments in Asia are not wholly impressive. In much of the continent its voice remains weaker than that of the US, China or even Japan. Much of this weakness results from the mismanagement and neglect of Asian affairs that characterized Soviet policy well into the 1950's, but restraints imposed by geography, resources, lack of vision and the strengths of rivals continue to play a large role. Even in South Asia, Moscow's ability to influence events positively is still limited. In Southeast Asia the situation is much less favorable, and in the critical East Asian area Soviet policy towards Japan has been sterile. Perhaps the best illustration of Soviet inability to capitalize on its investments are the hardily independent Communist regimes in North Korea and North Vietnam.

The USSR also failed in two less tangible ways: it has not been accepted as an "Asian" power, and it has made practically no ideological breakthroughs. The Soviets have remained outsiders looking in, and much of their success has been purchased at the price of submerging ideological aspirations. Moscow's hopes in both of these areas had always been illusory, and by writing them off, Brezhnev and Kosygin have rid their policy of considerable dead weight. Yet for a nation that claims to have a special mission in the world, the renunciation of internationalism is a hard sacrifice to make.

In moving forward from its present position, the USSR must repair the remaining weaknesses in its policy structure and go further along the more promising lines that it has laid out. Having successfully asserted its membership in the balance of power, Moscow must now play its part creatively in specifically Asian matters and especially in managing the US-Sino-Soviet triangle as it impinges on Asia. This multi-sided relationship will present increasing problems and opportunities as the emergence of Japan as a major power adds still another dimension to it. On the one hand, Moscow views the possibility of a Sino-Japanese rapprochement with considerable trepidation, and, as mentioned earlier, has real concerns about the role that a powerful Japan can play. At the same time, Japan's increasing independence from American influence and the strains put on US-Japanese relations as the United States develops new financial and China policies, offer the Soviets some excellent opportunities for improving their position with Japan. The Soviets have only begun to exploit these openings in dealing with the Japanese; the development of a satisfactory relationship with Tokyo is probably the greatest challenge facing Soviet policy over the next several years.

All aspects of the USSR's Asian policy will be further complicated by uncertainties over how far America will lower its posture. This in turn will depend considerably on the outcome of the conflict in Indochina—a variable that will also have a direct effect upon the role that the USSR will be able to play in Southeast Asia.

Soviet policy planners thus face an extremely labile situation in Asia, but without doubt they expect the seventies to be a decade of growing Soviet influence. Both the situation on the ground and the past trend of Soviet policy suggest that they will enjoy success in moving towards a more positive involvement. But it is hardly likely that their position during this decade will even approach that which they hold in Europe. Indeed, it would be a major triumph were Moscow able to extend the South Asian pattern eastward—and this is probably their objective for the coming years.

The easy gains in much of Asia have already been made and from here on, Soviet advances will have to be bought with increasing levels of effort, especially in political terms. Also, a more forward policy will make the USSR a more inviting target and entail greater risks. There is every reason to believe that the Soviet leadership will seek to keep the risks low. It has more pressing concerns elsewhere; something approaching the status quo, modified by trends that are already in motion, is compatible with Soviet desires; and hopes for an ideological breakthrough are likely to be kept from view. Indeed, Soviet policy will be likely of success to the extent that it accepts the primacy of state-to-state relations and aims for small gains, rather than indulging in foredoomed attempts to impose new forms of social order or disturb generally accepted patterns of international relations. The full arrival of Moscow on the world scene—and particularly in Asia—will result from Soviet ability and willingness to play the traditional role of a great power—with all of the advantages and disadvantages that this implies.

PART FOUR

Functional Dimensions of Asia's International Interaction

Towards a New Balance of Power in Asia

HARRY G. GELBER

Asian affairs appear; at the beginning of the 1970's, to be
undergoing several fundamental changes. These changes
are occurring at several levels—cultural and economic
as well as political. In consequence, though this
chapter is primarily concerned with foreign policy and
security, these matters should be understood to be
dependent upon changes in other areas. Perhaps the
most important clusters of such factors—none of them
adequately explored by recent scholarship—are the
following:

First, there are the ways in which the focus of political
loyalties, and therefore the character and content of the
concept of the nation-state, is changing in subtle but
important ways. The criteria by which groups of
individuals distinguish between "we" and "they", the
terms upon which they concede legitimacy to authority,
the causes which they regard as important, have much
more significant transnational elements, or elements
to which the normal distinctions between nations
are irrelevant, than was the case 20 or 30 years
ago. This is not to say that these phenomena can
be adequately described as "declining patriotism"
or even that patriotism, where it remains relevant, is
declining. It is merely to say that the assumptions
which underlie such concepts as "patriotism" tend to
be seen as a hindrance rather than a help in the
fulfillment of some of the socio-economic purposes of
certain power segments of society. Whereas "liberalism"
and "nationalism" were allied and largely coextensive
as recently as the latter part of the 19th century, in the

advanced countries of the early 1970's they tend to conflict. Second, there are the changes in economic transactions together with the ways in which electorates[1] expect their governments to control such transactions and their consequences. It seems evident that the national economies of most advanced countries have come between, say, 1950 and 1970 to depend upon their external environments in ways which are more complex and politically more sensitive. An increasing number of phenomena, such as the operations of multi-national corporations or multi-national trades unions, are beyond the control of any single government, however powerful. At the same time, electors expect their governments to exercise ever more subtle and finely-tuned controls over economic life, with a view to fulfilling ever more complicated and detailed economic and social aims. It seems very likely that the requirements imposed upon policy-makers by these internal and external factors will not always be reconcilable. It is far from clear whether this problem can be solved by reliance upon present forms of state authority or, indeed, in ways compatible with the maintenance of the nation-state structure as we have known it in the past.[2]

Third, modern states are also under great strain in their capacity as information and learning and decision-making systems. They seem to be caught between three conflicting pressures. There is the quantity of detailed information, increasing at an exponential rate with the spread of electronic data processing and high-speed communications. This leads to a dramatic rise in the number of socio-political choices to which public authorities can be asked to address themselves. There is also the increasing velocity of change in public emphasis on what problem should be accorded priority. The speed of this change of focus, together with the public desire for a "can do" approach by governments, tends to produce increased pressures for instant solutions. Not merely

---

[1] By this I mean real electorates, whether composed of all adult citizens, as in the US, Britain or Australia, or a quasi-electorate like the party in the USSR, or the still narrower group which comprises the effective political constituency in a state like North Korea.

[2] This involves one of the minor ironies of our time. One aspect of the "youth movement" is its concern with what it sees as a runaway technocracy or economic system. Yet it seeks to restore political control very largely by reference to criteria which imply the continuing legitimacy and usefulness of the nation-state. It seeks to combat the real revolutionaries of the last quarter of the 20th century —IBM and Standard Oil and various biochemical laboratories—by reliance upon the socially conservationist and politically conservative "revolutionary" slogans of simpler societies and less complex times. One is reminded of Marie Antoinette playing at being a shepherdess. I do not, of course, wish to suggest that every aspect of the "youth movement" is conservative; still less that conservatism is necessarily and everywhere mistaken.

do such solutions tend to produce more problems than they pretend to solve, but they lead to increased public irritation and frustration with the governmental process as a whole once the initial solutions are seen not to work. Alternatively, government must seek to slow down the swift change of focus of public demands or to divert it towards secondary or dispensable policies. From this point of view, also, it seems likely that there are growing built-in contradictions between the idea of centralized government (indeed, perhaps of consistent government) and the principle of "government by the people." Finally, there is the problem that too much information and advice may be functionally quite similar to having too little. If a decision-maker has before him a multitude of recommendations urging every conceivable course of action, his problem is very similar to the problem he would have if he had no recommendations before him at all. Here, too, the structural inadequacies of the nation-state and of centralized government may point towards the need for radical reform. The question may be nothing less than whether a more efficient information, learning and control system than the nation-state needs to be devised, and how it could be made effective.

Subject to these very large qualifications, the major movements in foreign policy and security relationships in Asia seem to involve four sets of problems: the strategic balance between the United States and the Soviet Union; the triangular relationship between the US, and USSR and China; the position of Japan; and the affairs of Southeast Asia following the US disengagement in Vietnam. I shall examine these, briefly, in turn.

It has become one of the truisms of international politics to observe that during the 1960's the international system moved away from the bipolarity achieved after World War II and towards more complex and multipolar patterns of relations. But it is equally evident that one of the major limitations upon operations within that international system, and the acting out of conflicts within it, is the strategic nuclear balance. The most important elements of this remain bipolar. Its condition has been affected, over the last decade, by four important developments. First, the numerical increases in the strategic forces on both sides, first by the US, more recently by the USSR. Second, the increasing complexities and uncertainties which flow from developments and refinements in weapons technologies and have brought quite novel forms of weapons into the time-scale of practical forward planning. Third, the dangers of accident or miscalculation which this process creates. Fourth, the changing attitude to defense within the US. From these have flowed a number of consequences. As the nuclear establishments of the two sides have grown in numbers and sophistication, so the balance between them appears to have become less sensitive to merely quantitative increments by either side. At the same time, it appears less and less likely that these armaments would be used in response to anything short of a major strike by the opponent. In consequence, the political benefits derived from the possession of large nuclear forces seem to have diminished.

Against this background the two sides have begun fresh efforts to control the strategic competition between them, especially through the Strategic Arms Limitation Talks (SALT). Though at the time of writing (August 1971) it seems much too early to predict what the results of the talks will be, the purposes of the two sides in pursuing them can be outlined. Each side wishes to avoid strategic war and therefore to reduce the uncertainties which new weapons developments threaten to introduce into their strategic relations. Each wishes to reduce the possibility of war through miscalculation or accident. Each wishes to increase its control over the consequences of technical developments on both sides, to ensure that the balance of such developments does not work to its own disadvantage and to encourage the development and maintenance by the opponent of secure and stable command and control arrangements. Powerful groups on both sides would like to reduce arms expenditures. Each also has more specific aims. The Soviet Union appears to be trying to use the talks to head off, or at least slow down, qualitative advances in US weaponry which could more than balance the quantitative advances of the Soviet Union in recent years. This refers especially to Multiple Independently Targetable Reentry Vehicle (MIRV) technology and possibly to novel ABM devices a generation beyond the components of the Safeguard system. Doubtless Moscow also wishes to make maximum use of the talks for propaganda purposes and in order to encourage disunity and disagreements among the western allies. Similarly, the US wishes to use the talks for broader diplomatic purposes, for example, as evidence that it is fulfilling its obligations under the Nuclear Non-Proliferation Treaty to seek arms control agreements. At the same time it may be possible to create pressures for the limitation of Soviet offensive systems, while using the fact that talks are proceeding as a way to defuse a variety of domestic criticisms. Though both sides appear committed to the proposition that no third party must be allowed to acquire substantial leverage on their strategic balance, as distinct from their general political relationship, they wish to pursue that aim at the lowest practicable cost not only in fiscal terms but in terms of propaganda vulnerability and of strategic armaments.

It seems safe to say that there are several things which SALT will not do. It will not lower hostility between the US and the USSR. It may contain that hostility,[3] but the two sides are separated by complex and genuine conflicts of interest whose resolution is not yet in sight. Nor is SALT likely to cut off new weapons developments. The increasing complexity of defense technology will make it impossible to draft any legal document to cover developments in this area, or to create a mutual understanding in which both sides could repose confidence. Still less can one foresee an agreement to prevent new discoveries not yet made. SALT will therefore not end the arms race, though it may establish novel limitations upon it and new conditions for the way in which the race is run. Though a success in SALT, in the sense of a signed treaty or even a clear mutual understanding, could stop some kinds of arms developments, it would, almost by definition, redirect research and development on both sides into areas not specifically covered by the SALT agreement.

A single, comprehensive arms control agreement is, however, not the only possible aim. Another may be "To think of the task of SALT as that of producing over time not a single system of limitation but a series of agreements."[4] A variant of this idea might be to maintain the conference in semi-permanent session to serve as a constraining mechanism on the activities of the two defense structures. But it is not clear whether this would prove acceptable or, if acceptable, successful. If the mechanism looked like it would be effective it would be criticized in Washington as a permanent gift to the anti-defense lobby. If not, it would be a political liability without corresponding payoff. Similar points might be made about Moscow, especially from the point of view of the Red Army command. On the other hand, the talks may prove extremely effective as a way of stimulating internal debate within the bureaucracies of each side. These debates might lead to important readjustments in the administrative perspective on each side. What these will be cannot now be predicted, but they might include an increasing perception of common or convergent interests. Or they might lead to more subtle and effective ways of safeguarding the perceived national security interest against domestic criticism as well as against external foes.

From the point of view of the balance of power in Asia, SALT is likely to have three kinds of consequences: the arms limitations actually achieved, and the consequences of those limitations upon the Soviet-American strategic relationship; possible future lines for weapons

[3] Not least by persuading important groups in the bureaucracies of both sides to pay more attention to their common interests.

[4] Hedley Bull, "Strategic Arms Limitation: The Precedent of the Washington and London Naval Treaties" (Occasional Papers on Arms Control and Foreign Policy, Center for Policy Study, University of Chicago, 1971).

technologies which will be left open by any SALT agreement; and the view which various Asian nations will take of the behavior of the superpowers in SALT and of the consequences of an agreement. On the first point, if there is to be an agreement it will probably be in two areas: the acceptance of some numerical limitation on land-based missile launchers and the confining of ABM cover to some very low level of deployment. If some variant of these ideas is adopted, each side would obtain assurance on a cut-off in some weapons deployments by the opponent, but without qualitative or developmental limitations and at the cost of continuing reliance upon mutual assured destruction. This concept of mutual assured destruction has become firmly established in recent years, especially in the United States. It has been supported by arguments which stress that so long as each side is absolutely vulnerable to the other, neither side can tolerate policies leading to war; that the deployment of weapons systems such as ABM and MIRV will tend to destabilize the Soviet-American strategic balance, create new uncertainties, and may even at some point create or increase pressures on one or the other side to strike first. It is therefore sensible for both sides to eschew such systems, especially defensive ones, in order to maintain the assurance that each side lacks the means to prevent the other from retaliating massively against any attack.[5]

The difficulty is that mutual assured destruction also involves great disadvantages. In a situation where there is no technical and political alternative, such a posture may serve. But once such alternatives become available, it requires reexamination. The chief disadvantages of mutual assured destruction (or assured vulnerability) are probably as follows: nothing in this strategy, or outside it, can guarantee that a war will not occur, either as a result of miscalculation or of a loss of control in a crisis situation by one side or the other or both. In such a case, mutual assured destruction institutionalizes a situation in which there would be maximum disaster for everybody. Moreover, the strategy is plainly immoral and must become politically unacceptable as soon as more humane alternatives present themselves. It is no coincidence that public opinion in the west, and the US in particular, has turned sour on defense policies at a time when defense means not merely Vietnam but a total nuclear threat. A permanent threat to millions of civilians is not an acceptable basis for a long-term defense policy. In democratic states it will therefore be necessary to find an alternative basis if there is to be political support for defense policy at all.

[5] See, for example, Herbert Scoville's remark "The primary aim of any arms control agreement is to provide greater confidence that this state of mutual deterrence is maintained and at the same time to conserve scarce resources that both nations need for many other programs." "The Limitation of Offensive Weapons," *Scientific American,* January 1971, p. 15.

There is, moreover, an inherent contradiction between the notion of sovereign nation-states and national governments on the one hand and a deliberate choice for mutual assured destruction on the other. Presidents and prime ministers are not elected, secretaries of defense and foreign ministers are not appointed, civil servants and officers are not promoted, in order to make or keep their own countries and its citizens vulnerable as a matter of deliberate political choice. At a technical level, too, a mutual assured destruction posture must remain vulnerable to an attack upon missiles prior to launch and the need to guard —probably expensively—against various system weaknesses. It seems entirely possible that additional expenses under this heading would be greater than the expense of an ABM system which might make those costs unnecessary. Finally, as the nuclear establishments of the two sides grow in numbers and sophistication, but in the absence of defense, so the balance between them must become less sensitive to quantitative increments by either side. This is beneficial in so far as it slows down the arms acquisition race. But it also makes it less and less likely that the arms could ever be used except in response to a major strike by the opponent (and perhaps not even then).

In consequence, the political payoff from the possession of these forces has declined. This, too, could be cited as an element reinforcing arms control efforts. But the difficulty is that the more absolute the strategic nuclear standoff between the US and the USSR becomes, the less can their nuclear weapons deter the launching of non-nuclear wars, especially by third parties; or even of future non-great power nuclear wars. It is not self-evidently a good bargain to buy some decrease in the already small risk of great power nuclear war with an increase in the possibility of other and especially conventional conflicts. Furthermore a Soviet-American balance of mutual assured destruction, in the absence of defense, is by definition vulnerable to destabilization by third parties. For this reason, as well as the increased rigidity of the Soviet-American standoff, it must further devalue the great powers' guarantees, including their nuclear guarantees, to various allies.

Beyond these very general considerations, however, an assessment of the consequences of SALT depends upon forecasts as to future weapons developments and their timing, and the relationship between these developments and the precise limitations which may be agreed upon. Certainty is impossible in this area, where most of the relevant information is classified. It remains to be seen whether an ABM limitation agreement, if reached, would prevent the deployment of new families of such weapons, ranging from the hard-point systems now being developed in the US to maneuverable defending warheads, reentry-vehicle-deflecting rather than reentry-vehicle-killing methods, and various possible non-nuclear, anti-ballistic missile systems. A limitation on the number of land-based offensive missile launchers, on the other hand, might leave the Soviets free to concentrate on mobile rather than fixed base launchers, the US free to lengthen its lead in MIRV technology and both sides free to compete in developing longer range and quieter submarine systems. It also seems possible that both will develop fission free and miniaturized nuclear weapons, not only in the single figure kiloton but in the subkiloton range. If such weapons are developed,[6] they will probably be used to increase the fire-power of comparatively small bodies of professionals, and especially in conflicts which do not directly involve the other superpower. At the opposite end of the weapons spectrum, it seems probable that both great powers will put more effort into satellite surveillance and the use of space as a hiding and dispersal area and perhaps eventually as an arena for combat. It is, for example, by no means clear that the elimination of another power's satellite need cause an armed conflict on earth, let alone a nuclear exchange. It will certainly be possible to put into space many of the electronic systems needed for strategic or theater operations. If necessary, they could be left unattended and activated as required without the use of politically vulnerable overseas facilities.

The technical uncertainties involved here are so great that they raise a quite different and extremely interesting possibility. It is a commonplace that the lead-time between advanced research and the deployment of weapons systems based upon that research has been increasing. At the same time, production and engineering on both sides have been refined to the point where a large variety of systems, once researched and developed, can be deployed at relatively short notice.[7] Indeed, R&D efforts are used on both sides not merely to develop systems for deployment, but to create short-lead time options with which to threaten the other side. At the same time, defense R&D has proved incomparably more resistant to political critique than defense deployment. It follows that the R&D effort on both sides has come not merely to sustain the broad political and strategic competition between the great powers, but has itself become the arena in which much of that competition is carried on. R&D, occasionally complemented by judicious leaks of technical information, has become a way of maneuvering in peacetime for a developmental advantage which might be decisive in case of conflict but which, once it is per-

---

[6] It is necessary to treat this proposition with great caution. Fission free bombs have been forecast before but do not seem to have yet appeared. Cf· Freeman J. Dyson, "The Future Development of Nuclear Weapons," *Foreign Affairs*, April 1960.

[7] Assuming, of course, the necessary funds are made available. And the process of making them available can be a signal to the opponent.

ceived by both sides to exist, itself helps to make conflict unnecessary. The management of R&D policy has therefore itself become a vital area of Soviet-American competition.[8] This novel emphasis upon R&D, rather than on deployment, plays a role which has some interesting analogies with campaigning in the age of Turenne, when prebattle maneuvering not merely decided battles themselves but was often understood, by both sides, to make actual fighting superfluous.

There remains the view which Asian powers will take of SALT and its results. It is clear that many of the more likely SALT outcomes could produce unfavorable reactions. In so far as the conduct of the talks, and the administrative and political debates about them in Washington and Moscow, emphasize purely bilateral Soviet-American concerns, they will be regarded as further evidence of the superpowers' willingness to disregard the interests of smaller states. If the talks produce a freeze in the numbers of offensive missile launchers, but without further qualitative limitations or restrictions on the numbers of deliverable warheads, smaller powers will argue that the US and the USSR have failed to fulfil their arms control obligations under the Nuclear Non-Proliferation Treaty. They will resist the notion that these arrangements should help to dissuade them from developing their own weapons. The outcome of SALT could encourage proliferation in other ways. An agreement to limit defensive weapons to insignificant levels would be seen as consolidating the Soviet-American standoff in ways which decreased the credibility of great power guarantees to others. This would increase the perceived need for smaller powers to have their own nuclear forces.

The argument should not be overstated. It may well be that some

---

[8] So has its funding. Soviet military R&D expenditure at the end of the 1960's was growing at some 10–13 percent per annum. In 1971/72 Soviet spending in this area was estimated to be 20–40 percent higher than US expenditure. See the testimony of Dr. John S. Foster Jr. in ABM, MIRV, SALT and the Nuclear Arms Race, Hearings before the Subcommittee on Arms Control, International Law and Organization of the Committee on Foreign Relations, US Senate, 91st Congress, 2nd Session, Washington, 1970, p. 500. According to Defense Secretary Melvin R. Laird the US RDT&E budget for FY 1972 was about $7.9 billions, but the Soviet Union was spending some $3 billion more (in 1968 equivalent dollars). See the Secretary's Statement before the House Armed Services Committee on the FY 1972–76 Defense Program and the 1972 Defense Budget, March 9, 1971, p. 56 and table 1, p. 163. See also Dr. Thomas W. Wolfe's testimony in The Limitation of Strategic Arms, Part 2, Hearings before the Subcommittee on Strategic Arms Limitation Talks of the Committee on Armed Services, US Senate, 91st Congress, 2nd Session, Washington, 1970; and William R. Kintner and Robert L. Pfaltzgraff Jr., Soviet Military Trends: Implications for US Security, Special Analysis paper No. 6, American Enterprise Institute for Public Policy Research, Washington, June 1971.

proliferation of nuclear weapons is likely to the point of inevitability. It would certainly be difficult to argue that different SALT outcomes, or a different American strategic posture, would be sure to stop it. But SALT could well affect the character and pace of proliferation, as well as the surrounding political circumstances and the patterns of strategic relationships once proliferation has gone further. The probable SALT outcomes suggested here may help to spread nuclear weapons more widely, or more quickly, than might otherwise be the case, and do so in ways more injurious to international stability. The grounds for such a spread would be three. Smaller powers may consider that the possession of comparatively elementary nuclear forces would be useful in disputes with other smaller powers, especially where the superpowers had no interest in intervening or had deterred each other from doing so. Possession would also confer diplomatic advantage and international status.[9] Such weapons could also be useful against the superpowers themselves. They could be used to deter an unprovoked attack from either. Beyond that, and especially in the absence of high-confidence superpower defenses, their presence would impose a variety of psychological and political constraints upon the superpowers in areas of potential dispute with smaller nuclear powers. They might even make it possible, in some situations, to play off one superpower against the other.

Such considerations would be reinforced if the outcome of SALT helps China to derive just such benefits from the acquisition of her own force. Some superpower vulnerability to China already exists, following the start of deployment of a Chinese MRBM force and the beginning of series production of a Chinese version of the TU-16.[10] It will increase as the Chinese force increases in size, mobility or hardening and sophistication and acquires long-range weapons. It is generally agreed that China has thereby acquired or enhanced an ability not only to deter US or Soviet attacks upon China, but, an

[9] The fact that President Nixon's overtures to China coincided with the development and deployment of Chinese nuclear weapons will not escape attention. The announcement that the President had accepted Chou En-lai's invitation to visit Peking came in mid-1971—just about the time when China's MRBM deployments were becoming significant. It may be noted that at about the same time the Soviet Government invited the CPR, as well as the US, Britain and France, to take part in five-power nuclear arms control talks. See *Tass* (Moscow), June 23, 1971. It was the first time that the CPR was invited in this way. The fact that China rejected this approach, and the Soviets may have desired this approach, does not alter the broader political significance of the Soviet move.

[10] Melvin R. Laird, Statement of March 9, 1971, before the House Armed Services Committee on the FY 1972–76 Defense Program and the 1972 Defense Budget, US Government Printing Office, 1971, pp. 47–48.

ability to impose constraints on superpower intervention in a variety of conflict situations where Chinese interests are involved. A failure by the US and the USSR to impose qualitative restraints on their own, or each other's weapons developments might, in fact, have beneficial effects here. Increasing sophistication of their force structures, and especially the development of defensive systems,[11] will diminish the possibility of Chinese leverage against them. It will also diminish the expectation of near-nuclear powers that the possession of even small and unsophisticated forces will automatically imply the acquisition of great power status.

This would not, however, necessarily affect the local or regional reasons which might lead near-nuclear powers to acquire such weapons. It is important to note here that great power arms control discussions do not stand alone. They take place in a political and strategic setting which includes the Sino-Soviet relationship, the US withdrawal from Southeast Asia, the decline in US support for Taiwan and the increasing constraints on the US military presence in Korea and Japan. Of prime importance here are theater forces-in-being, including theater deterrent forces. American protection of South Korea, for example, has become more suspect. This is not primarily because of the reduction in US troops there, but because a progressive abandonment of US bases in Japan could involve ones essential for the provision of American air or naval support for South Korea. The circumstances in which such Japanese bases, once abandoned, would again be made available to the US are quite unclear. South Korean bases, on the other hand, would be too vulnerable. And in any case, the run-down of the US Navy has made some forms of support by surface vessels or naval air power also suspect. It is true that US long-range missiles pointed at the Soviet Union are not directly relevant to this situation; and to this extent the outcome of SALT may not have a direct bearing on the problem. But it is equally true that long-range missiles are no substitute for effective and disposable power in the region, and SALT could easily produce a political or arms control climate in which the run-down of theater forces becomes significantly easier. Similar points might be made about US commitments in other areas.

The Soviet Union and China

At this point it seems useful to turn to the second set of problems, the triangular relationship between the USSR, China and the

---

[11] Whether such systems should be, or need to be, of the kind represented by the US Safeguard system, may be a very different question.

US. Though these relationships move within parameters set by nuclear strategy, their substance has been concerned with lower-level conflicts and political maneuvering. One of the main elements has been the Sino-Soviet dispute, whose current manifestations can perhaps be traced back to the open disagreements between the two powers which emerged towards the end of the 1950's. Since then the conflict has taken on many of the characteristics of classic great power rivalries. Its elements can be summed up under four broad headings. There are the disputes caused or accentuated by the fact that these two powers live next to each other, divided by a very long border on whose legal status they do not agree and which is in any case not everywhere clearly defined. The Chinese argue that large areas of Siberia were subject to the sovereignty of Peking until 1860, when China was forced to cede them to Russia. Peking has not demanded the return of these regions, but it does want the Russians to acknowledge that these territories were acquired by Tsarist aggression as a preliminary step to negotiations on a new border agreement. The Chinese have hinted that they might not insist on this prerequisite and that once negotiations begin they would not ask for very significant amendments to the present borders.[12]

The difficulty from the Soviet point of view is twofold. If such a Chinese prerequisite for negotiations is presented or revived, its acceptance would, in the absence of prior Chinese undertakings on points of detail, leave Peking free to raise very large claims indeed. At the same time the Soviet position in the face of such claims would, ipso facto, have been undermined. Moreover, Soviet acceptance of the Chinese view would by implication invalidate a whole series of other Tsarist Russian agreements on other borders and in other areas of policy. The grounds for Sino-Soviet dispute on these matters, complicated as they are by traditional enmities and historical differences, are obvious.

A second reason for conflict has been the dispute about Soviet technical and economic aid to China. During the middle and late 1950's, in particular, the Soviet Union provided large-scale economic aid. The development of some areas of Chinese heavy industry became de-

---

[12] The extremely defensive CPR Government statement of October 7, 1969, dealt with the Sino-Soviet border disagreements without mentioning such a prerequisite. *Peking Review,* October 10, 1969, p. 3. It is, however, not clear that Peking is in any great hurry to settle this border issue, as distinct from preventing a Soviet attack on China. An unresolved border claim provides a useful diplomatic card against the Russians, without amounting to provocation which would cause or justify a Soviet attack. At the same time the border difficulties help to energize public support while also promoting domestic discipline.

pendent, to a significant degree, on Soviet technicians, machines and blueprints. The Chinese nuclear program, whether for power production or a weapons capability, was begun during these years largely with Soviet help. In 1957 the two countries concluded an agreement which Peking interpreted as a Soviet promise to help China acquire nuclear weapons. Between 1959 and 1961 aid in all these forms was abruptly withdrawn following a series of Sino-Soviet political and strategic disagreements. Chinese industrial development was badly affected; and Moscow has not yet been forgiven.

A third cluster of disputes has concerned ideological differences, competition for the leadership of the Communist group of nations and for influence among noncommitted and especially underdeveloped states. At the heart of these matters are differences over the proper way to organize Socialist society, the priority to be accorded to violent revolution as a means for Socialist parties to achieve power, and the support to be given to national liberation wars. The Chinese "great leap forward" and, later, the formation of communes, were assertions that China had discovered new and by implication better forms of Socialist organization; that the Soviet model for organization and modernization need not apply to other developing and especially Socialist states. The Cultural Revolution embodied the notion that special measures were required to maintain revolutionary enthusiasm, to prevent the deterioration of Socialist societies and the growth of revisionism. At the same time the Chinese leaders made it very clear that in their opinion the Soviet leadership had deteriorated in just this way: to the point, indeed, where they were betraying the cause of world Socialism.

Moscow has emphasized the cohesion and unity of outlook of Communist nations and the need to safeguard the achievements of Socialism in any one Socialist country both from internal deviations and from dangers external to the group.[13] China has emphasized the nationalist bases and elements of the different approaches to Socialism, the requirement of consensus rather than coercion among them, and her own role as an alternative source of ideas and leadership. Moscow has argued that conditions in the world at large, outside the Socialist camp, have changed, that the parliamentary road to power for Socialist parties is now feasible and that the risks of violent overthrow have become too great in an age of nuclear armories. From the Chinese point of view, however, capitalism will never surrender

[13] This is the foundation of the Brezhnev doctrine, used to justify Soviet intervention in Czechoslovakia. Very similar arguments were heard in Moscow in 1969–70 during the debates about possible Soviet intervention in China.

peacefully. Though changes have taken place in the world, capitalism will fight back as bitterly as ever, and exaggerated fears of capitalists and great power weapons will merely serve to disarm the revolutionary peoples and render them helpless. Very similar arguments apply to the question of support for peoples' wars, though it is true that the Chinese arguments in favor of such support have been loudest where it was the Russians who would risk most by giving it. China's own behavior has been much more discreet than her rhetoric would suggest.

It is against this background that the two powers have debated the problem of their relations with the capitalist world in general and the US in particular. Here again, it has been Moscow which has argued for caution, a measure of accommodation and an interpretation of "coexistence" which combines the pursuit of détente in Europe with some strategic arms control and other inter-governmental agreements useful to Moscow, with a continuation of political and diplomatic pressures calculated to weaken the west's position without exposing the Soviet Union itself. China has accused the Soviet Union of cowardice, betrayal of the revolutionary cause and, worse, of collusion with the capitalist world.[14] In particular, Soviet-American discussions on such matters as arms control have been viewed with deep suspicion as intended to consolidate Soviet-American strategic dominance in the world and, more specifically, as aimed at a joint containment of China.[15] Moscow, in turn, has accused the Chinese of adventurism and of harboring neo-Trotskyist views.

By the mid-1960's debates on these matters had become not only the chief feature of relations between China and the Soviet Union but a major aspect of the internal affairs of each. The reason for this was not merely the importance which each state had for the other. It was rather that the ideological elements of the dispute had potentially profound consequences for the character of the state and the principles of social organization on each side. No doubt the fall of

[14] See, for example, a Soviet report on one of the earliest of Mao's public denunciations of the Soviet leaders, *Pravda*, September 2, 1964.

[15] It is true, on the other hand, that some forms of Soviet-American arms agreement would benefit China and, in particular, certain groups in the Chinese bureaucracy. A Soviet-American "zero ABM" agreement, for example, or an agreement to limit ABM to a very low level, would confirm the CPR's medium-range retaliatory capability against the USSR or US bases and allies in the Far East. This would be in the interests of the Chinese defense authorities. It would also be good for some economic planners, in that it would limit the military's claims for a larger share of national resources. It might even be good for Maoists if it appeared to underline their arguments about the need for domestic unity and discipline in the face of Soviet-American collusion or the need not to be misled by an American Presidential visit to Peking.

Khrushchev in 1964 was mostly due to a variety of domestic factors, especially economic ones. But the consequences of the Cuban crisis of 1962, of the Sino-Soviet dispute and, in particular, of the mutual detestation between Khrushchev and Mao, made their own significant contribution. By 1965/66 the dispute had also become a major factor in the internal affairs of China. Questions such as the proper response to the growing US involvement in Vietnam, the future of relations with the Soviet Union and how to structure Chinese defense policies played an important role in the debates which culminated in the disgrace of Liu Shao-chi and Lo Jui-ching. Certainly the outcome of these debates became clear, and the cultural revolution began, in a flurry of antirevisionist declarations which had the clearest implications for the now-dominant Chinese attitudes to Moscow and what came to be termed social imperialism.

These trends culminated in the March 1969 border clashes on the Ussuri River. Though they were neither the first nor the last of the small armed clashes along the Sino-Soviet border, they constitute in retrospect an important turning point. Both sides responded with increased military preparations and political mobilization. Soviet troops along the border were reinforced and reorganized. Moscow declared that the Soviet Union would be protected against an obviously unreasonable and aggressive China; and the Communist commonwealth would be protected against Maoist excesses. The Chinese response was much more clearly defensive. Lin Piao's report to the Ninth Party Congress on April 1, 1969 warned of intensified Soviet threats and the possibility that Moscow (as well as American imperialism) might launch a war of aggression.[16] Chinese forces were redeployed towards the northern borders, but in primarily defensive ways. There was increased emphasis on civil defense and air raid precautions and the government stressed the Chinese peoples' readiness to absorb any hostile strike and annihilate any enemy on Chinese soil. But the government also stressed that China would not attack unless she was herself attacked, and quoted Chairman Mao to the effect that "As far as our own desire is concerned, we don't want to fight even for a single day."[17]

The Soviet threat to China contained important ambiguities. It was never clear how far the military preparations were intended as a preface to an actual attack, or how far they were intended to put pressure on the CPR to come to terms with Moscow. In any event the

[16] Text in *Peking Review* (special issue), April 28, 1969.

[17] CPR Government statement of May 24, 1969, New China News Agency, Peking, May 24, 1969.

Russian lines of communication to Peking were not broken off and by October Peking had bowed to Soviet pressure to the extent of agreeing to the opening of border talks. From the Soviet point of view the talks offered two possibilities. If the Chinese proved recalcitrant, Soviet arguments about China's unreasonable conduct would be strengthened. This would benefit the Soviet position vis-à-vis other Communist parties, increase China's isolation and help to prepare the ground for any military action which might become desirable later on. If, on the other hand, the Chinese came to terms, there would be benefits for the security of Soviet borders, the prestige of the Soviet government and the entire Soviet diplomatic position vis-à-vis China.

From the Chinese point of view, on the other hand, the opening of the talks itself implied a defusing of the danger of Soviet attack. This in turn allowed a firming up of the Chinese negotiating position and increased resistance to Soviet pressure. It may be that, in addition, both sides were somewhat alarmed by the brinkmanship of mid-1969. From late 1969 until the end of 1970 there were signs on both sides of a wish for some measure of accommodation. There have been persistent Soviet suggestions that, even if ideological accommodation between Moscow and Peking are impossible, the two states should cooperate in the fight against capitalism and the US.[18] On the Chinese side Premier Chou En-lai's visit to Pyongyang in April 1970 had clear implications for a softening of the Sino-Soviet conflict. The previous radical line, which coupled opposition to Soviet social imperialism with that of American imperialism was gradually played down in favor of hostility to US imperialism alone. During the second half of 1970 antiSoviet invective was either absent from major pronouncements in Peking, or comparatively perfunctory.[19] This is not to say that mutual hostilities have disappeared. They simmer on beneath the surface and can break out in the form of Chinese responses to Soviet actions in East Europe which imply a reactivation of the Brezhnev doctrine, or to Soviet moves towards arms control in concert with the United States; or of Soviet responses to Chinese moves towards an understanding with the United States.

[18] Cf. The Pravda editorial of July 5, 1970, or the official Soviet greetings to Peking on the occasion of China's national day in 1970, *Tass* (Moscow), September 30, 1970; also Izvestia. Mr. Leonid Brezhnev reiterated the theme in his report to the 24th CPSU Congress on March 30, 1971, text published by Novosti Press Agency Publishing House, Moscow, 1971, pp. 15–16.

[19] See, for example, Lin Piao's speech of October 1, 1970, *Peking Review*, October 9, 1970, pp. 14–15; and the joint editorial of *Peoples Daily*, *Red Flag* and *Liberation Army Daily* of October 1, 1970.

In principle, the two sides seem to have three kinds of options. One is presumably to continue a relationship ranging from mild accommodation to low-level conflict and acute verbal dispute. Many of these elements do indeed seem likely to persist. One would expect to see Sino-Soviet competition in ideological terms, or for the adherence of other ruling and non-ruling Communist parties, or as alternative guides, philosophers and friends to underdeveloped nations. They may come to compete in their relationships with Japan. The USSR seems likely to try to create and maintain a political constellation in southern Asia which is unfavorable to China or at any rate contains her. Southeast Asian countries may try to play off the two powers against each other for their own local benefit. There is likely to be conflict between Soviet and Chinese ambitions and commitments in the Middle East. A second possibility would be for either side, or both, to take greater risks of an armed clash between them. This seems improbable for the moment, though the possibility can never be ruled out. The elimination of some of China's nuclear facilities must be tempting. But the risks for Russia in any war with China would range from American or west European intervention in Eastern Europe to Chinese retaliation against the Soviet maritime provinces, some risk of a Chinese nuclear response against Central Asia and, by no means least, the risk of a long war of attrition on Chinese soil which might end ambiguously after causing very great Soviet losses. For China, the risks are equally great. Even if Lin Piao was right in saying that any foreign invader of China will be defeated by sheer numbers in the end, China's losses in the process would be very grave. In such a war, even if nuclear weapons were not used, China could lose most of her cities, her transport network, and her precious scientific and industrial base, not to mention the very large casualties which would be inflicted by the well-armed and sophisticated Soviet armies.

There remains the third possibility: moves towards an accommodation, an alternative which faces very great obstacles. Each side is vulnerable to the other, whatever any agreement between them may say. This extends from territorial problems to the widest political and ideological differences. Mutual trust will be hard to create and harder still to maintain. Each side is likely to seek safeguards which the other may regard as a threat, or at least an attempt to take unfair advantage. Much depends on the character of the post-Mao regime and of its policy preferences. It seems wholly unlikely that any Chinese regime would consider a return to dependence upon the USSR in any major area of public policy. Moscow, for its part, would find it difficult to accept a genuine partnership. Moreover, lasting accommodation would probably depend on ideological compromises by one side, or both, which seems improbable. But there are also factors pointing the other way. Two may turn out to be of particular importance. To say that China and the USSR are strategically and politically vulnerable to one another is also to say that for each the other has much to give. Territorial and political security for either is likely to be greatly enhanced by a settlement between them. In some circumstances this could prove a powerful attraction. It must also be obvious to both parties that no one benefits more from their hostility than the United States. The ability to play them off against each other, and to profit in oblique ways from their mutual suspicions, is a major American diplomatic and strategic asset. It seems entirely possible that both Moscow and Peking may at some point try to deprive the US of the comfortable certainty of Sino-Soviet hostility and suspicion. Better relations with each other may be a precondition for increased leverage by either party against Washington.

US and the Sino-Soviet Conflict

The fluctuations of this relationship have had important consequences for the global posture of the United States, and especially for its arms control and Asian policies. American protection of Taiwan against attack from the mainland was undertaken at a time when Chinese power was seen as an extension of world Communism led by Moscow. That protection has become more ambiguous as Sino-Soviet differences have multiplied. The US-Japanese relationship has been influenced, perhaps decisively, by Tokyo's uncertainties about both China and the USSR. And the state of Sino-Soviet relations has had important consequences for the course and conduct of the war in Vietnam.

Given Sino-Soviet hostility, American freedom of strategic and political action depends on displaying as much even-handedness as possible towards both parties. The less assurance Peking or Moscow has about future American actions, the better off Washington is likely to be. Even-handedness is likely to be accompanied by non-involvement, for open American moves to exploit Sino-Soviet hostility could easily legitimize a response disadvantageous to the US, as well as incurring direct risks. Playing down the US threat to Moscow and Peking may be a precondition to concentrating their attention on each other. In the circumstances of the Soviet-American relationship of the last decade, this has implied some improvement in American relations with China. This has, in turn, been consonant with an important school of thought within the United States.

It is worth noting that the role of American domestic opinion in relation to foreign policy seems to have undergone important changes. It is, of course, normal for foreign policy to be largely a function of domestic politics. Public opinion has almost always been an important determinant of US policies abroad, whether as motivating force or as limiting factor. But there has been a significant change of emphasis. As a broad generalization, whereas during the Truman-Acheson period the administration tried to lead, guide or manipulate domestic opinion so as to permit an American adjustment to the realities of the post-war world, in the 1968–1971 period the administration has increasingly tried to adjust the realities of the world, and the American global posture, so as to accord with US opinion.

As with any change of this magnitude, the reasons are highly complex. But three clusters of factors can be suggested as pertinent here. First, the pressures of post-industrial development have tended to concentrate attention on the important and difficult problems within America. Urban development, education, pollution, racial problems, social services, drugs, the maintenance of economic growth in a period of both inflation and unemployment, crime, transport and the problems of modern electronics, all provide endless causes for civic interest and action, as well as intellectual stimulation. Americans simply find their own society so much more fascinating than the dreary and comparatively conservative problems of the rest of the world, including their own involvement in those problems. Second, there are the growing complexities of administering a society which is so large yet changing so swiftly, together with the almost insurmountable problems of information flow and the formulation of decisions which are adequately considered, yet still relevant by the time they are taken. Decision-making tends to lag behind events. In consequence, affairs abroad can be attended to if they are routine. If not, they may not be dealt with until they have become crises. Third, America is suffering from the consequences of its own success in promoting a highly effective global security structure after 1950. Two results are especially relevant. One is the room for maneuver which the US now has in retrenching her responsibilities, especially in light of some comparatively novel domestic doubts about the efficacy of material power in politically ambiguous circumstances. The other is the obvious fact that many Americans have come to take their security for granted.

The very notion of a *real* external threat to the United States is apt to arouse disbelief. An important reason for American disenchantment with Vietnam has been the inability of many Americans to convince themselves that the costs in blood and treasure incurred there have any clear relationship to the interests, let alone the security, of the

United States. Few people believe that West Europe is in any danger. The nuclear threat, on the other hand, is at once horrendous and improbable. Since no threat to the US is perceptible, it is incredible that nuclear weapons should ever actually be used except as the result of some obscure, malign and irrational machinations. It seems significant that the enemy is frequently identified in terms, such as "the establishment" or "the military-industrial complex," terms which are rooted less in political analysis than in demonology. The very extent of American power has made it possible for many Americans to regard the means by which it is exercised as wasteful and unnecessary or, at worst, as a threat to their liberties and safety. Hence the return, after the historically exceptional period, 1948–68, to the normal American suspicion of, and hostility to, a forward foreign policy or to large-scale military preparations in peacetime. Introspection of this kind, moreover, can encourage other weaknesses, notably the disposition to analyze and debate a foreign problem in terms congenial to American political leanings and intellectual habits rather than in terms which do justice to the problem's foreign substance.

All this suggests that American policies are becoming more closely attuned to the vagaries of domestic public opinion than they have been in recent years—as well perhaps as less predictable. It does not, of course, follow that these policies are worse for the US. Less predictability can mean greater influence. And public opinion can be used to push an administration in directions which it regards as desirable, or to put pressures on a foreign opponent. Moves towards an accommodation with the CPR have been of great benefit in terms of US politics; but they have also put a squeeze on the Soviet Union and Hanoi. Moves towards an arms control agreement with the USSR incorporating a launcher limitation and a very low level of ABM deployment are advantageous both at home and abroad. But they also leave the way open for increased American ascendancy by way of multiple warheads and improved accuracies. They can increase Chinese concern about the Soviet-American relationship, yet confirm a Chinese medium-range retaliatory capability against the Russians and increase the pressures on Moscow to seek a European settlement as part of a policy of freeing its hands in order to cope with China. A Nixon Doctrine which stresses the maintenance of an American nuclear umbrella for smaller allies in Asia, coupled with greater local self-reliance in lower-level conflicts, has similar sorts of advantages. It is popular in the US in that it reduces engagements in Asia. It decreases the ability of Asian states, including America's allies, to take the US for granted. At the same time it does not preclude any American action which might later seem desirable.

From the Soviet point of view, a world without a Soviet-American arms control agreement may be even worse than a world with one, for an agreement would at least bring partial limitations on American weapons and might ease the great economic pressures on the Soviet Union caused by the present effort to consolidate "parity." But a Sino-American rapprochement is largely disadvantageous. It creates fresh uncertainties about both the US and the CPR. It strengthens China's international position and undermines Moscow's attempt to isolate Peking. It may involve some cooperation between Washington and Peking on a Vietnam settlement, which in turn would ease a running sore for American power, eliminate a major element of US containment of China and free China's attention and resources for affairs in the north. It will therefore increase the Soviet emphasis on defensiveness and military security. It may increase Soviet impatience with any signs of deviation in East Europe. But it may also increase the pressures on Moscow to seek a Central European settlement, and therefore its willingness to pay a higher price for it.[20] It may, by helping to bring the CPR into the United Nations, weaken the Soviet position there. On the other hand the pressure to give aid and support to North Vietnam could ease. The Chinese position as contender for Communist leadership would be weakened. The adjustment of South and Southeast Asian states to the circumstances of a novel Sino-American relationship could open up some new opportunities for Soviet diplomacy and perhaps naval enterprise. Most important of all, in the longer term, a new relationship between the Soviet Union and Japan becomes not merely possible but likely.

For China, an understanding with the US and United Nations membership must help to secure her status as one of the world's great powers. It may help to make China a party to a Vietnam settlement, combining a peace-keeping role with the removal of US forces from South Vietnam and, with them, of an important danger to China's own southern flank. At the same time a US withdrawal under conditions of agreement with China would make it easier for America to continue to play a role in East Asia than would be the case if such a withdrawal were accompanied by maximum humiliation. Such a role might be in China's interests, especially with respect to the balance against the Soviet Union and the containment of Japan. China's diplomatic position vis-à-vis Japan must therefore be strengthened. Deterrence of a Soviet attack upon China might also be marginally strengthened

---

[20] The four-power Berlin agreement of August 1971 appears to indicate such a trend.

by the addition of new uncertainties to Moscow's political calculus. Within Southeast Asia, a US withdrawal which left behind a self-sustaining South Vietnam might also be in China's interests, for a divided Vietnam would display less independence from, or resistance to, China while continuing frictions throughout Indochina would create or maintain grievances which could be exploited. The US withdrawal could, therefore, maintain a variety of opportunities for diplomacy and low-level pressures by the entire Southeast Asian grouping of "Indochinese Peoples" which Peking has sponsored and led; while maximizing such opportunities for Peking.[21] In addition, an understanding with Washington may move the Taiwan problem towards a solution on Peking's terms. The authorities in Taipei and Peking might even be moved to come to an arrangement between themselves.

As against this, it may prove difficult to reconcile a partial Sino-American accommodation with Chinese claims to the leadership of anti-capitalist and imperialist movements in the world, or with the maintenance of revolutionary enthusiasm, vigilance and discipline at home. The various Chinese gestures towards the US have made a clear distinction between the inter-state and inter-governmental level at which an accommodation may be possible, and the maintenance of China's ideological positions and continuation of the struggle against imperialism. During the middle months of 1971 there was a rash of statements about the applicability of the five principles of peaceful coexistence and the need for peaceful inter-state relations. But the maintenance, also, of China's ties with its own friends and its commitment to world revolution and the support of national liberation movements is also important to China.[22] Both logically, and in terms of Peking's prevailing ideological precepts, these ideas are, of course, compatible. But whether the attempt to couple them also proves compatible with domestic unity and discipline remains to be seen. Foreign hostility has in the past been an important factor in promoting domestic cohesion; and opposition to American imperialism has been an important part of the entire fight against both capitalism and revisionism. It has, indeed, been important for the maintenance

---

[21] This argument is subject to various limitations. Peking may well prefer, for example, to avoid Sino-American understandings over the heads of the North Vietnamese but with results detrimental to North Vietnam's interests.

[22] See, for example, the May Day 1971 editorials in *Peoples Daily, Red Flag,* and *Liberation Army Daily;* Chou's remarks about not abandoning China's friends and his interview with Mr. J. Pepin of Canada, *International Herald Tribune,* July 21, 1971, pp. 1–2; *The Times,* July 21, 1971, p. 1, July 30, 1971, p. 5; and the remarks about the five principles of coexistence by the Chief of Staff, Huang Yung-sheng, on July 30, 1971.

of Maoist élan. And in so far as Maoism has itself become a major unifying principle for the Chinese state and nation, a devaluation of this component of the Maoist ethic may have considerable—albeit perhaps long-term—consequences for the unity and power of China.[23]

For the United States, these newly emerging triangular relationships involve some important costs. Nixon's request to be received in Peking confirmed the Chinese leaders in the essential correctness of their policies. Together with the Nixon Doctrine, the new patterns could spell the end of the American ascendancy not only in Southeast Asia but in important segments of the western Pacific. Most particularly, they have had and will have important repercussions in Japan.

Quadrilateral Relationships in Asia

JAPAN

The security concerns of Japan are complex, and likely to grow more so. Japan, a great economic power which is only lightly-armed, lies between the three foremost nuclear powers in the world. Its security depends very largely on the relationship between these rather than upon its own unaided efforts. Tokyo must therefore look to ways of influencing that balance to promote its own interests, or else to the establishment of an alliance relationship with one of its great neighbors. This colors the consideration of each of Japan's more immediate concerns: the security of South Korea, the independence and prosperity of Taiwan, the state of the naval balance in the Pacific and the protection of Japan's shipping lanes, Japanese access through Southeast Asian waters to the oilfields of the Middle East, its wish to exploit the oil resources of the East Asian continental shelf and its claims to the return of territory at present held by the Soviet Union in Sakhalin and the Kurile islands. In none of these matters can Japanese interests be fully protected by Japanese power, as distinct from Japanese powers of persuasion.

There appear to be five approaches to these problems. Most of them imply a continuing dependence by Japanese policies on the postures and decisions of others. All of them are open to grave objections. The first is a maintenance and strengthening of the alliance and economic relationship with the United States; the second is a rapprochement with the CPR; a third would be a political and economic

---

[23] I have tried to argue these points in my "Limiting Factors in a Reconsideration of US-China Policies," *Orbis*, Fall 1970, esp. pp. 602–607.

settlement with the Soviet Union; the fourth would be to secure Japanese security by careful and subtle balancing among the three nuclear powers, while continuing a low military posture; and the fifth would be a policy of increasing not just Japanese independence but Japanese military strength, perhaps including an eventual development of nuclear weapons. Though these categories seem analytically useful it would be uncharacteristic as well as unnecessary for Japanese governments to make clear-cut choices between them. The reasons have to do not merely with Japanese ways of doing business but with two weaknesses in the Japanese position: constraints imposed by the party system and elements of fragility in Japan's economic miracle.

The Liberal Democratic party (LDP), which has been in power for about twenty years, shows some signs of potential weakness. The party's voting performance has remained remarkably steady since the early 1950's, but the totals have represented a declining percentage of an increasing electorate.[24] Japan's rural areas are an important part of the party's electoral base and there have been no signs that the government intends to permit an electoral redistribution which would undercut its strength there. At the same time Japan's economic and population changes, and especially the concentration of people in the cities, create a real and growing discrepancy between that electoral structure and the nation's social realities. In any case, there have even been signs of rural disaffection with the government associated with its rice support and other agrarian policies. There are also a variety of internal factional differences and disputes which might surface or even cause an LDP split in some circumstances, including a crisis over rearmament or in foreign policy. As against this, the party continues to be in command of both houses and indeed strengthened its hold on the Lower House in the elections of 1969.[25] It benefits from its strong ties with big business and the civil service,[26] though these also make it disliked among many moderates and intellectuals. Finally, it has benefited from the divisions of its opponents. Even if its own electoral strength were to continue to decline, it might at some point form an alliance with one of the smaller groups which are at present in opposition. Two potential candidates are the right wing Democratic

---

[24] Between the elections of 1953 and those of 1969 the LDP continued to obtain something over 22 million votes in every Lower House election. But as a percentage of the total, the LDP's share declined from 65.6 percent in 1953 to 47.6 percent in 1969. In the Upper House election of June 1971 the LDP's share of the votes dropped from 46.7 percent (in 1968) to 44.6 percent.

[25] The LDP increased its total to 288 seats, a working majority of 44.

[26] In 1970/71 roughly 25 percent of the LDP's Lower House and nearly 50 percent of its Upper House members were former members of the bureaucracy.

Socialists and Komeito, the political arm of the Soka Gakkai religious movement.

During the 1960's most of the electoral ground lost by the LDP was gained not by any other single party but by several groups. The leading opposition group, the Japan Socialist party, lost nearly two-fifths of its seats in the 1969 election, but its share of the votes rose again slightly in 1971. Komeito was notable in nearly doubling its Lower House representation (to 47 seats) in 1969, but may have reached a plateau at that level. Among the more remarkable gainers in recent years has been the Japan Communist party. With its new, relatively moderate image, its posture of neutrality between Peking and Moscow, its acceptance of the idea of Japanese self-defense and above all its social and urban policies, it has done well in a number of elections and in mid-1971 increased its share of the votes from 5 to 8 percent. In some areas and on some issues these groups have been able to cooperate. This has been especially notable in the megalopolitan belt which includes Tokyo and Yokohama, and at the local government level. Joint efforts by Socialists and Communists have scored impressive successes in areas where housing, transport, pollution, social services and the provision of social infrastructure such as roads, hospitals and schools, have become pressing problems.[27] At the same time big city living has produced signs of change not merely in party allegiances but in attitudes to politics as such and the balance between group consciousness and individual choice.

Against this political background a few tentative hypotheses seem plausible. There are important differences in outlook between many of these political groups on major aspects of defense and foreign relations. Though near-consensus has emerged on some matters—for example the general desirability of some improvement in relations with China—there is little common ground between the LDP and the Communists or left wing Socialists on such issues as the definition of Japanese interests outside the Japanese home islands, relations with the US or rearmament. It is therefore probable that clear-cut decisions in any of these areas, especially if they seemed new and moved away from the status quo, would cause much soul-searching. In so far as megalopolitan problems loom larger in Japan, they may find political expression in support for left wing groupings whose foreign policy attitudes will probably be low-posture and defensive ones. In

[27] I do not suggest that these problems are peculiar to Japan. Indeed, awareness of them, and the formation of radical groups propounding various solutions, seems to be a common feature of many situations where people are facing the unprecedented social, economic and administrative facts created by megalopolitan growth. New York, Los Angeles, Tokyo and Calcutta are obvious instances.

consequence, the more the LDP comes to perceive its electoral danger, the more it (and *a fortiori* any successor government based on a left-of-center or even a center-left coalition including elements of the LDP) might feel forced to adopt one of two sorts of attitude. A government faced by acute and inescapable security problems might feel compelled to adopt a comparatively authoritarian stance, with potentially unfortunate consequences for the whole future of representative democracy in Japan. Or, much more probably, the authorities would adopt a restricted and defensive interpretation of Japanese interests and, indeed, find it hard to pursue any determined or consistent foreign policy at all. Even this might not avoid anguished domestic debate, recriminations and divisions with obvious possibilities for, among other things, the exercise of foreign influence.

The second weakness arises, paradoxically, from the very success of the Japanese economy. The average annual growth rate of the Japanese GNP since the mid-1950's has been something over 10 percent. Towards the end of the 1960's it went up to around 16 percent. The result has been to put Japan into third place in the international GNP table, surpassed only by the USA and the Soviet Union. Most projections suggest that there will continue to be swift growth, though there is disagreement on just how dramatic it will be.[28] But this growth has been based on a number of factors at least some of which may change. Japan has enjoyed the advantage of spending less than 1 percent of GNP on its own defense. It has had to cope with less than 1 percent annual growth in its population, and has enjoyed political stability and extremely high rates of domestic saving—nearly 40 percent in 1968. Its business management and domestic transport systems have been excellent. So has its higher education system. And, like West Germany, it has had a new, post-1945 industrial infrastructure. Moreover, growth has also, inevitably, produced or encouraged various domestic stresses. Wages and consumer spending have risen by 9–10 percent in recent years. But labor leaders have pressed for still higher wages, supported by the facts of Japan's increasing manpower shortage. Added to this have been the consequences of urbanization. Japan's rural population, over 48 millions in 1955, is expected to decline to 32 millions by 1975. One Japanese estimate has suggested that by the end of the century the Japanese population will be some 93

---

[28] The US economic measures of August 1971 may, for example, create difficulties for Japan. For one lively discussion of some alternative projections see Herman Kahn and Max Singer, "Japan and Pacific Asia in the 1970's," *Asian Survey*, April 1970, pp. 399–412. An excellent survey can also be found in Peter Drysdale, "Japan in the World Economy: The Decade Ahead," paper delivered to a conference on "Japan and Australia in the 1970's," Sydney, June 12, 1971.

percent urban. The consequent problems of pollution, housing, schools and the provision of social services require not only a considerable technological effort but money in quantities which can only come from continued economic growth. Pressures for Japanese aid to under-developed countries, the claims of defense and the need for invest-ment to safeguard Japanese markets and sources of supply, all point in the same direction: economic growth and the maintenance of fiscal and balance of payments policies which will permit massive invest-ment at home and abroad. In sum, economic growth has produced problems whose solution requires a continuation of rapid growth. A decline in the growth rate could produce serious social and political consequences.

Growth is, however, singularly dependent upon foreign economic connections and therefore upon factors which Japan cannot wholly control. Japan's visible exports and imports combined are equivalent to over 20 percent of GNP, roughly twice the proportion for the US. In recent years Japan has imported increasing quantities of food, in-cluding 75 percent of its wheat and over 80 percent of its soybeans. Consumption of imported meat and butter has gone up. Japan's energy requirements more than tripled between 1955 and 1965 and continue to go up. By 1966 Japan was importing roughly 30 percent of its coal and over 90 percent of its oil. Consumption of iron ore has gone up from 17 million tons in 1960 to 85 million tons in 1969. Essential supplies of this sort have increasingly come from sources in the Americas and Australia, safeguarded by long-term contracts. Since the flow of imports must ultimately be paid for through an increased export program, Japanese prosperity and growth rely to a great degree on free and uninterrupted trading opportunities. The United States, Australia and Canada, in that order, have become Japan's most im-portant trading partners. Roughly one third of Japanese exports go to North America and one third of its imports come from there. This sector is even more important than such percentages imply, and for three reasons. Japanese exports to the United States include a high proportion of goods, such as iron and steel, machinery and electrical goods, which come from the growth sectors of Japanese industry. These sectors have therefore depended particularly on the US market. Second, Japan's financial ties, including the financing of significant portions of Japan's trade, are largely with the United States. Third, the Japanese balance of payments has in recent years been particularly dependent on trading and other surpluses earned in North America. In 1969, for example, when the global Japanese surplus on current account was about $2.2 billions, the surplus on trade with the US was just over $1 billion. In 1970 the global and US trading surpluses were

$1.4 billions and $500 millions respectively.[29] Nor do these figures take into account additional Japanese earnings in such areas as shipping charges on goods traded with the US. It would therefore appear that, at least for the time being, Japan's prosperity and ability to cope with its pressing population, big city and pollution problems depend markedly on its economic relationship with the United States.

Under these circumstances Japanese foreign policies labor under very great constraints. Any sudden damage to Japanese-American economic exchanges could have serious repercussions on the Japanese economy. But this same fact also makes Japan vulnerable to American action against Japanese goods or freedom of trade,[30] or to US pressure to permit the inflow of US investment capital into Japan, with the attendant risk that imported business habits may damage the unique relationships within Japan on which the nation's economic success has in large part been based. Similar constraints operate at the strategic level. Many Japanese doubt the usefulness or desirability of the US alliance and, whether for this reason or from a sense of national pride, would like to see Japanese bases returned to Japanese control. But the government is very much aware that no replacement for American protection, including the nuclear umbrella, is in sight; and that any policy for replacing it with Japanese forces, even defensive ones, would have to overcome grave political and legal difficulties within Japan. The defense, not only of Japan but of Japanese interests in Korea and Taiwan depends largely on the US commitment to defend those areas against direct attack. From the government's point of view, unless the US is encouraged to retain facilities in Japan and the Ryukyus, Japan itself would be exposed. It might then have to rearm at a pace which public opinion would dislike even more than the presence of US bases. On the other hand, reliance on the US makes Japan vulnerable to sudden shifts in US policy. President Nixon's announcement of his proposed visit to China, and the resulting embarrassment of the

[29] US figures on these exchanges differ markedly from the Japanese ones. This is due to technical differences in classification and accounting. I have assumed that in a discussion of Japanese policies, Japanese computations are more meaningful.

[30] The 1970/71 US-Japanese exchanges over the textile trade and the Japanese payments surplus with the US illustrate these difficulties. The textile problem has been handled with marked insensitivity in Washington, and to some extent in Tokyo, in spite of the voluntary restraints which Japan quietly applied to its textile sales in the US. The American attitude has come uncomfortably close to saying that Japan should liberalize its own markets while agreeing to the maintenance of American protection. And one wonders whether the manner, let alone the substance, of the US dollar defense measures of August and December 1971 took adequate account of the help which Tokyo repeatedly gave Washington between 1968 and 1971 in balance of payments accommodations on capital account.

Japanese government, are likely to have driven that lesson home in Tokyo.

The second option, a rapprochement with the CPR, faces Tokyo with different sorts of dilemmas. Until mid-1971 such a rapprochement was thought largely inconsistent with the relationship between Tokyo and Washington, with the growing Japanese economic interest in Taiwan, with Japanese strategic interests in Korea and Taiwan and with Tokyo's views about desirable future developments in Southeast Asia. It was not thought to be feasible at all during the Cultural Revolution or, on acceptable terms, after that movement began to fade out in 1969. The official Japanese approach to China was therefore cautious, limited and slow. On the other hand, important segments of Japanese opinion have wanted an accommodation. The traditional cultural ties with China have played a role here. So has the deep Japanese desire to avoid international disputes in its own area. Various Japanese groups have argued that Southeast Asian conflicts cannot be settled, or Korean conflict prevented, without China's participation and consent. Others have conceded at least the principle that the Taiwan problem is an internal Chinese affair. Many of these groups have agreed that one of Japan's most important roles in the international arena could be that of broker between China and the west.

This line of argument has been strengthened by some economic considerations. The lure of the Chinese market has attracted some Japanese businessmen. In the longer term, exploitation of the resources of the East Asian continental shelf can hardly proceed without some understandings between Tokyo, Peking, Taipei, Seoul and Pyŏngyang. Peking, for its part, has been able to influence Japan, especially by repeated criticism of Japanese defense planning, which has found a strong echo among antimilitary groups within Japan. The advancing US accommodation with Peking has no doubt strengthened the hands of those in Tokyo who wish to move faster towards an understanding with China. Prime Minister Sato has said that Japan is ready to hold talks with Peking. At the same time, moves towards accommodation may have to be finely tuned if they are not to involve an unnecessary weakening of South Korea or dispute with the Soviet Union. Most important, they could be "outflanked" if Sino-American accommodation came to imply containment of Japan.[31]

[31] No Japanese government can now exclude such possibilities. On July 28, 1971, less than two weeks after President Nixon's statement about his proposed visit to Peking, the Acting Foreign Minister of Japan, Takeo Kimura, told the LDP's China study committee that Japan's relationship with China was fundamentally different from that of America in that China and the US had historically been friendly before World War II. His audience was, admittedly, a comparatively hardline China policy group. But the remark has ominous long-term implications.

These considerations increase the importance of the third option: accommodation with the Soviet Union. This, too, has so far been incompatible with the Tokyo-Washington relationship. It has been equally incompatible with Japanese claims for the return of Soviet-held territory or Japanese fears about the security of its shipping lanes, or indeed of Japan herself, in the face of the growing Soviet Far Eastern fleet. Such fears must be rendered more acute by Soviet port-developing activities in Kamchatka—where Soviet ships would have much easier access to the broad Pacific, and one much freer from surveillance, than they now have from Vladivostok. Nor has Tokyo forgotten the Soviet role in the launching of the Korean war in 1950. Moscow has been immovable on the territorial issue. Though there have been repeated suggestions about Japanese participation in the economic development of eastern Siberia, Japanese businessmen have found Soviet terms and conditions uninviting.

On the other hand, new links with Moscow offer various potential benefits. Japan might reinforce the Soviet wish to dissuade North Korea from again invading the South. This might be of increased importance to Tokyo if moves towards Sino-American cooperation were accompanied by a continuing decline in the relationship of mutual confidence between Tokyo and Washington. Japan might try to adopt a balanced position between China and the Soviet Union—which is likely to imply some improvement in Japanese relations with the Russians. The Soviet naval threat might be somewhat devalued; a move which would not only benefit the security of the Japanese islands. If the opening of the Suez canal were followed by an increased Soviet naval presence in the Indian Ocean and along the southern shores of Arabia, the security of Japan's Middle Eastern oil supplies would make an understanding with Moscow even more desirable. There would be gains, moreover, in terms of Japan's increasing independence from the US and the offsetting of a developing Sino-American relationship. It is true that the costs of such moves could be heavy. But it may not be impossible to secure more advantageous terms from the Russians for economic cooperation in Siberia and to leave on one side, for the time being, Japan's territorial claims against the USSR.

The remaining options involve the degree to which Japan may wish to rearm. The first Defense White Paper, issued in October 1970, and the proposals for the Fourth Defense Build-Up Plan, had some intriguing aspects. Japan's defensive posture was stressed. Japan would not acquire weapons, such as ICBM's, which could threaten other countries. The policy against nuclear weapons would be maintained "for the present," though it has been argued that an acquisition of defensive weapons would not be in contravention of the Japanese constitution, Japan would continue to rely on US deterrence and the Mutual Security Treaty with the US, which was renewed in June 1970 after its initial term of ten years. Japan's own defense efforts should be based on autonomous and local self-defense efforts. Yet the Mutual Security Treaty is now subject to one year's notice of termination on either side. The US force presence in Japan is declining and Japan is resuming political control of Okinawa, following which the island is to be defended by Japanese forces, and US combat operations from there will be subject to prior consultation with the Japanese government.

The bases for an expansion of Japanese forces are being laid, but the pace and character of expansion have not yet become clear. A build-up of Japanese conventional, and especially naval, forces has begun. Japanese planners are also paying considerable attention to ways of countering urban guerrilla operations, including disruption by very small militant groups. The question of strategic weapons must be regarded as open. Japan has a significant rocket and space research effort. In 1970, Japan was the fifth country to orbit a satellite. The specifications for the Japanese MuIV rocket show some striking similarities to those for the US Minuteman military missile. Japan's electronic and computer industry is well able to back up an advanced weapons effort. On the nuclear side, Japan is due to have 5000 MW of nuclear generating capacity by 1975 and there has already been talk of uranium separation and enrichment facilities. While the antipathy to strategic weapons remains strong, public opinion polls and voting have in recent years shown an increasing acceptance of the idea that Japan will rearm and the younger generation of Japanese appears not to share the "nuclear allergy" of their elders. Japanese manufacturers have shown considerable interest in various arms production possibilities. It may, moreover, be possible to produce at least some varieties of non-nuclear strategic weapons.

International pressures appear to be pushing the Japanese government towards some combination of these various policies. It would be in character for the Japanese bamboo to bend with the wind and retain the strategic and economic benefits of the US connection. But Japanese postures will also be designed not to expose future governments to the kind of embarrassment which Sato suffered as a result of President Nixon's 1971 overtures towards China. Tokyo may parallel the US in trying to build diplomatic and economic bridges to Peking, even if it means sacrificing some Japanese interests in Taiwan. But if Peking is invited to sit on the UN Security Council while Japan remains excluded, or if the US too easily abandons Taiwan, lasting resentment may well be caused in Tokyo. This would give further impetus to moves for Japanese diplomatic independence and the acquisition of advanced weapons. There may also be a degree of accommodation with the Soviet Union.

At the same time Japan is likely to refine reactor and fuel handling capabilities, as well as rocket, guidance, radar and computer facilities in such a way as to give herself shorter lead-time options without the domestic and international embarrassment of an overt decision to go for weapons.[32] In the longer term, various kinds of sea-based second strike systems may become possible. Japanese research and development on defensive and non-nuclear weapons systems is likely to speed up. This may include non-nuclear ballistic missile deflection rather than destruction methods. Japan is also likely to seek a further diversification of its sources of supply and financial connections. Trading and financial ties with Europe, in particular, may become more important after Britain joins the Common Market. One would also expect to see great effort put into anti-pollution and pollution-avoidance technologies, into economically feasible methods of extracting a greater range of raw materials from low-grade and seabed deposits, and into a spread of Japanese-controlled consumer goods production to less developed countries with lower-cost labor. It is, however, a major difficulty that such policies would leave Japanese interests and policies dependent upon a careful balance between three great powers and domestic public opinion. This would be an inherently unstable and fragile situation. It might offend Japanese pride. It could also leave Japan unable to cope with many kinds of external crises without accepting grave diplomatic costs as well as domestic disunity and strife.

SOUTHEAST ASIA

At the start of the 1970's it seems clear that many of the reasons for instability within Southeast Asia not only persist but may be growing stronger. Ethnic and religious hostility within and between these states continues to exist. Mutual suspicions between Cambodians and South Vietnamese have weakened their military cooperation against North Vietnam. Similar mutual dislike persists between Khmers and Thais, Malays and Chinese, Burmese and Karens. Except in the presence of immediate and urgent common danger, cooperation between these groups and states has been very limited.

The difficulties are compounded by contemporary economic and

[32] If this prognosis is correct, Japan will probably not ratify the Nuclear Non-Proliferation Treaty.

social developments. Western medical techniques and dietary changes have produced or encouraged population growth in a way which has made old patterns of production and social organization inadequate. The new needs, together with security requirements in a world of competing and often hostile nation-states, have produced irresistible pressures for the creation of more modern and efficient national organizations. Competitive recipes for modernization have become important elements in the contest for political and social loyalty in these societies. Yet economic growth in many areas remains slow. Population growth can swallow up increased production. Even where per capita GNP figures are improving, there are unresolved problems about the distribution of these growing resources. Increasing wealth, moreover, is invariably accompanied by new forms of social conflict as patterns of social organization and lines of authority change under the impact of new economic processes. New elites arise, familiar with the novel technical and administrative needs. New tensions arise between them and the more traditional segments of society, many of which are concerned less with progress and individual achievement than with group loyalties and consensus, less with efficient management than with the maintenance of cultural identity or virtuous conduct by the ruler.

In some states, such as Thailand, Indonesia and perhaps South Vietnam, there have been attempts, supported or even led by the army as the most disciplined organizing force in society, to impose central rule on shifting political and social forces. The task, in a situation of social fragmentation, is to maintain and strengthen the modern nation-state as both a new focus of loyalty and an effective provider of security against the outside world. This requires the most delicate judgment about the ways in which the center of gravity of political opinion moves from traditionalist opinions to an acceptance of more modern social forms. The success of such a policy of transition depends on a variety of factors. Economic improvement must be fast enough to prevent chronic discontent which might provide a base for revolutionary groups; but the improvement must not be accompanied by social changes more abrupt than the constituency will tolerate. The elite must encourage technological progress, but without becoming alienated from the more traditional segments of its own society. It may have to search for foreign technical and economic help to speed the local modernization process, but must do so on terms which its citizens will accept as compatible with their own pride and independence. It must contain disaffection in a socially and ethnically fragmented society, but without being counter-productively oppressive. It must maintain cohesion within the new state but by methods which will not be embarrassing to its foreign friends. It may wish to guide the society away from traditional authority and towards westernized electoral politics. But in doing so it may have to steer carefully between domestic resistance to change, and foreign charges of undemocratic conduct.

In sum, many of the states of Southeast Asia have yet to establish adequate modern social organizations. The task of nation-building is not complete. Economic development has scored considerable successes, but in many cases prosperity remains vulnerable. The slow growth of the Communist states has made them unattractive models for economic development, though some aspects of the Chinese experience remain of interest. Instead, growth has been organized along more flexible lines. Success has tended to correlate with stable and effective political leadership, with sound economic policies and financial management, and with a steady and continuing access to foreign investment and markets, especially in Japan and the United States. But this has involved other costs. Investment has depended, in considerable part, on political stability. That stability, as well as production and marketing, have been liable to direct interruption, for example by insurgents, as well as to indirect limitations in the shape of the interest policies of creditor groups, the fluctuations of world commodity prices or the direct and indirect consequences of protectionism in the US or Japan. Many Southeast Asian states have earned substantial sums from US dollar expenditure with respect to the Vietnam war. South Vietnam itself has received US investment on a scale which makes rapid post-war economic recovery very likely. Japan has not only invested heavily in Southeast Asia but become the most important trading partner for many of its states. Yet the windfall earnings of "Vietnam dollars" will fall away and US investment in South Vietnam could end with the American troop withdrawal, while the availability of Japanese and American markets will depend not only upon the economic growth of those countries but upon trading relations between them. Moreover, the post-Vietnam period is likely to see a decline in US aid as well as military expenditure in the whole region.

There has been an improvement in the strength and self-confidence of many of the local regimes, but few of them have developed exportable power or found safety or stability through regional or collective security arrangements. North Vietnam, with probably the most efficient administrative and political structure in the region, has shown no signs of phasing out its overt and covert pressures on all Southeast Asian nations in its reach. Thailand, South Vietnam, the Philippines, Malaysia and Singapore have all, at various times, sought the protection of collective security arrangements, but many of their external difficulties remain. Insurgencies, promoted or supported from abroad, exist in most of the countries of the region. Yet regional cooperation has not been primarily concerned with security problems. These have been contained, though not solved, by outside military power. Organizations like ASPAC, ASEAN and the Asian Development Bank have not replaced this need for outside help in stabilizing regional affairs. There have been at least three important consequences. Within the region, there has been an emphasis on the skills of persuasion, manipulation and indirect pressure rather than military power in what one observer has called the Byzantine politics of Southeast Asia.[33] But these local states also remain dependent, in many important ways, on the decision of outsiders. If it is true, for example, that local hostilities have been contained by the presence of some of the great powers, then the withdrawal of that presence, and especially of American forces, is likely to lead to greater military expenditure by local states. This must, in turn, bring acute resource allocation problems, slower growth and a longer period of economic weakness.

Altogether, as long as the area remains divided into mutually hostile entities, incapable either of coalition or of conquest, it will remain an object rather than a subject of international politics. Its future position in the world balance of power will be determined less by local governments than by others. In making their calculations, those others will be guided by at least three clusters of factors. First, Southeast Asia has no political units which, like the major European or East Asian states, are of great importance to world politics; no major industrial or research centers; and no irreplaceable raw materials. Second, the attitudes of major states will be guided by the importance which their administrations attach to domestic as opposed to foreign problems. The powers do not have identical views on these matters and the movements of opinion within them tend in somewhat different directions. Third, the importance of Southeast Asia to the US and the USSR is not of the same order as its importance to China and Japan.

The US impact on Southeast Asia in the last two or three years has been profoundly affected by the twin policies of Vietnamization and the disengagement of US forces from Indochina as a whole. These policies rest upon a number of assumptions which differ from those of previous administrations: that the US cannot command or control political changes in Southeast Asia—at any rate at acceptable cost; that American economic and military power might be altogether tangential in shaping the internal futures of the societies concerned; that the cost of the US engagement in Vietnam has been disproportionately higher

---

[33] John H. Badgley, "The American Territorial Presence in Asia," *The Annals of the American Academy of Political and Social Science*, Vol. 390, July 1970, pp. 38–47.

than any useful aim which might be achieved thereby; that the US commitment has caused or accentuated US weaknesses elsewhere as well as at home. Indeed, the Vietnam experience helped to bring about a much broader reassessment of US foreign policy, with the Vietnam withdrawal itself only a partial result. The Nixon Doctrine emphasized, from mid-1969 onwards, the devolution of security responsibilities to allies. The US would adhere to its treaty commitments, continue to provide a shield "if a nuclear power threatens the freedom of a nation allied with us or of a nation whose survival we consider vital to our security." In the event of other kinds of aggression "we shall furnish military and economic assistance when requested. . . But we shall look to the nation directly threatened to assume the primary responsibility of providing manpower for its defense."[34] The object is explicit: to make American involvement more unlikely. The emphasis is on partnership and local effort. The US has stressed its expectation that Asian countries will display greater self-reliance and independence.[35] It has also emphasized its expectations from the development of regional cooperation, ranging from the five-power security arrangements for the defense of Malaysia and Singapore to the Lower Mekong Basin project.

The formal US withdrawal is therefore limited. The US will probably maintain a presence in Thailand and—assuming political stability in the Philippines—its bases at Clark Field and Subic Bay as well as support facilities at Okinawa. But it will probably be a presence which does not require the use of American manpower in politically ambiguous conflicts, and one which is not subject to domestic criticism in the same way as the Vietnam commitment has been. Altogether, US policies in Southeast Asia, and elsewhere for that matter, will be affected by the Vietnam experience for some years to come. This tendency will be apparent to all other powers involved. One of its more important results, therefore, will be to change the structure of expectations of all concerned regarding future power relationships in the Pacific and Southeast Asia. In particular, it is likely to change the expectations of Japan, and some of the more important past constraints on the foreign and defense policies of China.

Prospects for the Future of Southeast Asia

China has traditionally regarded Southeast Asia in general, and Indo-china in particular, as its own proper sphere of influence. At times,

[34] Richard Nixon, "US Foreign Policy for the 1970's: Building for Peace," The White House, February 25, 1971, p. 5.

[35] *Ibid.*, p. 32.

indeed, it has been considered as a lost dependency which it is China's duty to recover as part of the process of the reassertion of China's international rights and status following a century of national humiliation at the hands of foreigners. Influence in Southeast Asia can also yield more specific dividends, including leverage against a Japan whose industrial and military potential has caused Peking grave concern; an Indonesia which might, given adequate economic progress, become a counterweight to China within the region; and an India which is allied with the Soviet Union. The Chinese diplomatic effort over the past two years has improved Peking's position in Southeast Asia. There have been a number of other policies consistent with this sketch of China's aims, including road-building and protection programs in Laos, training and logistic support for insurgents in Laos, Thailand, Burma and Malaysia. Most importantly, of course, these aims have formed at least part of the rationale for the political, propaganda and military effort to secure a US withdrawal from the area. That effort has included the provision of arms and supplies, as well as political backing, for North Vietnam and the South Vietnamese insurgents. These various policies have made a significant contribution not only to the US withdrawal, but to the more accommodating postures which Thailand and Malaysia, among others, have begun to adopt towards Peking.

The promotion of Chinese influence has, however, been subject to a number of important limitations. Peking has been, and probably remains, primarily concerned with its tremendous domestic administrative, economic and political problems and the debates about resource allocation which must accompany any proposal about their solutions. So far, China lacks the industrial infrastructure, as well as the mobility of military effort, for large or sustained military offensives in any direction beyond its own borders. Its primary security problems, the Soviet armies along its northern border, fear of Japanese rearmament, and Taiwan, hardly permit any very high priority for Chinese efforts in the south. In general, the practical caution which China has displayed in the past is likely to persist. Nor are local states, and especially the Vietnamese, likely to welcome or even permit Chinese dominance. These are powerful arguments. Yet the US withdrawal will change the structure of constraints for China and present it with new targets of opportunity if it can, or will, take advantage of them. Any large-scale US re-engagement in Southeast Asia following the Vietnam withdrawal seems quite improbable. The Soviet Union lacks bases in the region. Japan is not yet rearmed. And China is in the process of acquiring a significant nuclear deterrent against each of them, as well as against the US. In terms of the great power balance, these are likely to be optimal conditions for an extension of Chinese influence in the region.

Moreover, it may be that Vietnam will remain divided following a US withdrawal. If so, any Vietnamese resistance to the spread of Chinese influence would tend to be weakened.[36] Nor would the weaknesses of the Chinese industrial structure, or the comparative lack of mobility of the Chinese forces, be decisive in conflicts which did not involve major powers outside Southeast Asia. Indeed, military action may be unnecessary in many situations. After a complete US withdrawal from Vietnam even American air and logistic support may become unwelcome to local governments faced with the task of making their peace with Peking. Archipelago states would be less affected by such considerations than mainland ones. It might be, therefore, that new lines of division would open up between a mainland Southeast Asia attempting to reach an accommodation with Peking in the absence of western or Japanese protection, and those archipelago states which, by virtue of distance or size or the operations of outside nations' sea and air forces, felt themselves under no such pressure.

Japan's interests in Southeast Asia are great, but may be expendable —at a price. Most of Japan's oil comes from the Middle East and through Southeast Asian waters. Japan's economic and financial aid to Indonesia may have been partly motivated by the need to have a stable and friendly Indonesia athwart those lines of supply. Japan has major investments and trading interests in the region. These might grow as Japan, with its stable population and high cost labor force, begins to transfer labor-intensive (and possibly also pollution-intensive) production to lower-wage Southeast Asian areas. Yet the maintenance and extension of such interests probably require political and economic attitudes by local governments inconsistent with a close relationship between them and Peking. Japan's growing energy requirements might be met by nuclear power production or alternative sources of hydrocarbon fuels. Yet the first must imply a military potential, while the second implies the security of other sea lanes or agreements with other Asian states on oil exploration and exploitation. No such agreements are in sight. As to trade, Japan might diversify its markets in other directions if the political and strategic costs of involvement in Southeast Asia became too great. And there are other low-wage areas to which

---

[36] The assumption here is that an effectively unified Vietnam, or Indochina, would be more resistant to such influence. This assumption may be mistaken, especially if (1) Soviet involvement in Indochina wanes following the US withdrawal, leaving Hanoi more clearly dependent on China; (2) If internal, including ethnic, disputes persist in Indochina and weaken both its government and the unity and discipline of its followers. If Hanoi did try actively to resist Peking, it might come to be in the US interest to support North Vietnam.

production facilities could be dispersed. But each of these moves would have political costs. The balancing of advantages and disadvantages in this matter is likely to cause long and perhaps bitter debates in Tokyo. Certainly any major limitations on the freedom of international trade, or on Japan's access to overseas markets, is likely to make the control of one's own markets seem more desirable. On the other hand, Japan's strategic weaknesses, in particular the urbanization and concentration of its population which deprive it of resiliency in case of major conflict, may persuade Tokyo to caution, at least until such time as it possesses what Japanese leaders regard as an adequate deterrent. But either way, the maintenance or devolution of Japanese interests in Southeast Asia will bring Tokyo into conflict with the aims of China.

There remains the Soviet Union, which has been an Asian and Pacific power for over a century. Some elements of a Soviet Southeast Asia policy can be identified. The Soviet Navy has made its presence felt in Southeast Asian waters. Moscow has been economically active in Malaysia, Thailand, Singapore and even Indonesia. North Vietnam has depended, at times vitally, upon Soviet supplies and weapons in the fight against the US. Indeed, Soviet aid at some points amounted to $1 billion per annum. Yet it is hard to perceive a vital Soviet interest in Southeast Asia, apart from the weakening of the US and China. If one Soviet response to danger from China, and to an improvement in Sino-American relations, is a move towards Japan, it would make little sense to offend Japanese political and trading interests unnecessarily in Southeast Asia. More importantly, the Soviet Union's concern with China has pushed it towards two other considerations. The first is a Soviet diplomatic and military link with India, accompanied as it has been by Soviet naval deployments in the Indian Ocean. As and when the Suez canal reopens, and direct communications are possible once more between southern Arabia and the Black Sea, that naval presence and Soviet support for India will become more important. The second may be that the security of the Siberian borders might best be secured by pinning China down in Southeast Asia rather than preventing a Chinese engagement there. From this point of view it could be in Moscow's interests for China to exploit its opportunities in Southeast Asia rather than forage in South Asia or the Middle East. It would, at the same time, be in the Soviet interest to encourage Southeast Asian instability, and an expenditure of Chinese energy and resources in coping with this, rather than stability and a settlement which permitted a redirection of Chinese attention. If these considerations are sound, the Soviet Union may confine its interests in Southeast Asia to the gaining of cheaply-available diplomatic points and a strengthening of its bargaining position for use elsewhere. But a major Soviet involvement in Southeast Asia would be unlikely.

The conclusion must be mildly pessimistic. Southeast Asian states are likely to remain mutually hostile or suspicious during the coming decade, without stable regional security arrangements and subject to the overriding influence of greater powers from outside the region. Economic and educational developments may provide the infrastructure for the more cohesive and internally stable states of the future. But for the time being Southeast Asia will, from an international point of view, be as important as the great powers let it be. One's pessimism goes further. A Pacific standoff between four powers, each of which insists on maximum freedom of action and a minimum of commitment vis-à-vis the outside world, is likely to be difficult to maintain. If none of the larger states can be certain of the diplomatic and strategic commitments of the others, the result may be a balance—but a hair-trigger one in which the very scale of uncertainty may bring overreaction from any of the participants at times of tension. While smaller nations will have little direct leverage against each of the four powers, their reaction will further complicate the great power balance as well as causing political problems within the large powers' own electorates. Together with these uncertainties will come the consequences of faster communications and the need, at times of crisis, for fast decision-making. This will be done on the basis of inadequately digested results of ever-increasing floods of information and data. It is, indeed, far from clear that the problems which face the Pacific nations, whether in matters of security or trade or of international finance, are soluble within the limitations which at present restrict both national policies and international systems.

The Asian State System in the 1970's

HOWARD WRIGGINS

The Strategic Setting

The Asian state system encompasses more than 75
percent of mankind in states with widely differing
capabilities, sizes, types of regimes and sources of
influence. It finds its main armature in the relationship
between two mainland giants—the Soviet Union, a
world power, and China, an Asian regional power.
Although geographically not an Asian power, the actions
of the US, another superpower, force its inclusion as a
member of the Asian state system. The island state of
Japan has a rapidly growing economy and is likely to
play a more important role in the future of Asia through
its dramatic economic growth and potential military
capability.

A number of smaller sub-systems lie within the larger
Asian state system. India, a case by itself, is neither a
world nor yet a major Asian power, but it does dominate
the South Asian sub-system. It has played a large role
in the Sino-Soviet rivalry and within 20 years is likely to
be of major consequence in the wider Asian system.
Indonesia in Southeast Asia is not a great power but can
be expected to be politically important in its immediate
Southeast Asian neighborhood and economically of
wider significance. The future of the Asian state system
will be shaped largely by the relations between these
six major states.

In this chapter we will first compare Asia and the
western state system before examining the trend toward
a quadrilateral balance of power between the US, the

USSR, China and Japan. We will then examine two sub-systems: (1) South Asia focusing on India, and (2) Southeast Asia, whose members have tended to be notably dependent upon outside powers. A third sub-system, in East Asia, where Soviet, Chinese, Japanese and American interests converge on and near the Korean peninsula, is not examined in such detail. Although more the focus of great power pressures than the other two sub-systems, at the present writing (July 1971) East Asia appears to have a greater inherent stability than the other two. At least so long as the Korean demarcation line holds firm, the converging powers are not likely to run any serious risks there. Areas of greater uncertainty and more likely movement are in South and Southeast Asia. The chapter concludes with some observations regarding possibilities for intensified regional relationships, particularly in Southeast Asia.

Asian and Western State Systems Compared [1]

It was once possible to talk of the western state system, with its geographical and political center in western Europe. The Asian state system does not have such a clearly defined geographical center. Nor is it virtually autonomous the way the European state system was from the time the Turks were halted at Vienna in the 17th century until World War I, which brought revolution to Russia and the presence in Europe of American power. Particularly since World War II, the Asian state system, like the European system before it, has been significantly affected by decisions made or avoided in Washington. However, as will be seen, the Asian state system is likely to become increasingly self-sufficient as the patterns of politics within Asia itself become more autonomous and as the American commitment to and capability for global security management diminishes. Nevertheless, the Asian state system cannot be considered without reference to the wider, international system of which it is a part.

At the same time, relationships between all members of the Asian state system are not equally intimate. Rather, beneath the overarching relationships among the four major Asian powers, one can distinguish a series of regional sub-systems. In South Asia, India, Pakistan, Nepal

[1] I am indebted to my colleague Stanley Heginbotham for this approach, although my formulation differs somewhat from his. See H. Wriggins, S. Heginbotham and J. Morley, *The Emerging Balance of Power in Asia and Opportunities for Arms Control, 1970–1975* (ACDA/IR-170, April 1971), Vol. II, Section I, by Heginbotham.

and Ceylon form one sub-system.[2] The states of Southeast Asia form another;[3] and in East Asia, Japan, the Koreas and Taiwan form a third. These, in turn, are directly affected, in different ways, by the external world. Accordingly, the Asian state system can properly be called a loosely articulated and poorly integrated state system.

Geography has an important role to play in this diversity. Europe, after all, is a small peninsula protruding into the Atlantic from the western end of the Asian continent. River systems draw the countries together willy nilly, crossing national and cultural areas, focusing movement and access away from the east into the central plains of Germany and France or into northern Italy. London to Paris is only 200 miles; Paris to Berlin only 500. In Asia, by contrast, huge rivers flow outward to the sea, but do not link diverse cultural and linguistic areas. Moscow and Peking are some 3,600 miles apart; from Moscow to New Delhi is 2,500 miles, across the Hindu Kush and the Himalayas. Only the jet age has made Asian capitals as convenient to each other as European capitals have been for generations.

The Asian state system is also marked by its historical diversity. In the heyday of the European state system, all participants generally shared post-Renaissance, Christian culture (Imperial Russia and southern Eastern Europe were exceptions), a history of Roman judicial practice, rationalist aspiration toward scientific thought and an evolution toward representative democracy conceived of either as a good or something to which all regimes would be driven sooner or later.[4] To be sure, the post-Waterloo settlement sought to hold back the sweep of popular legitimacy, but educational, technological and other trends all tended to bring into doubt legitimacy by inheritance and substitute for it a growing demand for popular democratic institutions.[5]

In Asia there is no such common civic or religious tradition or unifying linguistic or cultural substratum. Before the colonial era diversities were greater than in most of West Europe. "Disparate colonial

---

[2] Michael Brecher, "International Relations and Asian Studies: The Subordinate State System of Southern Asia," *World Politics*, Vol. XV, No. 2, Jan. 1963, pp. 213–236.

[3] Guy Pauker, "Southeast Asia as a Problem Area in the Next Decade," *World Politics*, Vol. XI (April, 1959). Also George Modelski, "International Relations and Area Studies: The Core of Southern Asia," *International Relations*, II (April, 1961).

[4] For a discussion, see L. Dehio, *The Precarious Balance* (New York: Knopf, 1962).

[5] R. R. Palmer, *The Age of the Democratic Revolution* (Princeton: Princeton University Press, 1964).

experiences heightened intraregional differences by imposing a multiplicity of trading and cultural foci."[6] While the idea and institutions of democratic legitimacy through competitive popular elections are presently viable in only a few places and single-party or no-party, militarily based authoritarian regimes tend to be typical, there are substantial differences between the authoritarian, mobilizationist regimes in Russia and China and the electoral practices of Ceylon, Japan, South Korea and India. Moreover, despite the early rhetoric about Asian solidarity immediately following the achievement of independence from European imperial rule, this common colonial experience has not counted for much in post-independence policy. It has, however, left an anti-western residue which affects their foreign policy approach to western countries. Revival of cultural traditions take contemporary leaders back to very diverse backgrounds—Hindus and Muslims found collective life impossible together; Hinayana Buddhism in Ceylon and Burma shows little in common with Japan's Mahayana Buddhism. Russia's Slavic cultural origins provide little fellow feeling or sense of mutuality to Russian relations with China, or vice versa, as a short-lived collaboration demonstrated. No cosmopolitan elite provides upper-level social and blood relationships among Asia's leaders to soften interstate rivalries and deepen mutual understanding as occurred periodically in western European history.

In the European state system, the principal actors tended to be roughly comparable—in size, and in military and governmental capability. Not so in Asia. China, by far the largest, after a century and a half of decline, has only recently succeeded in unifying the realm and in bringing some degree of consistent authority and managerial capability to the people of China. Japan's technological skills and energies far surpass all the other Asian states. Russia's forced draft industrialization and China's dramatic industrializing efforts far exceed anything the other major mainland countries have been able to achieve. Mountain geography, Hindu culture and a recent British imperial past combined to insulate the Indian sub-continent from other areas of Asia.

Given the size of Asian populations, it is not surprising that Russia, China and India should have three of the world's four largest armies. Russia's is by far the most technically advanced on the mainland, and its thermonuclear warhead and delivery capability is now roughly comparable to that of the United States. Its capability for action in Asia, however, is of course limited by European security problems.

[6] Margaret Roff, "Disintegrative and Integrative Tendencies in Southeast Asia" (unpublished paper).

China has a fledgling nuclear weapon capability, and a large conventional army. India's army, the smallest of the three at 1 million men, is perhaps more mechanized than the Chinese, but lacks the back up of even China's level of nuclear capability as yet. Although India has a developed nuclear technology and could produce a nuclear explosion within six to eight months of deciding to do so, it appears, for the present, unwilling to take the step before it has developed a substantial delivery capability—a matter of perhaps five to eight years without direct external assistance.

From these preliminary observations we conclude that the Asian state system is marked by its diversity and notable contrasts in size and capability, its loose articulation and dispersed character. Nevertheless, it is appropriate to call it a regional state system within the larger world state system.[7] Relationships within Asia are becoming more intimate and continuous than at any time in history. These may be essentially cooperative—as between Russia and India, for example, or Japan and the United States. They may also be conflictual, as between Moscow and Peking or New Delhi and Islamabad. In either type of relationship, statesmen are more attentive to each other's assessments and moves than they are to those other powers not in the system.

From 1945 to the early 1960's, most decisions and actions of the major Asian statesmen were responses to the cold war conflict between Washington and Moscow. Since then the Asian sub-system has become more autonomous, generating its own dynamic pattern of relationships independent of the Moscow-Washington conflict. Indeed, the latter relationship has itself been profoundly affected by developments arising within the Asian state system itself, as the Moscow-Peking conflict has eased Moscow's and Peking's approach to the US, for instance. Moreover, as the two major nuclear powers—the US and the Soviet Union—have been demonstrating how the delicate balance of terror restricts both, local, national, conventional and unconventional capabilities of smaller powers are gaining in importance. Neither of the two superpowers is able to assure its preponderance over others in the Asian system as was taken for granted until the late 1950's. Rather, changing relationships between any pair of the major states affect the calculations and policies of the others.

---

[7] Technically, it should perhaps be called a "sub-system," but the vocabulary is so cumbersome that we prefer to leave it tacitly understood that the Asian states do form a "sub-system" of the world state system.

Toward a Quadrilateral Balance

A MODERATE FOUR-PARTY MODEL

Instead of the harsh, predictable and rigid lines of the bi-polar confrontation, so familiar in the 1950's and up to the mid-60's, the 1970's are likely to be marked by more flexible, resilient, and to some extent versatile, relationships among the four major powers. Each of the four will act more independently of the others than in the past, and yet each will be more sensitive to the probable reactions of the others. It could well be an era of greater maneuver as well as of substantial caution.[8]

Russia is likely to make more of an effort to develop better relations with Japan, easing Tokyo toward greater independence of the United States. In order to improve its position vis-à-vis Russia, China is likely to open itself to more flexible relations with the United States. The US, in turn, is likely to be more open to varied relationships with both Russia and China, and to accept the fact that Japan will also be able to—and will want to—demonstrate greater independence of its American link.

In the Asian quadrilateral balance, one can expect more normal diplomatic relations, closer cultural exchanges, a style of mutual dealings typical of more relaxed periods of diplomacy. To be sure, moments of tension and hostility will not be excluded, followed by prompt readjustments in position. Trade exchanges are likely to increase amongst the four; there will be less passionately hostile rhetoric.

It is even possible that in this closely interactive quadrilateral relationship, each state will be more alert and attentive to the others' vital interests than in the past. And each may set stricter limits on its own ambitions than before. A quadrilateral system is conducive to such moderation. Each participant will want to ensure that it does not take steps which would be likely to precipitate closer intimacy among any two of the others directed against itself. Each is likely to be sufficiently attentive to the needs of the others to ensure that such a combination does not develop. For example, an unduly demanding Soviet policy toward China or undue adventurism in the Third World might induce the US and China to draw closer together at Soviet expense. Insistent Soviet questioning of Americans on this score prior to the modest thaw in Sino-American relations suggests it was considered in Moscow, at least, to be a real enough possibility.

[8] For the most sophisticated discussion of this possibility, see A. Doak Barnett, "The New Multipolar Balance in East Asia: Implications for United States Policy," *The Annals*, Vol. 390, July 1970, pp. 73–87.

Chinese aggressiveness in Southeast Asia or in Korea could induce closer Soviet-American and Japanese relationships, and might even precipitate Japan into developing nuclear weapons and rapidly expanding its military capability. Renewed military action on the Sino-Indian border might be expected to draw concerted American and Soviet support to hard pressed South Asian countries. Domestic opposition within the US will inhibit renewed American involvement on the Asian mainland. But the new Asian balance would make American involvement even more unlikely. For instance, undue American pressure on either the Soviet Union or China might induce both of them, under new leadership, to draw more closely together in some sort of diumvirate, dividing responsibilities between them for actively promoting each other's state-to-state or revolutionary interests at the expense of America's friends elsewhere.

The developing system will have much greater flexibility and will constrain all participants although it will not be immeasurably flexible. Japan or the US are unlikely to throw over entirely the interests supported by their close relationship. The economic and security links with America are too important for Tokyo, and Japan's association is too important for the US in security terms. The Sino-Soviet "bloc" is unlikely to be reconstituted—suspicions run too deep and manifest interests are too incompatible for that. And neither Moscow, Peking nor Washington are likely to develop genuine intimacy, unless either of the other two embarks on a truly hegemonic venture.

The quadrilateral balance is also likely to affect each one's approach to local conflicts. With the decline in bi-polar cold war confrontations, the outcome of any local conflict is likely to be seen as less consequential than before to any of the major powers. Each autonomous major power is likely to see things from a slightly different, less predictable viewpoint. Hence, smaller countries will be less likely than before to be able to count on the unquestioning support of a cold war sponsor; and there will be less of a tendency toward adventurism. Moreover, since there is greater unpredictability and flexibility about how the other major powers would react, each major power is likely to be more cautious in the advice it gives to its protégés and will be more cautious in intervening if a conflict does get started.

TOWARD QUADRILATERAL IMBALANCES OF POWER

However, other models than the quadrilateral balance are also conceivable.

1. A Moscow advance: For example, despite Moscow's sense of threat from China and its weakness from its unsolved problems in

East Europe, Moscow may see the American withdrawal from Asia as an opportunity to push forward at both Washington's and Peking's expense. Increasing naval energies may reflect a delayed response to American versatility developed in the 1960's. It also suggests a wider Soviet ambition for the 1970's. Should China experience a new time of troubles, perhaps associated with a succession crisis, or should American interests be turned inward because of domestic outcries, or should Japan's military effort remain limited and not strategically active, hard-liners in Moscow might seize such a moment for major Soviet advances. A series of coordinated coups in the Arab Sheikdoms, interventionist diplomacy in Iran, bold measures in western Pakistan or in India might alter the Asian balance substantially.[9]

2. **Chinese possibilities:** Similarly, successor Chinese leaders, frustrated at their status in the world state system, might attempt to utilize numerous vulnerabilities in Southeast Asia to exclude foreign interests and consolidate a Chinese realm. This would be achieved, of course, before Japan emerged as a full-fledged military state, and while the US was dealing with its domestic problems and the Soviets were themselves beset with a possible succession crisis or dramatic difficulties in their eastern European frontier.

3. **Japanese capabilities:** Alternatively, within the next decade, unexpected political changes within Japan could bring to the fore leaders bent on overcoming their present semi-subordinate position. Japan could regain its foreign policy boldness, particularly in Southeast Asia which is already experiencing rapidly increasing Japanese economic activity and consequent growing political influence.

If any of these developments should occur, the Asian state system could suffer intense stress and even devastating direct hostilities. But the chances that these internal developments will accumulate into foreign policy crises seem more remote than the more moderate quadrilateral balance suggested.

There is, of course, no guarantee that each of the major powers will see its interests served by moderation, permitting limited interests of all to be pursued at minimum cost to each. Indeed, as implied above, certain vulnerabilities on the periphery of the Asian state system may provide just such disastrous temptations as the Balkans and East Europe provided European statesmen in 1914 and 1939. The South Asian and Southeast Asian sub-systems therefore deserve consideration.

[9] For an evocation of this view, see Hanson W. Baldwin, *Strategy for Tomorrow* (New York: Harper & Row, 1970), Ch. 8.

South Asia—The Sub-Regional Politics of Hegemony

THE SPECIAL ROLE OF INDIA

The South Asian sub-system turns around India. India's incomparable relative size and longstanding religio-political tensions are peculiarly the mark of South Asia. To the smaller states of South Asia—Pakistan, Ceylon and Nepal—India's 530 million people and its growing military self-sufficiency are important considerations.

Despite the reiterated statements of peaceful intentions of India's leaders, Pakistanis have remained both anxious and unreconciled. Pakistan's vulnerability cannot be overcome, for its 55 millions in West Pakistan are divided by over 1,000 miles of Indian territory from the more numerous, politically articulate and administratively less influential 75 million East Pakistani Bengalis. Although under President Ayub Khan Pakistan had a surface integrity and capacity for decision and action, underlying political tensions between East and West Pakistan, ethnic divisions within West Pakistan and lack of consensus on constitutional matters more than offset the energy and organizing capacity of the West Pakistani bureaucracy. Though at one time better equipped than India, Pakistan's army is one-fourth the size of India's and is completely dependent upon imported equipment and material.

Tiny Ceylon with 12 million people, is experiencing growing internal difficulties as a rapidly expanding educational system contributes to rising expectations, competitive politics project inflated promises at each election and a stagnating export economy faces deteriorating terms of trade.[10] Devoting less than 1 percent of GNP to defense, Ceylon is hardly an independent factor in the South Asian state system. Yet it has been used in the past by more powerful outsiders, and its present or future political vulnerabilities could provide temptation to major Asian powers bent on exerting leverage in South Asia.

To the north, lying between massive India and China, Nepal finds its geographical configuration and economic and cultural links southward toward India; but it also seeks to ensure its independence. Whenever they have been able, Nepal's leaders have sought a policy of non-alignment between its giant neighbors, hoping that relations with one will be sufficiently intimate to discourage encroachment by the other, without at the same time involving the preponderance of either. More recently, it has opened relationships with many countries

[10] Donald R. Snodgrass, *Ceylon. An Export Economy in Transition* (Homerwood, Ill., 1966). Calvin Woodward, *The Growth of a Party System in Ceylon* (Providence: Brown, 1969).

on the apparent theory that small countries are most protected when they are most noticed, and that by broadening its diplomatic representation and accepting foreign assistance from numerous donors, its condition as an independent state can be best assured.[11]

But it is India which preponderates over the South Asian state system. Committed from the outset to non-alignment in the global system, India's leaders could never bring themselves to accept close working relationships with any of the western powers. On the contrary, India feared American's preponderating power more than any other during the Dulles period. American assistance to Pakistan seemed designed to force India to spend scarce resources on military preparations which were eventually required, not against Pakistan, but in 1962 against China. Sustained American economic development and food grain assistance to India and some security assistance following the Sino-Indian border conflict in 1962 were as far as either the US or India were prepared to go with each other.

From the time of the first Indo-Pakistan conflict over Kashmir in 1948-49, Pakistan has appeared to India as a major security threat. In the late 1950's the Sino-Indian border dispute added China as a second threat. The fact that Pakistan concluded a border agreement with China at the time of the 1962 Sino-Indian conflict and that China threatened action against India in 1965 during the second war between India and Pakistan, only confirmed in New Delhi the double, and possibly concerted, threat from both Pakistan and China. Pakistan threatens not so much because it is strong as because it has been irredentist, never having reconciled itself to Indian control of the Muslim-majority state of Kashmir. China was perceived as threatening because of its growing nuclear and conventional military capability, its commanding position on the upper slopes of the Himalayas, and its humiliating success in 1962.

Both countries represent conventional military capability Indians believe they must prepare against, and China, as we have seen, has a nuclear capability that threatens India. Both Pakistan and China can also play on the ethnic and religious vulnerabilities of India—Pakistan on the restless Muslims, particularly in Kashmir, and China on the hill peoples in the Assam and other hill areas of northeast India and, possibly, on peasant radicalism in stagnating rural Bengal. Political disorder and, the breakaway of East Pakistan from West Pakistan are believed likely to provide further opportunities for inconspicuous Chinese intervention in Bengali politics. These latter

[11] Leo E. Rose, *Nepal: Strategy for Survival* (Berkeley: University of California Press, 1971).

vulnerabilities are easily exploited by small numbers of well-trained organizers and could cause costly disorders capable of sapping New Delhi's energies without events ever coming to a test.[12]

Faced with these vulnerabilities, and unwilling to depend upon alliance-type arrangements, India has been aware that it faces a serious security gap.[13] It has sought to correct this by investing substantially in its own defense production. And it has come to depend heavily on a sustained flow of sophisticated weaponry from the Soviet Union and purchase arrangements in West Europe and to a lesser extent in the United States. The Soviet relationship has come to seem natural and expedient to the Indians as a result of the Sino-Soviet split, which Indians rightly predicted well before most western observers. As New Delhi sees it, Russia's geopolitical position and its policy of resistance to Communist China make it the most logical and reliable source of countervailing pressure to contain Chinese ambitions against India. The close-in-arms support role for Moscow allows it to make available equipment that is obsolescent on its western frontier at bargain prices while contributing to the military strength of a country on China's southern flank. Such a policy has the added advantage of limiting America's influence on Indian foreign policy—a step possibly of significance to long-run Soviet ambitions in South Asia.

Given the intensity of the Sino-Soviet polemic regarding India, it is fair to say that India has been a source of tension between the two.[14] An obvious Soviet interest in India's security capability suggests that for Moscow, India is seen as part of Moscow's anti-Chinese policy. Given India's limited military technology and its economic cramp, it seems unlikely that India can soon play a significant, independent role in the Asian state system of the major powers. But any Asian state interested in an active policy in South Asia cannot ignore India. And since foreign policy weighs political futures as well as present capabilities, India is unlikely to be discounted for the latter part of the 1970's.

CHINA, RUSSIA AND SOUTH ASIA

Moscow or Peking's foreign policy toward South Asia will affect their relations with each other. Should Soviet ambitions include gain-

---

[12] For a detailed discussion of India's security situation, see Heginbotham and Wriggins, eds., *India's Search for Security*, based on ACDA study, *op. cit.*

[13] See Wayne Wilcox, "Indian Security Environments, 1971–1975: China and Pakistan," ACDA, *op. cit.*, Vol. III, Ch. III.

[14] Bhabani Sen Gupta, *The Fulcrum of Asia* (New York: Pegasus, 1970), pp. 36–40.

ing major leverage over India as a way of consolidating Russia's position in the Indian Ocean area or to weaken America's global posture generally, this could contribute to Sino-Soviet rivalry. Similarly, should China pursue serious subversive opportunities in either Bengal or among the hill peoples of northeastern India, the Russians and Indians would be likely to consider this an undue penetration of Chinese influence.

Seen from this perspective, developments in India can have an effect upon relations among members of the Asian state system in another way. India's capacity for governance provides a considerable area of order on the periphery of China and Soviet Russia. A marked disintegration of governing capacity in India could lead to political disintegration. It is impossible to predict precisely what the outcome of such a disintegration would be, but it is safe to say that the level of inter-group and inter-regional violence would rise sharply. It is plausible to expect that both the Soviet Union and China would not ignore opportunities to improve their own position in South Asia. For instance, the Soviets might like to improve their naval power, by consolidating influence in the area of West Pakistan and western and southern India. Or, the Chinese might be tempted to consolidate their strength in the Bengals as a *point d'appui* on the Indian Ocean.

Abrupt political change in Pakistan also changed India's security position, and therefore its relationship with both Moscow and Peking. In the aftermath of Pakistan's failure to reestablish its authority in East Pakistan, new problems emerged. The guerrilla conflict encouraged activities of radical and clandestine organizations on both the Left and Right, and left large numbers equipped with weapons for the first time. The direct involvement of Indian forces speeded the end of the guerrilla conflict and accelerated independence, but deeply involved New Delhi in Bangla Desh's internal politics, willy nilly. West Bengal's antiDelhi and antiCongress extremists made the most of new opportunities and India's security problems, though eased in the west by the weakening of Pakistan, remained aggravated by uncertainties in the east. Commercial relationships between India and East Bengal improved while Pakistan in the west sought closer reassurances in the direction of China, Washington and Iran.

Contrariwise, conditions in South Asia could be materially affected by changes in Asian powers' approach to one another. If there were a close rapprochement between Moscow and Peking, for example, India would become immediately vulnerable. If Sino-Indian relations continued to be hostile, presumably Moscow's military assistance to India would quickly decline. If Moscow had decided to advance its influence in West Pakistan and in India and China its influence in

East Pakistan, Burma and eastward, India's government would find itself without close-in support, and would have to seek assistance from the US, Japan, or West Europe.

Alternatively, of course, India and China might reach border agreements, like China has reached with all its other southern neighbors. Friendly diplomatic commercial and cultural relations might be resumed between China and India, with a joint withdrawal of forces from the disputed frontier and other measures taken to allay mutual suspicions. Under such circumstances, India would reduce its dependence upon Soviet military arrangements and might even be likely to seek to ease relationships with Pakistan as well.

If there were a general détente among the major Asian powers, perhaps because all agreed to turn more resources to development and welfare, and they were intent upon allaying anxieties among their neighbors to the south, India would be freed of short-run anxieties about China. This might encourage India to pursue détente with Pakistan. Or, if xenophobic or religious fundamentalist leadership had meanwhile gained control in India, New Delhi might decide that now was the time to resolve the Pakistan problem once and for all.

Accordingly, there is a two-way interaction between the quadrilateral relationships among major Asian powers and internal relationships within South Asia. Major Asian powers do not control what occurs in the South Asian sub-system. However, their mutual relationships are affected by the opportunities, and the risks relationships between the South Asian states offer to the major powers. It can also be said that the way the major powers in the Asian state system relate to each other will affect the relationships among the South Asian states themselves. An exploration of the Southeast Asian sub-system will demonstrate similar considerations.

Southeast Asia: Comparative Diplomacies of Strategic Dependency

A DEPENDENT SYSTEM WITH SOME SHARED CHARACTERISTICS

Even more than South Asia, Southeast Asia has been the object of activities of outside powers; it has rarely been an independent actor affecting the fate of other state systems. For all the remarkable activities of Southeast Asia's successive empires, immortalized, for example, at Angkor or Borobudur, no one realm encompassed the total territory; no one projected power beyond the present confines of Southeast Asia.[15] Situated astride the great fault line separating Indic and Sinic Asia, recipient of additional influences of Islamic origin, Southeast Asians have had to learn the art of accommodating to innumerable external influences. This is not to say that the peoples of the area have not had a creative and unique cultural, artistic, religious and political life of their own. On the contrary, the richness and variety in the tapestry of their life and institutions can be matched perhaps only in China, India and in West Europe. But it is to remind the reader that no Southeast Asian Guptas pressed commerce, cultural and religious inspiration into neighboring India or China; no local Mings or Manchus acquired anything analogous to tributary rights beyond the area itself. During the nineteenth century, only Thailand retained its autonomy; all the rest came under the direct control, however diverse, of the European empires or in the case of the Philippines, the United States.

Despite many notable contrasts between them, however, it is possible to make some general observations about the Southeast Asian states.

1. **Frontiers** in Southeast Asia have had a different significance than in the western state system generally. In Southeast Asia historically, frontiers have been seen largely as zones where people intermingle, not as lines on the map defining juridically where one state's authority ends and another's begins. Rather, the limits of sovereignty have been defined in pragmatic, operational terms as that zone in which one regime's effective control gradually disappears and another's authority becomes manifest. Peoples have flowed across these zones virtually without hindrance except for nature's impediments.[16] The authority of states has been centered in their primate cities and the capacity to govern diminishes rapidly toward the frontier areas.

2. **Official "penetration"**: As modern means of statecraft have improved, with greater mobility and better administrative capabilities, the men of the capitals have gradually penetrated to the outer reaches of the realm. In this process, cultural diversities between capital and province have been dramatized, and the arrival of authorities presage new exactions rather than bringing badly wanted services. This is truly Thoreau's terrain, where that ruler governs best who governs least.

[15] For one of the most interesting and wide-ranging histories of the area, see David Steinberg, William Roff, et al., *In Search of Southeast Asia* (New York: Praeger, 1971).

[16] For a discussion, see Robert Solomon, "Boundary Concepts and Practises in Southeast Asia," *World Politics*, Oct. 1970, Vol. XXIII, No. 1, pp. 1–23.

Each state, therefore, is not territorially defined and possessing a monopoly of legitimate violence. Rather, each is imprecise in authority and highly permeable to the movement of uncommitted peoples.

3. Typically, there is a limited *capacity for governance*. Apart from Thailand, the state structures are new, and apart from Malaysia, bureaucracies are overstaffed and not notably competent. And most states lack integration.[17] Class differences are marked, as small, usually cosmopolitan elites man the decisive levels of government, business and the army, while an uneducated majority only periodically turns attention to issues beyond the monsoon or planting cycle. Domestic political institutions lack legitimacy, being either inherited from the colonial period, or inventions of charismatic civilian leaders or self-appointed military men.

4. **Many Minorities:** The permeability of frontiers, the looseness of governance and the inheritance from pre-colonial and colonial commercial practices have encouraged over the past several hundred years the rise of important minority communities. They sometimes play crucial roles in commerce, like the ethnically Chinese to be found in the centers of business, shopkeeping and money-lending roles throughout the area. Minorities feel vulnerable to periodic xenophobic passions turned against them, compounding their traditional tendency to trust only their own kind. Sometimes—and understandably—they seek the support of their land of origin.[18] Periodic communal outbursts against these minorities bring particularly acute instabilities to most polities, as was demonstrated in the communal slaughter in Indonesia in 1965 during Sukarno's decline and riots in Malaysia in 1969, following an electoral setback for the Malay party and growing impatience on the part of the ethnic Chinese minority.

5. **Parallel Economic Problems:** Economically all the states are beset by the limitations of exporting primary products and most are dependent on only one or two commodities for their foreign exchange earnings. Malaysian organizational skills have demonstrated how systematic improvement can prolong comparative advantage from natural rubber; Indonesia has promising varieties of primary products, including substantial minerals and petroleum deposits. Thailand has

---

[17] For a discussion, see H. Wriggins, "National Integration," in M. Weiner, *Modernization: The Dynamics of Growth* (V O A Forum, 1966).

[18] This is close to the "mosaic" society depicted in the Middle East by Carleton Coon in his *Caravan*. On the unique adaptive capacity of Thailand, see G. W. Skinner's *Leadership and Power in the Chinese Community of Thailand* (Ithaca: Cornell University Press, 1958) also R. Tilman's forthcoming study on *Ethnicity and Politics: The Changing Political World of Philippine-Chinese Youth* (New York: Columbia University Press, 1972).

shown ingenuity in switching from rice to corn for export in response to Japanese market demand, and is encouraging foreign capital to promote industrial growth. Nevertheless, all but Indonesia depend on a narrow export range.

For the producers of primary products, market prospects are not bright. The world economy is depending proportionately less on tropical products characteristic of the area. States such as Indonesia, with petroleum and minerals, have a brighter long-run future than the others. But for all, diversification is an important goal, and only through industrialization can high-return diversification be achieved. Yet only the city-state of Singapore and possibly Thailand show promise of rapid industrial development, and in the former, at least, there is a desperate race to keep ahead of a burgeoning population. Special difficulties arise for regimes interested in promoting economic growth when they attempt to take over the economic functions of the minority community entrepreneurs.[19]

Yet economic life also provides a number of nongovernmental processes and interests looking toward mutual accommodation and assistance. The Chinese commercial community, often working across national frontiers and frequently at cross purposes with specific policies of specific governments, provides a remarkably resilient framework for commercial and informational exchanges. Growing numbers of multinational corporations, with interests in many countries in the area (and outside), adjust and accommodate these interests. The special agencies of the United Nations and the Asian Development Bank may provide more important processes for mutual adjustment in the future.

6. Growing Domestic Difficulties: All the states face rapidly growing populations and other sources of growing internal tensions. Although population pressures do not yet strike sharply on public or official awareness except in Singapore, Mindanao and Java, rates of growth are accelerating everywhere. Land-man ratios are still more favorable than in India, Pakistan or Ceylon. However, already Thailand and Malaysia have reached the limits beyond which traditional modes of agriculture cannot be expanded, and Java's overcrowding is legendary.

During the 1970's the states of Southeast Asia will begin to experience increased internal tensions resulting from population growth, economic cramp and rising expectations. Political activation will lead more people to demand more from their government and growing

---

[19] For an extended discussion, see F. Golay, R. Anspach, et al., *Underdevelopment and Economic Nationalism* (Ithaca: Cornell University Press, 1969).

self-awareness will contribute to more explicit invidious comparisons between ethnic and class groups. Educational opportunities are expanding rapidly, but school and university curricula are not necessarily germane to contemporary productive needs. Educated unemployed are likely to grow in numbers, with unusual skills readily available for political organization and protest politics. These instabilities are likely to tempt outside powers to intrude.

7. **Leaders' Personal Diplomacy:** Most of the rulers have substantial scope for making their own foreign policy. Few have well-established foreign policy bureaucracies prone to appeal to precedent and to traditional concepts of the "national interest." There are few well-organized interest groups attempting to affect foreign policy. Each leader has a relatively free field for personal initiatives in foreign policy. And since each is unsure of his tenure in office, he may use foreign policy as one means of attempting to sustain himself in power. It is no wonder that Southeast Asia has been marked during the past fifteen years by many instances of personal diplomacy initiated by heads of state.[20]

Yet leaders face certain external and historical constraints in their foreign policy. Numerous *traditional antagonisms* set limits to policy alternatives and add to the region's vulnerability. The Annamese of Vietnam and the Thais have had longstanding rivalry, often competing for control in the area lying between them, now Laos and Cambodia. For generations, the Cambodians have been under pressure from the Vietnamese. Only the coming of the French stabilized their ambiguous zone of authority, which is again in flux as a result of North Vietnam's organizing abilities and South Vietnam's and American efforts to disrupt Hanoi's sanctuaries in Cambodia. Relationships between Malays and Indonesians have been complex. They are of similar ethnic origin and their languages have much in common. Sukarno sought to build a Greater Indonesia, to encompass peninsular Malaya, Sarawak and North Borneo as well as the balance of Indonesia in one realm. That his country contained over 110 million people and by far the largest army in the area contributed to suspicions which it will take Sukarno's successors many years to overcome.[21]

8. **Appeals to Outsiders for Help:** Such a pattern of divided interests, governmental weakness and diverse perspectives contributes to

[20] For a parallel discussion of a similar phenomenon in Africa see R. O. Mathews, *Inter-State Conflict in Africa* (1971), unpublished Columbia University dissertation. See also H. Wriggins, *The Ruler's Imperative* (New York: Columbia University Press, 1969), Ch. 11.

[21] For a convenient discussion, see Peter Lyon, *War and Peace in Southeast Asia* (London: Oxford, 1969).

the continued vulnerability of the area. During the past two decades most of the states have dramatized their vulnerability by calling on outside assistance to help cope with what each considered to be threats to its national independence or regime survival. Faced with the "emergency" in the 1950's, Malaysia accepted the help of Great Britain, in the process consolidating Malay political preponderance. During the 1950's and 1960's, Thailand sought—and received—substantial military assistance from Washington and provided facilities to Washington for the conflict in Vietnam. The former consolidated the position of one group of leaders and slowed the circulation of leadership hitherto effected by periodic coups d'état, while the latter was expected to weaken its ancient Annamese rivals. In Vietnam itself, one faction among several in the South called on the US and in the North, Hanoi called on both Russia and China, intensifying the conflict and making it less necessary for either contending group to come to terms with its Vietnamese opponents. Indonesia received substantial assistance from the Soviet Union, then developed close political links with China and, subsequent to the fall of Sukarno, turned to western countries and Japan for assistance. Thus, the need each regime felt for external support underlined traditional antagonisms, suggesting a persisting source of vulnerability for the future.

THE INTEREST OF OUTSIDE ASIAN POWERS

The major actors in Southeast Asia for the 1970's are likely to bring different relative weights to bear than in the 1950's and 1960's, contributing to continued uncertainties throughout Southeast Asia.

1. **American interests** in Southeast Asia are more derivative than direct, as suggested by the fact that changes in the overarching Asian state system quite as much as domestic reactions to the Vietnam war have fundamentally affected Washington's perception of its stake in Southeast Asia. To be sure, the US is committed to an orderly, though accelerating, disengagement from Vietnam and to provide some, though as yet ill-defined, forms of assistance to Thailand. Useful, though by no means critical, raw materials come from this area. Washington's close engagement in the future policy of Japan and Tokyo's strategic interest in the sea lanes through Southeast Asia and commercial interest in developing sources of raw material and markets there are considerations giving weight to Southeast Asia in American calculations. Indonesia's internal success and foreign policy approach could have a profound effect upon these interests, as well as on America's continuing concern for Australia's independent future.[22]

[22] For a more detailed and slightly different discussion see Melvin Gurtov, *op. cit.*

While Washington played a central role in the 1950's and 1960's, Southeast Asia will be less consequential in American foreign policy in the 1970's as already discussed. To be sure, commercial and investment activities in Indonesia, Singapore, Thailand and Malaysia have been considerable and are likely to continue. But these were not undertaken with state encouragement and are not likely to successfully lay claim to direct American official support in case of civil disorder, threatened nationalization or war.

2. **Soviet interest** by contrast, has been growing. Increased commercial links have developed around the purchases of Malaysian and Indonesian rubber and palm oil. Earlier substantial Soviet interest in Indonesia suggested more than commercial concerns in the 1950's although Chinese success in the mid-60's displaced Moscow, and Sukarno's overthrow subsequently overcame close-in Chinese influence. Soviet support for North Vietnam helped sustain Hanoi against American military pressure and prevented China from gaining preponderating influence in Hanoi. Soviet interest in containing possible Chinese ambitions in Southeast Asia is also suggested by a collective security proposal for Asia initiated by Moscow in 1969, which never received official elaboration. It was not enthusiastically taken up by leaders in either South or Southeast Asia, but it could be a card in a future Soviet diplomatic hand.

Restrained Soviet activities in the area, including periodic naval visits, would not necessarily run counter to the interests of local states or of the United States. With the decline of British capability and a lessened US involvement, statesmen in the area may well see a modest Soviet presence as providing another counterweight to the two potentially much more influential outside states—Japan and China. After all, Russia is far away along distant and exposed sea lanes and is not likely to concert with China or Japan at the expense of local state interests.

3. **China's intentions** remain obscure while its future role is bound to be more consequential. China looms large in the minds of the leaders of small states in Southeast Asia, and in Indonesia its intimacy with Sukarno before his demise is not forgotten. The notable contrast between revolutionary and interventionist rhetoric and cautious policy in practice only renders projections more unsure. *Four future alternatives* for Chinese policy in South and Southeast Asia are conceivable:

a. China can focus primarily on its huge and intractable internal problems, ignoring its small neighbors to the south so long as they do not allow themselves to become *points d'appui* for external powers hostile to China.

b. China can develop normal diplomatic relations with its southern neighbors, eschewing involvement in their internal affairs and seeking no special relationships with the governments or ethnic Chinese minorities, but nevertheless carrying on commercial, cultural and other working relationships with them as it does with most other governments in the world most of the time.

c. It could revert to traditional special relationships with states of Southeast Asia, seeking from them displays of fealty before their protector in Peking, ensuring that their foreign policies were aligned with and friendly toward China in all things while leaving their domestic affairs to themselves.

d. An intensified version of this latter approach would be a Chinese Communist system of neighboring satellites, where the form, personnel and policy of neighboring governments would be designed and manipulated in considerable detail from Peking.

The first two approaches would be quite compatible with the interests of the other major Asian powers. A limited low-key involvement by the others would make such a possibility credible to Peking on the assumption that reasonable over-all relationships with the US and the Soviet Union could be effected elsewhere, and both states were unambiguously committed to a low-key involvement in the area.

But given the vulnerabilities and internal weaknesses of the Southeast Asian states, there is a possibility that as Chinese capabilities improve over the next decade, Peking would be increasingly tempted to move toward the third or fourth type of relationship. A question for the other Asian powers in the late 1970's may well be this: how to discourage China from seeking type three or four control in Southeast Asia without at the same time so evoking Chinese anxieties as to precipitate it into seeking just such control as a measure of urgent defense?

4. Political Implications of Japan's Growing Economic Role: Within the decade, Japan will be substantially less dependent upon the US for security than it is today and its economic activity abroad will be greater. Even if it does not increase the proportion of economic resources presently going into defense above the present .9 percent of GNP, it will have a very impressive defense establishment. Already it is seventh in the world in the rate of defense spending, and it will be more impressive by the end of the decade.[23] In Southeast Asia its interest will be very substantial and different from those of the other three major Asian powers.

Japan is rapidly becoming the workshop of the area, importing raw materials to keep her own factories going and exporting capital and

---

[23] See James Morley, "Fiscal Restraints on Japan's Defense Policy," *ACDA, op. cit.*, Vol. IV, Ch. 1.

technical know-how. Increasingly, small-scale industries are being set up in southern Asia for preliminary processing of raw materials or even the manufacture of labor-intensive components for more sophisticated Japanese electronics and other gear. This developing network of economic links with Japan is far outstripping western, Soviet or Chinese activities. In this lies both great opportunities for economic development and perceived dangers for Southeast Asians, paralleling earlier fears from undue American investment.

As Japanese businessmen and their large agglomerations come to play an increasingly important role in local economies, these anxieties are growing. More and more it is feared that decisions consequential to local economies will be made in the board rooms of large Japanese combines, without regard for the economic consequences to the small, dependent economies. As Japanese investments grow, the time may come when political changes within Japan may bring to power men more determined than her present rulers to assert Japanese political preponderance, perhaps on the excuse of having to defend Japan's investments overseas.

To be sure, Japan's economic interests are now worldwide; they go far beyond Southeast Asia. Indeed, it seems probable that by the end of the 1970's, economic interests in Latin America will be more important to Tokyo than Southeast Asia. Nevertheless, Japanese economic activities in Southeast Asia will run into less opposition from third parties than elsewhere. And Japanese economic power is likely to loom larger to the people of the area than in most other areas, with the exception of Korea, Taiwan and the Philippines.

5. Conclusion Regarding the Interests of Outside Powers: If this analysis has validity, the defensive interests of all four major powers in Southeast Asia can be served if no one seeks preponderating influence. If all adopt a policy of mutual self-restraint, permitting access for commercial, intellectual and diplomatic relations for all, with none of the powers utilizing the states in the area to mount a possible threat to vital interests of the others, each one's most important interests can be served. Moreover, within such a framework of major power restraint, the most important interests of the indigenous countries can also be pursued.

To be sure, there is no guarantee that any of the outside powers will be thus restrained. The vulnerabilities of Southeast Asian states —the lack of national political integrity, the presence of substantial and often disadvantaged ethnic minorities, the historical tendency of each state, and of factions within each state, to seek outside assistance—could draw the major states of the Asian state system into mutual conflict over Southeast Asia.

Moreover, there is no guarantee that either of the proximate major Asian powers—China or Japan—will not during the next decade see major interests served by undertaking more direct action there. Ambition could lead them to aspire to greater control; or fear could lead them to seek to preempt suspected ambitions of any one of the other four major outside states.

A NEW REGIONALISM?—RECONCILIATION NOT INTEGRATION

Until the mid-1960's, the Southeast Asian states appeared to ignore the cost to each of allowing their traditional rivalries and desires for direct external assistance to override their shared interests in limiting the role of outsiders in their affairs. As each depended upon a single outside protector, they too often found themselves drawn into conflicts not of their own making.

Divisive Elements: There is little in their economic circumstances to draw them together. A detailed analysis of the direction of trade shows that with the exception of Thailand's exports, of which rice is a large component still, and the entrepôt Singapore, no country in the area sold more than 25 percent of its export values to all the countries of the region put together, and no country imported more than 17 percent from other economies in the region. For major trading countries like Indonesia and the Philippines, by 1968 Japan provided a larger recorded market than all Southeast Asian countries combined. And for all the countries of Southeast Asia, Japan has become the largest single source of imports, larger, indeed, than all the other Southeast Asian countries put together. Moreover, a commodity by commodity analysis suggests that export products are mutually competitive. Indonesia's and Malaysia's tin, vegetable oils and rubber compete in the world market; Thailand and Burma both export rice.

Well-planned industrialization, it is sometimes argued, could lead to closer economic relationships. It would free these Asian states from undue dependence on those tropical products which lead to competition for world markets. They could begin to produce locally those goods that would substitute for goods imported from the four corners of the earth—or more accurately, mainly from Japan and Hong Kong. To be sure, apart from North Vietnam, Burma and Sukarno's Indonesia, countries of the area have not sought to develop independently self-sufficient, inward-looking economies. On the contrary, most have been remarkably outward-looking, seeking the cheapest imports and exporting a major proportion of their total production to the best market. Nevertheless, should they alter their design and begin to work toward planned regional industrialization, they might gain closer regional economic integration. But these would be high-cost arrangements. And agreed investment for the region would inescapably imply that some statesmen would consciously choose to become more dependent on neighbors than is already the case. Who can predict that relationships with any one regional neighbor are sufficiently reliable to lead prudent men to seek such dependence in the name of economic integration? In sum, one cannot expect the working of economic forces to draw the states of the region together.

The structure of the Southeast Asia sub-system itself contributes difficulties. The contrast between the political (international and domestic) circumstances of the mainland states and the off-shore, island states is a divisive element. The dynamic, well-organized and determined North Vietnamese are seen by many in Southeast Asia as threatening the independence of Laos and Cambodia, as well as of South Vietnam. American withdrawal is widely expected to encourage Hanoi to push its position in all three areas. Indonesia's massive size though less overwhelming in Southeast Asia than is India in South Asia, nevertheless has in the past contributed to intensifying regional differences.[24]

Efforts at Reconciliation: On the other hand, post-Sukarno leadership has made a serious effort to allay the fears of Indonesia's smaller neighbors. Local statesmen have a good deal of initiative in foreign policy matters; personal relations amongst them can be important. On the whole, they do not have to negotiate and bargain with an array of well-entrenched, politically organized popular interest groups prior to making decisions on regional affairs.[25] It is quite conceivable, therefore, that should these leaders come to see their own interests well-served by reconciling their policies, historic antagonisms could be played down, minority problems held within bounds and competitive economic interests not allowed to impinge upon concerted foreign policies. If they were able to reach a closer harmonization of their own foreign policies, they could better insure themselves against undue influence from the larger world state system.

Increased Consultation: As we have seen, during the past decade, there has been a notable increase in consultation and interchange between these governments (with the exception of Burma and North Vietnam). Earlier, each elite tended to look toward the metropole of its former colonial rulers. Now, they look to one another more fre-

[24] S. Heginbotham, "Indian Perceptions of Japan and Southeast Asia" (ACDA/IR-70), Vol. III, Chapter 5.

[25] On this problem see Ernest Haas, "The Challenge of Regionalism," in S. Hoffman, ed., *Contemporary Theory in International Relations* (Englewood Cliffs, N.J.: Prentice-Hall, 1961), p. 236.

quently. It may be that a proportion of these consultations have been motivated by leaders who are concerned with their domestic political strength or their regional position, and who hope to be host or sponsor to the next consultation. Nevertheless, it appears that they are increasingly coming to realize that they can—and indeed must—assume greater responsibility for coping with their own domestic and foreign policy problems, and to broaden their international relationships rather than depend upon only one outside power for support.

Thailand has begun to reach beyond the American relationship to closer consultations with Indonesia, Malaysia, the Philippines and Singapore, as well as to broader relationships with China. Post-Sukarno Indonesia has been working more closely with its immediate neighbors on commercial and security issues. The controversy between Indonesia and the Philippines over North Borneo demonstrated how fragile have been the steps toward collaboration. There may be immediate domestic political advantage in trumpeting differences with neighbors. But this quarrel also dramatized the view that allowing such differences to gain momentum can only work to the national disadvantage of everyone.

More than ever before, local leaders seek to institutionalize mutual consultations and orderly examination of differences in order to reconcile their foreign policies. They now seek ways to obtain resources through multilateral institutions so as to minimize the direct involvement of any one of the major Asian powers in bilateral development assistance.

Numerous meetings of specialists on investment, finance, marketing, tariff and other economic measures under the auspices of ECAFE have given to responsible men in every Southeast Asian country a deeper knowledge of their neighbors' problems than at any time before. The Association of Southeast Asian Nations (ASEAN) has brought together leaders of Thailand, Malaysia, Singapore, Indonesia and the Philippines for regular consultations on common political and development problems. A tin agreement, reached under the auspices of ASEAN, is favorably influencing tin marketing. The Asian and Pacific Council (ASPAC) included Japan and South Korea in East Asia and Australia and New Zealand as well as most Southeast Asian countries. More concerned with security questions than ASEAN and in a wider area, it brings Ministers together for annual confabulations. The Mekong River Development Project focuses consultations on future collaborative development.

In May 1970, at the time of the Cambodian invasion, eleven nations of the region met in Djakarta to seek a joint area-wide reaction to the spread of the Vietnam war. Little direct result came of it, but the initiative represented a notable break with the past, as states in the area sought to concert a common policy toward a major development within the area. The Asian Development Bank (ADB), initiated largely by the Japanese with Washington's encouragement and located in Manila, seeks to channel development assistance from numerous outside contributors to insulate recipients from undue direct influence by any single donor country. And by concerting with others, proponents of the ADB hope to lever more resources from donors than they might be willing to contribute separately.

This discussion suggests that regionalism in Southeast Asia will not move in the direction of "integration." Rather, the more modest and realistic objective can be to develop the habit and practice of consultation, leading toward policy reconciliation. Such regular practice would reduce local divisions and help to insulate any one country in the region from undue dependence on any one large outside country by contributing to an increasingly complex network of multinational organizations, cross-cutting associational links and the process of mutual adjustment.

Consensus Among Major Powers on Agreed Self-Limitation

But if Southeast Asia is not to become an arena for competition between the four major Asian powers in the future, as it has been in the past, it will not be enough for the states in the region to make more efforts to concert and reconcile their policies. Each one's vulnerability and traditional rivalries are too deep for these modest steps at regionalism to prevail should local leaders seek help and outside major powers respond with substantial direct support. The external major powers must themselves reach some understanding on the terms of their relationship to states in the region and the scope they will permit themselves and accept for one another's activities.

For the 1970's the major Asian powers might well search for a consensus on their dealings with Southeast Asia. An overinvolvement by any one is likely to accelerate the counterinvolvement of the others. This should inhibit all from seeking exclusive relationships with any one local capital. The major powers might agree not to become involved in intraregional conflicts; foreign bases would be gradually— and surely—withdrawn. Insofar as each of the major powers refrained from seeking exclusive relationships with any one local regime or from forwarding its own exclusive interests by meddling in internal affairs, no one outsider would attempt to use Southeast Asian countries as proxies in an effort to undermine or to contain other outside powers.

To be sure, such general principles are fraught with ambiguities—and are therefore difficult to enforce without deepening misunderstandings and risking further conflict and outside involvement. For example, the political side-effects of growing Japanese commercial activity or Soviet commercial and naval interest will be difficult to assess. Maoist doctrine is likely to lead Chinese leaders to infer direct political influence from Japanese investment and Soviet commercial relations. The possibilities for inconspicuous Chinese activity in the area will persist. Local leaders will be prone to suspect such activities whenever their own minorities of Chinese ethnic origin organize to express grievances or to seek greater political influence. The pace and scope of American withdrawal will leave many uncertainties, as local regimes hitherto dependent upon American support or confident of American backing in the event of a major external challenge, will seek new ways to reinsure their own security, intensifying anxieties of their neighbors.

Nevertheless, a combination of greater regional collaboration between the states of Southeast Asia and more explicit mutual self-limitation on the part of the major Asian powers together could avoid the injection into Southeast Asia of great power conflict. Such steps could also avoid the reciprocal effect on the relationships among the four Asian powers of periodic Southeast Asian turmoil.

To seek to encompass in one chapter the full richness of possibilities and probabilities in Asian international political life is like pursuing the chimera. We have sought here simply to identify gross patterns of probable relationships among the four major Asian powers during the 1970's, as American power in Asia diminishes, Soviet power increases in western Asia, in the Indian Ocean and in Southeast Asia, Chinese capabilities improve particularly vis-à-vis Southeast Asia, while Japanese economic strength surges forward carrying with it growing political influence and an implicit future military capacity. To see how these shifting relationships in the overarching state system are related to the highly differentiated and particular relationships between the states of South Asia and Southeast Asia may have enriched our view of what real statesmen will have to grapple with.

There is no clear direction into the future. At the time of choice, the as-yet concealed unfolding of events reveals little of their shape and course. An essay like this can sketch the outer contours of what might transpire. It is the active men and women, in and out of responsible positions, as they make specific choices, sometimes with foresight and with reason, often with only half knowledge, misconception and undue passion, who help create the foreground of affairs on which real persons must play out their parts. Events, too, based on earlier choices, may have a momentum of their own which can only be diverted or channeled by the harshest kind of political and bureaucratic effort. However these choices are made or the momentum of events are affected, these, in turn, set the course to the far horizon of the more distant future. For it is the way individuals grapple with the momentum of events which sets the actual course; a pattern of abstractions like a "state system" and its elaboration can only be suggestive of the range of conceivable and of probable choice.

Index

243, 289, 290; United Arab Republic, 243; United
States, 237, 243
 society, 231–233
 Sri Lanka Freedom party, 236, 237
 Tamils, 231, 233
 United National party, 236, 237
Chiang Kai-shek, 257, 258
China:
 Chen Yi, 17
 Chi Peng-fei, 17
 Chou En-lai, 17, 112, 160, 259, 320
 economy, 12, 18, 19, 23–25
 foreign policy, 2–31; achievements, 29–31; capabilities,
 12, 13–16, 278; decision-making, 16–18; domestic poli-
 tics, 18–23; economic interests, 23, 24, 316, 317; environmental influences, 3–7, 81, 82; ideology, 3–5, 8–11,
 317–322; internal determinants, 8–13; military aspects,
 3–6, 12, 15, 16, 81, 82, 88–92, 317–322; nationalism,
 11–13; objectives, 8–11, 321, 322; restraints, 16, 278,
 325–327, 340–342
 Han Nien-lung, 17
 liberation wars, 25–28, 88
 Lin Piao, 20, 319, 321
 Liu Shao-chi, 6, 8, 18–20, 319
 Lo Jui-ching, 319
 Mao Tse-tung, 2–4, 8, 11, 18, 19, 22, 257, 319
 peaceful co-existence, 10, 11, 88
 political system, 18–23
 relations with African states, 29; Burma, 25, 26, 228,
 239, 242, 244; Cambodia, 25, 26, 29, 200; Ceylon, 28,
 240, 243; India, 25–27, 65, 79–82, 85, 86; Indonesia,
 25, 26; Japan, 24, 25, 33, 36, 54, 55, 59, 60; Laos, 25,
 26, 29; Malaysia, 25, 26, 207–211; Nepal, 28, 238;
 North Vietnam, 26, 29, 30, 176, 177; Philippines, 25,
 26, 222, 223; Pakistan, 27, 28, 30, 106, 112, 113; Soviet
 Union, 9–11, 23, 273–275, 277–289, 292, 315–327; Thailand, 25, 26, 188–191; United States, 4–7, 248, 322–
 327, 350–352, 369–371
 Western Europe, 24
 role in Asian balance, 248–250, 315–343, 350–352, 354–
 357, 363, 364, 369–371
Colombo, 230, 238, 244

Djakarta, 120, 121

East Bengal, 64, 65, 73, 77–80, 87, 94, 95, 113
Economic Commission for Asia and the Far East (ECAFE),
300, 368

Geneva agreement on Indochina (1954), 88, 174, 188, 258
Geneva agreement on Laos (1962), 198, 199
Greater East Asian Co-Prosperity Sphere, 33, 40, 54, 56, 293

Habomai, 293
Harriman-Sandys Mission, 110
Himalayas, 63, 64, 91, 95, 227, 228
Hungary, 71

India:
    Administrative service, 67
    Civil service, 67
    Congress party, 68–73
    Communist party of India (CPI), 69, 72, 86
    Communist party of India (Marxist), 13
    DMK party, 72
    economy, 72, 74, 75
    foreign aid, 74–76, 86, 87
    foreign policy, 61–92; achievements, 88–92; decision-making, 67–73; domestic politics, 67–73; environmental influences, 61–67; military aspects, 61–67, 83–92; objectives, 73–76, 86–88; restraints, 291
    history, 61–67
    Jana Sangh party, 69
    Kashmir, 62–65, 70, 77, 78, 85, 97, 99, 114
    Kerala, 72
    Ministry of Defence, 68
    Ministry of External Affairs (MEA), 67–69
    Ministry of Finance, 68
    Ministry of Home Affairs, 68, 71
    Mizos, 92
    Muslims, 70
    Nagas, 92
    Naxalites, 92
    nuclear weapons, 89, 90
    political system, 69–73
    Prime Minister Indira Gandhi, 71–73, 81, 86, 87, 289
    Prime Minister Nehru, 67–69, 71, 84
    Prime Minister Lal Bahadur Shastri, 71, 107, 291
    relations with Burma, 76, 244; Cambodia, 76, 83; Ceylon, 76, 243, 244; China, 25–27, 65, 76, 79–83, 85, 86; Eastern Europe, 75; Indonesia, 65, 82; Japan, 36, 76, 83, 84; Laos, 83, 198; North Vietnam, 83; Pakistan, 65, 76–80, 104–109; South Vietnam, 83; Soviet Union, 69, 75, 76, 84–92, 287–292, 299; United States, 75, 84–92
    religions, 61–63
    Socialist party, 69
    society, 61–63

204; environmental influences, 210; military aspects, 209, 210; objectives, 207–209

political system, 206, 207

relations with Britain, 203, 205, 206–207; China, 25, 26, 205, 207–211; Hungary, 207; Indonesia, 137–140, 206; Poland, 207; Rumania, 207, 208; Soviet Union, 204, 207, 208, 211, 298, 299; Taiwan, 209; Yugoslavia, 207

society, 203, 204

Tun Abdul Razak, 207, 208, 211

Tunku Abdul Rahman, 205–207

Marshall, Charles Burton, 110

Mekong River Development Project, 195

Middle East, 88, 99, 100, 109, 114, 334

Moscow, 86, 92, 274, 286–299, 303

Muslim League, 93, 95, 96, 98

Nepal:

economy, 237, 238, 239

foreign aid, 238

foreign policy, 226–245; achievements, 244, 245; decision-making, 233, 234; environmental influences, 227, 288

King, 233, 234, 241, 242

military aspects, 240–242

history, 227, 228

political system, 233, 234

relations with China, 28, 238, 241, 242; India, 238–240, 241

society, 230, 232

New Delhi, 63, 67, 72, 73, 75, 76, 78, 80–83, 85–87, 90, 91, 92, 105, 112, 234, 238, 240, 288, 292

North Korea:

foreign aid, 157–161

foreign policy, 156–165; decision-making, 157; objectives, 156–165

Kim Il-sŏng, 156–164, 294

political system, 156, 157

relations with Australia, 162; Britain, 162; Ceylon, 237; China, 157–161; Greece, 162; Holland, 162; Japan, 54, 162; South Korea, 162–165; Soviet Union, 157–161, 293, 294; United States, 163; West Germany, 162

North Vietnam:

foreign policy, 174–183; decision-making, 175–178; military objectives, 176, 178–182

history, 174, 175

Ho Chi Minh, 262, 263

political system, 174–176

relations with Cambodia, 200, 201; Ceylon, 237; China, 26, 29, 30, 176, 177; India, 83; South Vietnam, 178–181; Soviet Union, 176, 177, 296, 297; United States, 178, 262–264
Vietnam Workers' party, 174
Nuclear Non-Proliferation Treaty, 90

Okinawa, 37, 38, 53, 57, 58, 335
Organization for Economic and Cooperative Development (OECD), 34
Osaka, 44

Pakhtunistan, 114
Pakistan:
    armed forces, 98–100, 102–109, 111–114
    Awami League, 108, 109
    Z.A. Bhutto, 108
    Communist party, 109
    economy, 97, 98, 105, 112, 114
    foreign aid, 109–113
    foreign policy, 93–115; achievements, 113–115; decision-making, 101–104; domestic politics, 100–104; economic interests, 100, 106, 108–113; military aspects, 94–97, 101–113; objectives, 100, 102, 104–114
    history, 93–97
    Muhammad Ali Jinnah, 96, 101
    Kashmir, 47, 102–104, 106–108, 112–115
    Ayub Khan, 102, 103, 105–108, 110, 112, 113
    Liaquat Ali Khan, 96, 101
    Yahya Khan, 108, 112, 290
    People's party, 108
    political system, 97–104
    relations with Britain, 96, 97; China, 27, 28, 30, 106, 111–112, 113; India, 65, 77–80, 99, 102, 104–109; Indonesia, 111–113; Malaysia, 111–113; Soviet Union, 111, 287–292, 299; United States, 102, 103, 106, 109–112, 268–270
    H.S. Suhrawardy, 100
Pearl Harbor, 41
Peking, 81, 82, 84, 91, 113, 292, 316, 320, 333, 335
Pentagon, 38
Peshawar, 110, 111
Philippines:
    Chinese community, 221
    economy, 220–221
    foreign policy, 218–221; domestic politics, 219–221
    history, 218, 219

350–352, 363–366, 369–371; France, 249, 261, 262; India, 84–92; Indonesia, 249, 265, 266; Japan, 33, 36–39, 52–54, 57–60, 327–336; Laos, 198–200, 263, 264; North Korea, 259–261; North Vietnam, 178, 262–264; Pakistan, 109–112, 268–270; Philippines, 219, 220, 222–225, 340; South Korea, 148–152, 259–261; South Vietnam, 166–168, 262–264, 339, 340; Soviet Union, 248, 249, 257–259, 277–281, 284, 285, 322–327; Taiwan, 250, 257–259; Thailand, 190–194, 197
role in Asian balance, 307–327, 339–344, 350–352, 362–366, 369–371

Versailles Peace Conference, 40

Washington, 92, 111, 247, 253, 256, 257, 258, 266, 309, 334, 351, 363
World Bank, 72, 75, 112, 240

Yokosuka, 37